I0754232

Abbott Lawrence

LIVES

OF

AMERICAN MERCHANTS.

BY FREEMAN HUNT, A. M.,

EDITOR OF THE MERCHANTS' MAGAZINE, ETC., ETC.

VOL. II.

NEW YORK:

DERBY & JACKSON, 119 NASSAU-STREET.

CINCINNATI:—H. W. DERBY & CO.

1858.

R. C. VALENTINE,
Stereotyper and Electrotyper,
81, 83, and 85 Centre-street,
New York.

GEO. RUSSELL & CO.,
Book and Wood-cut Printers,
61 Beekman-street, N. Y.

CONTENTS OF VOL. II.

PORTRAITS.

Elias Hasket Derby

LIVES

OF

AMERICAN MERCHANTS.

ELIAS HASKET DERBY.

SALEM, fifteen miles east of Boston, is one of the most ancient settlements in the State, and before the Revolution was distinguished for its enterprise and commercial spirit. Embarking early in the fisheries and coastwise trade; building at first boats, sloops, and schooners, it gradually increased the size of its vessels, and sent them to the West Indies, Madeira, and the Mediterranean. Fish, oil, lumber, and provisions were exchanged for sugar, coffee, rum, and molasses, and these again were bartered for wine, fruit, silk, and iron, or bills of exchange on London. When the war of the Revolution checked the foreign trade, new models were adopted, and, in place of a navy, private armed ships were sent forth to encounter the British on the deep. Many of these met with brilliant success, in their conflicts on the ocean.

At the close of the Revolution, some of these were converted into Indiamen, and the ships of Salem were among the first to bear our flag to the Cape of Good Hope, the Isles of France, Bourbon, Surat, Bombay, Madras, Calcutta, Batavia, and Canton; and the fame of Salem was widely diffused through the great marts of Europe and Asia. When the port of Boston was closed, before the Revolution, Great Britain, in her anger, proposed to transfer its trade to Salem, and make it the entrepot and capital of the State.

But Salem declined the boon. It would not profit by oppression, although it had a fine harbor, and could have extended its piers to water deep enough to float ships which could not enter the harbor of Boston. Its wharves were then accessible to small vessels only, and its citizens were more alive to the wrongs of their country, than to their private advantage. When our volunteers had expelled the British army from Boston, it again became the seat of government.

Its ruined piers and edifices were rebuilt; capital returned to it; a navy-yard and fortresses were constructed; canals and railways were made, to connect it with the interior, and Salem, which had begun to rival it in commerce, upon the death of its leading merchants, was gradually overshadowed, and almost absorbed by the growth of the metropolis.

It is still, however, distinguished for wealth, enterprise, and refinement, and still holds in reverence the memory of those merchants, who, in the last century, laid the foundations of its prosperity.

Among them, no one is remembered with greater respect than Elias Hasket Derby. None have surpassed him in enterprise, or contributed more to improve the shipping, or extend the commerce of the country. No one has done more to rear up masters and merchants for its guidance.

Living at a period when banks were unknown—having few early advantages, he carved out, by his own genius, the way to wealth, and while achieving one of the largest fortunes made in America during the eighteenth century, he had the satisfaction to build up with it the fortunes of his native town, so that when he died, in 1799, although he had studiously avoided public life—rarely, if ever, held an office—his loss was mourned as a public misfortune.

The subject of this memoir was of English extraction. His ancestor, Roger Derby, born in 1643, emigrated to America in 1671, from Topsham, near Exeter, in the south of England.

He was a member of the society of Friends, and left home to enjoy religious freedom. He settled first in Ipswich, but having been fined for non-conformity, he removed to Salem, where he met with more liberality. Here he embarked in trade, reared a large family, and acquired a respectable property.

At his decease, in 1698, it appears, by his inventory, that he possessed a house, wharf, and warehouse; a stock of goods, some specie, and a silver tankard, which probably accompanied him from England, and, by his will, he settled his real estate upon his sons, Samuel and Richard.

His son Richard, born 1679, engaged in maritime affairs, but dying in 1715, at the early age of thirty-five, has left no record behind him, except that of his marriage, in 1702, with Martha, the daughter of Elias Hasket of Salem.

With respect to this somewhat peculiar name, the following entry appears upon the records of the General Court of Massachusetts:

"December 4th, 1703.

"Col. Elias, son of Capt. Stephen Hasket, of Salem, has lately removed to Boston, from this town. He had been for some time governor of Providence."

His station must have been at Providence, in the Bahamas; for it is a tradition in the family, that Elias Hasket, the subject of our memoir, was named for a governor of the Bahamas, who presented him, at his baptism, with a silver-headed cane. A large head of such a cane, inscribed J.

K. to E. H., has descended, with the name, from the infant to his grandson.

Richard Derby, at his decease, left a widow and several children, among them a son Richard, born in 1712, who was the father of Elias Hasket Derby. Losing his own father in his infancy, he was reared by an energetic mother, and soon gave proof of intrepidity, for we find him as early as 1736, in his twenty-fourth year, master of the sloop Ranger, about to sail from Salem for Cadiz and Malaga.

At a period when the mother country tried to repress the enterprise of the colonists, and confine their trade to British possessions; when the straits were infested by corsairs, we find this young man venturing to cross the ocean in a craft which would be deemed now scarcely safe to run from Salem to New York.

Among the shippers upon this voyage was James Lindall, of Salem, whose invoice and letter of instructions are still extant. In the letter, he directs Captain Derby to invest the proceeds of his fish in oil, fruit, and handkerchiefs, or in any other articles his good judgment may determine, and wishes him a prosperous voyage. A letter from Capt. Derby, when about to sail, refers to a previous voyage to the Island of St. Martins.

The Ranger appears to have made a good voyage, for we again find him, in 1739, about to sail in her for St. Martins, and, in 1742, he appears as master, and part owner, of the Volant, bound for Barbadoes and the French Islands.

His letter of instructions for this voyage gives a vivid picture of the difficulties which attended a voyage to Guadaloupe or Martinique.

In 1757 Capt. Derby appears to have retired from the sea, and to have relinquished his vessels to his sons John and Richard, and become a merchant of Salem; for we find among his papers the following letter from his eldest son, which is a good specimen of the mercantile correspondence of the day, and gives us some insight into the trade which he had cultivated between Salem and Spain:

"GIBRALTAR, 14th December, 1758.

"WORTHY SIR:—These I hope you will receive per your brigantine Lydia & Betsey, Capt. Lambert. I wrote you the 1st instant by way of Cadiz and Lisbon; since which I have landed my white sugar, and sold it for $17½ per cwt., and my tar I have sold at $8½ per bbl. I have not as yet sold any of my fish, nor at present does there appear to be any buyer for it; but as it is in very good order, and no fear of its spoiling, I intend to keep it a little longer. I am in hopes that this Levanter will bring down a buyer for it. I hope to get $12 for my brown sugar. We have this day had the Sally delivered up to us, and intend to sell her for the most she will fetch: as to sending her to the West Indies, I am sure if she was loaded for St. Eustatia, she would be seized by the privateers before she got out of the road; and having no papers but a pass, would be sufficient to condemn her in the West Indies, if she should be taken by an English cruiser. I have bought 140 casks of claret, at $10 per cask, which I intend to bring home with me. I have written to Alicant for 500 dozen handkerchiefs, if they can be delivered for $4 current per dozen. My cargo for home I intend shall be, 140 casks of claret, 20 butts of Mersilla wine, 500 casks of raisins, some soap, and all the small handkerchiefs I can get. I have written to Mr. Lane that I shall remit him £250 or £200. As to any thing else, Capt. Lambert can inform you, who is knowing to all my business. Not having further to write, I remember my duty to you and my mother.

"I am your obedient son,

"RICHARD DERBY, JR.

"Raisins, 27 to 30 rials; Malaga, $34 per butt; white sugar $17½ per cwt.; brown sugar, $10 to $12; fish, no buyer; Mersilla wine, $30 to $32 per butt."

The commerce in which Capt. Derby was engaged, was pursued in vessels ranging from fifty to one hundred tons. His vessels, laden with fish, lumber, and provisions, cleared for Dominica, or some Windward Isle in the British West Indies, and then run through the islands for a market; sometimes getting a license to discharge in French or Spanish ports. The returns were made in sugar, molasses, cotton, rum, claret, or in rice and naval stores from Carolina.

With the returns from these voyages, assorted cargoes were made of oil, naval stores, and the produce of the islands, for Spain and Madeira, and the proceeds remitted partly in bills on London, and partly in wine, salt, fruit, oil, iron, lead, and handkerchiefs, to America. The bills of exchange on London were sold at a premium in America, and contributed largely to pay for importations from England. In his voyage to Spain, Capt. Derby had chosen the house of Lane & Booth, afterward Lane & Frazer, of London, as his English correspondents, and, until the close of the century, they continued the faithful agents of his family. We subjoin one of their letters:

"London, 1st November, 1760.

"Capt. Richard Derby:—We are now to confirm the preceding copy of our last, since which we have received none of your favors. This is to advise you that Messrs. Lynch, of Gibraltar, remitted us last month two bills for your account, viz.:

"John Leweson, Denham-street	£87 13s. 9d
"Wm. Davis's bill on Francis Waldron, in Portsmouth	23 10 3
	£111 4s. 0d

"The former of which is accepted, and shall be placed

to your credit in course. The other is noted for non-acceptance, and we fear will not be paid, as Lieut. Waldron is out on the recruiting service, and has left no direction for the payment.

"We remain with due respect, sir, your humble servants,

"LANE & BOOTH."

"LONDON, 20th November, 1760.

"CAPT. RICHARD DERBY :—On the other side you will find copies of our two last letters, and we are now to reply to your favor of the 14th July. In answer, we are to acquaint you that Capt. Elkin has made us no remittance, in consequence of your orders to him to send us £500, nor have we received any from your son, which, indeed, we cannot expect, as all the produce of his cargo must go toward the discharge of his ransom bill. As Capt. Benj. Bates has not valued on us for any money for your account, we suppose he had no occasion for it, and that we shall not hear from him on the subject.

"We are glad you received your goods by Evers & Co.; the return due on his insurance will be passed to your credit. We shall observe to send you no further supply till we hear from you again.

"The bill on Lieut. Waldron is returned us with protest for non-payment, and we shall send it to-morrow to Messrs. Lynch, of Gibraltar, debiting you with 14s. 6d., for charges of protest and postage.

"We are with respect your most humble servants,

"LANE & BOOTH."

"SIR :—We are now at the 31st December, and confirm our last on the other side, since which we have your favor of the 22d September, inclosing your letter to Mr. Robert Scott, with a remittance for £150; both which we delivered to him, and have taken his receipt for the bill.

"We are glad you received your goods by Jacobson, in good order; and any returns of premium for insurance, made for your account, will be passed to your credit in course.

"We are with respect, sir, your most humble servants,

"LANE & BOOTH."

The commerce in which Capt. Derby was engaged was bold and adventurous. When he commenced life, the shipping of Massachusetts was estimated at 200 sail, and 8,000 tons. Few vessels exceeded 60 tons burden. His vessels were exposed not only to the dangers of the sea, but also to the bucaneers, and French and English cruisers, who were often reckless in the seizure of American property. Among his papers we find a protest of Michael Driver, one of his captains, bearing date December, 1759, against an English privateer, the King of Prussia, which robbed him of his specie, and sent his schooner, the Three Brothers, of 56 tons, to Tortola, to be robbed again by a court of admiralty. In the year 1762, we find another protest, of the same master, against a French cruiser, La Tigre, which had seized another of Capt. Derby's vessels, but more generously allowed him to ransom her, retaining the mate as a hostage. In the same year we find a third protest, stating that Capt. Derby and another merchant had procured a cartel, called the Mary, and sent her with the ransom money, in specie, to redeem their hostages, and that she also had been captured, and sent in for adjudication, by a British ship of war.

It appears, however, by the papers, that she was acquitted, and that the hostages were honorably redeemed, although the Mary was detained for some months in the French port, and the losses and expenses of Capt. Derby, by this series of captures, exceeded fifteen thousand dollars.

During the French war, from 1756 to 1763, Capt. Derby owned several ships, as well as brigantines; for in his letters to Booth & Lane, he directs insurance on his ships Antelope, Lydia, and Ranger, merchantmen of two hundred to three hundred tons burden.

They are described as mounting from eight to twelve cannon, principally six-pounders, with four cannon below deck, for close quarters. The letter-book of Capt. Derby is still extant, as are also his two ledgers, covering the space from 1746 to 1783, and closing with his will and the division of his estate. These books were kept with scrupulous care; are models for imitation, and throw much light on the commerce of the period.

During the French war, an event occurred which greatly exasperated Capt. Derby. With the proceeds of his shipments to Gibraltar, he purchased there a French prize, of three hundred tons, sold under the decree of a British Court of Admiralty, and gave her the expressive name of Ranger. Loading this ship with wine, he sent her, under the command of Capt. George Crowninshield, to the West India Isles, and exchanging her wine for sugars, dispatched her on a voyage to Leghorn. But this flight was too adventurous for an humble colonist; the Ranger was not destined to reach her port. She had proceeded but a few miles, before she was seized by four English privateers, and taken to Providence, in the Bahamas.

Capt. Derby met the exigency with spirit. After taking the advice of Mr. Pratt, one of the first lawyers of the State, he dispatched his son John, in one of his light vessels to the Bahamas, with funds and letter of credit. He addressed letters to the judge, a native of Massachusetts; but the vessel was confiscated, and delivered up to the privateers. The owner appealed, and filed his bonds to prosecute the appeal in England.

His letters to his counsel and correspondents in London

are still extant. In these he writes in an indignant tone, stating, that within three years, no less than two hundred sail of vessels have been taken to Providence, in the Bahamas; that none have escaped condemnation, except those which were able to pay more than the captors; that the judge of the Admiralty Court, Bradford, and the governor, Shirley, who went there penniless, had gone home with fortunes of £30,000; that his ship was on a lawful voyage, and was condemned because she had no register, which, being a prize, she could not get until her return to England; and upon the pretence that she designed going to Salem, when she was actually on her way to Leghorn, where she would have been sold, with her cargo, for $70,000. That she had been given up to captors, on a valuation of $17,000, or one-fourth part of his claim, upon bonds signed by bankrupts, most of whom had left the island; and that when his son had apprised the judge of their inability to pay, he told him it was none of his business. He assures his counsel that such seizures had set the country on fire, and would be taken up by the Province, and directs him to spare no pains to reverse the decree; and, if he deems it advisable, to sue the bondsmen and the owners of the privateers, and the governor and judge also; and, to show he is in earnest, he sends him a draft of sixty-three pounds, as a retainer, and a letter of credit on his bankers.

Capt. Derby sent another vessel to the Bahamas, to serve an inhibition on the court, and, for some years, pursued his appeal; but a colonist at that time seldom obtained redress in the Admiralty Courts of England, and, from his subsequent letters, in which he refers to his discouraging lawsuits, we may infer that he was forced to content himself with a moderate insurance for the loss of a voyage which would have doubled his fortune. The injustice of England; the corruptions of her courts; the spoliations made upon her colonists, and the check given to their rising commerce, must have made a deep impression on Capt. Derby and his son. The stories of his wrongs must have been oft repeated, and no doubt contributed to that indignant feeling which animated the Eastern seaports during the Revolution; the latent causes of which have been but partially developed by history.

It was reserved for the son of Capt. Derby, after independence was secured, and during another French war, to make the Leghorn voyage, with results more brilliant than the hopes indulged by his father; and it was the fortune of his grandsons, the Crowninshields, the sons of the captain of the Ranger, to adjust, during the war of 1812, the money account with England, with long arrears of interest, in their armed ship America.

But losses did not dishearten Capt. Derby. After ransoming another vessel, the brig Neptune, from the French, through the house of Gardoqui & Co., of Bilboa, he pursued his commerce in the ship Antelope, the brigs Neptune, Earl of Derby, and schooner Kate, until the Revolutionary war, and, by frugality and perseverance, made himself independent.

In early life he married Mary Hodges, of Salem, who became the mother of eight children. The race from which she sprung, was distinguished for its size. An anecdote is preserved of one of them, a young man, six feet six inches in height, who was captured by a British frigate. When asked if he was not remarkable for his height at home, he is said to have replied, "I am the shortest of six brothers?" The descendants of this lady have nearly all of them preserved this peculiarity of the race.

Capt. Richard Derby lived through the war. From 1769 to 1773, he was a member of the General Court; in 1774, 1776, and 1777, a member of the Governor's Council; and, in 1774 and 1775, his son Richard was a delegate to the Provincial Congress.

He was a sound whig, and retained his courage to the last; for Col. Swett, in his narrative of the march of Leslie to Salem, published a few years since, relates that Capt. Richard Derby was the owner of some of the cannon which Col. Leslie desired to seize. Meeting the old gentleman before his house, in Salem, he demanded the surrender of the cannon, and "urged him to deliver them up without resistance. Derby's reply was as significant as that of the old Spartan: Find them, if you can! take them, if you can! they will never be surrendered!"

The courage of the old man, who defied a regiment under arms, and the spirit of his townsmen, who raised their drawbridge and sunk their boats, preserved the cannon.

By the returns of Col. Mason, Nov. 15th, 1775, of the cannon he collected at Salem for the American army, it appears there were nineteen pieces, eight of which were received from Capt. Derby. These were of inestimable value to our forces.

Capt. Derby married a second time; lived to witness the independence of his country; and, by his will, proved in 1783, he left an ample provision to his widow, and divided nearly $70,000 among his children. A fine picture of the old gentleman remains, in a well-powdered wig, with a spyglass in his hand, and a ship in the distance. His widow lived to found the Derby Academy, at Hingham; his eldest son, Richard, was an ardent patriot, and another of his sons, John Derby, was an owner of the ship Columbia, which, on her second voyage, discovered the Columbia River. By a remarkable concurrence of events, and by the uncommon speed of two ships, owned by his father and brother, he carried to England the first news of the battle of Lexington, returned to Salem with the first intelligence of the effect it produced in London, which he laid before General Washington, at Cambridge, and at the close of the war brought to America from France the first news of peace. His second son, Elias Hasket, the subject of this memoir, was born in Salem, August 16th, 1739, and in early life appears to have kept the books and conducted the correspondence of his father, and to have been the accountant of his family. At an early age he married a Crowninshield, while his sister married a Crowninshield also; thus making a double connection between the families.

From 1760 to 1775, he not only took charge of his father's books, wharves, and other property, but imbibing the spirit of his father, and acquiring through him and his captains a knowledge of commerce, he engaged extensively in the trade to the English and French islands. At the commencement of the war, he was the owner of no less than *seven* sail of vessels, in the trade of the West Indies, varying from sixty to one hundred tons, and by frugality and industry had acquired a property of $50,000.

At this period, most of the rich men of Massachusetts clung to the mother country, but none of the Derby name followed their example, and the subject of our memoir espoused the cause of the colonies. A period had arrived adverse to commerce. The colonists possessed neither navy-yards nor navies, although entering into the conflict with Great Britain, and defying the great naval power of the world, and their merchantmen were soon swept from the ocean.

At the commencement of the war, nearly all Mr. Derby's vessels were at sea, or at the Islands. He had persevered in his peaceful pursuits to the last, and some of his last shipments had realized large profits. Sugar, coffee, and foreign goods had risen in value at home, but the question was, how to bring his property to Massachusetts.

His first effort was signally unfortunate, as appears by a letter of December 13th, 1783, by which he endeavors, without success, to obtain redress in England. He writes as follows:

"The most of my trade, before the war, was to Jamaica, at which time I had three vessels there: one of them, namely, the Jamaica Packet, Capt. Ingersoll, took out papers in the name of Mr. Gray, of the north side at Jamaica, and sailed for home. On his passage to Salem he was taken by a British cruiser, and carried into Boston. The captain who took him deprived him of all his papers, and kept them until the trial came on, when the bill of stores was missing from the papers. The court condemned one cask of rum, and one cask of sugar, for want of the bill of stores, but acquitted the vessel and cargo. Capt. Ingersoll could not get leave to sell the cargo. He applied, from time to time, to have the interest delivered, and could not succeed; but after a time, and when the enemy were near leaving Boston, he obtained leave to sell so much of his cargo as would be sufficient to repair his vessel, with a view to leave Boston with the fleet, which he was desirous of doing, hoping thus to save the interest. When the fleet and army were leaving Boston, they came and took most of the rum on board the transports; the soldiers, and sailors, and others, came in the time of confusion, and cut his sails from the yards, and made them into bags; they cut the hoops from the hogsheads of sugar, and took most of it away. Not being satisfied with that, the day they quitted the town, they came and cut the fasts from the wharf, when the schooner drove down river, and went ashore on one of the islands, and was there burned by the British, by which I lost better than £3,000 sterling."

After this capture, another vessel of Mr. Derby's, the schooner Nancy, Capt. Hallet, reached Cape François, and we find there Capt. Nathaniel Silsbee, in charge of three of his vessels and cargoes. Capt. Silsbee was the father of the late Nathaniel Silsbee, senator from Massachussets, and appears to have enjoyed the entire confidence of Mr. Derby.

The correspondence between them is still extant. Mr.

Derby writes to him under date of February 13, 1776, as follows:

"I advised you of the danger of coming home late in the spring. Taking all affairs into consideration, I must conclude it not safe or prudent for me or you to venture such an interest on this coast so late as you must, provided you think of coming. If this letter should meet you at the Mole, you may ship me, by any vessels bound to Cape Ann, Newbury, Ipswich, or near to it, some cotton, cocoa, sugar, molasses, duck, cordage, powder, or any other article you think may answer, as I make no doubt that any goods will make 100 per cent. For your government, I have sent the prices here, and have no doubt they will be much higher, if times hold as they are at present. But do not send any indigo, as that is contrary to the association, but any foreign goods you have a right to bring. I do not at this time mean to write any positive orders, as affairs may alter in the spring.

"There are many difficulties in carrying on business at this time, and I should be sorry to hear of your going to Halifax, or of your doing any thing, however small, contrary to the Association of the Continent; and you may depend upon it, that if the present dispute should continue the next summer, that there will be no less than 100 sail of privateers out from the continent, and I suppose the interest of mine, as Jamaica or Halifax property, must share the fate of other things, if taken. But may the Almighty Disposer of all things order the councils of the wicked administration to come to naught."

Mr. Derby adds a postscript by Capt. Hallet, in which he says:

"The times at present are such, I cannot determine what will be for the best, and must therefore leave it wholly to you, not doubting the business will be conducted with care. Should so large a fleet come on this coast in the spring as is talked of, I should think it not best to ship so much to the Northward or otherwise; but it is now said that commissioners are appointed to come over to accommodate affairs, but I doubt it. I commit you to the Almighty's protection, not doubting that we shall once more carry on business at Salem in peace and safety.

"From your friend,

"ELIAS HASKET DERBY."

Capt. Silsbee writes to Mr. Derby in reply, from St. Nicholas Mole, March 17, 1776, that he has received his letter, and has disposed of the principal part of his three cargoes to good advantage; dispatched Capt. Hallet on his return; shall visit Jamaica to learn the latest news, and govern himself accordingly; that he shall not ship the principal part of the property until he can do so with safety, and, after loading his vessels, shall leave sufficient to load a fourth, and concludes:

"I have sent you, per Capt. Hallet, a gun and pair of pistols, which you will please accept. I bought them for myself, but I think you stand more in need of them than I do, and I send them to you, sir, as a present.

"N. SILSBEE."

Capt. Silsbee continued in the service of Mr. Derby until the close of the war, when his health failed him; and Mr. Derby evinced the interest he felt in the family, by intrusting several ships to his son, the late senator, who made a successful voyage to the East Indies before he attained his majority. The elder Capt. Silsbee exercised his best judgment; but so vigilant were the British cruisers, that Mr. Derby lost two more of his vessels on their way homeward.

His trade was ruined, and his property seriously impaired. The war had now raged for more than a year, and thus far he had confined himself to the peaceful pursuits of commerce; but after the wanton and reckless destruction of his property, and the capture of two more of his vessels, it became apparent that he must either abandon the seas, which both he and his forefathers had followed for half a century, or meet force with force. Boston and New York had been occupied and nearly ruined by the enemy. Newport, Philadelphia, Savannah, and Charleston soon shared their fate; and the main reliance of the country to preserve its intercourse with Europe, and for supplies of arms and military stores, was on the shipping of Salem and a cluster of small ports around it, among which Marblehead and Beverly were conspicuous.

The blood of our mariners and merchants was up: they were indignant at the oppressive course of the government of Great Britain—aware that their country, almost destitute of ships-of-war, looked to them for service. Smarting under their own losses, they resolved, with one accord, to meet Great Britain on the deep.

Mr. Derby united with his townsmen, and took a prominent part in the equipment of at least 158 armed vessels, fitted out from Salem during the Revolution, mounting more than 2,000 cannon, and manned by the gallant seamen of Salem and the contiguous ports of Beverly and Marblehead.

It is impossible to define the precise part taken by Mr. Derby in the equipment of this fleet; but Mr. J. P. Felt, the antiquarian, of Salem, after careful examination of Mr. Derby's papers and other sources of information, writes to the author of this memoir, as follows:

"It is a very difficult thing to discriminate as to the privateers in which Mr. Derby was concerned, there being no particular account of them. It is to scraps like the inclosed, and other accounts and inferences, that I am obliged to resort to obtain my knowledge. In fact, I feel that, if I were to conclude that whenever a privateer was to be built, he told them—'Go on and build her, and fit her out; get what you can taken up, and I will take what remains'—I should not be far from correct."

Thus active was Mr. Derby in creating a volunteer navy, which was almost as effective as the army on land, in humbling the pride and crippling the resources of Great Britain.

One of the first armed vessels that sailed from Salem was the sloop Revenge, one of Mr. Derby's West Indiamen, armed with 10 guns. She appears to have taken, on her first cruise, four Jamaicamen, laden with 733 hogsheads of sugar, besides other cargo; and by an account settled with Miles Greenwood, of June 24, 1777, Mr. Derby appears to have realized a fourth part of the proceeds. There were other ships in which Mr. Derby took an interest, which were equally successful; and many of their officers performed exploits which rival those of Paul Jones and Decatur. In one of his letters, he requests one of his captains to bring him home from Bilboa "the guns left there during the war by Capt. Haraden;" and a brief sketch of his achievements will give some idea of the intrepidity of the men who commanded our privateers.

One of the bravest officers and best seamen who sailed from Salem during the Revolution, was Capt. Jonathan Haraden. He was born in Gloucester, Massachusetts, and when a boy was taken to Salem by the father of the late George Cabot. Very little is known respecting his early life, but that little redounds to his credit, and shows that he was not apt to shrink from his duty on any occasion. Soon after hostilities commenced between Great Britain and her colonies, Massachusetts built two small vessels, each of 14 guns, for the protection of trade. One of these, the Tyrannicide, was placed under the command of Capt. Fisk, afterward Gen. Fisk, of Salem, who appointed Mr. Haraden his lieutenant. On her first cruise, she fell in with a royal cutter, bound from Halifax to New York, having on board, besides her own crew, a number of picked men destined for some of the British ships-of-war. After a short contest, in which the guns of the Tyrannicide did great execution, the cutter was obliged to strike, and was carried in triumph into Salem. The British officers and men were astonished and indignant at being thus captured by a Yankee sloop. Lieut. Haraden afterward rose to the post of captain, but soon left the sloop to take command of the Pickering, a Salem ship of 180 tons, carrying 14 six-pounders and a crew of 45 men and boys. In this ship, built for a cruiser, but commissioned as a letter of marque, he sailed from Salem in the spring of 1780, with a cargo of sugar for Bilboa, then a place of great resort for American privateers and prizes. On his passage, May 29, 1780, he was attacked by a British cutter of 20 guns, and beat her off after a contest of 1 hour and 45 minutes.

Upon entering the Bay of Biscay, he fell in with a British privateer of 22 guns and 60 men. Having approached her in the night, unobserved, he run alongside, and commanded her through his trumpet, in a voice of thunder, to strike to an American frigate, or he would sink her. The privateer struck her flag, and the captain, when he came on board the Pickering, was mortified to find he had submitted to such inferior force. Mr. John Carnes, of Salem, was put in charge of the prize. Both vessels proceeded toward Bilboa, and, as they approached the land, they met a sail coming out, which the captain taken in the prize informed Capt. Haraden was the Achilles, a privateer from London, of 42 guns and 140 men, and added that he knew her force, as he had cruised in company with her a few days before. Capt. Haraden coolly replied, "I shan't run from her." As she approached, she first encountered the prize, and placed her third lieutenant and prize crew on board of her. She then made sail for her captor, who was prepared to receive her. Night coming on, and judging from her movements that she would defer her visit until morning, Capt. Haraden turned in to take some repose, directing the watch to call him in case the foe should approach. As the day dawned, June 4, 1780, the Achilles bore down upon the ship, and an officer went immediately to communicate the fact to Capt. Haraden, and found him in a profound sleep. Upon being awaked, he calmly rose, went on deck, as if it had been some ordinary occasion. Finding his force was small for the work to be done, as part of his crew were in the prize, he offered a large reward to his 60 prisoners for 10 volunteers. A boatswain and nine men joined him and took their station with the crew, thus increasing his strength to 47 men and boys.

He then went round to see that every thing was in order, assuring his men that, although the Achilles appeared to be superior in force, he had no doubt they would beat her if they were firm and steady, and did not throw away their fire. "Take particular aim," said he, "at the white boot-top."

The Achilles took position close alongside of the Pickering, who received her with a broadside, followed by others in close succession. Although the Pickering appeared little larger than a long-boat beside her foe, and was deep in the water from the weight of her cargo, yet this gave her some advantage, for nearly all of her shot took effect near the water-line of her adversary. The Achilles, on the contrary, was so large and so high above the water, she made a good target for her foe, and many of her shot passed over the Pickering. One of them, however, took off the head of the volunteer boatswain, and eight of her crew were wounded. During the conflict, Capt. Haraden showed a courage and determination almost superhuman. Close to the foe, constantly occupying the most exposed position, while the shot flew around him like hail, he was, in the language of one present, "all the time as calm and steady as amid a shower of snow-flakes." He had an uncommonly fine crew: they caught the spirit of their commander, and did their duty so thoroughly, that the Achilles found she must either run or sink. She at length sought safety in flight.

A broadside of crow-bars, fired at a particular time, is said to have had a prodigious effect, and to have hurried her decision. The Pickering, in her turn, gave chase, and Capt. Haraden offered a large reward to his gunner if he would carry away a spar, but fortune did not favor him. The Achilles was light, and, having a mainsail as large as a ship of the line, outsailed the Pickering and escaped, after a fight of 2 hours and 55 minutes' duration.

The prize was in sight during the action, and a conversation took place between the two prize-masters, which is worthy of record, since it shows the confidence which Capt. Haraden's crew had in his prowess and good fortune.

At the request of the English prize-master, Mr. Carnes had informed him of the force and character of the Pickering; but when he saw her engaging the Achilles, he thought he had been deceived, and inveighed bitterly against his informant. Mr. Carnes assured him that he had told the truth, and added, "If you knew Capt. Haraden as well as I do, you would not be surprised at this: it is just what I expected; and I think it not impossible, notwithstanding the disparity of force, that the lugger will at least be beaten off, and I shall have the command of this prize again before night;" and so it actually happened.

The Pickering returned, recaptured her prize, and carried her in safety into Bilboa.

The battle was fought so near the Spanish coast, that an immense concourse of spectators, estimated at 100,000, assembled along the shore, in boats and on the hill-sides, during the action; and before the Pickering and her prize had been at anchor half an hour, one could have walked (says an eye-witness) a mile from the Pickering, stepping from boat to boat. So great was the admiration with which the battle and victory were witnessed, that when the captain landed, he was surrounded by this vast throng of strangers, and borne in triumph into the city, where he was received with public honors and favors.

On another passage from Salem to France, the Pickering found herself one morning at daylight in close proximity to an English ship of the line, supposed to be the Foudroyant. She was in full pursuit, and gained rapidly on the Pickering, but refrained from firing, as she doubtless wished to take her without injury. It was soon obvious on board the Pickering, that she must be captured unless she increased her speed. At this juncture, Capt. Haraden put out his sweeps. Upon this, the ship fired, and shot away the blades of three sweeps; but, by great exertions, the crew actually pulled away from the Englishman, and reached France in safety. There she obtained a cargo of ammunition, and returned in safety to Salem, where her cargo was much wanted.

The Pickering was afterwards fitted out, under the same gallant commander, as a privateer, mounting 16 guns, and was very successful. In one of her cruises she came up with three armed vessels in company, bound from Halifax to New York. They formed in a line, and made a formidable appearance. Great as was the confidence of the officers and crew in the bravery and judgment of their captain, they evinced, by their looks, that they thought on this occasion he was going to hazard too much; upon which he told them he had no doubt whatever that, if they would do their duty, he would quickly capture the three vessels; and this he did with great ease by going alongside of each of them, one after the other.

The first was a sloop, mounting 12 guns; the second, a brig of 14; and the third, a ship of 16 guns.

On another occasion, while cruising near Bermuda, he was greatly annoyed by two sloops. They sailed very fast, and, keeping near him whenever he took a prize, would retake her. But Capt. Haraden was not to be foiled in this manner. He concluded to leave them by night; and, when out of sight, sent down his foretop-gallant-yard and mast, and otherwise disguised his vessel. He soon after fell in with them again: they were soon in pursuit, and he put out drags. One overtook him, and, when so near as to prevent escape, he opened his guns upon her, and soon captured her. Then, placing the English flag over the American on the Pickering, the sloop, with the English ensign flying, bore down upon her consort, and captured her also.

On his return home from one of these cruises, he fell in with a North Carolina schooner, which had been out to the Islands with a cargo of lumber, and was returning home with the small proceeds. She had been just before stopped by an English letter of marque, which in a piratical manner had robbed her of her quadrant, compass, and stores, unrove some of her rigging, and then left her to her fate. Capt. Haraden found her in this deplorable condition, supplied her necessities, and sent her home. Having learned the course taken by the letter of marque, he went in pursuit, overtook and captured her, and, after giving her captain a stern rebuke for his piratical conduct, he gave his own crew permission to make reprisals. He then allowed the letter of marque to continue her voyage. Imbued with that humanity which characterizes our seamen, he would not, even under these circumstances, sink or destroy a ship worthless as a prize, and thus ruin a brother sailor.

Off the Capes of the Delaware, he fell in with an English brig of war of equal or superior force, which struck to him almost immediately. The particular circumstances of this extraordinary affair were thus related by Captain Haraden:

He had a favorite boy on board his ship, whom he had at his request sent on board one of his prizes, that he might return to his home. The British brig had captured the prize, and had the boy on board. On the approach of the Pickering, this boy recognized her, was very much elated, and gave such proofs of his joy as were natural upon such an occasion. On being asked what was the cause of his exultation, he replied: "That is my master, and I shall soon be with him."

"Your master?" said they; "and who is he?"

"Why, Capt. Haraden," said the boy. "Did you never hear of him? He takes every thing he goes alongside of—he will soon have you."

The news soon flew to the captain's ears; the boy was sent for, and upon inquiry, gave the same account. In the mean time, the Pickering was coming up, and soon run close alongside of the English vessel, to leeward, so that the deck of the latter was completely exposed to the fire of the former. Capt. Haraden then said, calmly, "Haul down your colors, or I will fire into you." With a mere show of resistance, the colors were struck, and, the wind and tide being favorable, the ship and her prize in ten or twelve hours anchored in Philadelphia. The extraordinary courage of Capt. Haraden, and his power of imparting it to his men, had given him "a name of terror on the ocean."

In one of the last cruises of this gallant officer in the Pickering, he fell in with a king's mail-packet from one of the West India isles, homeward bound, which gave him a very warm reception. After an action which lasted four glasses, Capt. Haraden found it necessary to haul off and repair damages. Having done so, he again went alongside of the packet, with all the powder he had left in his cannon. He then hailed the enemy, and told him he would give him five minutes to haul down his colors, and if they were not down at the expiration of that time, he would sink him. At the end of three minutes the colors came down. The boat, on going alongside the prize, found the blood running from her scuppers, while the deck appeared more like the floor of a slaughter-house than the deck of a ship. On the quarter-deck, in an armchair, sat an old gentleman, the governor of the island from which the packet came. During the whole action he had loaded and fired a heavy blunderbuss, and in the course of the battle had received a ball in his cheek, which, in consequence of the loss of teeth, had passed out through the other cheek, without giving a mortal wound.

In the course of the war, Capt. Haraden is reported to have taken 1,000 cannon from the English. Toward its close, he carried several prizes into St. Eustatia, and with his ship and prizes, shared the fate of the island, when it was taken in 1781 by the fleet of Admiral Rodney. One of the prizes thus taken was a Boston vessel, which had been captured by a British ship and recaptured by the Pickering. The owners of this vessel sued Capt. Haraden for damages, for having carried the ship into St. Eustatia instead of sending her home or to some other port. He was compelled to pay a large amount; and as his owners, after the loss of their ship and prizes, were not ready to indemnify him, he commenced a suit for indemnity.

Such was the sympathy for Capt. Haraden, that when the case came on, the courthouse was filled with spectators, and the streets of Salem were thronged. The verdict was in his favor, and when it was known, the people in the streets rent the air with their acclamations. While volunteers upon the land, who rarely met a foe, have been rewarded by pensions and liberal grants of land, this volunteer upon the sea, with his brave associates, who rendered tenfold the service and incurred far greater perils, have received no honors and no rewards from government. His grandchildren in Salem still, however, treasure up a few memorials presented to him by the owners of the Pickering and the Julius Cæsar, in which he sailed after the loss of the Pickering—consisting of three massive pieces of silver plate, inscribed with the name of the invincible captain.

Capt. Haraden was in his person tall and comely; his countenance was placid, and his manners and deportment remarkably mild. His discipline on board ship was excellent, especially in time of action. Yet in the common concerns of life he was easy almost to a fault. So great was the confidence he inspired, that if he but looked at a sail through his glass, and then told the helmsman to steer for her, the observation went round, "If she is an enemy, she is ours!" His great characteristic was the most consummate self-possession on all occasions, and in midst of perils, in which if any man equaled, none ever excelled him. His officers and men insisted he was more calm and cool amid the din of battle than at any other time; and the more deadly the strife, the more imminent the peril—the more terrific the scene, the more perfect his self-command and serene intrepidity. In a word, he was a hero.

Capt. Haraden paid the debt of nature at Salem, in 1803, in his 59th year.

If his country has not yet evinced her gratitude for his services—if he has been suffered to die in obscurity—posterity will yet do him justice.*

---

* In compiling this brief memoir of Capt. Haraden, I have made liberal use of a sketch published by Col. Israel Thorndike, of Beverly, his lieutenant; of an oration, by Hon. C. W. Upham, of Salem; of a narrative, by Stephen Haraden, of Salem, his nephew; and of the statements of his shipmates, Robert Cowan and William Prosser, of Salem, and Samuel Newhall, of Marblehead, furnished me by Capt. J. P. Felt. They are undoubtedly authentic, and corroborate each other. Col. J. Jewett also has supplied some anecdotes.

But there were many captains of private armed ships in the war of the Revolution who have left behind them a brilliant name. Among them, Salem had her Fisk, Haraden, and Gray; Beverly, her Thorndike, Tittle, and Woodbury; Marblehead, her Mugford, Cole, and Tucker.

A few more particulars as to the Salem privateers must suffice for this memoir. They will show there was chivalry in the private service as well as in the navy:

Abstract of a letter from Capt. Wm. Gray, late Lieutenant of the Privateer Jack, of 12 *guns and* 60 *men, Capt. David Ropes, who was captured while on a cruise from that port.*

"SALEM, June 12, 1782.

"On the 28th May, cruising near Halifax, saw a brig standing in for the land; at 7 P. M. discovered her to have a copper bottom, 16 guns, and full of men; at half past 9 o'clock she came alongside, when a close action commenced.

It was our misfortune to have our worthy commander, Capt. Ropes, mortally wounded the first broadside. I was slightly wounded at the same time in my right hand and head, but not so as to disable me from duty. The action was maintained on both sides close, severe, and without intermission for upwards of two hours, in which time we had seven killed, several wounded, and several abandoned their quarters. Our rigging was so destroyed that, not having command of our yards, the Jack fell with her larboard bow foul of the brig's starboard quarter, when the enemy made an attempt to board us, but they were repulsed by a very small number compared with them. We were engaged in this position about a quarter of an hour, in which time I received a wound by a bayonet fixed on a musket, which was hove with such force, as entering my thigh close to the bone, entered the carriage of a bow gun, where I was fastened, and it was out of my power to get clear until assisted by one of the prize-masters. We then fell round and came with our broadsides to each other, when we resumed the action with powder and balls; but our match-rope, excepting some which was unfit for use, being all expended, and being to leeward, we bore away, making a running fight. The brig, being far superior to us in number of men, was able to get soon repaired, and completely ready to renew the action. She had constantly kept up a chasing fire, for we had not been out of reach of her musketry. She was close alongside of us again, with 50 picked men ready for boarding. I therefore called Mr. Glover and the rest together, and found we had but ten men on deck. I had been repeatedly desired to strike; but I mentioned the sufferings of the prison-ship, and made use of every other argument in my power for continuing the engagement. All the foreigners, however, deserted their quarters every opportunity. At 2 o'clock P. M. I had the inexpressible mortification to deliver up the vessel. I was told, on inquiry, that we were taken by the Observer, a sloop-of-war belonging to the navy, commanded by Capt. Grymes. She was formerly the Amsterdam, and owned in Boston; that she was calculated for 16 guns, but then had but 12 on board; that the Blonde frigate, being cast away on Seal Island, the captain, officers, and men had been taken off by Capt. Adams, in a sloop belonging to Salem, and Capt. Stoddart, in a schooner belonging to Boston, and by them landed on the main. Most of the officers and men having reached Halifax, were by the governor sent on board the brig, in order to come out and convoy in the captain of a frigate who was, with some of his men, coming to Halifax in a shallop, and that the afternoon before the action he and some others were taken on board the brig, which increased his number to one hundred and seventy-three men.

"Capt. Ropes died at 4 o'clock P. M. on the day we were

taken, after making his will with the greatest calmness and composure.

"Besides Capt. Ropes, were killed Nathaniel Trask, of Beverly, prize-master, and James Gregory, of Danvers, quarter-master. Enemy's loss more than double."

"July 18, 1782.

"Capt. Wm. Gray and five others, who were taken in the Jack of this port, arrived here last Tuesday on parole from Halifax. Capt. Gray wishes it to be published, that himself and other persons with him, in the hospital at Halifax, have been treated with great kindness and humanity, and that every attention was paid them by Dr. Halliburton and the subordinate surgeons of the hospital which they could reasonably expect or desire. There were 81 prisoners remaining on board the prison-ship at that place."

(*From the Nova Scotia Gazette, June* 11, 1782.)

"To the Printer: Sir—In justice to humanity, shown to all my officers and ship's company of his Majesty's ship Blonde by the commanders of the American private ships-of-war, the Lively, Capt. Adams, and the Scammel, Capt. Stoddart, I have the pleasure to inform the public that they not only readily received us on board their vessels, and carried us to Cape Bessue, but cheerfully supplied us with provisions till we landed at Yarmouth, when on releasing all my prisoners I had on board (64 in number), and giving them a passport, to secure them from our cruisers in Boston Bay, they generously gave me the same, to prevent our being made prisoners of or plundered by any of their privateers we might chance to meet on our passage to Halifax.

"For the relief and comfort they so kindly afforded us in our accumulated sufferings and distress, I most ardently wish and hope that if any of these privateers should ever happen to fall into the hands of our ships-of-war, that they will treat them with the utmost lenity, and give them every indulgence in their power, and not look on them (promiscuously) in the light of other American prisoners,—Capt. Adams especially, to whom I am particularly obliged, as will be seen by his letter herewith published. My earnest thanks are also due to Capt. Tuck, of the Blonde prize-ship Lion (letter of marque of Beverly), and all his officers and men, for their generous and indefatigable endeavors to keep the ship from sinking (night and day at the pumps), till all but one got out of her, and by the blessing of God saved our lives.

"You will please publish this in your next paper, and insert the undermentioned copies of Capt. Adams' letters to me verbatim, and desire Mr. Home will do the same on Friday next, which will oblige your humble servant,

"EDWARD THORNBROUGH,

"Commander of his Majesty's late ship Blonde.

"HALIFAX CAREENING YARD, June 3d, 1782."

"ON BOARD SLOOP LIVELY, OFF SEAL ISLAND, May 12, 1782.

"SIR:—It being my disposition to relieve distress (more especially that of those in your situation), I have sent my boat to your assistance, and at the same time my vessel is at your service, to carry you to the main, where you may provide yourself with a vessel to take your ship's company to Halifax or elsewhere. I should be glad you would come on board, or send such necessaries as you may want for your comfort, and believe me to be your humble servant and friend to the distressed, DANIEL ADAMS."

"ON BOARD SLOOP LIVELY, OFF SEAL ISLAND, May 13, 1782.

"DEAR SIR:—Your generous and candid behavior toward the American prisoners you had on board the Blonde does you the highest honor, and although I feel the most poignant distress for your sufferings, it gives me signal pleasure that it is in my power to relieve you. My situation is so critical here that it would not be consistent with my duty to go out of the vessel, but should be very glad to wait on you on board the Lively, and any of the rest of the gentlemen that should choose to take a passage to the main. If you will send me an estimate of what provisions you shall want for the remainder of the ship's company on the island, it shall be immediately sent on shore.

"I am your humble servant,

"DANIEL ADAMS.

"TO EDWARD THORNBROUGH, Esq."

In Felt's *Annals of Salem* will be found a record of most of the private armed ships equipped in Salem during the war of the Revolution—a large fleet for a town containing less than 6,000 inhabitants. When a Salem captain was asked by an Englishman during the war, "Where do you get your cannon?" he replied, "We cast them;" and when asked again, "But where do you get the patterns?" he replied, with a significant smile, "At Saratoga."

The armed ships of Salem intercepted the transport and supply-ships sent from England and Nova Scotia to the troops in Boston and New York. They resorted to the French islands for munitions of war, and captured the ships engaged in the sugar-trade. They cruised in the Bay of Biscay, English and Irish Channels, raised the rate of insurance on British ships to 23 per cent., and compelled England to employ most of her navy in convoying merchantmen; and, although a large number were captured, they rarely yielded to an equal force.

List of the private armed ships fitted out from the port of Salem, Massachusetts, during the war of the Revolution, viz., from March, 1776, *to March,* 1783.

	Guns.	Men.		Guns.	Men.		Guns.	Men.
Active†c	14	60	Griffin†	..	..	Pompey‡	6	..
Adventure†c	..	..	Hammond†	14	..	Poole‡	..	..
Astrea*lm	20	50	Hammond‡	10	..	Poole*	..	..
Aurora†	..	..	Hampden†c	14	..	Porus*	..	..
Banter	10	..	Harlequin‡	14	60	Putnam‡	..	..
Beaver‡	10	..	Harlequin*c	20	95	Rambler†	14	..
Belisarius‡	..	..	Hasket & John†c	..	..	Racehorse‡c	10	..
Blackford‡	10	..	Hawk‡	..	..	Ranger‡	7	20
Black Prince*	18	..	Hask't & John*lm	..	..	Rainbow§	..	..
Black Snake§	12	..	Harriet‡	14	..	Rattlesnake†c	20	95
Brandywine†	6	..	Hazard†	..	..	Raven‡c	..	..
Bloodhound†	14	55	Hendrick‡c	18	100	Recovery†	..	..
Brutus*c	20	100	How†	8	40	Renown*	14	..
Bowdoin§	8	..	Henry*c	..	..	Revolution*	..	..
Bunker Hillc	..	..	Henry‡	..	..	Revolt†	..	..
Cato‡c	14	55	Hind*	..	..	Rhodes*c	20	110
Chase†	10	..	Hyder Allyc	..	..	Roebuck‡	12	..
Chance‡	..	..	Hope†c	..	..	Romulus†	..	..
Centipede‡	6	..	Jack§c	12	60	Rover§c	14	60
Creature†	14	..	Jackall‡	..	..	Salem Packet*lmc	..	..
Certificate‡c	6	..	James*	..	..	Sally*	..	..
Charm'g Pollylm c	..	..	Jason*c	16	100	Saucy Jackc	..	..
Civil Usage‡	10	..	John*	..	..	St. Johns Packet†c	..	..
Concord†	..	..	Julius Cæsar*lm.	14	40	Scammel‡	16	40
Congress*c	20	130	Jupiter*	..	..	Scourge*	20	110
Cyrus*	..	..	Junius Brutus*c.	20	110	Scorpion§	6	..
Congress‡	8	..	Lark‡	12	..	Sculpin‡	10	..
Cutter†c	10	45	Languedock‡c	..	..	Sacharissa‡	..	..
Dart‡	..	..	Lexington†	8	..	Shaler	..	..
Delight‡	4	..	Lincoln†	12	..	Simon Forester*c	..	..
Dispatch†	..	..	Lion†	16	..	Shark§	10	..
Disdain*c	20	110	Lively‡c	6	..	Spring Bird‡	..	..
Don Galvez†	..	..	Lucy†c	..	..	Spitfire‡c	..	..
Dolphin†	6	25	Louis le Grand*.	18	100	Sturdy Beggar‡c.	..	..
Eagle†c	14	..	Macaroni†	14	..	Swett‡	..	..
Essex*	20	..	Mars*	..	..	Speedwell†c	14	55
Exchange*c	..	..	Marq. Lafayette*.	..	..	Surprise‡	12	60
Experiment†	..	..	Mary†c	..	..	Tatne Bush§	10	..
Fame†	16	..	Modesty‡	8	..	Thomas*c	..	..
Fanny†	..	..	Monmouth†c	12	..	Thorn‡c	..	..
Favorite	..	..	Montgomery†c	14	60	Thrasher‡	..	..
Felicity†	..	..	Morning§	8	..	Tiger†c	10	..
Flying Fish†c	10	45	Munroe†	..	..	Trenton*	12	..
Fly‡	10	..	Neptune†	16	75	True American‡	..	..
Franklin*c	18	100	New Adventurec.	14	50	Two Brothers†c	..	..
Fortune†c	14	60	O. Cromwell*c	16	100	Two Bros.*lm c	..	..
Fox†	14	45	Panther‡	14	50	Venus†	..	..
Gen. Gates‡	10	..	Patty*	..	..	Viper*	..	..
Gen. Greene†c	16	86	Pickering*c	16	45	Washington†	..	..
Gen. Lincoln†	..	..	Pilgrim*	18	110	Warren‡c	..	..
Gen. Putnam‡	18	66	Phœnix†	..	..	Wild Cat†c	14	75
Grand Turk*	22	110	Plato†	8	..	William & Anna‡	..	..
Greyhound‡c	8	35	Polacre†	..	..			

The marks in the above table are explained as follows:—The star (*) signifies ship; dagger (†) brig; double-dagger (‡) schooner; section (§) sloop; *lm* letter of marque; and *c* captured.

The number of these private armed ships, exclusive of those of Beverly and Marblehead, was 158. They mounted at least 2,000 guns, and carried, on an average, from 12 to 14 cannon.

They captured at least 445 vessels, nine-tenths of which reached port in safety. At least 54 of these privateers and letters of marque were captured, and many were lost by perils of the sea. The crews were composed almost entirely of Americans; and from a letter of E. H. Derby to the Secretary of State, in which he mentions that more than 100 men had signed the articles of the Grand Turk within three days after the notices were posted, we may infer that many seamen were to be found during the war who enlisted with alacrity. Several thousand men were furnished by Salem, many of whom, captured by English frigates, lingered for a long time in the Mill Prison and Jersey prison-ship.

The proceeds of the prizes were equally divided between the owner of the ships and the crews, including officers of the vessels.

Among the gallant officers who commanded the armed ships of Salem, were John Archer, John Brooks, C. Babbidge, Daniel Bigelow, Johnson Briggs, N. Brown, Nathaniel Brookhouse, Thomas Benson, John Carnes, John Cathcart, Benjamin Crowninshield, Samuel Crowell, J. Dollanson, John Derby, Benjamin Dean, E. Emerson, David Felt, John Felt, Simon Forester, Wm. Gray, Jonathan Haraden, Daniel Hawthorne, Benjamin Hammond, Gideon Henfield, S. C. Hobbs, Samuel Ingersoll, John Lee, John Leach, N. Lamprel, Stephen Marcoll, J. B. Millet, Jonathan Mason, J. Murphy, Jonathan Neale, Benjamin Needham, Gregory Powers, Joseph Pratt, Wm. Patterson, Thomas Perkins (the principal founder of the Salem Marine Society), Daniel Ropes, David Ropes, John Revel, Joseph Robinson, Daniel Saunders, Elias Smith, Israel Thorndike, J. Tucker, S. Tucker, C. Thompson, John Tittle, Joseph Waters, C.

Woodbury, Henry White, J. White, and Capts. Cook, Jones, Jewett, and Palfrey. Many of these were killed or wounded during the war of the Revolution. Immediately after the battle of Lexington, the above Capt. John Derby, a brother of Elias Hasket, in a fast-sailing ship from Salem, carried to London the first news of that engagement; and on his return, July 18, 1775, immediately waited on Gen. Washington, at Cambridge, with an account of the excitement and surprise produced in England by the intelligence.

During the war of the Revolution, Massachusetts contributed 67,000 soldiers to the armies of the Union—more than were supplied by any other State. But she has never had justice done to her for her services on the ocean. She manned most of the frigates and ships-of-war fitted out by government, and at least one-half the private armed ships which met the "queen of the ocean" on her own element, and successfully disputed her supremacy.

At least 6,000 seamen must have sailed during the war from Salem: if we allow three men to a cannon, and assuming that ratio for other seaports, it is safe to assume that the armed ships which sailed from all the ports of the State in the seven years' contest, bore with them at least 30,000 men. It is time that history should do full justice to the efforts and sacrifices of Massachusetts.

Although the armed ships of Salem captured many vessels from the enemy, her losses were severe. Her fishing-smacks and merchantmen were either swept from the sea by English cruisers, or decayed at the piers: and during the last year of the war, few vessels could enter or leave the port without encountering the fastest frigates of the British navy. From 1771 to 1785, the tonnage of the port actually declined, and did not revive until the opening of the India trade, when it moved onward with astonishing rapidity, as will appear from the subjoined table:

TONNAGE OF SALEM.

	Tons.		Tons.
1768	7,913	1791	9,031
1771	9,223	1800	24,862
1781	8,652	1807......252 vessels	43,570

Arrivals in last quarter of 1807 include 17 from Calcutta, 6 from Sumatra. Duties for the quarter, $511,000.

Shipping owned by Hon. William Gray in 1807, at Salem:—15 ships, 7 barks, 13 brigs, and 1 schooner—or one-fourth of the total tonnage of the port.

From 1791 to 1800, when Mr. Derby owned nearly one-fourth the tonnage, the annual ratio of increase was close upon 20 per cent. From 1800 to 1807, when the tonnage culminated immediately before the embargo, the ratio of growth was 11 per cent.

The disastrous effects of the embargo and war were subsequently shown by the diminution of vessels in foreign trade, from 152 in 1807, to 58 in 1815.

As the war progressed, Mr. Derby learned to appreciate the importance of speed, and as the enemy armed their large ships and sent out many privateers and letters of marque, he established ship-yards, studied naval architecture, and built a class of vessels vastly superior in size, model, and speed to any previously launched in the colonies, and able to cope with a British sloop-of-war. He did not materially increase his fortune during the war, although he took many prizes. He was not desirous to enrich himself by privateering, and gradually converted most of his ships into letters of marque; but he found himself at the close the owner of four ships—the Grand Turk, the Astrea, the Light Horse, and Hasket & John, of three hundred to three hundred and sixty tons; and of three brigs—the Henry, Cato, and Three Sisters, all of superior model, in place of seven sloops and schooners, which he owned at the commencement of the war. He had held his own, and made a fair interest on his capital in his contest with the British.

He had been successful, but he welcomed the peace with joy, for his tastes were pacific. And he was now prepared, by the speed and capacity of his vessels, to meet the mercantile fleet of England in fair competition on the ocean. He was now to embark on new paths of commerce, untried by Americans, and the courage and enterprise he had developed during the war impelled him onward. His ships had outgrown the humble trade he pursued before the war. They were no longer adapted to a small business, or the slow carriage of lumber, live-stock, and fish to the West Indies. He had began to look for new fields of enterprise, and his first step was to the north. In his letter of June, 1784, to Lane, Son, & Frazer, of London, he apprises them that—

"Capt. Buffington, in my bark, the Light Horse, sailed the 15th of June for St. Petersburg, in Russia. This vessel and her cargo of sugars cost me £8,000 sterling, and as the voyage is new to us in this quarter of the world, I wish you to make me £3,000 sterling insurance."

Thus was opened the American trade to St. Petersburg.

For a brief interval Mr. Derby sent his ships to transport mules from Spain to the West Indies to supply the deficiencies caused by the war; to Virginia, to load tobacco and flour for London; to Carolina, to take rice for France; but finding these routes preoccupied, he turned his eyes toward the Cape of Good Hope and the Indies, and determined to measure his strength against the incorporated companies of France, England, Holland, and Sweden, which then monopolized the commerce of the East.

In 1781, Mr. Derby had built at the South Shore, under the eye of Thomas Barstow, a fast-sailing ship of 300 tons, called the Grand Turk. Her armament was 22 guns, and her voyages had been remarkably successful. Of her first cruise no record remains, but on her second cruise, under Joseph Pratt, she went to the coast of Ireland, and there captured the ship Mary, from Jamaica, sugar laden, and on her way to Bilboa with her prize, took the brig John Grace, and carried both in safety to Bilboa, where the net sales amounted to $65,802. After refitting, she sailed for the West Indies, captured several prizes, which were sent into the French islands and condemned, and proceeds remitted to Salem. She subsequently captured the ship Pompey, of 20 guns, from London, which sailed after the proclamation of peace was signed, but was captured before it took effect in the longitudes in which she was taken. After this brilliant success the Grand Turk made two voyages to the West Indies. In November, A. D. 1784, she was dispatched, under the command of Capt. Jonathan Ingersoll, on the first voyage from Salem to the Cape of Good Hope. She was lying at Table Bay when Major Samuel Shaw arrived there on his return from Canton, and in his memoir, edited by the Hon. Josiah Quincy, he states that he sent his boat to the Grand Turk for Captain Ingersoll to come on board, and says of him :

" His object was to sell rum, cheese, salt provisions, chocolate, loaf-sugar, butter, &c., the proceeds of which, in money, with a quantity of ginseng, and some cash brought with him, he intended to invest in Bohea tea ; but as the ships bound to Europe are not allowed to break bulk on the way, he was disappointed in his expectations of procuring that article, and sold his ginseng for two-thirds of a Spanish dollar a pound, which is twenty per cent. better than the silver money of the Cape. He intended remaining a short time to purchase fine teas in the private trade, allowed the officers on board India ships, and then to sail to the coast of Guinea, to dispose of his rum, &c., for ivory and gold-dust, thence, without taking a single slave, to proceed to the West Indies, and purchase sugar and cotton, with which he would return to Salem. Notwithstanding the disappointment in the principal object of the voyage, and the consequent determination to go to the coast of Guinea, his resolution not to endeavor to retrieve it by purchasing slaves, did the captain great honor, and reflected equal credit upon his owner, who, he assured me, would rather sink the whole capital employed than directly or indirectly be concerned in so infamous a trade."

These views of a Massachusetts merchant and master, at a moment when the slave-trade was permitted by the laws, and this resolution of Capt. Ingersoll to sail in ballast from the coast of Africa to the great slave mart of the West, are peculiarly interesting at the present moment, when the topic of the slave-trade is again started at the South.

The Grand Turk sold her rum to an English East Indiaman, and delivered it at St. Helena. She returned in 1785, via the West Indies, and her sales proved sufficient to load two ships for home with Grenada rum. Capt. Ingersoll sent the ship to Salem, and returned with his shipment in the Atlantic, and on his way home he rescued the master and mate of the English schooner *Amity*, whose crew had mutinied, and set their officers adrift in a boat. After their arrival in Salem, Capt. Duncanson, of the Amity, was sitting one day with Mr. Derby in his counting-room, and, while using his spy-glass, he espied his own vessel in the offing. Mr. Derby promptly manned one of his brigs, put two pieces of cannon on board of her, and, taking with him the English captain, boarded and recaptured the Amity.

Mr. Derby was a man of action rather than of words; and, when he reported the facts to the Governor, he concluded his laconic letter of six lines in these terms: "The prisoners remain at your Excellency's disposal."

When the letter was printed, some one criticised it as not properly addressed to "His Excellency;" but Mr. Derby replied, "the address was there—they would find it in the conclusion."

Another anecdote of Mr. Derby at this period of his life, of a different character, may not be out of place. He was cheated by a merchant to whom he had sold some merchandise. When the loss was ascertained, he called his clerks around him, and charged them not to trust a man again who wore nankeen small-clothes in midwinter; "For if he cheats himself, you may expect he will cheat you." A few weeks afterward, one of the first merchants of Boston drove down to Salem, while Mr. Derby was absent, to buy an invoice of goods; but the clerks, observing his dress, and taking Mr. Derby at his word, refused to trust him; and he returned without his merchandise. His anger was appeased when he discovered what part of his costume had destroyed his credit.

On another occasion, Mr. Derby sold a country clergyman a piece of broadcloth on credit, and after two or three years he sent his clerks several times for the pay, but they returned empty-handed. Mr. Derby told them they did not understand their business, and added, "Let me see him if he ever comes here again, and I will show you what can be done." The clergyman came, the clerks ushered him into the inner room, and awaited the result. They were not a little amused to see him walk out after an hour's conversation with Mr. Derby, without squaring the amount, with another piece of broadcloth under his arm.

Although the voyage of the Grand Turk to the Cape did not realize all the hopes of Mr. Derby, the provisions, ginseng, and other articles, gave a fair profit. He had learned, too, the wants and prices of the Indian market. His eldest son, Elias Hasket, had also left college, landed from one of his ships in Scotland, visited London, Paris and L'Orient, in France, learned the French language, and gained some insight into the English and French trade to the Indies. Thus encouraged, Mr. Derby, December 5, 1785, dispatched the Grand Turk, under the command of Capt. Ebenezer West, on the first voyage from New England to the Isle of France, India, and China.

The Grand Turk reached home with a cargo of tea, silks, and nankeens, in June, 1787; and the letters from her officers had been so satisfactory, that, before her arrival at Salem, Mr. Derby dispatched the bark Light Horse and brigantine Three Sisters for the East, and was largely embarked in the East India trade.

In December, 1787, Mr. Derby again dispatched his ship Grand Turk on a voyage to the Isle of France, under the charge of his son, Elias Hasket, with a promise that he would send the ship Juno in a few weeks afterward to his consignment. The Juno foundered at sea, and proved a total loss, without insurance. The Grand Turk, however, was sold, with her cargo, at a great profit, by his son, who remained a year in the Isle of France, until relieved by the ship Atlantic, dispatched after the loss of the Juno, when he proceeded to Surat, Bombay, and Calcutta, and first displayed our ensign at those ports.

Elias Hasket, Jr., remained three years in India, and there formed an extensive mercantile acquaintance, and laid the foundations of the extensive trade subsequently developed by his father. August, 1788, he purchased at the Isle of France, from the proceeds of his cargo, the ship Peggy and brigantine Sultana, and sent them to Bombay for cotton. The Peggy returned to Salem, where she arrived June 21, 1789, with the first cargo of Bombay cotton. In 1789 he dispatched the Sultana to Madras, and loaded the Light Horse and Atlantic at Bombay, with cotton, for China. After visiting Surat, Bombay, Madras, and Calcutta, he sent the Astrea to Rangoon. She was impressed by the natives, and sent with troops to Siam, where she first displayed the flag of America. Returning in the brig Henry, in January, 1791, the immediate result of his voyages was found to be a profit of nearly $100,000. He soon after sent a ship on the first voyage made from America to Mocha, in the Red Sea.

During the years 1787 and 1788, his father having dispatched the Light Horse and other vessels to the Isle of France and India, no less than four of Mr. Derby's ships found their way to Canton in 1789, viz., the Atlantic, Three Sisters, Light Horse, and Astrea.* Of these, the Astrea was one of his favorite ships: she was distinguished for speed, having in one voyage to the Baltic made the run in 11 days from Salem to the coast of Ireland, and she was rated at 360 tons. This ship first appears on the books of Mr. Derby in 1783, and seems to have been a letter of marque during the last year of the war. After the peace, she made several voyages to London and the Baltic, and continued to run many years in the service of Mr. Derby.

Early in 1788, Mr. Derby planned, for the first time, a direct voyage to Batavia and Canton, and selected the Astrea for that purpose: but in those days a Canton voyage was a serious undertaking; and, as six months were required to provide the specie, ginseng, and other cargo, the ship was sent in the spring up the Baltic for iron; a schooner was sent to Madeira for wine, and letters were addressed to Mr. Derby's correspondents at New York, Philadelphia, and Baltimore for ginseng and specie. The Astrea, on her return, met with stress of weather, and put into Newfoundland. This detention delayed her voyage until the close of the year. Upon her arrival from Russia, Mr. Derby had her thoroughly repaired, and then submitted her to a sur-

* The Astrea was built by Mr. Derby, and made her first passage as a letter of marque, in 1783, to France in 18 days, and returned in 19 days.

vey of three experienced merchants, who reported her to be in fine order for an Indian voyage.

In February, 1789, he dispatched her for Canton with an assorted cargo, backed up by shipments of specie by David Sears, Samuel Parkman, and other distinguished merchants.

Her manifest gives the assortment then deemed proper for such a voyage, with a list of the adventures and terms of shipment, and may interest the merchant of the present day:

MANIFEST OF THE CARGO ON BOARD SHIP ASTREA, JAMES MAGEE, MASTER, FROM SALEM, FOR BATAVIA AND CANTON.

Mark	Cargo
[S]	50 barrels salmon.
	100 tons iron, 5,757 bars.
[W]	39 pipes Madeira wine, 4,290 gallons.
	50 barrels tar.
ED	50 boxes chocolate, 2,500 lbs.
	598 firkins butter, 32,005 lbs.
[SC]	345 boxes spermaceti candles, 8,933$\frac{1}{4}$ lbs.
[D]	153 hhds. and tierces ginseng, 55,776$\frac{3}{4}$ bls.
[R]	11 pipes red port wine, 1,339 gallons.
[F]	6 pipes Teneriffe wine, 721 gallons.
	24 hhds. beer, 2 barrels each.
	24 bbls. beer, 40 gallons each.
	115 tubs steel.
[B]	48 barrels beef.
[F]&A	336 bbls. common flour.
This belongs to Tenney & Brown, of Newbury; $\frac{1}{3}$ the net proceeds you are to credit E. H. D.'s account for freight—the other $\frac{2}{3}$ to lay out on account of T. & B. in light goods. B & T A 1009	9 kegs snuff.
FD	2 boxes women's shoes, 407 pair.
[D]d	14 hhds. N. E. rum, 1 hhd. stores, } 1,792 galls.
	19 dozen handkerchiefs.
[F]	7 hhds. codfish, 9 quintals each, 63 quintals.
This belongs to Folger Pope, and after deducting commissions, the net proceeds is to be credited to E. H. D.'s account, as friend Derby is to have the use of the money for freight.	1 phaeton and harness complete, with saddles, bridles, &c., cased up.

This belongs to James Bott, and goes on the same terms as the above.	EED	J. Bott, 1 box saddlery.

ADVENTURES.

	ID	4 hhds. ginseng, 1,998 lbs. 10 half bbls. beef. 1 box shoes, 94 pair. 6 cases Geneva. 2 pipes red port wine, 237 galls. 9 firkins butter.
Capt. Nathaniel West.	NW EW	15 boxes spermaceti candles. 1 pipe Teneriffe wine, 118 galls.
James Jeffry.	I7I xx No. 1	1 cask ginseng, 274 lbs.
Ezekiel H. Derby.	ED 1 cask Nos. 1&2 1 bag	Ginseng, 310½.
Ezekiel H. Derby & Co.	D&C	1 cask of siftings of the ginseng, 138 lbs.
George Dodge.	[W]	810 dollars. 1 pipe Madeira wine, 110 gallons (marked with marking irons GD near the bung).
Benjamin Pickman, Jr.	BP.	2 pipes Madeira wine, 220 gallons.
Josiah Shippey & Co. This goes one-fifth for freight.	[S] No. 1 a19	8 boxes containing 4,000 dollars. 19 tierces ginseng, 4,086 lbs.
Josiah Shippey & Co. This goes at 33⅓ per cent. for freight.	[W] No. 1 a16	16 tierces ginseng, 3,547 lbs.
Josiah Shippey & Co. This goes one-fifth for freight.	17S No. 1 & 2 No. 1 a24	2 boxes containing 1,000 dollars. 23 tierces 1 bbl. ginseng, 4,719 lbs.
John Seaman. This at 33⅓ per cent. for freight.	A No. 1 a3	11 tierces ginseng, 639 lbs.
David Sears. This at one-fifth for freight.	DS No. 1 a16	Boxes containing 15,000 dollars. 16 casks ginseng, 5,570 lbs.
David Sears. This at 33⅓ per cent. for freight.	DS No. 17 a31	15 casks ginseng, 4,793 lbs.
Edmund Seaman. This at one-fifth for freight and commissions.	ES No. 1 & 2	200 Spanish milled dollars. 2 tierces ginseng, 430 lbs.

Shipper	Marks	Goods
Samuel Parkman. This at one-fifth for freight and commissions.	P No. 1 a7	7 hhds. ginseng, 2,444 lbs.
	SP No. 1 a5	5 boxes containing 5,000 dollars.
Eleazer Johnson. This at one-fifth for freight and commissions.	EJ No. 1 a5	5 casks ginseng, 1 keg samples, } 1,988
	No. 1 a7	7 bags dollars, 4,000.
James Magee and Thomas H. Perkins.		1 pipe Madeira wine, 103 galls. 1 pipe port wine, 122 galls. 250 lbs. loaf-sugar. 4 cases Geneva, 18 galls. 20 gallons brandy. 95 doz. 9 bottles rappee snuff, 1,449 lbs. 552 lbs. manufactured tobacco.
Wm. Cabot: freight and commission as others pay.	W7C	A box containing 23 pieces plate, weight 255 oz. 16 dwts. 12 gr.
Oliver Brewster; at 9 per cent. freight home.		A bag containing 500 dollars.
Robert Breek; at 25 per cent. for freight and commissions.		A bag containing 200 dollars.
People—Adventures.		4 bbls. N. E. rum, 104¼ galls. 50 cases Geneva, 225 galls. 2 bbls. snuff, 260 lbs.
Elias H. Derby; to be disposed of.		4 casks ginseng, 965 lbs. " " 30 lbs. } 995.

It will be noticed that many of the shipments by merchants paid a large freight, and that it was the custom for the officers and children of the owner to take an interest in the voyage. The cargo of the Astrea was intrusted to the joint care of Capt. James Magee and Thomas Handasyd Perkins. The last-named gentleman laid the foundation of his fortunes in this voyage, by establishing a house in China, and for many years was a leading merchant in Boston, and one of the founders of the Boston Athenæum and Asylum for the Blind. His memoir has already appeared in the preceding volume, and his character at this early period of his life may be inferred from the following extract from a letter to Mr. Derby, of February 3, 1789, from the late David Sears, an eminent merchant of Boston: "We may rest easy; and were our whole fortune depending on the honesty of Magee and Perkins, I think, by what I know of them, that it would be as safe as if we were in the ship ourselves."

The following letter of instructions from Mr. Derby for this voyage is still extant;

"SALEM, February, 1789.

"CAPT. JAMES MAGEE, JR., MR. THOMAS H. PERKINS:

"GENTS—The ship Astrea, of which James Magee is master, and Mr. Thomas Perkins is supercargo, being ready for sea, I do advise and order you to come to sail, and make the best of your way for Batavia, and on your arrival there you will dispose of such a part of the cargo as you think may be most for my interest.

"I think you had best sell a few casks of the most ordinary ginseng, if you can get one dollar a pound for it. If you find the price of sugar to be low, you will then take into the ship as much of the best white kind as will floor her, and fifty thousand weight of coffee, if it is as low as we have heard—part of which you will be able to stow between the beams and the quintlings—and fifteen thousand of saltpeter, if very low; some nutmegs, and fifty thousand weight of pepper; this you will stow in the fore peak, for fear of its injuring the teas. The sugar will save the expense of any stone ballast, and it will make a floor for the teas, &c., at Canton.

"At Batavia you must, if possible, get as much freight for Canton as will pay half or more of your charges—that is, if it will not detain you too long,—as by this addition of freight it will exceedingly help the voyage. You must endeavor to be the first ship with ginseng, for be assured you will do better alone than you will if there are three or four ships at Canton at the same time with you. If Messrs. Blanchard & Webb are at Batavia in the brigantine Three

Sisters, and if they have not stock sufficient to load with coffee and sugar, and if it is low, and you think it for my advantage, then I would have you ship me some coffee or sugar, and a few nutmegs, &c., to complete his loading. If his brigantine can be sold for a large price, and sugar and coffee, &c., are too dear to make any large freight—in that case it possibly may be for my interest to have her sold, and for them to take passage with you to Canton: but this must not be done unless you, Dr. Blanchard, and Capt. Webb shall think it *greatly* for my interest. Or possibly they may sell their brigantine to advantage, and find some Dutch ship that would take their freight to St. Eustatia or Curaçoa, so as to make it very advantageous. But there are too often difficulties attending the sale of ships so far from home; it therefore must be well thought of before it is undertaken. One thing I have against it is, that I shall have too much property in the Astrea, and not know it in time to make my insurance; which ought to be taken into consideration. On your going round the Cape, no doubt, you will see some India ships bound home; you will put letters on board two or three of them for me, acquainting me with the situation of the ship, and every thing you think I may wish to know. Capt. Magee and Mr. Perkins are to have 5 per cent. commission for the sales of the present cargo, and 2½ per cent. on the cargo home, and also 5 per cent. on the profit made on goods that may be purchased at Batavia and sold at Canton, or in any other similar case that may arise on the voyage. They are to have one-half the passage money—the other half belongs to the ship. The privilege of Capt. Magee is 5 per cent. of what the ship carries on cargo exclusive of adventures. The property of Mr. Perkins, it is understood, is to be on freight, which is to be paid for like the other freighters. It is orders that the ship's books shall be open to the inspection of the mates and doctor of the ship, so that they may know the whole business, as in case of death or sickness it may be good service in the voyage. The Philadelphia beer is put up so strong, that it will not be approved of until it is made weaker: you had best try some of it first. The iron is English weight: you will remember there is 4 per cent. that you will gain if sold Dutch weight. As the ships will be about leaving Batavia at the time you are there; if so, you will best barter the small ginseng for something those ships may have on board, as no doubt it will do better in that way than at Canton. You will be careful not to break any acts of trade while you are out on the voyage, to lay the ship and cargo liable to seizure, for my insurance will not make it good. All freight out and home, it is understood, belongs to the ship, as Capt. Magee is to fill his privilege with his own property. Be very careful of the expense attending the voyage, for I more fear that than any thing else; and remember that one dollar laid out while absent is two dollars out of the voyage. Pay particular attention to the quality of your goods, as your voyage very much depends on your attention to this. You will not forget what Mr. Shippey says to you on that head, of the green tea and nankeens. You are not to pay any moneys to the crew while absent from home, unless in a case of real necessity, and then they must allow an advance for the money. Annexed to these orders you have a list of such a cargo for my own account as I at present think may do best for me, but you will add or diminish any article as the price may be.

"My own property, I suppose, will take the room of 500 chests, and your freight that you already engaged will take the room of about 500 chests, and then I compute you will have room for 500 chests more on freight, to make up the 1,500 which you think the ship will load on cargo. You must, at Canton or Batavia, endeavor to fill the ship with light freight; and, provided you can do it to advantage, you have leave to put my property into more valuable goods, so as to take the less room: but this must not be done unless by calculation you find it greatly for my interest. And I again repeat that I would have the doctor and Mr. Bray made acquainted with the whole business of the voyage, for fear of accident, as, in case Mr. Perkins should fail, one or both of them might be of great service to the voyage. It is likewise my order that, in case of your sickness, you write a clause at the foot of these orders, putting the command of the ship into the person's hands that you think the most equal to it, not having any regard to the station *he* at present has in the ship. Among the silks, you will get me one or two pieces of the wide nankeen satin, and others you will get as directed. Get me two pots of twenty pounds each of race ginger, that is well put up; and lay out for my account fifteen or twenty pounds sterling in curiosities. There will be breakage room in the bilge of the ship, that nothing dry can go in; therefore, in the crop of the bilge you will put some boxes of China, such as are made suitable for such places, and filled with cups and saucers, some bowls, and any thing of the kind that may answer.

"As to the sale of the ship Astrea, it will not do to think of it, on account of the freighters' goods; but if at Batavia or Canton you can agree to deliver her the next season for $20,000 or $25,000, you may do it, the danger of the seas, &c., excepted. Attend particularly to the writings for this contract. Provided that you wish to obtain more property home in the ship, it will be most agreeable to me to take such a part of the profit, or take it to come at their risk, and for me to have all above 40 per cent. for Hyson tea and light goods; but the goods must be of the best quality, and put in at the cash value; but do not take it on my risk without the property is insured before you leave Canton. If any goods are shipped from Canton in the ship, you will endeavor to get me the consignment, as it may serve some of my family at Boston. It is understood where I have one-third of the ginseng for the freight and commissions, as mentioned in the agreement, I am to allow Magee and Perkins the commission for the whole sales out. In case Mr. Blanchard is at Batavia, and purchasing coffee, sugar, and other articles, if he can, by taking those articles, put off some of your goods and give you this money, in any way not to injure his voyage, then I would have him do it. Provided you, by information, are fully convinced that you can make a freight from Batavia on coffee, sugar, cotton, rice, or any thing else, and you can sell my ginseng for a dollar a pound this weight, then I wish to have a third of my quantity sold, but not for less; but in a barter way you no doubt will do better.

"Capt. Magee and Mr. Perkins—Although I have been a little particular in these orders, I do not mean them as positive; and you have leave to break them in any part where you by calculation think it for my interest, excepting your breaking acts of trade, which I absolutely forbid. Not having to add, I commit you to the Almighty's protection, and remain your friend and employer,

"ELIAS HASKET DERBY."

"SALEM, 15th February, 1789.

"We acknowledge the above to be a true copy of our orders this day received.

"JAMES MAGEE.
"THOMAS HAND. PERKINS."

The Astrea sailed with brilliant prospects, but American ships were already following the lead of the Grand Turk, and, between the fall of 1788 and 1791, no less than fifteen American vessels arrived in Canton.

Mr. Perkins found the market overstocked with ginseng, and sold the large invoices of Mr. Derby at $20,000 less than the prime cost. He found there, also, three other ships of Mr. Derby. The Light Horse, Atlantic, and Three Sisters, influenced by temporary high prices of produce in the Isle of France and India, had come on to China; so that four of his ships were lying at Canton in the summer of 1789.

Pursuant to the orders of Mr. Derby, two of these ships were sold, and the proceeds of all their cargoes were shipped in the Astrea and Light Horse, which arrived safely in Salem, with no less than 728,871 pounds of tea for Mr. Derby. This importation was unprecedented; so also was the entire importation of the same year into the United States, viz., 2,601,852 pounds of tea. And the result was disheartening to the merchants who first adventured in the China trade. Down to this period, most of the teas had come at high prices via Sweden, Holland, England, and France. The nation was exhausted by the war, and less than a million of pounds sufficed for the consumption of a country which now absorbs forty millions of pounds annually, in addition to cocoa and coffee.

Still another event had occurred during the voyage to dishearten Mr. Derby. The government had been organized under the constitution of 1788, and an unexpected duty been imposed on teas, which amounted to $25,000 on the invoices of Mr. Derby. This duty took immediate effect, without any exception for the cargoes on the way.

Under these circumstances, Mr. Derby addressed to Congress the following memorial, in which, and the letters which accompanied it, he presents the oppressive weight of the duty, and shadows forth the idea of the present warehousing system of the United States.

"*To the Honorable Senate and Honorable House of Representatives of the United States of America, in Congress assembled:*

"The memorial of Elias Hasket Derby, of Salem, in the commonwealth of Massachusetts, merchant, humbly showeth—

"That your memorialist, previous to the fourth day of March, in the year of our Lord one thousand seven hundred and eighty-nine, fitted out and ordered to places beyond the Cape of Good Hope four vessels, laden with cargoes of the growth and produce of this country, and principally the property of your memorialist, to the amount, nearly, of all his stock in trade; that only one of those vessels, to wit, the Astrea, was ordered and designed for Canton; that from the unexpected and particular circumstances of the markets at the Isle of France, India, and Batavia, the factors of two of his said vessels thought it advisable, and did sell them and their cargoes, and meeting with his two other vessels in those seas, put the proceeds thereof on board of them; that the factor of the ship, the Light Horse, one of the two remaining vessels, being ignorant of the great number of vessels which had sailed from the United States for Canton, judged it most for the interest of your memorialist to proceed also to Canton, there to load with tea and return home; that his said two ships, the Astrea and Light Horse, have within a few days past returned from Canton to the port of Salem with the proceeds of their own cargoes, the other two vessels and their cargoes, principally in teas.

"That no fewer than eleven sail of vessels have been at Canton the last season, taking on board teas and other Chinese goods designed for the markets of the United States, amounting to three thousand one hundred and fifty tons of shipping, a schedule of which he herewith begs leave to exhibit; that some of those vessels have already arrived in the United States, and the rest are daily expected; that the teas which will be imported in all those vessels will, on the most accurate calculation, be more than sufficient for the consumption of the United States for three years; that the surplus produce of these teas cannot be exported to foreign markets without great loss, and that of course it must principally, if not altogether, be consumed in the United States.

"That from the badness of the markets to which he originally intended his property, and not from any plan, nearly all his capital at this time consists of teas, and that in consequence of the impost law, made since his property left the United States, he shall be obliged within six months to raise a very large sum of money to discharge his bonds given to secure the payment of the duties; that no property now remains by him from whence to raise the sums necessary therefor, unless it is teas, which, from the great abundance at market, cannot be used without a sacrifice is made of them; his situation is peculiarly distressing, requiring him to sell his property at so low a price as to make him, in fact, pay the duties out of his own pocket, without the most distant prospect of ever receiving a cent therefor, instead of his becoming the collector, and advancing them to government, for the consumer, or to suffer his bonds to be put in suit, and thereby to have his credit impaired, and lose his reputation of punctuality, and receive but temporary relief, with the loss of what is most dear to him; and this appears to him the only choice left, and whichever step he takes, it will be a painful, a really painful one to him. Under this melancholy impression, he flies to your honors for aid and relief; and from you it is that he expects assistance under this his most grievous burden, and which he could never have incurred if he or his factors abroad had known or could have foreseen the operation of the impost laws. He therefore, and with the fullest confidence, appeals to you, the guardians of the liberty and trade of the citizens of this rising empire, for redress, not doubting that when the amount of the duties of impost on two cargoes of tea, the great scarcity of specie, and the difficulty of raising some thousands of dollars in this young nation almost destitute of capital, are considered, your wisdom and candor will determine that so much time shall be given him for payment of the duties, and such provision be made for him, as that the consumers of that article shall eventually pay it, and not that he shall be compelled to pay it within the time limited by law, thereby throwing into the hands of watchful speculators an opportunity of enriching themselves, and rendering your memorialist the sole sufferer.

"He would only further add, that it is with the greatest cheerfulness that he advances to government the duties required by law; and, should the idea be thought not becoming and improper, would suggest that he would not hesitate to pay to the United States all the duties on his teas in that article, at a much less price than it would have sold for at market at the time when the impost law was made.

"Your memorialist therefore humbly prays your honors that he may be allowed to pay to the United States the duties on his cargoes of tea as he from time to time shall sell them, and no sooner, or otherwise grant him such relief as in your wisdom shall seem best; and as in duty bound will ever pray.

"ELIAS HASKET DERBY.

"SALEM, June 10, 1790."

The petition of Mr. Derby presented so strong a claim, that it was immediately granted. Ample time was allowed him for the disposal of his teas. Importations were checked; the low prices stimulated demand; the funding of the debt increased the means of the merchants; and we may infer, from the energy with which Mr. Derby embarked in the trade to India in 1791, that his means were not impaired, if they were not increased, by his tea voyages.

During the years 1789 and 1790, while the subjects of the duties on foreign merchandise and the funding of the State and national debt were under discussion, Mr. Derby carried on an active correspondence with his friends, the Hon. Benj. Goodhue and Fisher Ames, members of Congress from Massachusetts, in which he evinces his commercial information. When it was proposed to put a duty of twelve cents on Bohea tea, he pointed out the oppressive character of a tax amounting to nearly 100 per cent. on the prime cost, and the injustice that would be thus done to merchants who had embarked in voyages to China, and the danger of illicit importations. He suggested, too, the importance of a system of drawbacks to a commercial nation.

In discussing the question of the public debt, in his letter of February 3d, 1790, to the Hon. Benj. Goodhue, he incidentally remarks:

"At the time of Lexington battle, I loaned to government a large proportion of the supplies for the army, and took their obligations for so much specie, which obligations I have by me, and should think such debts were as justly due me as any private obligation whatever. To have the foreign debt put on a better footing than the domestic debt, or to put the interest at 3 or 4 per cent. without the consent of the holders of such obligations, will not, in my opinion, ever raise the credit of the government."

The loan he refers to was not the only aid rendered by Mr. Derby to his country. When General Sullivan marched to Rhode Island, he supplied his troops with boats to cross from the main to the island; he furnished the French fleet with coal; and at a later period took the lead in building a frigate for the nation; and when that nation, in her prosperity, tendered to him in requital 3 per cent. interest or a 3 per cent. stock for his active capital loaned to her in an hour of peril; when, too, that nation imposed an unexpected duty on his tea, while he was opening to her the way to oriental wealth, he submitted to her injustice.

Perhaps he might not have so readily acquiesced, could he for a moment have imagined that this same nation, after assuming by treaty the payment of his just claims on France, and allowing him no chance to enforce them with his own cannon, would for sixty years have withheld from his posterity both principal and interest of a just debt of $40,000.

From 1788 to 1799, he pursued the India trade with vigor, but he seems to have been surfeited with tea. His principal voyages after 1790, were either direct to the Cape, the Isle of France, Bourbon, Calcutta, Madras, or from Salem to England, Spain, France, Sweden, or Madeira, and thence to the East Indies, taking return cargoes, which were either sold in Salem or Boston, or shipped coastwise to his valued correspondents, Ludlow & Gould, of New York, James Carey & Co., and Pickering & Hodgdon, Philadelphia, or other consignees at Baltimore or Richmond. Some of his shipments paid large profits. By a letter to Stephen Codman, Esq., it appears that it was the custom of the day to sell muslins and calico from Calcutta by invoices marked 100 per cent. above the India price. An instance occurs of a shipment of twelve thousand plain glass tumblers, costing less than $1,000, and sent to the Isle of France by the ship Benjamin, Capt. Silsbee, and arriving when there was no glassware in the island, and selling for $12,000; and another instance in which a cargo of common red wine from the Mediterranean, arriving at an opportune moment, sold for sufficient to load two vessels with coffee, which was worth twenty-five cents per pound in America. From the disturbed state of Europe, trade was irregular. Voyages occasionally resulted in loss, but the ripened wisdom, courage, and perseverance of Mr. Derby were triumphant, and in the brief period from 1790 to 1799, a space little longer than the war of 1776, he increased his property at least five-fold, and made liberal advances to his children.

When Mr. Derby first engaged in the trade to India, there were no banks, and little active capital, in Massachusetts. His first cargoes were of moderate value: they consisted of an assortment of provisions, naval stores, spars, cordage, wine, spirits, iron, lead, and ginseng. These cargoes were swelled by shipments of goods, or specie on freight, paying from 20 to 30 per cent. upon returns for carriage. Mr. Derby rarely sold or purchased on credit, as debts, before the day of banks, were not punctually paid. While his large ships were on their voyages to the East, he employed his brigs and schooners in making up the assortment, by sending them to Gottenburg and St. Petersburg for iron, duck, and hemp; to France, Spain, and Madeira, for wine and lead; to the West Indies for spirits; and to New York, Philadelphia, and Richmond, for flour, provisions, iron, and tobacco; and made his remittances therefor, as far as possible, in the teas, coffee, pepper, muslins, and silks which he imported from the East, often bartering the one for the other, and sometimes drawing moderate advances from his consignees and London bankers. He rarely insured more than half the outfit, and, by dividing his risks, in his extensive commerce, could occasionally lose a ship and cargo without a serious interruption of his business. His views were always prospective, and his solicitude seemed to be to make his importations the basis of his future adventures, without incurring debt. After a few successful voyages to the East, his capital increased, and he became able to cope with the largest undertakings.

In the brief space of fourteen years, from 1785 to 1799, we find among his papers the record of one hundred and twenty-five voyages, by at least thirty-seven different vessels, of which voyages forty-five were to the East Indies or China.

The records have suffered by lapse of time and removal. A number of voyages are doubtless omitted, and many of the ships made intermediate voyages, of which no account remains; but we have ample memorials of the enterprise and activity of this distinguished merchant.

Among the ships sent by him to the East, to the Baltic and Mediterranean, were the ships Hasket & John, Grand Turk, 180 tons; Astrea, 360 tons; Henry, 190 tons; Recovery, John, Benjamin, Martha, Grand Sachem, Grand Turk (new), 560 tons; Active, Three Sisters, Juno, Atlantic, Peggy, Eliza, Light Horse, Mount Vernon, Bunker Hill, Benjamin (new), 450 tons.

The John was sometimes rigged as a ketch; the armed ship Benjamin was coppered to the bends. After her purchase by Capt. Silsbee in 1796, Mr. Derby adopted the practice of coppering his ships, then a novelty in America.

The Henry, built of white pine, proved a very buoyant and durable ship, and lasted nearly half a century. Among his small vessels were the brigs Dolphin, Conger, Brothers, Nancy, Ranger, Cato, Three Friends, Chance, Rose, Peggy, Henry, Antelope, Jutland; and schooners Hannah, Polly, Porga, Hope, Fanny; and sloops Sally and Alice.

Among the officers of these ships who afterward became distinguished for talents or success, were Hon. Nathaniel Silsbee, Dr. Nathaniel Bowditch, John Prince, Joseph Ropes, J. Magee, Joseph Pratt, Benjamin Hodges, Esqs., Capt. Richard Cleveland, Capt. J. Nichols, Hon. Thomas H. Perkins, Benjamin Crowninshield, Jacob Crowninshield, D. Saunders, Esqs., Capt. Richard Derby, Gen. Samuel Derby, Capt. Benjamin Webb, Capt. J. Ingersoll, Capt. Stephen Philipps.

Among the officers who rose most rapidly to distinction in the service of Mr. Derby, none is more prominent than the Hon. Nathaniel Silsbee, late Senator from Massachusetts. His father had enjoyed the entire confidence of Mr.

Derby, and after his death, Mr. Derby transferred that confidence to his son.

In 1790, he appears as the mate and captain's clerk of a small vessel bound to Madeira. In 1792 he is master of a sloop in the trade to the West Indies, which Mr. Derby empowers him to sell for $350. In 1793, at the early age of twenty years, he is on his voyage to the Isle of France, in command of the new ship Benjamin, of 142 tons. From the Isle of France he proceeds to the Cape of Good Hope, returns to the Isle of France, and brings his ship home with large profits.

In 1796, Mr. Derby dispatches him in the ship Benjamin to Amsterdam, and thence to the Isle of France, with a credit of $10,000 for his own private adventure. After selling his cargo at a great profit, he purchases a new ship of 450 tons, and returns to Salem with a full cargo of East India goods for his owner, and such favorable results for himself, as to enable him to commence business on his own account, in which he soon achieved a fortune.

When Mr. Derby first went into the India trade, there were few officers in the country able to take charge of an Indiaman on such long, untried voyages, and he was obliged to improvise not only ships, but officers, for the occasion. To obviate this difficulty, he gave gratuitous instruction to many lads of his native town. He admitted the most promising of these, when young, as masters or supercargoes, into his ships. If they displayed tact and ability, he soon gave them command, and laid the foundations of their fortunes, by liberal commissions and salaries, and an interest in the voyages. While his ships were absent, Mr. Derby devoted himself to the improvement of models and the supervision of his vessels on the stocks; or found his recreation on his farm, or in importing new flowers, shrubs, plants, trees, and animals, for his own amusement, and the improvement of his State.

The following letter, inclosing a receipt for £20, illustrates the mode in which Mr. Derby aided his young townsmen:

"SALEM, June 17, 1794.

"SIR:—Among so many men of learning as there are in the town of Salem, your having preferred me to be one of the teachers of the young seamen, whom you generously gave the learning of navigation to, I receive as a particular favor, and shall remember it with gratitude many days; and the more so, because, as to my appearance, I cut no great dash, being fully convinced that powdering my hair would add nothing to my understanding.

"Having accomplished the business assigned me, in furnishing those that attended on my tuition (whose names are hereunto subjoined), in the theory of the most useful part of the business of conducting a vessel from one port or part of the world to another as well as I was capable of, and as well as their different capacities would admit of, I have now only to add, that I am to request you to believe me, sir, when I say, that I wish you health and long life, and that I am in all services

"Your obedient servant,

"JONA. ARCHER, JR."

(Twenty names are subjoined.)

Frequent complaints are now made of an increase of marine losses. This is doubtless due in part to the fact that there is more rivalry among clipper-ships than in former days, that there is a less proportion of native seamen, and that our ships are not as well manned as formerly, although our improvements in model and rigging, and the superior intelligence of our officers, enable us to sail them with a less number of men than are required by English ships of the same tonnage.

Mr. Derby rarely lost a ship by marine perils; the only

instance of such loss in the record of one hundred and twenty-five of his voyages, is the loss of the Juno, purchased by him of Thomas Lee, in 1787, and which foundered at sea, from some latent defect, in moderate weather, soon after she left Salem. The remarkable exemption of Mr. Derby from such losses is doubtless due to several causes.

After the war, it was his uniform rule to have none of his ships come upon our coast between November and March, and although often urged by other merchants to reduce the liberal compensation he gave to his officers, no persuasion could induce him to change his policy.

He employed young and energetic men, gave them a large interest in their voyages, and consequently was uniformly well served by those in his employ.

Capt. Richard Cleveland, who was in his employ from 1788 to 1795, and who still lives in a green old age at Salem, after a life of singular vicissitudes, bears the following testimony to his ability and character, in the first page of his "Narrative of Voyages and Commercial Enterprises," published at Cambridge in 1842:

"In the ordinary course of commercial education in New England, boys are transferred from school to the merchant's desk, at the age of fourteen or fifteen. When I had reached my fourteenth year, it was my good fortune to be received into the counting-house of Elias Hasket Derby, Esq., of Salem; a merchant who may justly be termed the father of the American commerce to India; one whose enterprise and commercial sagacity were unequaled in his day, and, perhaps, have not been surpassed by any of his successors. To him our country is indebted for opening the valuable trade to Calcutta, before whose fortress his was the first vessel to display the American flag; and, following up the business, he had reaped golden harvests before other merchants came in for a share of them. The first American ships seen at the Cape of Good Hope and the Isle of France, belonged to him. His were the first American ships which carried cargoes of cotton from Bombay to China; and among the first ships which made a direct voyage to China and back, was one owned by him. He continued to prosecute a successful business, on an extensive scale, in those countries, until the day of his death. In the transaction of affairs abroad, he was liberal—greatly beyond the practice in modern times—always desirous that every one, even the foremast hand, should share the good fortune to which he pointed the way; and the long list of masters of ships who have acquired ample fortunes in his employment, is a proof both of his discernment in soliciting and of his generosity in paying them.

"Without possessing a scientific knowledge of the construction and sparring of ships, Mr. Derby seemed to have an intuitive faculty in judging of models and proportions; and his experiments, in several instances, for the attainment of swiftness of sailing, were crowned with a success unsurpassed in our own or any other country. He built several ships for the India trade, immediately in the vicinity of the counting-house, which afforded me an opportunity of becoming acquainted with the building, sparring, and rigging of ships. The conversations to which I listened, relating to the countries then newly visited by Americans, the excitement on the return of an adventure from them, and the great profits which were made, always manifest from my own little adventures, tended to stimulate the desire in me of visiting those countries, and of sharing more largely in the advantages they presented."

Mr. Derby must have possessed striking qualities, both of head and heart, to have made so deep an impression on young Cleveland, to have been thus held in such vivid and grateful remembrance for half a century. In 1799, serious difficulties arose with France, and the country, still without a navy, appeared to be upon the eve of a war with that powerful nation. Salem had once before provided a navy, when the country was destitute of national ships. She had prospered in her commerce, and she was now ready to volunteer again in commencing a navy.

Mr. Derby was a member of the Federal party, and with his townsmen had given a cordial support to Washington. In 1798, his successor, John Adams, commenced a navy. The Navy department was organized; the frigates Constitution, Constellation, and United States were launched, but funds were wanting. The government was obliged to borrow at eight per cent., and patriotic subscriptions were tendered to build vessels for the federal navy. In Salem, the Federal vote stood at 500 to 50, and the opulent merchants of the town and country were ready with voice and purse to aid in the enterprise.

The administration in June, 1798, passed an act authorizing the President to accept such vessels as the citizens might build for the national service, and to issue a six per cent. stock to indemnify the subscribers. The county of Essex was electrified, and in October the Merrimac, a ship of 28 guns, was launched at the month of the Merrimac. Subscriptions were opened in Salem, to which Mr. Derby contributed $10,000, and in a brief period some $74,700 was raised, and the decision made to build a frigate for the navy. Her construction was intrusted to Enos Briggs, who had built many of Mr. Derby's fastest ships. William Gray was appointed chairman of the committee, Benjamin Pickman was chosen treasurer, and Joseph Waters general agent.

In a few days the following notice appeared in the Essex Gazette, which well illustrates the spirit of the day:

"THE

SALEM  FRIGATE.

Take Notice!

"To Sons of Freedom! All true lovers of the liberty of your country! step forth and give your assistance in building the frigate to oppose French insolence and piracy. Let every man in possession of a white-oak tree be ambitious to be foremost in hurrying down the timber to Salem, where the noble structure is to be fabricated, to maintain your rights upon the seas, and make the name of America respected among the nations of the world. Your largest and longest trees are wanted, and the arms of them for knees and rising timber. Four trees are wanted for the keel, which altogether will measure 146 feet in length, and hew 16 inches square. Please to call on the subscriber, who wants to make contracts for large or small quantities, as may suit best, and will pay the ready cash.

"ENOS BRIGGS.

"SALEM, November 23, 1798."

So prompt was the response of the farmers of Essex, that in one month all the timber required for the frigate was delivered, and the contractor was obliged to insert the following notice in the Gazette to check the supply:

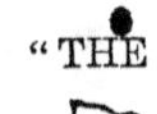

"THE

SALEM  FRIGATE.

"Through the medium of the Gazette, the subscriber pays his acknowledgments to the good people of the county of Essex for their spirited exertions in bringing down the trees of the forest for building the frigate. In the short space of four weeks, the complement of timber has been furnished. Those who have contributed to their country's defense, are invited to come forward and receive the reward of their patriotism. They are informed, that with permission of a kind Providence, who hath hitherto favored the undertaking,

Next September is the time
  When we'll launch her from the strand;
And our cannon load and prime,
  With tribute due to Talleyrand.

"ENOS BRIGGS.

"SALEM, Jan. 11, 1799."

The keel of the Essex was laid on the 13th of April, 1799, and on the ensuing 30th of September, her guns announced her launch by a federal salute to assembled thousands. The following account of the affair appeared in the next Gazette:

"And Adams said, 'Let there be a navy, and there was a navy.'

"To build a navy was the advice of our venerable sage. How far it has been adhered to, is demonstrated by almost every town in the United States, that is capable of floating a galley or a gun-boat.

"Salem has not been backward in this laudable design. Impressed with a due sense of the importance of a navy, the patriotic citizens of this town put out a subscription, and thereby obtained an equivalent for building a vessel of force. Among the foremost in this good work were Messrs. Derby and Gray, who set the example by subscribing ten thousand dollars each. But alas! the former is no more—we trust his good deeds follow him.

"Yesterday the stars and stripes were unfurled on board the frigate Essex, and at 12 o'clock she made a majestic movement into her destined element, there to join her sister craft in repelling foreign aggressions, and maintaining the rights and liberties of a 'Great, Free, Powerful, and Independent Nation.'"

The frigate Essex bore testimony to the energy, skill, and honesty of her builders. She proved the fastest as well as one of the cheapest ships in the navy; captured property to the amount of two millions of dollars from the enemy; lasted thirty-nine years; and when taken at disadvantage by a superior force, fought a battle which did honor to the country. Her entire cost, exclusive of stores and armament when ready for sea, was but $75,473.59.

The spirit of the Revolution still survived; for we find among the builders of the Essex the name of Jonathan Haraden, late captain of the Pickering, who supplied a part of her cordage. Her large cables were borne in procession to the ship, preceded by martial music.

The command of this frigate was very properly given to Richard Derby, a nephew of Mr. Derby, then absent on a foreign voyage. He however never took the charge, and retired from the navy, his sensibility having been wounded by the appointment of Capt. Preble to the Essex before his return.

Mr. Derby's apprehensions of difficulties with France were realized. In 1798, his ketch, the John, on her return from the Isle of France with a valuable cargo, was seized and sent as a prize to the West Indies, on the ground that she had no roll of equipage, although she had made several passages between France and the Isle of France, and no such paper was required in either country. She was recaptured by a British ship of war, and the following letter, from Mr. Derby to one of his agents in London, will further illustrate the proceedings in the admiralty courts of Great Britain in her colonies:

"SALEM, 3d July, 1798.

"MESSRS. LANE & FRAZER:

"GENTLEMEN:—Inclosed I send you sundry papers relating to the capture of my ketch John, that was taken some time since by a French privateer and sent into Porto Rico, and was afterward retaken by the frigate Amiable, Capt. Hobb, and carried into Tortola. Capt. Derby, who went from Salem as commander of the vessel, tarried at the Isle of France, to close his business, and dispatched the ketch for Salem under the command of Mr. Tibbets, the mate, who was taken from on board when she was captured by the French; so that there remained, to defend my property, only a young man, who was quite inexperienced in business, and who had gone out as a clerk to the captain. This young man, of his own accord, undertook to claim the property, and act as an agent (unauthorized by me), in the settlement of this business, and has been most shamefully imposed on by the judge and agent for the frigate.

"They obtained a sentence against one-eighth of the vessel and cargo, although it was clear that she was no prize to the French, and, of course, could not be one to them, vessels under similar circumstances, coming from the Isle of France to the United States, having been cleared in the admiralty at Guadaloupe. Not content with taking this eighth, at a fair and impartial valuation by disinterested persons, or an eighth of the goods as they rose, the agent insisted on valuing the vessel and cargo as he pleased—nearly 200 per cent. above what it ought to have been,—in this unprecedented manner fixing the *amount* of the eighth; and then demanding his payment out of those goods in the cargo, that he had purposely stated at a lower rate than the others; threatening, that unless a compliance was made with his infamous demands, that he would obtain an order from the judge, to have both the vessel and cargo sold at auction, and, in this manner, take from them both their neutral quality. Unless the payment of a prohibitory duty could be submitted to, it must have been sent to London in British bottoms. Besides this, he must have submitted to a rule established by the judge, of allowing 5 per cent. to the agent for sales, 2½ auctioneer's fees, 2½ wharfage, storage, etc., and other charges, amounting in all to 22½ per cent. Knowing it to be the judge's determination to expose him to these difficulties, he complied with their exactions, and I am deprived of nearly one-quarter part of the property, instead of one-eighth—or of no part, had justice been done.

"When I first heard of this vessel's being in trouble, I dispatched an agent expressly to look after her, who found her at Tortola, and entered a formal protest, and an appeal, against their proceedings, which accompany the within. To prosecute that appeal, he was under the necessity of giving bonds to the amount of £500 sterling. My wish is, that you would put those papers into the hands of some intelligent and trusty counsel, and ask their opinion of the probability of recovering any thing, from the means that these papers afford; and unless there is a moral certainty that something can be effected, I had rather the whole proceedings should subside, on being released from my bonds. I can submit better to this imposition, than to expose myself to further expenses, mortification, and disappointment.

"I am, gentlemen, your very humble servant,

"ELIAS HASKET DERBY."

Mr. Derby's agents placed the case before Dr. Nichols, an English proctor, and under his advice withdrew his appeal, and submitted to the loss of nearly one-fourth the cargo of the John; but in his prosperous business, the loss, although large, was not seriously felt. He had now risen to great affluence, at a time when wealth was rare; but while he allowed his family all the comforts of life, he had no love for display. If he ever evinced any pride, it was in his long-continued habit of assembling his seven children, and their families, every Saturday afternoon at his farm, and after spending a pleasant afternoon with them, of riding back in a long procession to Salem—the elder taking the lead. His wife, however, was more ambitious; she desired an elegant mansion, and he indulged her wishes. She erected a costly edifice, on the site now occupied by Derby Square, and laid out walks and gardens, extending from Essex-street to a terrace which overhung the river. To these a conservatory and choice collection of books were added. In his letter of December, 1798, to his London agents, he alludes to this fancy of Mrs. Derby, as follows:

"Mrs. Derby wants something to complete her house; she will write you. It is business I know nothing of. I have given her an order for £120; you will do as she may direct with it.

"From your friend,

"ELIAS HASKET DERBY.

"Messrs. LANE & FRAZER."

This mansion was finished, but was occupied by Mrs. Derby and her husband for a few brief months only. It survived the builders, and was for some twelve years afterward in the possession of their oldest son, and the seat of a generous hospitality. The life of Mr. Derby was now drawing toward its close; but one of his last letters expresses so well his kindness to his officers, and explains so clearly the reverence in which he was held by them, that we must give it insertion.

He had sent his fast-sailing ship Benjamin to his friends Lane & Frazer, to obtain a license from the British government to take a cargo of saltpeter from Calcutta. The order was obtained, the funds provided, and the ship about ready to sail, when her commander, Capt. Bullock, made a misstep, fell through the hatch, and nearly lost his life. The voyage, in consequence, was abandoned. Mr. Derby, while still suffering from the disappointment, writes to him as follows:

"SALEM, 13th June, 1799.

"CAPT. BENJAMIN BULLOCK:

"I have received your several letters dated London, and most sincerely sympathize with you in your distress, and I am still in hopes that you will receive such aid from the medical assistance you are able to procure, that you will be able to reach your home. I would not have you allow yourself to be discouraged, but endeavor to keep up your spirits, even if you have no prospect of ever being as well as you were before the accident; for, be assured that I always was, and still continue to be, your friend; and provided upon your return you have not regained your health, so as to be able to take charge of some one of my vessels, we will consult together, and endeavor to create some business for you.

"I should have written before this, but my mind has been so much engaged with the loss I have myself experienced (by the decease of Mrs. Derby), that I have not been able to do it before. You will, therefore, not impute it to my want of feeling for, and interest in, your situation. I have written Mr. Lane, by this opportunity, should you have occasion for money, that he would advance you £100 sterling, and to charge it to my account, which is agreeable to your wishes. You will receive this by Capt. Samuel Derby, of my brig Antelope. I have desired him to call on you, and to be of as much service to you as is in his power. If you feel it proper to return home, he will endeavor to procure you a passage in some of the ships for America; or in any way he can be useful to you, if you will propose to him, I am satisfied he will perform it with pleasure.

"Your sincere friend,

"ELIAS HASKET DERBY."

Mr. Derby made one more brilliant voyage before he closed his career, although he did not live to ascertain its results.

Hostilities having commenced between the United States and France, American trade had been checked, and a great demand had arisen for sugar and coffee in the ports of the Mediterranean. Mr. Derby, reviving a little of his revolutionary spirit, had built a new ship of four hundred tons, called the Mount Vernon, equipped her with twenty guns, six and nine pounders, manned her with fifty men, and, after loading her with 800 cases of sugar, placed her in charge of his son, Elias Hasket, with a sailing-master under him, and sent him up the Mediterranean. The cost of the cargo was $43,275, and the history of her voyage is given in the following extracts from the letter-book of the Mount Vernon, which is still extant:

"GIBRALTAR, 1st August, 1799.

"E. H. DERBY, Esq., Salem:

"HONORED SIR:—I think you must be surprised to find me here so early. I arrived at this port in seventeen and one-half days from the time my brother left the ship. In eight days and seven hours were up with Carvo, and made Cape St. Vincent in sixteen days. The first of our passage was quite agreeable; the latter, light winds, calm, and Frenchmen constantly in sight, for the last four days. The first Frenchman we saw was off Tercira—a lugger to the southward. Being uncertain of his force, we stood by him to leeward on our course, and soon left him. July 28th, in the afternoon, we found ourselves approaching a fleet of upwards of fifty sail, steering nearly N. E. We run directly for their center; at 4 o'clock found ourselves in their half-moon; concluding it impossible that it could be any other than the English fleet, continued our course for their center, to avoid any apprehension of a want of confidence in them. They soon dispatched an 18-gun ship from their center, and two frigates, one from their van and another from the rear, to beat toward us, we being to windward. On approaching, under easy sail, the center ship, I fortunately bethought myself that it would be but common prudence to steer so far to windward of him, as to be a grape-shot's distance from him, to observe his force and maneuvering. When we were abreast of him, he fired a gun to leeward, and hoisted English colors. We immediately bore away, and meant to pass under his quarter, between him and the fleet, showing our American colors. This movement disconcerted him, and it appeared to me he conceived we were either an American sloop-of-war or an English one in disguise, attempting to cut him off from the fleet; for, while we were in the act of wearing on his beam, he hoisted French colors, and gave us his broadside. We immediately brought our ship to the wind, and stood on about a mile—wore toward the center of the fleet—hove about, and crossed him on the other tack about half grape-shot distance, and received his broadside. Several of his shot fell on board of us, and cut our sails—two round-shot striking us, without much damage. All hands were active in clearing ship for action, for our surprise had been complete. In about ten minutes we commenced firing our stern-chasers, and in a quarter of an hour gave him our broadside, in such a style as evidently sickened him; for he immediately luffed in the wind, gave us his broadside, went in stays in great confusion, wore ship afterward in a large circle, and renewed the chase at a mile and a half distance—a maneuver calculated to keep up appearances with the fleet, and to escape our shot. We received seven or eight broadsides from him, and I was mortified at not having it in my power to return him an equal number, without exposing myself to the rest of the fleet; for I am persuaded I should have had the pleasure of sending him home, had he been separate from them.

"At midnight we had distanced them, the chasing rocket signals being almost out of sight, and soon left them. We then kept ourselves in constant preparation till my arrival here; and, indeed, it has been requisite, for we have been in constant brushes ever since. The day after we left the fleet, we were chased till night by two frigates, whom we lost sight of when it was dark. The next morning, off Cape St. Vincent, in the latitude of Cadiz, were chased by a French lateen-rigged vessel, apparently of 10 or 12 guns—one of them an 18-pounder. We brought to for him; his metal was too heavy for ours, and his position to windward, where he lay just in a situation to cast his shot over us, and it was not in my power to cut him off: we, of course, bore away, and saluted him with our long nines. He continued in chase till dark, and when we were nearly by Cadiz, at sunset, he made a signal to his consort, a large lugger, whom we had just discovered ahead. Having a strong breeze, I was determined to pass my stern over him, if he did not make way for me. He thought prudent so to do. At midnight we made the lights in Cadiz city, but found no English fleet. After laying to till daylight, concluded that the French must have gained the ascendency in Cadiz, and thought prudent to proceed to this place, where we arrived at 12 o'clock, popping at Frenchmen all the forenoon. At 10 A. M., off Algesiras Point, were seriously attacked by a large latineer, who had on board more than 100 men. He came so near our broadside as to allow our six-pound grape to do execution handsomely. We then bore away, and gave him our stern guns in a cool and deliberate manner, doing apparently great execution.

Our bars having cut his sails considerably, he was thrown into confusion, struck both his ensign and his pennant. I was then puzzled to know what to do with so many men: our ship was running large, with all her steering-sails out, so that we could not immediately bring her to the wind, and we were directly off Algesiras Point, from whence I had reason to fear she might receive assistance, and my port (Gibraltar) in full view. These were circumstances that induced me to give up the gratification of bringing him in. It was, however, a satisfaction to flog the rascal in full view of the English fleet, who were to leeward. The risk of sending here is great, indeed, for any ship short of our force in men and guns—but particularly heavy guns. Two nines are better than six or eight sixes; and two long twelves, or thirteen pounders, do better than twenty sixes, and could be managed with few men.

"It is absolutely necessary that two government ships should occasionally range the straits and latitude of Cadiz, from the longitude of Cape St. Vincent. I have now, while writing to you, two of our countrymen in full view, who are prizes to these villains. Lord St. Vincent, in a 50-gun ship, bound for England, is just at this moment in the act of re-taking one of them. The other goes into Algesiras, without molestation.

"I find that nothing is to be done here to advantage, except to obtain information from above. I have been offered $30 to deliver my sugar at Naples, where I think I shall go; but rather expect to sell at Venice, Constantinople, or Genoa, in case the French are driven from there. I have concluded to touch at Malaga, with Capt. Young, of Boston, and obtain what information I can; and think I may direct Mr. White how to lay out the property in his hands, against my return, as I think it for your interest to have it out of Spain. You need have but little apprehension for my safety, as my crew are remarkably well trained, and are perfectly well disposed to defend themselves; and I think, after having cleared ourselves from the French in such a handsome manner, you may well conclude that we can effect almost any thing. If I should go to Constantinople, it will be from a passport from Admiral Nelson, for whom I carry a letter to Naples.

"Your affectionate son,

"Elias Hasket Derby."

"Naples, 29th October, 1799.

"Gentlemen:—You undoubtedly have heard from Mr. Degan, ere this, of my arrival at this place. I have till this deferred writing, as my business has been in a very unsettled state. I have now to request that you will send by the first opportunity to America, copies of this letter to my father, in order that he may be apprised of my situation and the state of his business. My sales here amount to about $120,000, which, from the particular state of the place, I have found impossible to invest immediately in a cargo proper for America. I have, therefore, contracted for $60,000 in silks called ormazene, some satins, silk malice, gloves, brushes, and six tons of manna, six tons of liquorice, and sixteen brass guns, and eighteen swivels of the same, at one shilling sterling the English pound. These last serve me to arm two polacca ships that I have bought, and which are now ready for sea with my own. They will cost about $16,000, in complete order for sea, and are extraordinary fine, new ships, and great sailers, of 290 and 310 tons, and 14 guns. With these I am now ready to proceed to Manfredonia, for cargoes of wheat, for Leghorn, in the expectation, and almost certainty, of employing my time to advantage, till my silks, etc., are ready. I shall write you from Manfredonia, on my arrival. Till then,

"I am, sir, your friend and humble servant,

"Elias Hasket Derby.

"Messrs. Lane, Son & Frazer, Merchants, London."

"NAPLES, 29th October, 1799.

"HONORED SIR:—That this may find you in better health than when I left you, is my sincere wish. It has been an unhappy circumstance in my voyage, that I cannot bring it to a close, agreeable with your wishes, this fall, without too great sacrifices. My manufactured silks cannot be ready, and the red wine of Port Iolo is not yet in season to ship. My sales have been handsome, though not so great as I could have wished. I have been obliged to use a great deal of address, and exercise all my patience to effect them.

"They are now complete, all to 200 quintals of roll tobacco, brought by Capt. Allen from Gibraltar, who is discharged, and is now on his passage from Palermo to Charleston. They will amount, with the tobacco, to $120,000. I have bought 16 brass guns, at one shilling sterling per pound, expecting them to be as good a return as almost any thing. Also 65 boxes of manna, containing about 8,332 pounds, together with $50,000 contracted for principally in ormazine silks, satins, and about 700 casks of wine, in 58 gallons (French-fashioned casks), at about $12, which I expect will compose the Mount Vernon's cargo for America. In the mean time, whilst the silks are in the loom, I have thought it for your interest to purchase two polacca-rigged ships, of 290 and 310 tons—both of them very fine ships, almost new, and great sailers. They are now ready to proceed with the Mount Vernon for Manfredonia, to take, on your account, cargoes of wheat to Leghorn, which, from the rising state of the market, I think will more than clear the ships. They cost, with all expenses, about $16,000. By means of the brass guns, and others bought with them, they mount 12 and 14 sixes. Wages, $9 per month. I think, if I have the good fortune to bring them home, you will allow either of them to equal the Mount Vernon. My present intention is, to make all the dispatch in my power, to return with the three vessels to this port, and load them with wine for Salem—which will be in some preparation for them. I hope the arrangement will meet your approbation, for I assure you I did not know how I should otherwise invest my funds.

"Exchange on London, besides the uncertainty of it, is very disadvantageous. To invest $100,000 in silks, would not certainly do; and to leave property in a distracted country like this, where they guillotine six a day, three or four times in a week, would be madness. Mr. Bruce takes the Lucy, and Mr. Dana the Nancy, named for my sister Pickman. They are both well off for officers; and I trust, with Mr. Collins and others, I shall do perfectly well. If we are fortunate, I shall be here in two months, or, at farthest, I hope, in ten weeks, to take my manufactures and wines for home, as I think, with a good voyage. We are all in fine health and spirits.

"I am, with many wishes for you and the family's welfare, your affectionate son,

"ELIAS HASKET DERBY, JR.

"P. S.—The English minister, Lord Nelson, and Commodore Trowbridge, have been very polite to me."

The writer of the above letter was invited by Lord Nelson to dine with him and the officers of the fleet, at Naples, and was called upon to relate his encounter with the French fleet, for which he was much commended. In the course of the evening, one of the English officers, becoming a little excited, began to inveigh against the ingratitude of the United States, in throwing off her allegiance to the mother country. Mr. Derby disarmed his opponent, and restored the good-humor of the company, by stating that they did not understand the true causes of the Revolution; that the colonists, like themselves, had a great fancy for punch and Madeira, and were disturbed by a set of custom-house harpies, who were constantly seizing their wine, and spoiling their lemons, by running their rapiers through the boxes, and they fought, as any true Briton would, for their punch and their Madeira.

The beautiful Lady Hamilton was present on this occasion; and just at this moment, Napoleon, availing himself of Lord Nelson's stay at Naples, was making his way from Egypt to France.

A few more letters will show the results of the voyage, and the melancholy news from home of the death of his father, which reached Mr. Derby at Manfredonia.

"MANFREDONIA, 29th November, 1799.

"DEAR SIRS:—Your letter of the 16th has conveyed to me such distressing news, that indeed I know not how to answer it. The very kind and soothing way in which you were so good as to announce it, afforded me some alleviation to the pain I endured in parting with one who was infinitely dearer to me than my own life, which I feel I could have willingly sacrificed for him. My loss is beyond what I can count, and is certainly the greatest that could possibly befall me. But I ought to thank God for having preserved to me such an example till the present time. My wheat is all ready, and I hope in a fortnight to be able to proceed for Leghorn. We arrived here yesterday, after a most tedious passage—13 days in sight of Corfu; were fired on by two Turkish polaccas, but, on answering their shot, they made off: one of them, a 20-gun ship, went, after leaving us, and anchored under Cape Colone; the other, 18 or 20 guns, was off Cape Otranto. They have succeeded in taking, from what they tell me here, eleven different polaccas. Remember me to Mr. Costa Hall and the family, and believe me "Your sincere friend and humble servant,

"ELIAS HASKET DERBY, JR.

"Messrs. SCHWARTS & DEGAN, Merchants, Naples."

"MANFREDONIA, 27th December, 1799.

"SIR:—The Nancy being now ready for sea, I do direct that you proceed to sea, in company with the Mount Vernon and Lucy, and with them proceed to Leghorn, for the disposal of your cargo of wheat. Should any thing create a separation, you will address yourself to Messrs. Dupin & Co., to aid you in the sale; or should I be separated from you entirely, you will consult with Capt. Bruce, and close your business at Leghorn, and proceed to Naples, where the property in the hands of Messrs. Degan and Mr. Vallin, belonging to my father, will be delivered to you; with which proceed to Salem, in America.

"I suppose it will take nearly the amount of your sales of wheat to pay what those gentlemen may be in advance for the purchase of wines, silk, etc.; but should the Lucy, as well as the Mount Vernon, be entirely separated, in that case it will be necessary to sell a considerable proportion of the wine, as your ship cannot take it. Do all in your power to protect yourself from Algerines and Frenchmen,

"And believe me your friend,

"ELIAS HASKET DERBY.

"Capt. LUTHER DANA."

"LEGHORN, 8th February, 1800.

"MESSRS. JOHN DERBY & BENJAMIN PICKMAN:

"DEAR BROTHERS:—I have received from you several letters, containing the afflicting intelligence of the death of my father, which you may well imagine, from your own feelings, has overwhelmed me with the deepest affliction; and I must confess it has extremely disheartened me in my undertakings, which hitherto have been quite equal to my sanguine expectations. My voyage to Manfredonia has been considerably longer than I expected, and the weather excessively disagreeable; but had my detention been only fourteen days longer, it would have been an advantage to the voyage of so many thousand dollars, in the sales here; though I feel myself amply paid for the undertaking, as I shall now decidedly be able to invest more than $160,000 for home, including the ships. The weather has been such as to overcome us all, but is now settled for the better. That God will bless and protect you, is the sincere wish of a brother's heart. ELIAS HASKET DERBY."

"LEGHORN, 10th February, 1800.

"DEAR SIR:—You will be surprised at not hearing from me before this, but I have been out of the way of the different opportunities that may have offered. I have just completed a voyage to Manfredonia for wheat, which has turned out very fortunate. Two polacca ships which I had bought with my own funds, have cleared me near $30,000, in 2½ months. If I stop at Gibraltar, I trust you will see me in about six weeks; till then I am,

"Dear sir, your very humble servant,

"ELIAS HASKET DERBY.

"Messrs. ROBERT ANDERSON & Co., Merchants, Gibraltar."

The Mount Vernon arrived safely in America with her valuable cargo of silks, wines, and brass cannon, and realized a net profit of more than $100,000 on a capital of $43,275, the cost of the cargo, when she sailed from America, the voyage having been aided by a purchase at Gibraltar.

Before her arrival, however, her owner had closed his career. He left an estate which, with the advances to his son, exceeded a million, and was supposed to be the largest fortune left in this country during the last century. But this was not all. He had contributed still more to the growth of his native town, to the defence and commerce of his country. He had gained, too, a character for integrity, liberality, and mercantile honor, still more valuable.

The mansion in which Mr. Derby lived while acquiring his fortune still stands in Washington-street, Salem, and is now occupied by R. Brookhouse, Esq. But a few months before his death, Mr. Derby had finished his large and tasteful house in Essex-street, in Salem, with a conservatory, terraces, and garden. He had enriched it, also, with a large library, and secured the services of the late Mr. Heussler, a scientific horticulturist from Germany, who adorned the conservatory and garden with a choice collection of exotic plants and flowers. Upon his decease, it was set off to his eldest son, whose letters we have given. But with the embargo and war there came a check to the prosperity of Salem; ships decayed at the wharves, or were captured by the enemy.

Although Mr. Derby left seven children, in prosperous circumstances, and many merchants had risen to wealth in Salem, none of them were then willing to cope with the expenses and style of living attendant in such a structure. The buildings and gardens were closed for years, and finally gave place to the square and market, which now bear the name of Derby.

Mr. Derby, in his will, showed his appreciation of the services of his eldest son, who made two voyages, which contributed largely to his fortune—the one to the Isle of France, the other to Naples—in the Mount Vernon, and although he had previously advanced him his proportion, he allowed him to share equally in the final division.

The voyage of the Mount Vernon, however, was not the last voyage of the son. For ten years he occupied the paternal mansion, when, finding his fortune impaired by expenses of living and the adverse course of trade, he purchased the ship Mount Hope, of Newport—a vessel of 500 tons—and embarked for Rio Janeiro. with an intent to take a cargo of sugar to Russia. The voyage, as originally planned, would have surpassed his two previous voyages, but on his arrival in Brazil, he was induced by the agent of a great London house to take funds they wished to remit, and load with coffee upon advances from that house, with the assurance that he might proceed from England to the continent, if he found it advisable. But on her arrival at London, such was the state of affairs, that his consignees refused to risk their property on the continent, and he was obliged to sell at a loss.

From London he proceeded to Lisbon, and finding large flocks of merinos had crossed the mountains to escape the French armies, he concluded to take a flock to America. Down to this period the export of merinos had been prohibited in Spain; a few only had reached the country under the auspices of Consul Jervis and Gen. Humphreys; and the wool of this country was so coarse, that an English traveler had predicted we should never rival England in cloth. Mr. Derby lived to refute this theory. He embarked a flock of 1,100 merinos of the Montarco breed in the Mount Hope; and in 1811, after a tempestuous passage, he landed two-thirds of them in New York, whence they were sent to his farm at Ten Hills, near Boston, and gradually diffused over the country.

During the war, Mr. Derby, then known as General Derby, set up the first broadcloth loom ever erected in the State, and supplied many gentlemen with broadcloth of his own manufacture. He died in Londonderry, N. H., September 16, 1826, much loved and respected, leaving four daughters and two sons, Elias Hasket and John C. Derby.

But we cannot, in justice to the subject of this memoir, the first Elias Hasket, finish this sketch without giving the following obituary notice, which appeared in the Salem *Gazette* a few days after his decease, which is ascribed to the pen of the Hon. Benjamin Pickman:

Extract from the Salem Gazette of Sept. 10, 1799.

"Died, in this town, on Sunday last, at the age of 60, Elias Hasket Derby, Esq., having survived his amiable consort but a few months. Though Mr. Derby's natural disposition led him rather to retire from public observation, yet his character has been of too much importance in the community of which he was a member, for his departure out of life not to be sensibly felt and regretted. By a regular application to commercial pursuits, by a careful attention to all parts of his business, and by a remarkable course of good fortune, he arrived to a high degree of opulence. He possessed an uncommon spirit of enterprise, and in exploring new channels of commerce, has frequently led his countrymen to sources of wealth. He was among the first who embarked in the trade beyond the Cape of Good Hope, which has since become so extensive and lucrative; he made various improvements in navigation, and the many excellent vessels built according to his own plans and under his immediate direction, are proofs of his skill in naval architecture.

"If that man is deserving of the gratitude of his country 'who makes two blades of grass grow where one only grew before,' the memory of Mr. Derby has a claim to the affectionate regards of his fellow-citizens, for he possessed a good taste in gardening and agriculture, and most judiciously—both for his own enjoyment and the benefit of his country—applied a part of his wealth to improvements in that department. By his successful experiments in his excellent garden and farm, in Danvers, he taught the neighboring farmers that their lands are capable of productions which they had before thought could be prepared only in more genial soils. It was in these improvements that Mr. Derby found some of his most tranquil enjoyments, and they imparted delight to all who had the curiosity to visit them.

"In all his dealings, Mr. Derby uniformly regarded the

principle of justice, and his engagements were sacredly fulfilled. In the possession of riches, he did not forget the duties of charity. Providence had blessed him with abundance, and others partook of the gift; his hand often cheered the heart of poverty and affliction, and his charities were always applied with judgment—often in secret, never with ostentation. His deportment was modest and grave. In the hours of relaxation he was affable, mild, and cheerful.

"In the interesting domestic character of husband and father, he was particularly amiable, and possessed the unbounded affections of his family. He was a sincere believer in the Christian religion, which he evinced by an habitual regard to its precepts, by a uniform attendance upon public worship, and by a firm expectation—expressed through his last sickness—of inheriting its promises. In short, he has well discharged the duties of life, and we trust he is removed to a better world."

Mr. Derby was a tall man, of fine figure and elegant carriage. His deportment was grave and dignified; his habits regular and exact. He left at his decease the following children:

Elias Hasket, late of Londonderry, N. H.

John, late of Salem.

E. Hersey, late of South Fields, Salem.

Richard, late of Newport, R. I.

Elizabeth, wife of Capt. Nathaniel West, of Salem.

Anstiss, wife of Hon. Benjamin Pickman, of Salem.

Patty, wife of Hon. John Prince, of Jamaica Plains.

Their children completed the Derby Wharf, commenced by Richard Derby and continued by his son, extending it 2,000 feet into the harbor of Salem. They contributed largely to the construction of a bridge and avenue leading to the South Fields, now known as Lafayette avenue, and leveled and improved the Common.

They aided in establishing the East India Marine Society, composed of shipowners and masters only, most of whom have doubled Cape Horn or the Cape of Good Hope, and whose members already exceed 500;* whose collection of curiosities is the pride of Salem, and whose funds for charity, now greatly increased, exceed $39,000. The children of Mr. Derby have all passed away; but one of the sons-in-law, Capt. West, will be honored in Salem for his recent donation of $35,000 to found a school of science. While another son, the late John Derby, will be remembered for his enterprise in sending the second American ship to Japan in the year 1800, viz., the Margaret, Capt. Samuel Derby, which, during that year, visited that isolated empire.

In closing this memoir, a sense of duty impels us to make our acknowledgments to Capt. J. P. Felt, a member and officer of the East India Marine Society, for many facts and papers which have proved useful in compiling this narrative, and which were gathered and preserved by his industry. Let it be his satisfaction that they have aided in perpetuating the life and the virtues of a liberal and honorable merchant of Salem.

---

* At least 100 members took part in the Revolutionary war.

SIR WILLIAM PEPPERRELL, BART.

In a collection of the Lives of eminent American merchants, that of Sir William Pepperrell deserves a conspicuous place. He was a great merchant when the commerce of America was in its infancy, and in relating the events of his career, even in the summary record permitted us in this volume, we shall have occasion to notice many particulars which are highly interesting to those who are curious in the history of trade and navigation previous to the American Revolution.

During the colonial period many important changes took place in the course and direction of commerce; and, as a natural consequence, in the objects of American industrial activity. Such changes occurred during the lives of Colonel William Pepperrell, and of his son Sir William, embracing a period of nearly three-fourths of a century, in which they were prominent actors on the stage of busy life, and rose to mercantile renown and opulence, and to exalted stations both civil and military. It is proper to consider them here chiefly as merchants, their career in other spheres of action coming in only incidentally.

Previous to their day (1675), the commerce of New England consisted in the fur-trade, fisheries, and lumber, which furnished the staple articles for exportation in exchange for salt and manufactures, and for tropical productions from the Caribbean islands, and in provisions and naval stores from the southern provinces. The Pepperrells soon beheld the decline and extinction of the fur-trade, and the introduction of a more lucrative business in ship-building, and in the supplying of masts and spars for the docks and yards of England. They embarked early in these several branches of industry, and by a circle of operations, hereafter to be noticed, became the leading mercantile house in New England.

§ I.

The father of Sir William Pepperrell was a native of Tavistock, near Exeter, in Cornwall. His family being in humble condition, he was apprenticed for a term of years to the owner of a fishing-vessel employed on the coast of New England eastward of Cape Ann. At the age of twenty-two he left home, with a person named Gibbons, for the Isles of Shoals, where they embarked in the fishing business about the year 1675; and after four or five years, Gibbons left for the Kennebeck River, and Pepperrell soon changed his residence for Kittery Point.

This Point forms the southwestern apex of the State of Maine, at the mouth of the Piscataqua,—Great Island or Newcastle being on the opposite side of the river. The Piscataqua is navigable fifteen miles from the ocean, and receives large tributary streams from both shores, which penetrate many miles inland, and formerly supplied numerous mill-sites and places for shipyards, where, in the days of the Pepperrells, the hum of active industry continually echoed through the surrounding forests. At the head of tide-waters, saw-mills were in motion within three or four years after the landing of the Pilgrims, and, in process of time, they occupied every waterfall on all the branches of this beautiful river. But how changed is the scene! No forests are left for the axe-man, and no saw-mills are heard; but everywhere in their places stand magnificent factories, surrounded by beautiful villages, that are giving profitable employment to innumerable happy operatives. Ship-building too, excepting near the ocean whither timber floats from the banks of rivers in Maine, has nearly ceased on both shores of the Piscataqua; while, by the substitution of factories, the towns of Exeter, New Market, Dover, and South Berwick, previously only insignificant villages, are densely peopled, wealthy, educated, and refined.

The Isles of Shoals lie nine miles southerly from Kittery Point. They were visited by Capt. Smith in 1614, and for many years went by the name of Smith's Isles. Their whole number of acres is about six hundred, and the population varied, in the last two centuries, from two to six hundred persons. In early times they constituted one township, called Appledore, and sent two representatives to the General Court of Massachusetts, when a like number was sent from each of the towns of York, Kittery, and Wells. A portion of the islands now belongs to New Hampshire, and the rest to Maine. They afford a safe harbor to small vessels in stress of weather. The inhabitants were formerly more engaged in fishery than at present, and had many stagings and flakes for drying. It is here that the *dunfish*, so much valued by epicures, and which bring three times the price of common codfish, are obtained. They are said to be thicker than the common cod, and are caught and cured in the winter season, and named dun from their color. The character of the original islanders for sound morals, industry, and intelligence acquired for them great respect in the estimation of their contemporaries. They supported an able ministry at the time of Mr. Pepperrell's residence there.

While upon the islands, Pepperrell had frequent occasion to sail to Kittery Point for the purpose of traffic, and for the purchase and repair of boats. A shipwright there, named John Bray, supplied his wants, and in the course of their dealings welcomed him to the hospitalities of his house. Mr. Bray had arrived at the Piscataqua from Plymouth, England, about 1660, bringing with him his family, among whom was a child, named Margery, then only a year old. He purchased land at the Point, where the ancient Pepperrell mansion now stands, and was engaged in ship and boat building during a long life. Margery had arrived at the age of seventeen when she first saw Mr. Pepperrell, who, smitten with her youthful charms, was not slow in making his impressions known. He probably expected to drive a bargain for her, with her father, with the same facility that he had often done for a boat. But her tender years were offered as an objection to the match, though it was conjectured that lack of the needful on his part had some influence. Time, however, served to lessen both objections; she grew older, and he, by the first vessel he was able to send abroad, added much to his property; consequently, having passed through her teens, she obtained her father's willing consent to the alliance.

About the time of their marriage, Mr. Pepperrell changed his residence from the Shoals to Kittery Point, where Mr. Bray gave him the site of the present Pepperrell mansion. The south part of this structure was built by the elder Pepperrell, and the north part by Sir William. It has recently been curtailed in its dimensions, by the removal of ten feet from each end of the building. Here was the birthplace of Sir William, and here dwelt the two families, till the father's decease in 1734, which left the son's family sole occupants till 1759. It was in this period, of little more than half a century, that the largest fortune then known in New England was gradually accumulated. It was, however, increased by a legacy left to Mr. Pepperrell by his father-in-law, besides an estate in Plymouth, which also descended from Mr. Bray to Mrs. Pepperrell, and from her to her son (Sir) William.

Opposite to Kittery Point, and near the New Hamsphire shore, is Newcastle, an island which, during the first century after the settlement, was the principal seat of commerce, especially of New Hampshire, and was fortified at an early period. Two miles north of it was Strawberry Bank, now Portsmouth, which, as the savages disappeared and the country was settled, became a more convenient place of trade, and gradually absorbed most of that which had belonged to Newcastle. Near the southwest line of Portsmouth, a cove makes in and forms *Little Harbor*, where the first emigrants pitched their tents and commenced fishing.

When Capt. Smith arrived at Piscataqua, in 1614, there was a large Indian population on both its shores, called Newichewannocks, whose sachem resided at Quampegan (now South Berwick). Soon after, a pestilential disease swept off a large portion of his tribe, and opened a space for English settlers.

The first house erected was by Thompson, at Little Harbor, in 1623, and probably the next settlement was at South Berwick, where mills were erected in 1624, and immediately after followed the settlements of Newcastle, Portsmouth, Kittery Point, Dover, Sturgeon Creek, and Exeter. Between all these places there was constant intercourse, and "some political connection."

The number of mills increased on the small rivers, and lumber and ship-timber soon floated down in gondolas to Kittery Point and Newcastle, and were shipped to various ports, European and American. But the most lucrative, extensive, and durable business was the fisheries. It required small outfit, rarely failed of a good return and a ready sale in American and foreign ports, or a profitable exchange at the South for corn, tobacco, and naval stores; in the West Indies, for tropical produce; and in England, Spain, and Portugal, for dry-goods, sails, cordage, wines, and fruit.

Although civil dissensions and political changes occurred to impede the general prosperity, yet population and wealth gradually increased, until the disastrous war of King Philip, in 1675, which lasted three years, and was attended with savage murders and conflagrations, and a suspension of trade and of agriculture. Mr. Bray, father-in-law of the elder Pepperrell, arrived at Kittery Point some fifteen years before this war, and, at the close of it, had suffered less than those engaged in other occupations. Fishing-vessels and boats were indispensable, and yielded to shipwrights and owners a good profit. At the return of peace, therefore, Mr. Bray was able to extend his business upon a large and lucrative scale.

Ship-building was an early, and in time a very extensive branch of industry, on the Piscataqua and its tributary streams. Foreign merchants could supply themselves with vessels at a lower price than elsewhere. The Pepperrells built and sent many to the West India islands, laden with lumber, fish, oil, and live-stock, to exchange for cargoes of West India produce for home consumption; others to European markets, to exchange for dry-goods, wine, and salt, or to sell both vessel and cargo. They also traded extensively in Southern colonial ports, exchanging cargoes of fish and West India goods for provisions and naval stores. But a much larger amount of business was done in the fisheries. They sometimes had more than a hundred small vessels at a time on the Grand Banks, part of which they manned themselves, but more of them were let on shares. They also extended their business to other rivers. The following letter, written by the elder Pepperrell in the year in which Sir William was born, illustrates the times. It was addressed to Capt. John Hill, who commanded Fort Mary, at Saco, and acted as Pepperrell's agent.

"KITTERY POINT, November 12, 1696.

"CAPTAIN HILL:

SIR:—With much trouble I have gotten men and sent for the sloop, and desire you to dispatch them with all speed;

for, if all things be ready, they may be fitted to leave in two days as well as in seven years. If you and the carpenter think it convenient, and the ground has not too much descent, I think it may be safer and better to bend her sails before you launch her, so as to leave immediately. But I shall leave it to your management, and desire you to hasten them day and night; for, sir, it will be dangerous tarrying there, on account of hostile savages in the vicinity, and it will be very expensive to keep the men upon pay. I send you a barrel of rum, and there is a cask of wine to launch with [doubtless intended to treat female spectators]. So with my services to yourself and lady, hoping they are all in good health, as I am at present, who am your humble servant at command,

"WILLIAM PEPPERRELL."

The launching of vessels was, in those days, attended by all persons of both sexes living in the vicinity, who expected an ample supply of good cheer—rum for the men, and wine for the fairer sex. A barrel of each was the allowance on this occasion. The bottle was attractive and probably indispensable in all gatherings for mutual aid, whether log-rolling, corn-husking, rafting of timber, or raising of houses; and a militia company could drill only under the excitement of a treat from the captain. Even at ordinations the reverend divines must have a glass to quicken the fervor of their devotions. In a bill of expenses incurred on such an occasion, in the vicinity of Kittery Point, there are charged eight quarts of rum and two of brandy, for the clergy and council. And still worse, funerals were made an occasion for circulating the intoxicating cup, where the sighs and tears of sympathizing friends were awakened by the customary beverage, *spiced rum*. We have before us several bills for funeral expenses, incurred in the early part of the last century, in which this is mentioned. One of them specifies the ingredients thus: "Five gallons of rum, ten pounds of sugar, and half a pound of allspice, to make spiced rum." With such a network of temptations spread over society, it is wonderful that any escaped—that all were not rendered confirmed inebriates: but the Pepperrells, it is believed, always remained temperate.

Kittery, which included the present towns of Kittery, Elliot, and the Berwicks, grew faster than any other town in Maine. The Point was accessible by water and convenient for ship-building, both as respects security against savage depredations, and facility for obtaining timber, by water, from the interior, and rigging and stores from Boston. In addition to this, sessions of the Supreme Court met here many years. In 1646 the town paid nearly one-half of the amount of a tax assessed on the whole province of Maine.

In 1671, the militia of the province amounted to 700, of whom 180 belonged to Kittery, 80 to York, 100 to Wells, and 80 to Saco.

The elder Pepperrell was, like all the early settlers about the Piscataqua, trained to the use of fire-arms. His military services, during his first few years, were performed at the fort on Great Island, or Newcastle. A garrison-house was, however, previously erected and maintained at the Point, near his house, to which families might resort when threatened by sudden assaults from Indians; and as early as 1700 a fort was erected which went by his name. The celebrated warrior, Col. Church, in his eastern expedition in 1704, with 550 men, had orders "to send his sick and wounded to Casco, now Portland, or to Pepperrell's Fort at Kittery Point" (*Williamson*). This fort was probably a private concern, or at most built at village expense. But in 1714 the province of Massachusetts, in order to prevent the levying of improper duties by New Hampshire, made Kittery Point a port of entry, and adopted measures to retain it as such. A breastwork was erected northerly of the Point, a platform laid for six guns, a naval officer and notary public appointed, and all sea-captains and persons trading at the river were required to pay imposts, powder-money, and other duties, according to law. Pepperrell had command of this fort, which gave him the rank of captain. He also commanded the company of militia at the Point, and finally rose to the rank of lieutenant-colonel.

Mr. Pepperrell held the office of justice of the peace from 1690 to 1725. His trial-docket is still preserved, and exhibits the modes of punishing slight offences—the whipping-post being in frequent requisition, which gradually yielded to fines and imprisonment.

In 1715 he was appointed judge of the Court of Common Pleas, and continued on the bench many years; and his son (Sir) William, while a minor, served as clerk of the court.

The elder Col. Pepperrell educated his children, consisting of two sons and six daughters, in the best manner the time and place permitted. They were all taught reading, writing, and arithmetic, and their chirography was very fair. Beyond this, very little was attempted. The daughters, like most of their neighbors, were well trained in domestic duties, but had little opportunity for mingling in polished society. Several of them married sea-captains who commanded their father's vessels. They derived from their father a fondness for trade, and often sent ventures to Europe and the West Indies in his ships, such as fish and furs, to exchange for fruits and fine dresses. Several of them were part owners of small vessels, bills of sale of which are still preserved. Nor does it appear strange that, secluded as they were from more appropriate female enterprises and employments, they should imbibe some of the peculiar tastes of their father, and find him ready to gratify them.

The elder Pepperrell ever retained a strong attachment

to his fatherland, and seemed to anticipate the pleasure of returning to it after he should have acquired an independent fortune. But the machinery necessary for doing this, when once in motion, was too extensive and complex to permit of his removal or even temporary absence without great sacrifice: it required his constant superintendence. It appears, however, that in early life he made one voyage to Rotterdam. At the age of sixty, he wrote to his friend Mr. Roe, merchant in Tavistock, to purchase him an estate near him. One was named to him soon after, but reverses of fortune by shipwrecks, and the capture of many of his fishing-vessels, had intervened, and drew from him the following reply: "You wrote me that the Colson estate was for sale, but I have met with so many losses of late, that the sum asked is more than I can raise; but if I could purchase one worth four thousand pounds, I would soon pay for it. The times have been such that I have lost more than three thousand pounds. If it be possible, I hope to come and see you once more before I die. I pray you remember my love to all my friends in general, wishing you all happiness." He writes again some years after, and repeats his desire to purchase an estate, intending it rather for his son William and daughter Dorothy, than for his own occupancy. Mr. Roe writes, in 1723: "I am very glad to hear your son William and daughter Dorothy have a mind to settle in our country, but I cannot think of an estate near the sea-side at present; but if you have a mind to one seven or eight miles from me, in Ugburrow parish, worth fifty to sixty pounds a year, you can have it." It does not appear, however, that either of the Pepperrells, excepting Capt. Andrew, ever visited England, until 1747, when Sir William entered London, and was, by both king and people, greeted as the hero of Louisburg.

Col. Pepperrell, as before observed, reared a family of two sons and six daughters. Grave historians mention only one son (Sir William) and two daughters, who married Hon. John Frost and Hon. John Newmarch. A want of accurate information respecting his family is attributable to the remote situation of the parish records. The village in which he lived, though a place comparatively of great note and extensive trade in his day, sank into obscurity soon after the Revolution, and became the residence, chiefly, of a few fishermen, who even occupied his own former stately mansion. In addition to this, Sir William died at the close of the French war, in 1759; and the Revolutionary war, which ensued soon after, engrossed public attention, to the exclusion of preceding scenes and events in which the Pepperrells were engaged. Hence the traces of their family ties and relationships were nearly effaced from memory. The name, moreover, becoming extinct, is almost forgotten even by some in whose veins the Pepperrell blood circulates.

The parish records show that he had the following children, all of whom arrived at maturity, and were married—namely, 1. Andrew; 2. Mary; 3. Margery; 4. Joanna; 5. Miriam; 6. William (the Baronet); 7. Dorothy; 8. Jane.

1. *Andrew* was born July 1, 1681; was employed as clerk in his father's store; joined him as partner under the firm of William Pepperrell & Son; was supercargo and captain of a merchantman; resided at Newcastle, and was agent for mercantile houses abroad. He married Jane, daughter of Robert Elliot, Esq., in 1707, who bore him two children, Sarah, who married Charles Frost, and Margery, who married William Wentworth. Andrew Pepperrell died about 1713, and was buried at Newcastle. His widow married Charles Frost, of Kittery.

2. *Mary*, born September 5, 1685, married Hon. John Frost, and had sixteen children, eleven of whom reached maturity. Her second husband was Rev. Benjamin Colman, D. D., and her third, Rev. Benjamin Prescott, of Danvers, Mass. She died 1766, aged eighty.

3. *Margery*, born 1689, married Peletiah Whitemore, and had four children. He was lost near the Isle of Shoals. Her second husband was Elihu Gunnison, judge of the Court of Common Pleas, who resided at Kittery Point.

4. *Joanna*, born June 22, 1692, married Dr. George Jackson; had six daughters, and died 1725.

5. *Miriam*, born September 3, 1694, married Andrew Tyler, merchant in Boston, and had two sons and three daughters.

6. *William* (the Baronet), the subject of this memoir.

7. *Dorothy*, born July 23, 1698, married Andrew Watkins, who commanded one of Pepperrell's vessels. She had two sons, Andrew and John. Her second husband was Hon. Joseph Newmarch.

8. *Jane*, born 1701, married Benjamin Clark, of Kingston, N. H., and after his decease, 1729, she married William Tyler, brother of Andrew, of Boston; and in 1760 she married Ebenezer Turell. She had two children by Clark, named William and Benjamin.

The elder Pepperrell lived to see his son William advanced to the highest stations in the gift of the provincial government or of the people. As he approached the term of fourscore, the infirmities of age weighed heavily upon him, and finally terminated his useful and exemplary life on the 15th of February, 173$\frac{3}{4}$. His widow survived him until April 24, 1741.

To his son William he left the bulk of his estate. To the church at Kittery Point, sixty pounds to buy a service of plate for the communion-table; sixty pounds to the parish to buy corn for the poor, and fifty in money; thirty pounds to his nieces in Tavistock, and five pounds to the poor of the church there; to his mulatto servant his freedom; to Colonels Wheelwright and Gerrish, five pounds each, and Rev. John Newmarch ten pounds.

Letters of condolence from Col. Waldo and others were

written to his son William after the decease of his father. A few extracts from one, by Governor Belcher, so effaced as to be hardly legible, show the kind feelings cherished by him for both of the Pepperrells:

"BOSTON, March 11, 173¾.

"MY MUCH-BELOVED FRIEND:—I have received the token of respect to Mrs. Belcher and myself, with your sorrowful favor of the 1st instant, on the melancholy occasion of the death of my late worthy old friend, your father.

"I heartily condole with your honored mother, yourself, and all the good family, who have lost a tender head and father. God had blessed him with a large share of prudence and understanding. . . . . The blessing of the God of Jacob always rest upon you and yours, and may you greatly honor yourself in being (under God) the stay of your honored mother. . . . . Sir, I have exceeded on this head, since every one knows that Madam Pepperrell is blessed in a dutiful son. I wish much peace and love among the whole family; and am, honored sir,

"Your assured friend and humble servant,

"JONATHAN BELCHER."

§ II.

William Pepperrell, Junior (Sir William), was born June 27, 1696. His boyhood was passed at the village school, where he learned to read, write, and cipher. Under a private instructor, he was taught the art of surveying land, and of navigating a ship, and acquired some knowledge of geography. His early manuscript letters evince ignorance of the rudiments of English grammar. His chirography was beautiful, which rendered him very useful to his father. When not more than ten years old, he assisted in writing his father's justice docket, in copying his letters, and keeping his accounts, and probably, soon after, acted as clerk in his store. This brought him into immediate contact with those who traded with his father, including nearly all the persons settled on the banks of the Piscataqua and its tributaries. His education was, therefore, exclusively practical, and imparted early and clear insight into human character, and into the ways and means of successful trade and financiering.

Cradled amid the dangers of savage warfare, and while the lurking foe was prowling about the very neighborhood, and ever and anon lighting upon unsuspecting victims, his young mind must have become familiarized to tales of horror. While nestling in his mother's arms, we may well imagine him often listening to the recital of what she had seen and heard of exciting incidents and dire alarms in her day,—how her neighbor and intimate friend, Major Charles Frost, was waylaid and shot while returning from church, —how her neighbor, Mr. Shapleigh, was killed, his son taken captive, his fingers bitten off, and the bleeding vessels seared with a hot iron,—how her intimate friend, Mrs. Ursula Cutts, after spreading her hospitable board for the Waldron family, and while awaiting their arrival to dinner, was pounced upon by lurking savages, and herself and field-laborers tomahawked and scalped,—how twenty-one persons were killed or taken captive at Sandy Beach (Rye), only three or four miles distant,—how another party came there and killed fourteen and captured four others, and burnt the village,—and how numerous massacres and savage cruelties were perpetrated only a few miles distant, at Cocheco, Oyster River, and Salmon Falls.

Such were some of the scenes and events that transpired in the vicinity of Kittery Point. The Indian war was raging when Pepperrell was born, and continued three years. After four years' suspension it was renewed, and lasted till 1713, making thirteen years of hostilities during the first seventeen of his life ; and during the last ten of them, the war raged from Portland to the Piscataqua, destroying nearly all the settlements, excepting a garrison or two, and even in Kittery and its vicinity were a large number of murders, many of them among the friends and acquaintances of the Pepperrell family. Such a training must have awakened in his impressible mind a desire for revenge, and for deeds of heroism. Nor were there wanting other incentives calculated to foster a martial spirit. He was, in youth, a frequent spectator of military parades and exercises in his father's company drills, and of the exercise of cannon at the Fort, and at Great Island, all which had their influence ;—even worshiping assemblies had sentinels posted around, and those within were wont to pray with their hands resting on their firelocks, and public safety required that every man should be a soldier. No wonder, then, that young Pepperrell was imbued with a military spirit at an early age. At sixteen he bore arms in patrol duty, and in keeping ward and watch.

On the death of his only brother, Andrew, the firm was changed from William Pepperrell & Son to William Pepperrells, which continued more than a quarter of a century, until his father's death. The occupation of the firm was not that of a fancy goods shop. They dealt in lumber, naval stores, fish, and provisions, which required strong muscular exercise, and doubtless tended to give William his robust frame. His juvenile exercise was probably mostly aquatic, as nearly all intercourse with other places, whether for business or pleasure, was held by water. This early taught him the use of the oar, than which no exercise is better adapted to promote muscular development and the power of enduring fatigue. Nor was his mind under less favorable influences for vigorous growth. Removed from the enervating effects of refined society, and associating daily with lumbermen, ship-builders, and the hardy sons of Neptune, he was familiar with the rough and rugged aspect of human life, and imbibed its hardier influences both in body and mind.

The Pepperrells extended their sphere of business, and for some years were the largest merchants on the Piscataqua, or even in New England. Lumber and ship-timber floated down the river in gondolas from the head of tidewaters; and fish from the Grand Banks and the Shoals were poured into their warehouses; and cargoes were sent to the West Indies, to Portugal, the Mediterranean, and England, or exchanged. Often their vessels and cargoes were sold together, which promoted the extension of shipbuilding, one of the chief sources of their wealth. The lumber and carpenter's work were paid for in merchandise and provisions. Naval stores and provisions were obtained from the Carolinas, in exchange for fish and West India and European goods; and cordage, iron, hemp, and fishing-tackle from England, for vessels and cargoes sold there. Their bankers in Plymouth and London received the proceeds of cargoes and vessels sold in the Mediterranean, Portugal, France, and England, and answered the bills of exchange drawn on them in favor of Boston merchants, to whom they were sold at a great advance, and paid for in such goods as were needed to complete Pepperrell's assortment, and in provincial money. This money was expended in real estate, bought at low prices, and which rapidly increased in value. Such was the circle of operations by which the Pepperrells amassed a princely fortune.

But they greatly augmented their estate by the purchase of an extensive tract of land on the eastern side of Saco River. In 1716, they bought of the representatives of Benjamin Blackman, who had purchased from the original proprietors, Gibbons and Bonython, a large part of the present township of Saco, extending from the sea several miles along Saco River, including all the mill-sites on which stand the present large cotton factories, and also most of the land in that flourishing town. The bargain was made by the younger William, first for two-thirds of the land, which he bought of Samuel Walker, of New Jersey, and immediately afterward the other third, bought of Thomas Goodwill, of Boston. Being a minor, the transaction was performed in the name of the elder Pepperrell, who paid Mr. Goodwill for his third one hundred and forty pounds, current money, and took the deed in his own name, and afterward conveyed it to his son. In 1729, the younger William bought of William Corbain, of Boston, an adjoining tract eastward of the former, and became thus sole proprietor of the greater part of the towns of Saco and Scarboro'. The rise in value of these lands, added to the profits yielded by the mills they erected, were of themselves an ample fortune for one house.

After the purchase of Saco, young Pepperrell, at the age of twenty-one, seems to have assumed the duties of an outdoor partner, in directing improvements on this large estate, and in contracting for the building of vessels on Piscataqua and Saco rivers.

Ship-building was rendered particularly profitable by the policy of the home government, which favored this branch of industry more than any other, insomuch that the ship-carpenters in the Thames complained, in 1724, that their trade was hurt, and their workmen emigrated, caused by the building of so many vessels in New England. Parliament had prohibited the manufacture of woolens in America, for exportation from one colony to another, and the hatters in London were favored by a law forbidding the hatters in New England to employ more than one apprentice. But the board of trade despaired of any remedy for the ship-carpenters, "since it would hardly do to prohibit the building of ships by the colonists." Pepperrell, therefore, found it profitable to embark extensively in this business. He also managed the affairs of the firm in Boston, assisted by his brother-in-law, William Tyler, a merchant of that town. Meanwhile the elder Pepperrell attended more to in-door trade, particularly to the fishing interest, and much of his time was necessarily devoted to the care of his numerous family.

The ascendency which the Pepperrell firm enjoyed over any other mercantile house in New England, gave it a large agency in the transaction of the pecuniary affairs of the province with the mother country. This branch of business was conducted by the younger Pepperrell, and brought him into an intimate acquaintance with public men in Boston; and this, while it cultivated courtly manners and an easy address, for which he became distinguished, introduced him into the best society, and favored his advancement in military and political life. He had no sooner passed through his minority than he was commissioned justice of the peace, and captain of a company of cavalry. He was soon after promoted to be a major and lieutenant-colonel, and at the age of thirty, was made colonel, which placed him in command of all the militia of Maine.

It was about the same time (1726) that he was chosen representative of Kittery, which then included Elliot; and next year he received the following notice of his appointment to the board of councilors:

"BOSTON, June 1, 1727.

"SIR:—I am directed by the Honorable Lieutenant-governor and Council to acquaint you that you are elected and appointed a councilor or assistant for the ensuing year, and that your attendance at the council-board is desired as soon as may be. Your humble servant,

"J. WILLARD."

His appointment was renewed thirty-two successive years

until his death, during eighteen of which he served as president of the board.

Among the families of distinction in Boston to whom young Pepperrell was presented, was that of the late Grove Hirst, Esquire, deceased, an opulent merchant, whose wife was daughter of Judge Sewall of the Supreme Court. The Hirst family were connected by marriage with Rev. Samuel Moody of York, whose wife was a Sewall, and whose niece, named Mary Hirst, occasionally visited there. Mr. Pepperrell had met her at her grandfather's, Judge Sewall, in Boston, and on the strength of the acquaintance there formed, called on her at York more than once. This gave much annoyance to the parson's son, who, in his journal, has recorded that he was bewildered by the attractions of the young lady. Young Moody was then a schoolmaster, and afterward settled in the ministry in the north parish of York. It is no wonder that his pretensions were outrivalled by those of Mr. Pepperrell, the heir of a fortune, and favored with engaging manners and the tact which fashionable life and political eminence confers. With assiduity and much skill, making presents of gold rings, a large hoop and other ornaments, he soon succeeded in winning her affections, and their marriage was solemnized the 16th of March, 1723, when he was twenty-seven years of age. The happy couple resided in the family mansion at Kittery Point, which was enlarged by an addition to the north end, giving the whole a stately appearance. On the death of his parents, the whole came into the possession of the son.

In 1730, Governor Belcher appointed him chief-justice of the Court of Common Pleas, immediately after which he endeavored to qualify himself for its duties by the study of law.

By an invoice still preserved, he ordered from London a small law library. Among these books were Danvers' Abridgment of the Common Law, a law dictionary, The Complete Solicitor, and some others.

He was not ignorant of the forms of judicial proceedings when he took his seat upon the bench as chief-justice. The courts had for several years been held in or near the family mansion, and his father had served many years as an associate judge, and he had himself, while a minor, held the office of clerk of the court.

With all their vastly extended and diversified commerce and navigation, it should be mentioned to the credit of the Pepperrell firm that they never imported slaves from Africa. Like all persons of their day who possessed the means, they owned a few slaves, probably ten or a dozen, whom they purchased in the vicinity. One of these was a cooper named Lymas, whose occupation was an essential part of the establishment, in making casks for fish and oil, and for carrying supplies of water for ship's use. Lymas was one day missing, and a vessel commanded by a Capt. Ward had just sailed for Portugal. Pepperrell wrote to his correspondents in Oporto and Lisbon to search said vessel. It appeared, on inquiry of the crew, that Lymas had concealed himself on board before sailing, and was not discovered till some days subsequently, when he made himself known. In a few days after, he was missing; and never being found, it was supposed by the crew that he had fallen overboard in the night.

On one occasion, Benjamin Bullard, a merchant of Antigua, shipped to Kittery Point five negroes, consigned to the firm of Pepperrells. He received the following answer, dated June 25, 1719: "Sir,—I received yours by Capt. Morris, with bills of lading for five negroes and one hogshead of rum. One negro woman, marked Y on the left breast, died in about three weeks after her arrival, in spite of medical aid which I procured. All the rest died at sea. I am sorry for your loss. It may have resulted from deficient clothing so early in the spring."

The following letter shows that commerce and navigation experienced vexations and trials in provincial times that are unknown at the present day, under a federal government and judiciary. It was written to an attorney in North Carolina, June, 1722: "Sir,—This comes by Mr. Samuel Walker, late master of our sloop *Hannah and Sarah*, who went from Barbadoes to North Carolina with a large cargo of rum and molasses. When arrived there, he had unfortunately lost his clearances, and although security was offered by the best gentlemen in that region to produce his clearances in any reasonable time, yet that was refused, and they condemned both sloop and cargo, and sold both within two days after; and in that country too, where they live so scatteredly, they bought every thing at their own prices. She being a good sloop, well found, with new sails and rigging, did not sell for half her value; and then you will perceive by their charges that they designed to share the whole among themselves.

"An experience of several years in shipping has furnished no case so outrageous in any court. No man can accuse us of attempting to defraud his majesty of any of his dues, and we have paid thousands of pounds. We do not suppose that his majesty ever appointed officers to trick his subjects. Papers may be lost in a thousand ways. It is the opinion of our lawyers here that we must be relieved by application to his majesty in council. We desire you to proceed in the matter for us, and inclose you a power of attorney."

Pepperrell sent also to the attorney letters from Boston merchants, explanatory of the proceeding, and urging an equitable settlement of the affair, and he sent Capt. Walker to Barbadoes for evidence of his regular clearance from that island. But it all availed little or nothing in the way of relief.

Few other incidents worthy of recital occurred in the life of Pepperrell, during the first ten years after his father's decease. His mercantile and other operations were continued, his real estate rose in value, and though he sustained occasional losses by shipwrecks and bankruptcies, his fortune on the whole was augmented.

On the death of his father, in 1734, he seems to have received strong religious impressions, which proved to be lasting, and led him to an open profession and union with the Church. His letters to relatives and intimate friends, from this time forward, are imbued with religious sentiment. In reply to a letter from his friend Col. Samuel Waldo, he writes: "I take kindly your expression of sorrow for my great loss in the death of my aged and honored father, and desire that God in his great goodness and mercy would be pleased to fit and prepare us all for that untried state of existence to which we are all hastening." In all his letters to his clerical friends, he solicits their intercession in his behalf. He often entertained the clergy as visitors at his house, and, among others, the itinerant Whitefield met with a cordial reception. In 1741, his only daughter Elizabeth was admitted into full communion in the Church.

When ordinations occurred in the neighboring churches, he was usually appointed one of the delegates from his parish to assist, especially when not engaged in official duties as councilor or judge.

At the funeral obsequies of his father, Mr. Pepperrell bestowed every mark of respect that filial affection dictated. He shortly after ordered from London the marble structure that now stands over the vault containing the mouldering remains of the Pepperrell family, which was erected about the year 1736. This is almost the only relic of Pepperrell's day now remaining as it was at Kittery Point; and even here, the vault beneath became so dilapidated a few years since, that water gained admission through its crumbling roof, and washed the dissolving remains of the tenants into an undistinguishable mass; and, but for the respect entertained for the memory of the illustrious dead, by a female remotely descended from the Baronet, the whole structure would long since have fallen into ruins. By her exertions and limited means the tomb was put in good repair.

The legacies left by the will of the elder Pepperrell were numerous but not large, the great bulk of his property descending to his son. As a matter of course, the other heirs were disappointed and dissatisfied. The numerous ships, farms, mills, stocks, warehouses, merchandise, etc., were known, and each daughter's husband anticipated a large bequest. But he directed only about five hundred pounds current money to be paid to each daughter, in addition to their marriage portions and other advancements, with half of his household furniture after his wife's decease, and from twenty to fifty pounds to each grandchild. Some of the sons-in-law had already anticipated a portion of their bequests, by indebtedness to the deceased. But they discreetly remained silent under their disappointment.

After the decease of the elder Pepperrell, the management of the extensive and diversified affairs of the firm devolved entirely on the son, added to which were the duties of the several offices he sustained, as justice of the peace, chief-justice of the Court of Common Pleas, councilor, and colonel of the Yorkshire regiment, together with the care of his own family, and of his widowed sisters and their children, and many poor relatives.

Residing in a part of the country more exposed than any other to the ravages of a cruel and perfidious enemy, he felt the importance of vigilance and constant preparation for defence. He accordingly issued orders frequently to all the captains to muster their companies, inspect their arms, and report their condition. Many orders of the kind are still preserved as autographs. In 1738, impressed with the difficult and responsible duties devolving upon him, he called a meeting of the commissioned officers at Portland, with whom he consulted and made overtures for a better organization, equipment, and discipline of the militia under his command. More ardor and military spirit were now diffused among the officers and soldiers: their ranks were filled, and new companies were formed. They all knew how to use the firelock, were marksmen, and in Indian warfare had been employed in scouts and ambuscades; but exercises and evolutions in large bodies, beyond single company trainings, they had yet to learn. In order to favor battalion and regimental muster, the Yorkshire regiment, comprising all the troops of Maine, was divided into two regiments. The western one, comprising the present county of York, he continued to command (1739–40), and the eastern or new regiment was transferred to Col. Samuel Waldo, of Falmouth, who had previously been his lieutenant-colonel. The former consisted of one thousand five hundred and sixty-five, and the latter of one thousand two hundred and ninety soldiers.

Massachusetts and New Hampshire were united under one governor, each province having a lieutenant-governor. In 1717 John Wentworth was appointed lieutenant-governor of New Hampshire, in place of Vaughn removed, Shute being governor of both provinces. He was succeeded by Governor Burnet, who died in 1729, and Jonathan Belcher was appointed the following year. Wentworth and his two sons, Benning Wentworth and Mark Hunking, were in trade in Portsmouth, and a spirit of rivalry existed between their house and the Pepperrells. The office held by the former gave them an advantage over the latter, in the exercise of which they seized one of Pepperrell's vessels for a violation, real or pretended, of the revenue laws. The case was to be tried in London. Pepperrell writes to his agent, who went out in 1723 to defend the suit.

"PISCATAQUA, February 9, 1723.

"ELISHA COOK, ESQ.:

"SIR:—Inclosed you have several affidavits, which we took with thoughts that, if there were occasion, they might serve us in our case relating to the seizing of our ship by the instigation of Lieutenant-governor Wentworth. But if they will not be serviceable for that, they will show how that man will strain at a gnat and swallow a camel. He and his two sons, being considerable traders, will endeavor to monopolize all the trade of this place, and to discourage and depress others. But you know the man; therefore I shall not trouble you further on this head. We would not have it exposed or known that we send you the above affidavits, you being sensible that, situated as he is, it lies in his power to hurt trading men.

"We are, with respect, etc., etc.,

"W. P."

While it was uncertain whether Belcher or Shute would be appointed governor of Massachusetts and New Hampshire, both of them striving for the office, Lieutenant-governor Wentworth wrote a complimentary letter to Belcher in London. On his first visit to New Hampshire, Belcher accepted an invitation from Wentworth to reside at his house. But he soon learned that Wentworth had written a similar letter to Shute, which he highly resented as savoring of duplicity. In this originated a feud attended with great persecution on the part of Wentworth, until his death in 1730; and his successor, David Dunbar, continued the same course, until finally, by unfair means, he and his friends, and Wentworth's friends, effected Belcher's removal in 1741. William Shirley succeeded Belcher as governor of Massachusetts.

Wentworth arrived in Portsmouth amid the acclamations of all the populace, who had assembled to welcome his return as governor.

In 1740, when paper money had increased throughout New England to an alarming extent, relief was sought in a "Land Bank," based on mortgages upon real estate. Governor Belcher opposed it in every stage of its progress, much to the dissatisfaction of the house, who soon after united with his enemies in New Hampshire and in England, in a petition for his removal. Although the crown approved of his course on the bank, his enemies assailed him on other subjects with such zeal and virulence, that he was recalled without a trial or investigation, and was succeeded by Governor Shirley. He sought redress in England, and on the eve of his departure his friends united in a fair representation of his conduct to men of influence at court. His friend Pepperrell was appealed to in his favor, by Councilor Allen, in the following letter:

"Honored Sir:—Mr. Foye, the bearer, waits on you with your friend Governor Belcher's letter, relating to his intended voyage to Great Britain, which he undertakes upon good encouragement of success; and as you have ever been of the number of his steady friends upon honorable terms, and a true patriot of your country upon the best principles, he flatters himself you will on this important conjuncture to himself and family, as well as of the province, give a further proof of your friendship, in assisting him with your interest on the other side of the water. And from the great regard I pay (without even a suspicion of flattery) to your noble and generous principles, for the best interest of your country, I take the liberty to beg and entreat your favor for our friend who has been so greatly abused. To the plea of friendship, allow me to add that this voyage (as I apprehend) is the last remedy to save a sinking country from being the prey of land-bankers and beggars, which, as they are now playing the game, is nothing but buying and selling the country. This I take to be a point in which every gentleman of fortune is interested, and so of great consequence to a gentleman of your superior fortune. On this account, particularly, have several good gentlemen here given their assistance, and I allow myself no room to doubt of your kind and generous aid, which I can urge with the better grace, as I am heartily engaged in the affair so well calculated for the good of my country and the security of my own little fortune. Excuse this freedom, and believe me to be, with great regard,

"Your most obedient servant,

"JAMES ALLEN."

Pepperrell joined most cordially in the effort to sustain and help his old "friend and his father's friend," which resulted in Belcher's appointment as governor of New Jersey, where he passed the remainder of his days, enjoying the esteem and respect of his old friends in New England, and in the interchange of friendly sentiment by letter.

The children of William Pepperrell, Esq., and Mary Hirst Pepperrell, were—

1. *Elizabeth*, born December 29, 1723.

2. *Andrew*, born January 4, 1726.

3. *William*, born May 26, 1729, and died the following February.

4. *Margery*, born September 4, 1732, who also died in infancy.

The two surviving children of Mr. Pepperrell, Elizabeth and Andrew, received the best education the province afforded. Their mother had been highly educated in Boston, and was well qualified to direct their instruction. Elizabeth attended the best schools there, residing, much of her time, in the family of the Hirsts and the Sewalls, where Andrew also was a frequent inmate while fitting for college, which he entered at Cambridge in 1741. Col. Pepperrell and lady passed much of their time in Boston—he in the General Court and in mercantile pursuits, and she with her children. The colonel had felt the need of learning very sensibly, and was determined that his only son and heir to his name and fortune, should enjoy all the advantages which it could confer. Naturally kind and affectionate, comely in person, graceful in manners, Andrew was the idol of his parents, and won the favor and esteem of a large circle of acquaintances among the élite of Boston. He graduated at Harvard at the age of nineteen, with distinguished honors.

Elizabeth, having completed her education, returned home to requite, with filial duties and affection, the fostering care and solicitude of devoted parents. Few if any belles of her day possessed equal attractions. An heiress of rare accomplishments and winning manners, high-bred maternal connections, and the only daughter of a distinguished merchant, high in official station, military, political, and judicial, and of commanding influence, and, withal and above all, a lady of sound religious principles and abounding in Christian graces, she was truly "a gem of the first water." Many were the admirers that clustered around, ambitiously courting her benignant smiles.

Among those who sought her favor, and the one whose assiduous attentions at length gained her affections, was a young merchant named Sparhawk, son of a clergyman of Bristol, Rhode Island, who, dying early, left a widow and two sons, John and Nathaniel. The widow married Jonathan Waldo, Esq., a wealthy merchant in Boston, who educated the two sons—John, who settled in the ministry at Salem, and left many descendants, and Nathaniel, who entered a commercial house as partner in trade with Benjamin Colman, of Boston. Nathaniel Sparhawk and Miss Pepperrell were married May 1, 1742. Their permanent residence was in Kittery, near the Pepperrell mansion, where

Mr. Sparhawk opened a mercantile house, whilst he still maintained his copartnership with Colman. As his father-in-law retired, or was obliged to absent himself to fill the public stations he held, Mr. Sparhawk gradually succeeded him, as will hereafter appear.

Early in 1744, Andrew Pepperrell, the son of Sir William, became a copartner in trade with his father, who notified mercantile houses accordingly.

§ III.

In 1744, a new scene opens in Pepperrell's life, in which the part he performed gave him great military renown, and inscribed his name on the enduring page of history : it was the siege and reduction of Louisburg, the strongest fortress on the seaboard of America, and which it had cost the French six millions of dollars to construct. This glorious victory was achieved by New England volunteers. Pepperrell was selected as commander-in-chief on account of his popularity and influence, which favored voluntary enlistment. One hundred armed vessels and transports, carrying four thousand men, sailed from Boston, and after a siege of forty-nine days and enduring incredible hardships, and throwing nine thousand cannon balls and six hundred bombshells into the city and fortress, compelled the commander to surrender and throw open the gates. Commodore Warren with several large ships aided the land forces during the siege, by cutting off supplies coming to the garrison. The French flag was continued at the top of the flagstaff many weeks after the capitulation, which served to decoy richly laden merchantmen into the port of Louisburg. The goods taken in them were sold at auction to Boston merchants and others, some of whom doubtless realized fortunes.

By the rules of the British service, and which now exist in the American navy, the proceeds of one-half of all prizes (unless the enemy be of superior force), goes into the national treasury, and the other half is divided among the captors; and where the prizes are taken by a fleet or squadron, all the vessels share alike in the proceeds, although only one may have done the work, provided they were all in sight of the capture. The army at Louisburg being in sight of the capture of the rich prizes, amounting to near a million of dollars, they naturally expected a share of the prize-money. Pepperrell writes to the Duke of Newcastle: "Your Grace will be informed of the capture of a rich South Sea ship, two East India ships, and some other valuable prizes, that were taken in sight of the troops, some weeks after we had possession of the fortress, to which they will think it a hardship not to share in." But they were entirely cut off from any share of prize-money, which was any thing but fair, since the army took the fortress without the aid of a single gun being fired by the fleet, and thus furnished the flagstaffs to hoist false colors upon, to decoy the French merchantmen. The army, in fact, "beat the bush," and the navy "caught the bird." They were told that their portion of the plunder was to be gathered on the land, and that the crown would probably divide the island of Cape Breton among the soldiers. But the only thing they ever realized was a mere trifle, accruing from the sale of provisions, soap, and candlewicks, which the commissary purchased of them at auction, perhaps a few shillings for each soldier.

The several legislatures of the provinces voted Pepperrell thanks and congratulations, soon after the capture, to which he made appropriate replies. The Duke of Newcastle, on receiving from him his official account, replies at length, saying among other things, "I lost no time in transmitting copies of your dispatches to my Lord Harrington, at Hanover, to be laid before the king. I have now the pleasure to acquaint you that the news of the reduction of

Louisburg was received by his majesty with the highest satisfaction, which the king has commanded should be signified to all the commanders and other officers, both of land and sea, who were instrumental therein: in consequence of which, I am to desire you would acquaint the officers under your command with his majesty's most gracious approbation of their services upon this occasion. It is a great satisfaction to me to acquaint you, that his majesty has thought fit to distinguish the commanders-in-chief of this expedition, by conferring on you the dignity of a Baronet of Great Britain (upon which I beg leave most sincerely to congratulate you), and by giving a flag to Mr. Warren." To Pepperrell was also given the commission of commander of a regiment of royal troops, with power to appoint a large portion of his officers.

The announcement of this brilliant achievement filled America with joy, and Europe with astonishment. All the seaports of England celebrated it by ringing of bells, salutes and illuminations, and volumes of congratulations were received by the king from all quarters. In London, the cannon of the Tower and Park were fired by order of the Lords of the Regency, and the city and large towns were in a blaze with bonfires and illuminations.

Both commanders were highly complimented by the government for their harmonious co-operation. More credit is however due to Pepperrell in this particular than to Warren. They both strove to be faithful to their trust, but Warren knew less of character and the springs of human action than Pepperrell. He never could have raised an army of volunteers like Pepperrell's, nor have controlled them by such gentle measures. Not a soldier was punished till long after the capitulation. But when their opinions varied on any measure, Warren was on many occasions captious and unyielding. He had the *fortiter in re*, but not the *suaviter in modo* of Pepperrell.

Sir William was detained at Louisburg with most of his army from the day of surrender, June 17, till the following May. In all which time his mercantile affairs were in the charge of his son and copartner, and his son-in-law, Sparhawk. They, and other merchants in Boston and elsewhere, derived some profit from the conquest, by the privilege of sending supplies to the garrison. The royal regiment which he raised there and in New England, was stationed in the fortress two years, and then disbanded,—the officers on half-pay.

The legislature of Massachusetts voted a congratulatory address to Pepperrell and his officers and soldiers, tendering them grateful acknowledgments for the important services they had rendered; and also to Admiral Warren and his officers and men, for their hearty and successful cooperation.

(*Pepperrell's Reply.*)

"LOUISBURG, April 5, 1746.

"GENTLEMEN:—I am extremely obliged to the Honorable Council and House of Representatives of the province of the Massachusetts Bay for their congratulation and compliments to me on the happy issue of the expedition against this place; and for his majesty's most gracious approbation of my services therein, which I had the honor of receiving from you the 2d instant. Next to the consciousness of my having engaged in the important enterprise out of zeal for his majesty's service and the welfare of my country, and that I have made it my constant aim to discharge the trust reposed in me with fidelity, nothing can give me a more sincere and lasting pleasure than my royal master's approbation, and my country's kind acceptance of my services.

"May the Lord of Hosts, who has given us the victory, ever defend and prosper this valuable acquisition, and grant that it may effectually answer the noble purposes for which our country was animated to attempt its conquest, in the prosecution of which the generous concurrence of the province of the Massachusetts Bay with his Excellency Governor Shirley's wise counsels and indefatigable application had so great a share; and may the happy consequences of our success be extensive as its fame, and lasting as the honor due to the heroic resolution and exemplary bravery of the officers and soldiers, whom I shall always esteem it my great honor to have commanded.

"It is with pleasure that I observe my country's gratitude for the good services and assistance of the brave and worthy Admiral Warren, whose singular vigilance and good conduct rendered his having the direction of his majesty's ships employed against this place peculiarly happy; and I flatter myself that the harmony which had subsisted between us in the prosecution of his majesty's service, has also had an happy effect; and I esteem it an auspicious aspect of Divine Providence upon this place, that a gentleman so peculiarly qualified and disposed to promote its prosperity, is appointed by his majesty to the government of it.

"As I shall ever retain a most grateful sense of the many honors I have received from my country, nothing will give me greater pleasure than any opportunity further to approve myself a true friend to its interest and prosperity; to which, if the honor and command conferred on me by his majesty can any way contribute, it will enhance their value.

"WM. PEPPERRELL."

Warren and Pepperrell embarked at Louisburg in the Chester, Capt. Spry, leaving the fortress under the command of Commodore Charles Knowles, and arrived in Boston about the 1st of June. They were received with a salute of cannon at the castle in the afternoon, and entertained by the governor. They arrived in Boston at 5 P. M., and were saluted by all the ships of war and town batteries. Upon their landing at Long Wharf, his majesty's Council and the House of Representatives received them, and they all were escorted by his excellency's company of cadets to the council-chamber. It being training day for the Boston regiment, the soldiers were drawn up in two lines in King's (now State) street, by his excellency's orders, and the officers paid the standing salute to the three, namely, Shirley, Pepperrell, and Warren. As they passed, the street, windows, doors, and balconies were crowded, and the regiment fired three volleys, and gave three hurrahs, in which the whole populace joined.

Sir William soon after took his seat at the council-board, to which he was re-elected president. The House of Representatives, then in session, being informed that he and Admiral Warren were in the council-chamber, went thither, when the speaker addressed them in the following manner:

"The House of Representatives of this province have a high sense of the services you have done for his majesty's subjects in general, and for the people of New England in particular; and it is with the greatest pleasure they embrace this happy opportunity of acknowledging it.

"In their name, and by their order, I congratulate you on your safe arrival in the province, and most heartily bid you welcome."

To which Admiral Warren replied:

"MR. SPEAKER:—I am obliged to this honorable House for the great respect they have shown me. They may depend upon my zeal and service while I live, for the colonies in general, and this province in particular."

Sir William replied as follows:

"MR. SPEAKER:—I am heartily obliged to the honorable House for the respect they have shown me; and I shall be always ready to risk my life and fortune for the good of my dear native country."

Soon after the above ceremony, Warren left Boston for England, where he was employed in the British Channel.

On the 4th of July, Sir William, attended by divers officers and gentlemen, set out for his seat in Kittery. He was met at Lynn by a troop of horse, and entertained, and was there received by a company of gentlemen and conducted to Salem; on entering which, he was saluted with cannon and ringing of bells, and conducted to the town hall to partake of a magnificent entertainment. After dinner, the royal healths were drank, Governor Shirley's, Sir William's, Admiral Warren's, Brigadier Waldo's, and those of all the officers and men at the siege of Cape Breton: at each toast the cannon were fired, and a treble discharge made by the troop of horse. On leaving Beverly ferry, a cavalcade met him from Ipswich and Newbury, and conducted him to the latter place, where his arrival, at eleven o'clock at night, was announced by a salute from the town cannon and by various fireworks, and the whole party were entertained with an elegant supper by Hon. Major Greenleaf. Next morning at ten, he crossed the Merrimac River, attended by the high-sheriff and a cavalcade from the county of York. He was attended from Hampton to Portsmouth by his majesty's council of New Hampshire, the high-sheriff, and numerous officers civil and military, with many other gentlemen, and two companies of horse. On entering Portsmouth, a troop of horse led the van, followed by officers of Louisburg with music and colors flying, then Sir William in a barouche, then the council, sheriff, and a long train of gentlemen; and a troop of horse brought up the rear. He was conducted to the governor's house to dine, and was saluted on his departure in the evening, as he had been on his arrival, by artillery, and was conveyed in the castle barge to his own house at Kittery.

We have dwelt longer on the siege and reduction of Louisburg than the brief period of time it occupied of Sir William's whole life would seem to justify. But it is to be remembered that this achievement was the main pillar of his fame, and inscribed his name on the enduring page of history. Here it was, too, that the prominent traits of his character present themselves in bold relief: his spirit for daring enterprise, his prudence, patience, forbearance, perseverance, self-devotion, patriotism, and reliance on Divine aid, shone conspicuously, and seemed to rise and. increase in proportion to the increasing demand for their exercise.

Here, too, it was that the hardy sons of New England took their first lessons in military service, preparatory to the grand drama of the Revolution, soon to follow. The same old drums that marched into Louisburg, rallied the troops in their march to Bunker's Hill; and the same Colonel Gridley who planned Pepperrell's batteries, marked and laid out the one where General Warren fell: and when Gage was erecting breastworks across Boston Neck, the provincial troops sneeringly remarked that his mud walls were nothing compared with the stone walls of old Louisburg. Thus the confidence and self-reliance its recollections inspired, proved a favorable preparation for the Revolutionary struggle; while the three years' delay of reimbursements, the refusal to give them a share of the prize-money, and the occasional disparaging taunts of individuals, underrating their services, fired them with the indignation requisite to bring their early experience into action, as soon as colonial oppression called for their services. Thus General Wooster, who commanded a company under Pepperrell, fell mortally wounded at Norwalk; Thornton, of New Hampshire, signed the Declaration of Independence; and Nixon, Whiting, Colonel Gridley, the engineer, and many other distinguished officers and men of the continental army, had served with Pepperrell at Louisburg.

Mr. Hartwell said, in the House of Commons, in 1775, that the colonists "took Louisburg from the French single-handed, without any European assistance—as mettled an enterprise as any in our history—an everlasting memorial to the zeal, courage, and perseverance of the troops of New England." "The conquest of Louisburg," says Smollett, "was the most important achievement of the war of 1744;" and it is remarked in the Universal History, that "*New England gave peace to Europe by raising, arming, and transporting four thousand men,*" *whose success* "*proved an equivalent for all the successes of the French upon the continent.*"

In concluding this brief sketch of the comparative actual services performed by the army and fleet, it must be conceded that the land-forces, in the moral aspect of their deeds, won imperishable fame. Warren was bred to arms; his home was on the deep, and his officers and men had dedicated and trained their energies, body and mind, for deadly strife, and were now in their chosen element, and in the ordinary line of their duty. Not so with the army. Pepperrell, a wealthy merchant, unaccustomed to the sea, with no expectation of military preferment to incite him, obeys the call of his countrymen, leaves all the comforts and endeared attractions of home and his peaceful occupations, to brave the dangers of an ice-bound coast, and the fatigues, dangers, and responsibilities of a perilous enterprise of doubtful success—yet sure to be disastrous to the colonies and to his own fame in the event of failure: and he is followed by four thousand farmers, mechanics, and fishermen, impelled by no forced levy or press-gang, but voluntarily shouldering their firelocks and girding themselves for a deadly conflict, and patiently enduring the hardships and toil of a seven-weeks' siege;—surely, this presents a spectacle of glowing patriotism and self-devotion far transcending the deeds of Warren and his crews.

§ IV.

The French government was exceedingly exasperated at the audacity of the provincial troops in capturing their strongest fortress in America, and immediately prepared a large force for its recovery, and for the punishment of the New Englanders, by sacking and destroying their principal seaports. The force consisted of forty large ships-of-war, besides transports, under the command of the Duke D'Anville, fitted out at Brest, and bringing three thousand to four thousand regular troops—" the most powerful armament that had ever been sent into America."

Intelligence reached Boston of the impending danger, which alarmed the colony and threw it into the utmost consternation. In a few days six thousand four hundred of the inland militia marched into Boston; to whose assistance six thousand men were, on the first notice, to march from Connecticut. The old forts on the sea-coast were repaired, new forts erected, and military guards appointed. The country was kept in a state of alarm and anxiety for six weeks.

Sir William, who still retained the command of the western regiment of the militia in Maine, on the announcement of approaching danger, issued his orders to the captains to muster their companies and examine their accoutrements, and hold themselves ready to march at a moment's warning. At the same time he ordered sentinels to be constantly on the look-out from commanding heights, to give the signal of approaching fleets.

At length the alarm was allayed by intelligence that the enemy was crippled by tempest and shipwreck; that an expected junction of M. Conflans with three ships of the line and a frigate from Hispaniola had failed; that pestilential fevers had prevailed among the French troops, and had destroyed two thousand of them. Intercepted letters which conveyed intelligence that an English fleet was approaching, disconcerted them. D'Anville's anxiety produced sudden death, and D'Estournelle, next in command, in extreme agitation, fell on his sword, their fleet was overtaken and dispersed by tempest, and the vessels returned singly to France. Thus ended the expedition that threatened desolation to the seaports of New England. A more remarkable instance of preservation seldom occurs. "When man is made the instrument of averting calamity, the Divine agency ought still to be acknowledged; but this was averted without human power."

In 1747, the British government ordered the building of four ships-of-war in New England; one of them a forty-four, at Portsmouth, under the contract and supervision of Pepperrell. He addresses a letter to Governor Wentworth, informing him that Col. Messerve (who commanded a regiment at the siege) had engaged to construct the ship, and requesting him to appoint three trustworthy referees to estimate the value of such a ship when completely fitted with forty-four guns, who reported nine pounds per ton as a fair price.

This undertaking opened a correspondence between Sir William and the Lords of the Admiralty, who furnished him with models and directions, and honored his drafts while the vessels were building. When finished, they were loaded with spars and naval stores, and sent to London under convoy, having only one tier of guns mounted. The ship was called the America, and was esteemed one of the best frigates in the British navy.

It seems almost incredible that one man should be able to attend to so many and such diversified branches of business at once,—a merchant, chief-justice of the Court of Common Pleas, senior colonel of a regiment, and thereby commander-in-chief of the militia of Maine, president of the governor's council, colonel of a regiment in the regular British army, and superintendent and accountant of the recruiting service, commissioner to treat with the Indians, manager of the largest landed interests in New England, owner of saw-mills, extensively engaged in the fisheries, superintending the building of a frigate, and all the while corresponding with persons engaged in these various pursuits, with the recruiting officers of his regiment, and with his old companions in arms. Yet his biographer and pastor, Rev. Dr. Stevens, says that it was a common remark of him, that whatever he undertook was always sure to succeed.

Early in 1748, Sir William notifies his foreign correspondents, that he had retired from mercântile pursuits, and recommends to them his son as his successor. About this time he was severely afflicted with rheumatic fever, from which he was ever after a periodical sufferer; which, in a letter to Governor Shirley, he attributed to the cold during the long siege against Louisburg, and to the shattered condition of his head-quarters during the following winter. To his friend General Waldo he also writes of his ill health, and thanks him for advice to quit business, which he says he has already done, excepting some affairs that none but himself can well settle.

It was in the autumn of 1746 that the French fleet was dispersed and wrecked or disabled, and returned to France. The following year another fleet of thirty-eight sail was fitted out from France, under M. de la Jonquière, who was the third officer in rank in D'Anville's fleet. One part of this fleet was appointed to convoy six East India ships, and the rest, with the transports and merchantmen, full of soldiers' stores and goods, were destined for Canada and Nova Scotia. The English admirals, Anson and Warren, sailing in pursuit of this fleet, fell in with it on the 3d of May, when, after a regular and well-fought battle, the French struck their colors. Six of their men-of-war and all their East India ships were captured, and between four thousand and five thousand French were made prisoners. This was the third disaster that befell the French navy within less than three years,—the first at Louisburg, when the Vigilant was captured, with other armed vessels, off the harbor; the second in 1746, under the Duke D'Anville, when a large fleet was dispersed by tempests and nearly unmanned by pestilence; and in this third defeat, the loss of ships was attended by the loss in property of a million and a half. For this glorious achievement Admiral Warren was in turn made a baronet.

Sir William was delighted at the success of his old companion in arms, and after congratulating, encourages him that his nephew will be provided for with a commission in his regiment. He then adverts to their accounts at the siege, and the difficulties of getting them passed.

"I am much concerned to hear you meet with difficulty in getting our accounts passed. Mr. Green is now having the vouchers compared and signed by Governor Knowles to go by this conveyance, and I have ordered Messrs. Apthorp and Sparhawk to hasten theirs, and I design to take my passage for New England next week. If they have not sent them before, I shall hasten them. I am sure all our accounts are honestly kept, and considering the difficulty we labored under after we came into this place, in having the French to take care of, the houses torn in pieces, the rain, no fuel in the garrison, and the long cold winter, that it was impossible to do things in a regular manner, as might have been done in a regular garrison. I am sure we made no advantage to ourselves, and to suffer in our estates would be very hard."*

---

* The deficient vouchers amounted to twenty-six thousand pounds sterling, but new certified vouchers were obtained for about the whole sum.

Governor Hopson having written him a request to pay a tailor's bill for work done for his regiment at Louisburg, his answer shows his sensitiveness at being thought remiss in the fulfilment of his engagements.

"* * * As to what you are pleased to mention relating to the making of the waistcoats for the regiment, I have to say, that I had advanced considerable money for said regiment, in recruiting money, which I sent two years past toward paying the non-commissioned officers and soldiers. I expected this tailor's bill to be deducted out of it. It cannot be expected that I should be acquainted with all the rules of the army, but so far as I do know, I shall endeavor faithfully to perform my duty in every particular.

"I do think it is the first time that ever any complaint was made against me for not paying my debts; and if any person had given me a hint that the bill in question could not have been deducted out of that money which I had advanced for the regiment, payment should have been ordered long since.

"Your excellency's most obedient, W. P."

Sir William's only son graduated at Harvard, 1743, and was soon after engaged to be married to a daughter of General Samuel Waldo, a distinguished merchant and extensive landholder in and about the present county of Waldo, which derives its name from him, and was second in command of the Massachusetts forces at the siege of Louisburg. The lately published *Life of Sir William* gives a circumstantial account of this engagement and of its unfortunate termination, much to the disappointment of both families. It commenced while the baronet was at Louisburg, 1746, and was dissolved in 1751, during which time Andrew was the active partner in his father's mercantile affairs.

Sir William writes to his merchant in England from Piscataqua, August 1749, that "Louisburg is delivered up to the French, and the English are settling Chebucto (Halifax) on Nova Scotia side, and I hear they go on bravely. I hope it will make a fine colony of Protestants and good subjects. Land is good, and mast timber is abundant. I have no thoughts of entering again into trade. As my son, Andrew Pepperrell, has taken my place in trade, you may recommend him to any of your friends. I will be bound for him.

"My regiment is disbanded, and I design to turn farmer. I am sure I spent a good part of my estate in the reduction of Louisburg. I am obliged to you for your wish that I might be governor, but you know I am a west countryman (Cornwall), and they dislike to put such men in for governors."

In August, 1749, Sir Peter Warren writes him:

"I would not, by any means, though much hurried, omit assuring you of the perfect regard I have for you.

"This conveyance carries the money voted by parliament for reimbursing your Province, and I hope sincerely that it will have a good effect, by establishing and keeping a silver medium of trade among you. I have exerted myself in every necessary shape to get the money away to you."

William Bollen, who married a daughter of Governor Shirley, was sent to England to solicit reimbursement of Louisburg expenses, which, with the joint agency of Commodore Warren, was obtained, after three years' toilsome and anxious service, and amounted to the sum of £183,649 sterling, or $800,000. It arrived in the shape of six hundred and fifty-three thousand ounces of silver, and ten tons of copper. "The money was landed on Long Wharf, placed in wagons, and carried through the streets with much rejoicing, and was divided between the four New England colonies, New Hampshire, Maassachusetts, Rhode

Island, and Connecticut—Massachusetts, including Maine, receiving most of it, New Hampshire being entitled to about $16,000." The paper currency of Massachusetts, previously reduced to the rate of seven to eight for one in silver, was now redeemed at a rate about one-fifth less than the current value.

It was the opinion of both Shirley and Pepperrell, that the New England vessels of war which were at Louisburg when the rich prizes were captured, were entitled to a share of the prize money equally with Warren's ships. But little or nothing was ever received.

Sir William was confined with rheumatism during February and March, 1749. He writes to General Waldo, March 29, thanking him for the friendly concern shown for his recovery, and says, "through God's mercy I am now so far recovered as to be able to walk out of doors. . . . . . I now find there are orders sent to Louisburg for the disbanding of Colonel Shirley's and my regiments, which is no more than I expected."

Governor Hopson notifies him of the disbanding of the regiment forthwith, on the arrival of transports to remove them, and urges him in friendly terms to send money to enable the non-commissioned officers and privates to pay their debts before embarking. He replies: "I have always been fond of your opinion, and shall endeavor to follow it. My design was to wait on your excellency by this conveyance, but considering that the regiment is disbanded, and that you daily expect the French there to retake possession, and as his majesty's ship America is this day (May 4, 1749) to be launched, and as I have had directions from the Right Honorable the Lords Commissioners of the Admiralty to assist in completing the ship, etc., you will be pleased to excuse me; but it will give me a vast pleasure to wait on your excellency here. In respect to supply of money, I now send to Colonel Mercer one thousand four hundred and twenty heavy dollars, which I have found very scarce and with great difficulty to be had, and very dear, costing fifty, fifty-one, and fifty-two shillings each in our currency. If Colonel Mercer had drawn on me, it would have been a saving to the crown. If your excellency should order away the transports with soldiers belonging to these parts, the same conveyance might bring what things I have at Louisburg to this port, which would lay me under new obligations to you."

Pepperrell had long contemplated making a visit to London, and late in September, 1749, he took his departure, and on his arrival was cordially received by his agent, mercantile and military, at Spring Gardens. His old companion in arms, Sir Peter Warren, residing at Westbury, soon made his appearance in London to give him a hearty welcome, and General Waldo soon joined them, which gave them a fine opportunity to fight over again the battle at Louisburg. They were soon presented to the king, who gave Pepperrell a very gracious reception, complimenting in strong term his glorious achievement in the siege, and expressed a desire to render him some service. Sir William replied that protection to the fisheries, in which he was employing many hundred of his majesty's dutiful subjects, was the chief favor he had to solicit. The Prince of Wales sought frequent interviews for conversation, and bestowed upon him many civilities, as did Lord Halifax and other noblemen. The Mayor of London waited on him, and caused a service of plate to be raised and presented as a token of respect for his military services. He was invited to visit the public institutions of the city by their respective governors, and was made a guest at the table of the nobility, whilst the impression on the public mind of his victory at Louisburg rendered him an object of universal interest among the whole people.

Early in August, 1750, Sir William took leave of London and returned to Kittery. In the same vessel, Sir Peter Warren sent two elegant black horses as a present to Massachusetts, purchased with his commissions as agent for receiving and forwarding the reimbursements. The remainder of his commissions was appropriated to support a school for Indian children in Stockbridge, Massachusetts. He requested that the horses might be sent into several parts of the province, and that those who profited by them should pay the expense of their keeping. Pepperrell, in notifying the Secretary of State of their arrival, asks that one of them might be sent to Maine (then a part of Massachusetts), adding, that "one-third part of the forces that went on the expedition to Louisburg were enlisted from that district." Maine is entitled to more credit for services rendered in that expedition than she ever gained in all subsequent wars.

After his return from England, he was ambitious of maintaining a style of living suited to his elevated rank. He was president of the council, chief-justice on the bench, colonel in the royal army, and a baronet, all which necessarily drew many distinguished visitors to his house, whom it was his choice as well as duty to greet with an elegant reception. His walls were hung with costly mirrors and paintings, his sideboards loaded with silver, his cellar filled with choice wines, his park stocked with deer, a retinue of servants, costly equipage, and a splendid barge with a black crew dressed in uniform. All these, especially after his return from Europe, were maintained in baronial style.

But he had an ambition that transcended this, in regard to his only son, the heir of his title and estate, the main pillar of his house and object of his fondest anticipations. To prepare him to act well his part in the elevated sphere in which he appeared destined to move, was the all-absorbing object of his ambition; and we may reasonably imagine that much of the information collected while abroad was, during the winter evenings after his return, fondly imparted, mingled with lessons of wisdom suited to his years and future necessities.

But how limited is human foresight! On the 20th of February, Andrew attended a gay party in Portsmouth, and in returning across the Piscataqua, late in the night, was exposed to the cold air, which, on the day following, caused a fever, that soon assumed a typhoid character. The best medical aid proved unavailing, and the imminent danger of the case was announced to his anxious parents. Trembling with alarm and dismay, their grief was inconsolable. Despairing of human skill, and believing firmly in the special providence of God, and that "the prayer of the righteous availeth much," and ever deeply impressed with the belief that the success at Louisburg was in answer to the earnest pleadings of Christians throughout the province, they now implored intercession for an afflicted family, of all the clergy in the neighboring parishes, and a special messenger was sent to the ministers in Boston with the following touching appeal:

[*To Rev. Dr. Sewall, Mr. Prince, Mr. Foxcroft, Dr. Chauncy, etc., in Boston.*]

"KITTERY, February 28, 1751.

"DEAR CHRISTIAN FRIENDS:

"The great and holy, just and good God is come out against us in his holy anger. Oh! may it be fatherly anger! He is bringing our sins to remembrance, and seems to be slaying our only son. Oh, pray! pray! pray for us, that the Lord would keep us from dishonoring his great name in our distress and anguish of soul; that he would support us under, and carry us through what he shall, in his sovereign pleasure, bring upon us; and, if it be his blessed will, that our child may yet be spared to us, and sanctified, and made a blessing. Pity us, O our friends, and cry mightily to God for us!

"We are your distressed friends,

"WILLIAM PEPPERRELL,

"MARY PEPPERRELL.

"P. S.—Dear cousin Gerrish, let our case be known to Christian friends along the road; and carry this letter, as soon as you get to town, to each one of the ministers to whom it is addressed."

Young Pepperrell died the 1st of March, after a sickness of ten days. A large concourse of friends attended the funeral, deeply sympathizing with the bereaved family. "The afflicted mother, mourning her only and beloved son; the fond sister, deprived of her accomplished brother; and the bereaved father, reeling under this heaviest blow which his house had ever sustained, presented a scene of distress truly appalling. His earthly hopes were blasted forever." His pillar and support was gone, and the old hero commenced preparations for his own summons, which he felt might be near at hand. Many were the letters of condolence that poured in upon him, especially from the clergy, with whom he was in high favor, and from several members of the council-board. To one of them, Colonel Rowland Cotton, whose letter is beautiful and appropriate, he replies: "I have received your kind and sympathizing letter on the death of my dear and only son, for which I am much obliged to you. I cannot enlarge, but must say, with that holy man of old, *Have pity upon me, have pity upon me, O ye my friends, for the hand of God hath touched me.* I beg your prayers, and am, dear sir, etc. W. P."

[*To Sir Peter Warren.*]

"KITTERY, in New England, April 26, 1751.

"HONORABLE AND DEAR SIR:—As I have written you several letters since I left your seat at Westbury, and not receiving any of your favors, I shall be very brief. I acquainted you in some of those letters that I had arrived safely, and found my friends and family well. A great mercy that I was preserved abroad, and then returned in health. But that mercies and prosperity are not always to be our experience, I have lately been taught; for on the first day of March, my dear and only son, after an illness of nervous fever of ten days—a healthy, strong, and promising young man, was taken from us by death—a very great bereavement. May God be graciously pleased to sanctify this affliction for our eternal good, that we may more and more realize the uncertainty of life and of all earthly enjoyments, and that we may be more earnest in securing an interest in the blessed Lord Jesus Christ, which is the only thing that can avail us in a dying hour. I hope you and your lady will never meet with so great a bereavement and trial.

"I have written to Mr. Kilby to send yourself and lady a mourning ring, in remembrance of our dear departed son, which I beg your acceptance of.

"I had thoughts of paying you another visit, but I know not what to do. Oh! that God would graciously be pleased to enable me to acknowledge him aright in all my ways, and then I shall be safe in life or death!

"Wishing you and yours much of His presence, my wife joins with me in best respects to yourself and lady, and your dear but uncertain comforters.

"I am, much respected and dear sir, your distressed friend, and faithful, humble servant, W. P."

[*Sir Peter Warren's reply.*]

"My Dear Sir:—I have received your favor of the 26th of April, and am sorry to assure you it is the only one I have had from you since I saw you, though you say you have wrote me several. I most sincerely condole with you on the great affliction with which you have been visited by the hand of Providence in the death of your only son; but if I know you rightly, I think you have fortitude and resignation sufficient to bear it as becomes a good man, and to submit to that great Power whose will it was to call him from this vain world, and to bereave you of so great an earthly comfort as we look upon our children to be. But why should I, who have felt the same distress myself, say so much to renew your grief? My wife joins with me in wishing you to bear with patience this trial, and in thanking you for the memento of rings sent to us both.

"Our portraits should have been with you ere now, could we have got the painter to finish them. Mine is pretty forward, and I hope you will have it this fall, and the other as soon as possible.*

"I came here a few days ago to drink the waters, by the advice of my physician, for the scurvy, and I think I derive benefit from them.

"I believe you and I have been together more than once at my neighbor, Mr. Naith's. His son is appointed consul at Madeira, is a man of business, and his father has prevailed on me to recommend him to you and your friends for commission business, which I take the liberty to do most heartily.

"Symbert has not sent me your and Captain Spry's portraits, which I admire [wonder at]. Sir Harry Frankland had commissions from me to get them sent to me.

"My dear Sir William, your most faithful obedient servant, P. WARREN."

[*Extract from Mr. C. Kilby's letter.*]

"October 7, 1751.

"I executed your commission to Sir Peter and Lady Warren, but did not see it necessary to go any further than

* These portraits are in the Athenæum, Portsmouth, N. H.

to accept of that melancholy token of your regard to Mrs. Kilby and myself, at the expense of four guineas in the whole. But, as it is not unusual here on such occasions, Mrs. Kilby has, at her own expense, added some sparks of diamonds to some other mournful ornaments to the ring, which she intends to wear, the whole of which is finished, and we recommended it to the maker to wait on Lady Warren, in order to give her an opportunity to express her regard for the present, which it is probable she may have already done. I have been silent under a deep feeling of sympathy, nor do I now find myself at present able to discharge the duties of a relation and friend with propriety. Our religion teaches us that it is our confidence in God only that can support us."

Little did Lady Warren expect, when she sent the kind message by her husband to Sir William, that it would so soon fall to her lot to receive a message of condolence from him in return. In less than a year after, he writes her:

"KITTERY, New England, November 18, 1752.

"MY LADY:—I do heartily sympathize with you in your sorrows for the death of my honored and dear friend, your late beloved husband, New England's friend. Your ladyship, I trust, and your dear fatherless children, are not forgotten in the prayers of the good people of this land. Many and exceedingly precious are the promises made to the widow and the fatherless, recorded in the Scriptures of truth. They were written, you know, for our instruction and consolation. Had it not been for Divine recruits from them, poor Lady Pepperrell and I should have perished in our late sore affliction and bereavement. But blessed is the man, the woman, whom the Lord chasteneth, therefore let us not despise nor faint under his chastenings. O may our profiting appear unto all! May we study and find out wherefore the Lord contendeth with us, and if we have done iniquity (as there is not a just man upon earth that doeth good and sinneth not), may we do so no more. Is any afflicted, let him pray. May we pray always, and remember each other in our daily addresses to the throne of grace, social and solitary. And may we thus hold a sweet Christian communion with each other in the house of our pilgrimage, till a few sorrowful days are rolled away, and then may we have a happy and joyful meeting with our dear departed friends in the presence of our holy, and blessed, and glorious Redeemer! I wish the best of blessings to your ladyship and your dear children, and I should be glad to do them any service, if it lay in my power.

"I am, dear lady, your ladyship's most faithful and most obedient humble servant,

"WILLIAM PEPPERRELL."

§ VI.

In forming the numerous treaties made with the eastern Indians by the legislature of Massachusetts, Sir William was for thirty years one of the commissioners, and generally president of the Board.

The first bridge erected over Saco River was effected by his influence and exertions, partly with aid of a lottery, of which he was chief manager. Many buildings were erected by him, and saw-mills put in motion. This immense estate, including most of the present towns of Saco and Scarboro', was even then a princely fortune. Saco, the Indian name, was in his day changed to Pepperrellboro', but after the extinction of the family, the original Indian name was restored.

The late Col. Thomas Cutts, the most prominent merchant and capitalist of his day in Maine, was in his youth a clerk in Sir William's store, and with a capital of a hundred dollars commenced trade in Saco. By industry and frugality, and judicious foresight, he gradually accumulated property enough to buy up, piece after piece, a great deal of the Pepperrell estate, partly by the rise of which he amassed his immense fortune.

The French war of 1744, which ended by treaty 1748, was renewed in 1755. Pepperrell received notice from the Duke of Newcastle of the near approach of hostilities, and directions to prepare accordingly. Soon after, he received a new commission as colonel, with orders to raise one thousand men immediately. He accordingly opened several rendezvous in New England, and soon raised a few companies. But Governor Shirley, who had received like orders for raising a regiment, monopolized the eastern provinces, and Pepperrell was ordered to New York to recruit. But in a few weeks he received a commission of major-general, which released him from this unpleasant duty. He was then appointed commander-in-chief on the eastern frontier, which, considering that it was a district near his house and well known to him, was a judicious selection. He was also appointed commander of Castle William in Boston harbor.

About this time Governor Shirley was called home to England to give an account of his doings, which left the chair of state to Lieutenant-governor Phipps. By the death of Phipps, in March, 1756, the government was administered by the council, of which Pepperrell was president and *de facto* governor, until the arrival of Governor Pownal. On the following August, Pownal took formal possession of Castle William. When Sir William presented the keys, he observed that *that* fortress was the key of the province, which gave the governor an agreeable opportunity of complimenting the conqueror of Louisburg. "The interest of the province," he replied, "is in your heart; I shall therefore be always glad to see the keys of it in your hands."

In 1757, while General Loudoun was loitering about Halifax with the regular and provincial army under the pretence of going to Louisburg to recapture the garrison, Montcalm, the commander in Canada, left Montreal with a force of regulars and Indians, and entering Lake Champlain, laid siege to Fort William Henry. The commander at Fort Edward, instead of hastening to raise the siege, thought only of flight, and wrote doleful appeals to the New England governors to hasten to their relief. The legislature of Massachusetts being then in session, awoke with alarm; and apprehending that the province would be overrun with fire and sword, the governor and council gave the command of all the military forces to Pepperrell, who marched forthwith to Springfield with several regiments. But he there learned that the enemy had retreated from Fort William Henry to Montreal, and the army returned in safety. This affair is briefly alluded to in the history of the times, and is here mentioned as an evidence of the confidence reposed in the old hero of Louisburg in times of imminent danger, all classes being ready to drop their implements of husbandry in the field, and to march under his banner.

Sir William writes, February 7, 1758, to his old friend, Sir Peter Kenwood, M. P.: "I have not been upon any campaign yet, as we had no governor here until lately; and Lieutenant-governor Phipps dying, and apprehending a visit from the French, the whole council desired me to take command of the castle and all the militia of the province, so that considerable part of last year, I spent my time and estate in visiting the frontiers, and getting the militia ready for action. I am allowed nothing for my time and expenses, neither have I had another opportunity to thrash the French, which I should like to have done.

But as I grow old, it is time for me to retire from the field."

Early in 1758, the British ministry was changed, and the helm of State, as respected the management of the war in America, was given to Pitt, which pleased the colonies, and excited them to extraordinary exertions. Massachusetts alone furnished 7000 men, and the other New England provinces in proportion. Taxes were enormous; individual merchants in Boston paid two thousand dollars, and the tax on real estate exceeded two-thirds of its income, and produced numerous bankruptcies.

Louisburg, with the whole island of Cape Breton, which Pepperrell captured in 1745, and which was restored to France by treaty in 1748, surrendered a second time to the British and provincial forces in 1758, under Lord Amherst and Admiral Boscawen. They did not, like Pepperrell, take the garrison by surprise, and consequently they sustained greater losses. The French sank four ships of from sixty to twenty guns each in the harbor's mouth, to obstruct the entrance. After the lapse of nearly a century, these ships are now being raised.

When the former ministry was changed to make room for the energetic Pitt, Sir William doubtless felt the loss of the Duke of Newcastle and of Lord Halifax, who had honored him with every token of respect when he was in London, and had since corresponded with him in a free and friendly manner on provincial concerns. They had twice sent him the king's commission of a colonel in the royal army, and in 1756 that of a major-general. On their removal from power he must have apprehended that all his past services would, in a measure, be overlooked by young Pitt, to whom he was almost, if not entirely, a stranger. But such was not the case. The conquest of Louisburg was indelibly inscribed on the page of history, and Pitt learned from all quarters that no man in America wielded an influence like Pepperrell's. He had recently seen, too, that when Massachusetts was threatened with invasion from Fort William Henry, and the whole population were in the greatest consternation lest the enemy should overrun the settlements with fire and sword, the eyes of all turned to the old hero of Louisburg as their leader; that they dropped their implements of husbandry in the field, seized their fire-locks, and marched forth in a mass under his banner to repel the enemy from the borders of the province.

The moral influence of such a man on the masses Pitt knew how to appreciate, and felt the importance of enlisting it to the uttermost in the existing crisis, in the service of the crown, by such merited tokens of respect for his character and past services as it was in the power of the king to bestow. Accordingly his majesty honored him with a commission of lieutenant-general in the royal army, bearing date February 20, 1759, an honor never before conferred on a native of America. But Sir William was not permitted to take the field. His health had failed, his end was approaching, and he could only cheer his countrymen and urge them onward to victory.

Among others who were compelled to succumb to the pressure of heavy taxation in 1758, as before noticed, was Sir William's son-in-law, the Honorable Nathaniel Sparhawk. In February, commissioners were appointed to receive his effects, and divide the proceeds among his creditors.

His property was advertised for sale at auction, September 15. In the same Gazette, Sir William publishes notice to all persons to settle with him immediately, and in December following, he advertises several farms for sale.

Sir William was impressed with the firm conviction that his earthly career was drawing to a close, and that it was his duty to be intent on putting his house in order. He employed an eminent lawyer, David Sewall, to write his will, which was duly executed in January, 1759.

Early in the ensuing spring he journeyed to Boston for medical advice, and on his return home, through Danvers, visited his sister, Mrs. Prescott, formerly the widow of Hon. John Frost, and subsequently of Rev. Dr. Colman. Judge Prescott writes him from Danvers to Kittery, April 23, acknowledging the receipt of a letter, dated 16th instant, containing discouraging accounts of his health, and adds :

"I pray God direct you into the best remedies, and to give a blessing to the means used for your recovery. . . . . I am told his excellency Governor Pownal thinks of making you a visit next week or the week after. Mrs. Prescott joins me in sending our love.

"Your affectionate brother,

"BENJAMIN PRESCOTT."

In accordance with this, the New Hampshire Gazette of May 4, 1759, contains the following notice:

"Last Wednesday came to town his excellency Governor Pownal, Esquire, governor of Massachusetts, attended by Captain Moulton's troop of horse, who was ordered by his excellency, our governor, to receive him at the province line. He passed through the town at ten o'clock, and was escorted to his excellency Governor Wentworth's seat, where he dined and lodged, and went next morning in his excellency's barge to the seat of Sir William Pepperrell, Baronet. In Kittery he received a handsome salute as he passed by the castle. We hear that Sir William Pepperrell lies dangerously ill at his seat in Kittery."

At the close of the campaign of 1758, the right and left extremes of contested territory, Pittsburg and Louisburg, had fallen into the hands of the British and provincial forces.

Three expeditions were planned for 1759, all to concentrate upon Quebec, the capital and palladium of Canada,—one through the Gulf of St. Lawrence under Wolf, another through Lake Champlain under Amherst, and the third under Johnson at Fort Niagara. The first and third were successful, and were fatal blows to French power in America.

Although Sir William was prevented by sickness and death from taking any active part in the campaigns of 1759, it is gratifying to know that his life was spared until the British and provincial armies had approached to the very verge of conquest,—till he had seen one fortress after another surrendered, and powerful armies marching on triumphantly, conquering and to conquer,—that he could contemplate savage warfare as about to cease on the confines of New England, and that the reports of tomahawking and scalping, of conflagrations and captivities and Indian tortures that had rung their changes in his ears, from boyhood to his old age, were no more to be heard within our borders. As it was with the leader of Israel who toiled on through many years and trials, and reached at last the summit of Pisgah, from which the beauty of the promised land burst upon his enraptured vision, only to close his eyes forever,—so with Pepperrell, who now beheld the conquest of a vast region soon to be added to the realms of his sovereign, and to become the future abode of peace, civilization, and Christianity, and inland seas hereafter to be whitened with the canvas of peaceful commerce. Well may we imagine him offering up the pious ejaculation of Simeon, "Now lettest thou thy servant depart in peace, for mine eyes have seen thy salvation."

Sir William Pepperrell died on the 6th of July, 1759. His funeral obsequies were attended by a vast concourse. The drooping flags at half-mast on both shores of the Piscataqua, the solemn knell from neighboring churches, the responsive minute-guns from all the batteries, and the mournful rumbling of muffled drums, announced that a great man had fallen and was descending to the tomb.

In contemplating the career of Sir William Pepperrell from the uneducated son of a fisherman, rising gradually by the force of his genius to princely opulence,—to the command of the military forces of Maine,—to the first seat on the bench of justice, and to the presidency of the governor's council, and all this before he had arrived at middle age,—enjoying, too, a popularity so transcendent that in a projected military expedition of greater magnitude and peril than the colonies had ever undertaken, he was selected as their leader, under whose standard all classes were willing and eager to enlist, from the hoary-headed Governor Wolcott down to the humblest axeman of the forest,—we naturally inquire what were the elements of his character that were so attractive and gave him such influence and success, and which drew from his sovereign the commissions, twice of colonel, then of major-general and lieutenant-general, and the title and dignity of a baronet, honors never before conferred on a native American. The word *tact* conveys a comprehensive idea of the nature of his power, a quick perception with sound common sense, derived not from books, but from the study of man, of his character and springs of action in all the diversified conditions and relations of life, by constant intercourse and observation; in which study he was an early and an apt scholar, and enjoyed an ampler field for instruction through life than usually falls to the lot of any one. It was this practical knowledge, stimulated by aspirations for honorable fame and distinction, and sanctioned by an enlightened conscience and Christian principles, that crowned his career with unparalleled success, and distinguished him from men of more education and equal purity of intention. It fixed upon the best attainable ends, and resolutely pursued them; it selected the most efficient means, and made judicious use of them.

His perceptions were clear, resolution strong, his judgment sound, and he ever formed his plans with due caution. It was a common saying in his day, that whatever he willed was sure to come to pass,—attributable, probably, as much to caution in willing as to stern inflexibility in acting.

He was particular in exacting from others the performance of their engagement, and equally so in fulfilling his own. He not only spoke often of the importance of punctuality, but more than once remarked that he did not remember ever to have promised payment and failed either as to time or sum. Such a course of policy tended to healthy trade and commerce, whilst it insured in his case both prosperity and popular favor.

Let "young America" pursue a like prudent course, and the public would hear less of assignments and bankruptcies, growing out of extravagant living and of hazardous speculations, and neglect to meet engagements promptly.

Sir William owned real estate in nearly every town on the seaboard, from Hampton to Portland, and also in the towns bordering on the Piscataqua River. During the two or three years after his return from England, his attention was occupied in looking after these estates, and in closing his mercantile accounts. The historian of Saco remarks, that the baronet was often in that town, and his appearance is described by several aged persons. "He passed much time at the house of Rev. Mr. Morrill, and always attended meeting when here on Sunday. His dress was usually in the expensive style of those days, of scarlet cloth trimmed with gold lace, and a large powdered wig. When strangers were present at meeting, it was common to solicit a contribution, the avails of which were the perquisites of the minister. Pepperrell would sometimes, it is said, throw a guinea into the box, in token of friendship and regard for the worthy pastor."

Sir William's education, though very deficient in early life, even to his orthography, was always progressive. Frequent intercourse with his library and extensive correspondence with persons of education, trained him to a good degree of accuracy in orthography, in the structure of sentences, and in the logical arrangement of his thoughts, insomuch that the rough draughts of many of his letters are written, not only grammatically, but frequently in good taste. As a public speaker he is said to have been always ready, and like most other men exclusively practical in their education, he spoke to the point, regardless of polished sentences and rhetorical flourish.

He was distinguished for popular and engaging manners and elegant address, had a high relish for the innocent and refined pleasures of society, was the delight of his friends and the life and spirit of every company; and however engrossed with public duties and domestic cares, he could readily lay them aside in the social circle and play the easy, affable companion. Amid the perplexities that beset him on every side during the siege, he preserved equanimity, and his cheerfulness inspired with hope and confidence all around him. That he was devoutly religious is abundantly shown in the foregoing pages.

Sir William expended liberally in the purchase of books. Guided, in some degree, in his selections by the advice of his pastor, a large portion of them were religious, with some historical, and but few miscellaneous. The graceful biographer of the Rev. Dr. Buckminster remarks that his father-in-law, the Rev. Dr. Stevens of Kittery Point, enjoyed such privileges during a winter's day as rarely fell to the lot of clergymen of that time, in his free access to the library of Sir William Pepperrell, which consisted of the best English editions of standard works imported by himself. When his library had grown so as to be burdensome, a large number of volumes were selected to form, in conjunction with contributions from other individuals, what was called the Revolving Library, for the benefit of the first and second parishes in Kittery, and one in York, each parish enjoying its use a certain portion of the year.

It is to be regretted that he made so few endowments for educational, humane, or religious purposes; but he was surrounded by a very destitute population who needed daily relief. Nor were public benefactions frequent and fashionable then as at the present day, and his will shows that he had many poor relations who had anticipated their legacies and might require further aid. He contributed liberally to his parish and church, and gave a four-acre lot for a church in Saco, a liberal sum to New Jersey College at Princeton, and a bell to the church in Pepperrell, Massachusetts, which town was named for him at the desire of the minister who had been a chaplain at Louisburg.

"Few were blessed," says a contemporary, "with a stronger constitution of body, and his mind was equally firm. Difficulties and dangers served only as occasions to draw forth his resolution, boldness, and intrepidity." But the siege of Louisburg subjected him to exposures, and laid the foundation of rheumatism, which occasionally returned, and finally terminated his useful and eventful life in the sixty-third year of his age.

The eventful life of Sir William Pepperrell closed a few years before the outbreak of the Revolution. Patriotism in his day implied loyalty and fidelity to the king of England;—but how changed the meaning of that word in New England after the Declaration of Independence! Words and deeds before deemed patriotic were now traitorous; and so deeply was the idea of their moral turpitude impressed on the public mind, as to have tainted popular opinions concerning the heroic deeds of our ancestors, performed in the king's service in the French wars. We have no sympathy with the joyous acclamations then bestowed on the successful victor returning from the field of glory to be crowned with laurels. We have felt no desire to perpetuate the fame of his achievements, although characterized at the time by patriotism as pure and disinterested as any exhibited during or since the struggle of the Revolution. The latter war absorbed and neutralized all the heroic fame of the illustrious men that preceded, and the achievements of Pepperrell, of Johnson, and of Bradstreet are now almost forgotten.

The extinction of their fame by the Revolution was not more remarkable than the wreck of their fortunes. The Penns, Fairfaxes, Johnsons, Phillips, Robinson, and Pepperrell were stripped of their immense possessions by confiscation, who, up to that hour, "had been but little less than hereditary colonial noblemen, and viceroys of boundless domain." Pepperrell, it is said, could travel from Piscataqua to Saco river, nearly thirty miles, on his own soil; and his possessions were large in Scarboro', Elliot, Berwick, Newington, Portsmouth, Hampton, and Hubbardston. In Saco alone, he owned 5,500 acres, including the site of that populous town and its factories.

In his will, rewritten with great care in January, 1758, he gives, after the decease of his wife and daughter, portions of her real estate to his grandchildren, Nathaniel, Andrew, Samuel, and Mary Sparhawk; but the great bulk of it, including his Saco lands, was left, unspecified, to a fourth grandson, William, as residuary legatee, on condition of his changing his name from Sparhawk to Pepperrell. All these grandsons remained loyalists or tories, and left the country, and these vast domains passed into other hands. A life-interest in the Saco lands was enjoyed by Lady Mary, the relict of Sir William, and her daughter Mrs. Sparhawk, devised to them by the baronet's will. In exchange for the right thus arising, the State assigned two-ninths, in absolute property, to Lady Pepperrell and her daughter Elizabeth Sparhawk, by a deed executed in 1788. Mrs. Sparhawk appointed Charles Chauncy, Esquire, her agent, by whom several lots were sold, and among them the mill lot, to Colonel Thomas Cutts, who purchased from time to time, as before stated, a large portion of the Pepperrell lands in Saco.

Thus the princely fortune of Pepperrell, that required a century to construct, from the foundation laid by John Bray the shipwright, to the massive structure raised by the fisherman William Pepperrell, and completed by his son Sir William, fastened and secured though it was, by every instrument that his own skill and the best legal counsel could devise to give stability and perpetuity, was in a brief hour overthrown and demolished, and its fragments broadcast, by the confiscation act of 1778 ; and two of his daughter's grandsons have since been saved from the poor-house by the bounty of some individuals, on whom they had no claims for favor. "Surely every man walketh in a vain show. He heapeth up riches, and knoweth not who shall gather them."

His plate was given to his grandson, Sir William, and was allowed in the confiscation act to be taken away from the dwelling of the deceased at Kittery Point. Colonel Moulton of York, with six soldiers, guarded its conveyance to Boston, whence it was shipped to England. Two or three pieces were presented to individuals and are still preserved. The sword he wore at Louisburg is in my possession. Another sword, richly mounted with gold and jewels, given him by Sir Peter Warren, is in possession of Dr. Jarvis of Claremont, New Hampshire. A gold snuff-box, said to have been given him by the Prince of Wales, afterwards George III., is owned by George A. Ward, Esquire, of New York, who prepared for the press the Journal of Curwen his ancestor, which is so much admired by every reader.

After the death of Sir William, Lady Pepperrell caused a neat house, in modern style, to be erected near that of her daughter, and the village church, both of which still remain. Here she died, on the 25th of November, 1789, after being a widow thirty years. The old mansion she left, built by the first Colonel Pepperrell, and enlarged by his son, is plain in its architecture and contained a great many rooms before it was curtailed ten feet from each end. "It was well adapted to the extensive domains and hospitalities of its former owners. The lawn in front extends to the sea, and the restless waves over which Sir William successively sought fortune and fame, still glitter in the sunbeams, and dash around the disconsolate abode. The fires of hospitality are extinguished, and the present inhabitants of the mansion (families of poor fishermen) seem to wish to exclude all visitors and strangers. The hall is spacious and well finished; the ceiling is ornamented, and the richly carved banister bears traces of former elegance. On ascending the staircase, paintings of angels' heads decorate the hall window."* A few years ago there was a noble avenue of trees of a quarter of a mile in length, leading to the house of Colonel Sparhawk, east of the village church. The large hall of this mansion was lined with some fifty portraits of the Pepperrell and Sparhawk families, and of the friends and companions in arms of Sir William.

Very few of the descendants of Sir William can be traced in America. He had only one married child, the wife of Colonel Sparhawk, and she left four sons and one daughter. The eldest son, Nathaniel Sparhawk, Jr., has a granddaughter, Mrs. Jarvis, of Maine, who has a fine family of children. There are two others, elderly maiden ladies, named

---

* Extracted from Curwen's Journal, by George Ward, Esquire.

Humphreys, residing in Conway, N. H. Mrs. Hampden Cutts, of North Hartland, Vt., has a family of five likely children. An only sister of hers married D. Everett Wheeler, Esq., an eminent attorney in New York, and died recently, leaving a promising son and daughter. These two sisters were also granddaughters of N. Sparhawk, Jr. Lastly, there is an elderly maiden lady named Sparhawk, residing in Portsmouth, descended from Samuel; and after her decease, there will not be left a Pepperrell nor a Sparhawk, of Pepperrell blood, in America.

Sir William, as before remarked, adopted his grandson, the son of Colonel Sparhawk, as chief heir to his estate; who left the country as a loyalist in 1778, accompanied by his brothers, and taking his lady with their four small children, three of them daughters. The mother died on the passage to London. The daughters married eligibly, and left a numerous list of descendants, who hold a high social position in England. Their father saved a small plantation in Surinam, and funds in the bank of England, as the remnant of his inheritance; and the British government allowed him a liberal pension in consideration of his losses in America. He died at an advanced age in 1816. It should ever be held in remembrance that he rendered all the assistance in his power to his suffering countrymen, whether banished for their loyalty or incarcerated for their rebellion; and he was among the founders of the British and Foreign Bible Society.

It was a leading and intense desire of the baronet to perpetuate his name and fame (rendered illustrious in the annals of history by his own brilliant achievements) to future generations. Doubtless his grief at the loss of his only son, the heir-apparent to his title and princely fortune, was intensified by the appalling thought that the name of Pepperrell would soon be blotted out of existence. He strove hard to thwart the seeming designs of Providence, by adopting and substituting his grandson as heir and residuary legatee, on condition of his legally assuming the name of William Pepperrell, in the place of William P. Sparhawk, thus giving him the great bulk of his property to hold for his natural life, and then to descend to his son, who was to assume the name of William Pepperrell, and to his son's son forever, so long as there shall be one of the name in his line. . . . . . But in case he should have no son, but a daughter, then the said estate was to remain in his eldest daughter, on condition that, if she marry, her husband shall legally assume the name of William Pepperrell; and after her decease, to go to the male issue, and to the heirs of such issue, and heir male successively forever. But if she shall have no son, then said estate shall be to her eldest daughter, and her male heirs, in manner aforesaid, successively forever, provided that he legally assumes the name of Pepperrell.

But if his said grandson William shall not leave any issue male or female to inherit the estate and name, then his grandson, Andrew P. Sparhawk, is substituted, with his heirs, in like manner and on like conditions;—and in case of failure in this line, then Nathaniel and his descendants are in like manner substituted; and in case of failure in this line, then Samuel Hirst Sparhawk and his heirs and descendants are in like manner substituted; and in case of failure in this line, then the son of his daughter (should she have one) and his descendants are in like manner substituted; and in case no grandson succeeds to the inheritance as aforesaid, then "my granddaughter's husband shall, he assuming the name of Pepperrell, be in like manner substituted; and next to her, in case of failure in this line, my daughter's second daughter (should she have one) shall be substituted." And in case of failure of all his direct descendants of issue, Joanna Frost, of Falmouth, and her children are substituted; and next to Joanna is substituted

Pepperrell Frost, son of widow Sarah Frost, of Kittery; and next, the oldest surviving son of his kinswoman, Margery Wentworth, deceased.*

But in defiance of every safeguard and security his own fertile mind and the best legal counsel could devise, the colossal fabric of his fortune was overthrown by the confiscation act of 1777; and,

> "To strangers now descends the heapy store,
> The race forgotten and the name no more."

The adopted grandson and heir received the title and dignity of baronet in 1770, and was called the second Sir William Pepperrell. He resided at the time at Jamaica Plains, near Boston, having married the daughter of Hon. Isaac Royal. Amidst the trials attending his banishment and the loss of his wife and fortune, there yet remained one luminous spot in the darkened horizon of the future,—one oasis amid the desolate waste,—the fondly cherished hope that his only son would live to inherit the baronetcy of his father and grandfather, as Sir William Pepperrell the third. But alas! as if doomed to disappointment and misfortune in every conceivable form and manner, this son, at the age of twenty, fell a victim to consumption, and the baronetcy as well as name have passed away forever. *Sic transit gloria mundi.*

---

* And in case all the above fail of issue, then the said estate is to be kept in repair,—also the family tomb; and one-third part of the residue of the rents and profits of said estate to be applied toward supporting a Congregational minister, where the present meeting-house now stands; and a free school near to it to be supported by the remaining two-thirds, under the care of the minister and his executors, within half a mile of his dwelling-house.

Engraved by J C Buttre

Stephen Allen

STEPHEN ALLEN.

THERE is an exalted as well as a low and groveling idea of trade. The latter ministers to man's acquisitiveness solely. The proclivity from the cunning and thrifty merchant to the sordid and miserly usurer is rapid, and brings discredit to the mercantile profession in the eyes of most liberal-minded men. To "buy as cheap and sell as dear as you can," seems entirely to address itself to the selfish part of our nature. "No friendship in trade," strictly carried out, will in the end most assuredly petrify the human heart. But as no path in life is not beset with temptations, that wherein they abound most, seems best calculated to perfect our humanity, provided fortitude is given us to withstand as well as profit by them. An ancient moralist has well observed, "that there is a vast difference betwixt forbearing to sin, and not knowing how to sin."* If trade then, as some have asserted, leads to low and debasing thoughts, surely they are to be so much the more admired, who, in spite of its appeals to human frailty, rise superior to knavery, and become distinguished as honorable merchants instead of low hucksterers.

Of the former was Stephen Allen, the subject of this memoir. He was born in the city of New York, on the second day of July, 1767. His mother, whose maiden name was Sabina Meyers, was born in Germany, and emigrated to the city of New York with her parents during her childhood. On the twentieth day of October, 1756, she

* Seneca Epist., quoted by Montaigne, p. 229, ed. 1711.

was married to John Allen. Their issue was five children, all males, the youngest of whom was Stephen. It is a remarkable fact, that of these five children, the three who survived early childhood (two having died young) unfortunately met with an untimely end. The eldest, John, at the commencement of our Revolution, became one of the drafted militia under our Continental Congress, and left his home at the period of the occupation of the city by the British. Since then, naught was heard of his existence, and the presumption is doubtless correct that he became a victim in some of the northern expeditions, which grew out of the early campaigns of our army on the Canada frontier. The next eldest brother, William, was lost at sea during a voyage from his native city to the Island of Antigua; and finally, the youngest (who is the subject of this present notice) became a victim of that dreadful tragedy on board the steamer Henry Clay: the occurrence of which adds an additional stigma to our character as a people most reckless of human life.

In the year 1769, Mr. Allen's father, who was a builder, was selected by government to superintend the erection of extensive barracks for the army stationed at Pensacola, East Florida. He there died of yellow fever, leaving his widow dependent upon her own exertions for the support of herself and three children. At the time of his father's death, Mr. Allen was an infant two years of age. Frequently has he testified to the benign example of that good mother, who taught him truth, virtue, and religion. To her influence may be traced that principal trait in his character, of *honesty*, which in his native city has rendered his name proverbial. We love to dwell upon the character of this noble mother, who not only taught her children to speak the truth fearlessly, but respected and upheld them for so doing. In a familiar letter to a friend, Mr. Allen has so conspicuously portrayed this characteristic of his mother, that we venture to present the story at some length in his own words.

"A short time after our return to the city (1776), I was placed by my mother at a school, kept by a man named Belcher. He was a man of very moderate attainments as a teacher, and moreover possessed an ungovernable temper, a disposition of all others the most unsuitable for an instructor of youth. My own disposition was warm, and there was a kind of ardor and pride in my temperament that always inspired me with a wish to excel others of my school-fellows in the progress of our studies. There was a boy at this school several years older than myself, who commenced the study of arithmetic at the same time that I did. In working our sums or learning our tables, I was always before him; still, by some unaccountable assistance given him during the recess of the school, he the next day was placed above me in the class. This having occurred several times in succession, I concluded the master assisted him. I accordingly, at the dismissal of the school, hung behind, after having finished my sum and shown it to the master for approval. The boy alluded to had been poring over his slate for more than an hour, and was no nearer completing his task than when he commenced; and at the dismissal of the school he was called up by the master, and assisted to work out his sum. On observing the master instructing him how to work, I said to him, 'You ought not show that boy, sir, how to work his sum, as you do not show me;' upon which he drew himself up, and without speaking a word, struck me with such force with the flat of his hand as to knock me down. I immediately rose up, ran home to my mother, and informed her of the treatment I had received, and the cause of it. She called on Mr. Belcher, and as he was unable to allege any thing against me, except the transaction as I had stated it, she withdrew me from the school, and placed me at another in the lower part of the city, kept by a Mr. Wingfield. At this school I continued about one year, and until I was again withdrawn on account of bad usage by the master. I have not the vanity to presume that I was any better in disposition or behavior than other boys of my age. But I am unable to recollect a single instance of disobedience to my teachers, in the performance of any act within my capacity to execute. To be perfect in my lesson was my highest ambition. I was at all times fond of my book, and the pious lessons, inculcated by my mother, had taught me to avoid evil acts and to be obedient to my instructors at all times. This Mr. Wingfield was an excellent teacher, but very severe in his discipline. One of the methods he used in punishing his scholars was by striking a certain number of strokes on the flat or palm of the hand with a piece of board, called a clapper, prepared for the purpose. In all the schools of that day there was an evident partiality shown by the master in his treatment of the children of those persons in eligible circumstances. This was the fact here; for it was plain to me that the children of those who were considered rich, were not only treated with more consideration and lenity than others differently situated, but they were seated in more conspicuous places in the school. . . . . . I had been writing from a copper-plate copy, then in common use in the schools. This copy, by frequent use, had come apart, and when I took it, formed two pieces. By some means or other, one part of it had fallen from the desk, where I was writing, to the floor. At that moment a boy by the name of ——, the son of doctor ——, was passing by the form where I sat, and, taking up the copy, inquired who was writing from it. I told him I was. He replied, 'Then you have torn it, and I will inform the master of it.' It was in vain that I protested my innocence, and that the copy was torn when I took it; for he appeared bent on mischief, and therefore repaired to the seat of the master with the broken copy in his hand, and there told his story. The result was that I was called up and charged with the fact. I denied it, and told the truth. But it would not avail, particularly as the charge was made by one of the favored scholars, and the clapper was therefore resorted to, of which I received three strokes on each hand, that entirely disqualified me from writing. The master nevertheless directed me to produce a copy equally as well written as the one torn, or receive further punishment. This was utterly impossible apart from the disability which had been inflicted, and with it still worse, and I therefore made no attempt, but took my seat. In a short time I was again called up, when the same punishment was repeated; and so for a third time, when one of the larger boys, by the name of Brevoort, and who was also one of the favored scholars and wrote an elegant hand, undertook in my stead to produce a copy. This was accepted by the master, although he was perfectly aware that the writing was none of mine; in fact, he saw it performed by Brevoort, whose desk was immediately in front of his. This treatment was both brutal and unjust, and excited in my breast a feeling of resentment against the boy who was the cause of it, and the man who inflicted it, which I was unable to control; and, accordingly, on the dismissal of the school I pursued this boy, gave him a sound beating in return for his baseness, and never after entered the premises of Mr. Wingfield. *My mother was perfectly satisfied with my conduct, inasmuch as she implicitly believed what I told her of the usage I had received;* and the precept she had inculcated on all occasions was, to hide nothing, but always to declare the whole truth—let the consequence be what it may. This is a rule I have always endeavored to steer by, and trust, therefore, that neither she or others have had reason on any occasion to doubt my veracity. . . . . ."

The underscoring is ours, and we wish that every parent

might ponder upon the moral deduced therefrom. What a proper pride appears in this simple recital—that truthfulness had been solicited from, and not beaten into the child, by its parent; and that mutual confidence and love was the result of such solicitude!

At the age of twelve years, the boy commenced an apprenticeship in the sail-making business with James Leonard, his brother William being engaged in the same loft as journeyman. From their earliest youth the brothers had imbibed principles of liberty from an uncle, who took great pains to explain to them the cause of the oppression which the mother country was then visiting upon her struggling colonies. Their employer was an ardent tory, and these youths were the only ones among the apprentices and journeymen who ever rejoiced at every success of the American cause, and were accordingly abused therefor. The lads had frequently to encounter the English press-gangs, which at that time prowled about the city; and at one time the younger barely escaped impressment, having been chased into his mother's house. His expertness in the business of sail-making was honorably noticed by his employer, and excited the envy of his companions. This became an incentive to his ambition, and he soon learned how to assist his employer in cutting out sails.

Peace having been declared, Mr. Leonard discontinued his business in the city, and set sail with his family for Nova Scotia. Mr. Allen was one of those who witnessed the entrance of the American troops into the city of New York with Washington at their head, and heard him address the citizens at his head-quarters in Broad-street.

Shortly after this, at the age of fifteen, he was turned loose upon the world to seek his fortunes. His brother William having left the city for Philadelphia, Mr. Allen was employed by Thomas Wilson, a Quaker, and continued with him till the year 1787. At this time his employer offered him a share in the concern, which he accepted. In May, 1788, he became connected in marriage with Miss Marschalk, when he was not quite twenty-one and she seventeen years of age. Wilson having contracted habits of dissipation, he was compelled to dissolve the connection; and in December, 1791, he commenced business on his own footing. During the Revolution of France he began to prosper; and, having amassed a small capital, he was enabled to purchase his material at first cost for cash, thus increasing his profits. At this time arose the two parties of Federalists and Republicans, with the latter of which he was not slow in sympathizing. For this he was proscribed, and suffered the loss of some of his best customers. Such persecution did not, however, shake the integrity of his opinions. With assiduity, perseverance, and economy, he was enabled to baffle the tyranny of such intolerance. On the 10th November, 1802, he entered into partnership with Joseph Lathrop, which connection was dissolved in 1809, in consequence of the ill health of his associate. In the following year, Mr. Augustus Wright became his partner. His wife having deceased, he had (in 1807) contracted a second marriage with Sarah, daughter of Joseph Roake.

The war with Great Britain in 1812 was the era of fierce and rancorous party spirit between Republican and Federalist. The latter strongly opposed the war, and endeavored to dissuade their friends from aiding Government by way of loan. The Convention of Hartford plotted treason and the dissolution of the Union. Mr. Allen did not hesitate to exert all the influence and means he possessed to oppose the unpatriotic attempts of Federalism. He joined a volunteer company, which threw up redoubts on Long Island, and loaned the Government all the money he was enabled to spare from his business. Business was of course prostrated, and his partner concluded to retire with the competence already earned, rather than risk the uncertain events of the future. The conclusion of this war, at the close of 1814, was sudden and unexpected. To Mr. Allen it brought additional prosperity. Several large vessels had been ordered to be built at Sacketts Harbor, and others, smaller, at Lake Erie; sail-duck was exceedingly scarce, and the credit of Government very low. Mr. Allen was consulted by the United States navy agent as to the readiest method of furnishing a supply of duck. The proposal of Government was to purchase such cloth as was needed on Government credit of ninety days, payable at maturity in Treasury notes, at the market price. To those possessing the material, his most earnest appeals to their patriotism was unavailing; they feared the risk, and refused negotiation, except upon terms the most exorbitant. After this unsuccessful attempt to enlist the sympathy of those who were far more able to incur loss than himself, Mr. Allen accepted the terms, and sold his whole stock to Government. His goods were duly forwarded, but had proceeded only half the distance, when the news of peace reached the city. Treasury notes, from a depreciation of ten per cent., rose rapidly to par, and thus a handsome profit was realized.

From this period Mr. Allen's career as a public man began. In April, 1817, he became a member of the common council of New York, and in March, 1821, mayor of the city. During the summer of 1822 the yellow fever appeared, the first case being reported in Rector-street, near the North River. Previous to this, the mayor had called the attention of the Board of Health to the inconsistency of our quarantine laws, which enjoined upon foreign vessels their purification at quarantine, but permitted their goods to be brought immediately to our city and landed on our wharves. The health officer and resident physician, both medical men, insisted that the disease was endemic, and could not be brought from abroad. Mr. Allen's remonstrances were therefore disregarded. He, however, was unremitting in his attentions to the most filthy localities of our city—visiting them personally, pointing out nuisances, and personally attending to their abatement. Throughout the prevalence of the disease, which continued until the 1st of November following, not a single day was missed in attending to these duties. On the 25th of this month the mayor addressed a message to the common council on the subject of the late pestilence, suggesting an amendment of our health laws, the erection of a fever hospital in the city, the proper construction of sinks, privies, &c., a more prompt and efficacious method of cleaning our streets; and "that connected with the health and prosperity of the city was the bringing in a good and wholesome supply of water, which ought never to be lost sight of until its accomplishment was consummated." Thus it appears that at this early period, to his earnest wish and desire for so great a blessing as the city now enjoys, may be traced his subsequent energy and ability in bringing to a successful completion the New York Croton Aqueduct.

On the 19th of January, 1824, Mr. Allen was superseded in his office of mayor by William Paulding. On the evening of his resignation the common council passed a unanimous resolution of thanks to the late mayor for the able and faithful manner in which he had discharged the arduous duties of his office. Scarcely an institution of benevolence, trust, or responsibility existed in his native metropolis which did not count him as an efficient member, and which did not experience his sagacity, his prudence, and his laborious activity. Among these may be enumerated the Mechanics' Society, the Tammany Society, the Mechanic and Scientific Institution, the Public School Society, the High School Society, the New York Hospital and Lunatic Asylum, the House of Refuge for Juvenile Delinquents, and the New York Prison Discipline Society.

Over several of these institutions he presided as first officer.

In April, 1824, in connection with Geo. Tibbets of Troy, and Samuel M. Hopkins, of Albany, he was appointed commissioner to visit the State Prisons, one at Auburn, and the other in the city of New York, and to report upon the efficacy of punishments inflicted on convicts, and to recommend such alterations in discipline and government as might be deemed useful and salutary. In accordance with these instructions, a long circumstantial and able report was prepared, a thorough revision of our prison laws suggested, and a sale of the old prison at New York and the purchase of a marble quarry either at King's Bridge or at Sing Sing recommended. Annexed to the report was a digest of all the laws on the subject of prisons scattered at large through our statutes, with a careful revisal to suit the suggestions of the commissioners; all of which was the sole labor of Mr. Allen. A subsequent act reappointed the same commissioners, and directed them to consummate their previous suggestions. The result was the purchase of land and the erection of the State Prison at Sing Sing.

Mr. Allen retired from mercantile business on the 1st of November, 1825. In the possession of a competence, his ardent desire was to refine his taste, elevate and improve his mind, and by reading and reflection pass the remainder of his life in the possession of that happy independence which constitutes a man neither rich nor poor. Trade to him possessed no further fascination than as a means to this end. Of simple habits, there appeared to be an ingrained moderation in his temperament which led him to seek rather the middle, and to avoid extremes. Luxurious habits of living, which are so easily contracted, and which so ruthlessly enslave and enervate most men, possessed no charm for him. Activity, mental and bodily, were his luxuries, and he has often contemplated with horror such an infliction of ill health as should render its victim inactive and dependent upon the care of others. To the more congenial duty of devoting himself to the cares of his family, and those benevolent and useful city institutions of which he was a member, were opposed the paramount claims of his party, which insisted upon conferring upon him public office.

In May, 1826, he became member of Assembly of the State of New York, and in 1829 was elected senator. During this session the now exploded safety-fund project was recommended by Governor Van Buren, and suggested by Mr. Forman, who borrowed its principal features from the regulations of the Hong merchants of China. These have a monopoly of trade with foreigners, under the stipulation that all are responsible for the individual pecuniary delinquency of any. This safety-fund project was opposed by Mr. Allen, who labored to show its injustice and inequality in a pamphlet of some length. The more correct principles of banking which now prevail were not then sufficiently appreciated to prevent the enactment of this law, which finally passed, with only six votes against it. While in the Senate, Mr. Allen, as member of the Court for the Correction of Errors, was constant in his place, hearing cases of appeal from the Supreme Court. Every case argued at this term, save one, he heard, and gave written opinions upon sixteen out of the nineteen cases heard. This was the first time in which written opinions were given in the Court of Errors by a layman. The able manner in which he executed this arduous duty excited the wonder and admiration of many of our judges and most distinguished members of the bar. To accomplish this arduous duty, his wonderful self-reliance and energy successfully aided him. He forthwith furnished himself, at considerable expense, with a law library, and laboriously studied the digests and elementary treatises. To aid himself in understanding the Latin terms abounding throughout these works, a Latin grammar and Ainsworth's dictionary were resorted to, and with no other aid he plodded his weary way to the accomplishment of his purpose.

In 1833 Mr. Allen was nominated and appointed as one of the water commissioners under an act passed the previous session of the Legislature, for supplying the city of New York with pure and wholesome water. His previous recommendation in 1822, and the fact that he had acted on a committee appointed to investigate the subject at that time, probably induced his appointment. It may not be irrelevant briefly to present the claims which entitle his name to be handed down to posterity as one of the originators of this noble project, and in the consummation of which he bore such a conspicuous part. We have in a former part of this memoir, alluded to his communication to the common council, while mayor, in 1821, advocating the propriety of bringing into the city a good supply of pure and wholesome water. Therein he suggested the introduction of the Bronx River, which in 1798 and 1799 was recommended by Dr. Brown, then street commissioner, and Mr. Weston, civil engineer, as the only feasible source. A committee was thereupon appointed. Mr. Allen, as chairman, reported the result, and recommended the following resolution:

"*Resolved*, That five hundred dollars be appropriated for the purpose of obtaining a survey and profile of the whole line of country between this city and the main source of the River Bronx, commonly called Rye Pond; together with an estimate of the probable cost of completing the project of supplying this city with good and wholesome water." This resolution was passed unanimously, and the mayor selected Canvass White, Esq., civil engineer, to run the necessary levels and surveys of the whole country from this city to the various sources of supply in the county of Westchester. In his instructions to Mr. White, he was particular in recommending him to go to the Croton River. Deeming the supply from the Bronx sufficient, Mr. White neglected this injunction. The ill health of the engineer prevented the presentation of his report till the year 1824, when Mr. Allen had been superseded in the mayoralty by Mr. Paulding.

We trace Mr. Allen's strong predilections in favor of the Croton in items of correspondence with several gentlemen on the subject of supplying the city with pure water. In 1823, in a letter to John Cotton Smith, he observes: "You are no doubt apprised of the circumstance that the corporation of this city have authorized the survey of a line of country between this and the Croton." Again, the same year, he addresses John L. Sullivan relative to bringing in the water of the Passaic River as follows: "It is more than a year since the common council adopted measures to ascertain the practicability of bringing in the waters of the Croton." Again, in correspondence with Mr. George W. Cartwright, of Sing Sing, relative to the practicability of obtaining a supply of water from the Croton, that gentleman writes to Mr. Allen: "If you resort to the Croton, it must be six or seven miles from its mouth. It may then be taken with advantage, and at a moderate expense, by an aqueduct, with a current of one and a half or two feet per mile, to within a few miles of the city." Mr. White's report seems to have been unattended to in the common council, as in 1826 a company of private citizens applied to the Legislature for an amendment to a charter which had been granted them the year previous, for supplying the city with good water. Mr. Allen was then a member of Assembly, and as chairman of a committee to whom this application was referred, reported in its favor. Therein reference is again made to the Croton as follows: "The situation of the city of New York, being on a narrow strip of land, and surrounded with marine waters, precludes a possibility of a supply from any source within its own limits. . . . . The result was, an appropriation was made by the common council of 1822 for the purpose of employing a competent and experienced engineer to make a correct survey of the whole line of country between the city and the Croton River." (*Assembly Journal*, 1826, p. 685.) It therefore may be concluded that when the able report of De Witt Clinton appeared in 1832 (which, by the way, was merely conjectural), recommending the Croton for a supply, Mr. Allen's convictions had been long and previously well matured in favor of this source.

In his report, Mr. Clinton confesses "that his opinion is formed under great perplexity and embarrassment," the result of which was a recommendation on the part of the committee of the common council to whom his report was referred, "That a law be applied for simply providing for the appointment of the board of commissioners, who should be invested with full powers to examine all the plans which have heretofore been proposed; to cause actual surveys to be made; to estimate the probable expense; to test the water; and generally to do whatever in their judgment may be necessary to arrive at a right result as to the best mode of effecting the proposed object." This law being subsequently obtained, Mr. Allen and his colleagues commenced their duties; and their report of November, 1833, may be taken as the first definite official settlement of this momentous question. The subsequent prosecution and completion of this noble monument of the energy of the people of the Empire City reflects the greatest credit upon all concerned. When the construction of the aqueduct was nearly completed, Mr. Allen and his fellow-commissioners were superseded by the appointment of gentlemen whose politics coincided with the then triumphant party.

The following honorable mention of the services of the original commissioners is made by Charles King, Esq., in his "Memoir of the Croton Aqueduct:" "It would be eminently unjust, in parting with these commissioners, to withhold from them the praise of having faithfully, intelligently, and assiduously fulfilled the trust which they had held for so many years. The chairman of the board in particular, Stephen Allen, has left upon the work, from its commencement to the advanced stage in which he relinquished it to his successor, the stamp of his energetic character and strong inquiring mind."

Having been removed in 1840 from the office of water commissioner by Governor Seward, on grounds purely political, he again fondly hoped to be relieved of the cares of public life, and to give his attention more closely to various benevolent institutions of which he was a member. But the Independent Treasury scheme having been passed upon, he was earnestly sought by President Van Buren to accept the office of Receiver-General of New York. Aware of his previous intentions to refuse any tender of public office, the President deputed his son, John Van Buren, Esq., to seek a personal interview with Mr. Allen, and endeavor to influence him to change his intentions. Sensible of the high honor and consideration of the President, the following letter, declining the office, was sent:

"New York, June 27th, 1840.

"M. Van Buren, Esq.,

"President of the United States.

"Dear Sir:—Your son has just now permitted me to peruse a letter from you, requesting him to inquire whether I would serve as Receiver-General for this city, should the bill now before Congress pass into a law. I feel much honored by the preference given me over others who are seeking the office, particularly coming from one whom I have ever held in the highest esteem. I must, nevertheless, decline being a candidate, not from any fear of the responsibility or trust reposed, but simply from a wish for relaxation from the public duties in which I have been engaged for the last four or five years, and of which I was lately relieved by my good friend *Governor Seward.*

"The office is one of great importance in a public point of view, and will require unceasing vigilance and attention from the incumbent. I have no reason to doubt, however, that you will be able to select a person to fill it, much more competent than I am, and to whom it may be a pecuniary benefit, which, to me, is of no manner of importance.

"Your request that the proposal should not be promulgated will be strictly observed on my part.

"That you may continue in the highly important station which you have filled with so much credit to yourself, and benefit to our beloved country and its institutions, is the wish of every true-hearted democrat; and which wish shall not fail of its fulfillment for the want of the best exertions of

"Your friend and humble servant,

"STEPHEN ALLEN."

Nearly simultaneous with the dispatch of this letter to the President, the following was received from the Hon. Silas Wright, at that time a member of the United States Senate:

"WASHINGTON, June 30, 1840.

"MY DEAR SIR:—I learned from the President, yesterday, that he had tendered to you the office of Receiver-General at New York, under the Independent Treasury bill—the final passage of which, in the House of Representatives, we hope may take place this day; and what causes this letter is, that I learned further from him that you had declined to take the office. I confess to you that this news has afflicted me deeply, inasmuch as I have for a long time known that his mind was fixed upon you for the place, and I have therefore felt at rest about it.

"My concern at your declination is greatly increased by the state of the question, your name being withdrawn. The only applicant of whom I am informed, and who has been much pressed by petitions and letters from your city, is ———, and a call from him at this moment has forced me to make an appeal to you, in the hope that the devotion which you have always manifested to the success of the democratic party may persuade you to yield your private wishes and personal convenience to the public good, at least for a short period.

"It may be a whim, but I hope you will pardon me for feeling an abhorrence at the idea that a ——— is to be selected in our State, to put this great measure into operation. I do not know any thing of ———, except from the papers which have been sent to me in his behalf, and from two very short visits he has made us during our present session, These papers would be greatly in his favor, if I did not know how easily papers are got up in your good city; and his visits would have been more highly prized by me, if they had not seemed to be too nearly connected with his application, and especially the one which has brought him here this day. Still, I do not permit these things to prejudice him in my mind more than I can help; and my great objection to him, after all, is the name, and these evidences that he belongs to the family. Still, he has upon his papers your mayor and almost all the official strength of your city; and to pass him, and go out of the city for a man, may endanger the harmony of feeling among our friends there; while to appoint a man of his own age and standing, resident there, may be worse.

"I appreciate fully your wishes to be retired and able to devote yourself to your private affairs; but can you not consent to give your name and character to the beginning of this new system, without doing violence to your personal duties or personal feelings? It is a delicate period. A dreadful contest is pending over the democracy, while embarrassment and distrust pervade the land. The success of the Independent Treasury plan must depend, in a great degree, upon the public confidence drawn around it at the start; and the appointment of men whom all the world know to be honest and beyond temptation is one of the most plain steps of policy and duty on the part of the President.

"I am at this moment favored with a note from him, urging me to do just what I am doing: to write to you; to say, that if you can consent to take the office for one year, and shall then wish to leave it, he will be under the greatest obligation, and will so consider your consent. He may be selfish; but he wants your aid, and your standing with the democracy of the city, and state, and country, to help start the system. He says, in his very short and hasty note, that you once told him you were always called upon to help break in a bad job, but that I must tell you he hopes this will not be a bad job, while you shall never have cause to regret the associates he will give you in the receivers at the other points. He charges me, also, to assure you that the duties of the office will be plain and simple, and in no way perplexing; while they intend to give you such means for physical security, that your mind may be at ease when the keys are in your possession. I cannot, myself, suppose that the duties can in any way be made complex and difficult, and I am sure, the responsibility alone excepted, that you would find the office a very pleasant one.

"But I must close as my time is consumed, and I fear your patience will be before you read this long letter.

"Will you give to me, or directly to the President, the earliest reply consistent with your unalterable conclusion? If the bill passes to-day, he will desire to make the nominations early in the next week, and urges me to request you to answer as soon as shall be consistent, but to take a day or two for deliberation, if it shall be desirable to you.

"A messenger this moment comes in with your letter to him, which he says he has received since writing his note to me, and he remarks, what I think, that it should not prevent my writing to you.

"Do not, my dear sir, consider me as obtrusive in this letter. It seems to me, if I were with you, I could persuade you to say yes to this request, and yet I would not make it if I thought it would be received as unkind, or that yielding to it would do you injury in your fortunes, or make you unhappy in your mind. I shall wait anxiously your answer, and in the mean time hope you will believe me to be, Very respectfully and very truly, your, &c.,

"SILAS WRIGHT, JR."

An appeal so urgent, and couched in terms so persuasive, had the desired effect of inducing him to accept this responsible office, which he did in the following reply:

"NEW YORK, July 5, 1840.

"HON. SILAS WRIGHT, in Senate, Washington:

"DEAR SIR:—I received your letter of the 30th ult. on the 2d instant, and have availed myself of the privilege allowed, 'to take a day or two for deliberation.'

"Your language is so friendly and inviting, and the general tenor of your reasoning so pressing, that I have experienced more difficulty in arriving at a conclusive decision than has occurred in any case within my memory. My reasons for having declined the office of Receiver-General are mostly of a domestic character, and, perhaps, so far as they relate to my private concerns, under the emergency of the case, they ought not to be a barrier to acceptance; but I I have in addition pledged all my spare time to certain benevolent institutions in this city, in whose prosperity I feel a lively interest. I am chairman of a committee of the governors of the New York Hospital, requiring my attendance each day from 10 to 11 o'clock, and on the last Saturday of each month the whole day. As president of the House of Refuge, once in each week I meet a committee, and once in each month the Board of Managers. As member of the Public School Society, I have with three or four other gentlemen the oversight of one of the schools, to which I give as much attention as circumstances will admit; and in addition the care of a pretty large family on my hands. The office I lately held as president of the Board of Water Commissioners did not materially interfere with the performance of these duties—that office not requiring attendance at fixed hours daily, and the only privation was that I could not leave the city for more than a few days at the same time: consequently this is the first summer for a period of years that I have found myself free, and have accordingly promised my family a tour of five or six weeks through this and adjoining States.

"The acceptance of the office of Receiver-General, therefore, would not only, in a measure at least, prevent me from fulfilling my pledge to the institutions alluded to; but would be a complete bar to my leaving the city for any one business day in the year. The presence of the Receiver-General, as I view it, would be required daily from ten to three—bank hours; for he should both receive and pay, or at least be present at all receipts and payments. These are matters which may weigh light with some; but circumstances alter the relative force of facts upon different persons.

"My objections to the office were briefly—first, the confinement to be endured by the incumbent; second, the necessity under the act of obtaining security, which has never been required of me in any trust I have heretofore executed; and third, the limit of $800 per annum for each clerk, as the services of competent persons cannot be obtained in this city at so small a salary.

"Your good opinion I value highly, and for the promotion of the democratic cause I am disposed to make considerable sacrifice. I think, however, you place much more importance on my acceptance of the office than it deserves, and that there are many good men and true that might be selected who would do credit to the office, and at the same time benefit the party—Flagg, Marcy, Dix,—and a host of other names throughout the State, better known to you than to me; for I see no good reason for confining the appointments to the city. Your view of the character of Mr. —— is correct. Such an appointment would be much more unpopular than the selection of a person away from the city.

"I ought to apologize for the length and uninteresting character of this letter, as perhaps all that was required of me was to say, whether I still adhered to the opinion expressed in my letter to the President. I therefore state, that unless I can be allowed a few weeks to arrange my private concerns, I must adhere to my previous determination. But if the public business will not be injured by the delay, and I can be allowed the time alluded to, then I will accept the office, should the question still be open and another not having been selected by the President for the place.

"Very respectfully yours, &c.,

"STEPHEN ALLEN."

It was ever thus. Not an office was ever conferred upon Stephen Allen but came to him unsolicited, and in many cases, like the one above, by means of pressing importunity from those bestowing it. One year passed, and glad to avail himself of the condition accompanying the appointment, he tendered his resignation. One of our daily journals, politically opposed to him, in eulogizing him for his honesty, ventured to predict, that when Stephen Allen delivered up this trust, instead of defalcation a balance would appear to his credit. Singularly enough, upon accounting to his successor, it was found that there actually was an excess of cash of fifty-one dollars and fifty cents.

A retrospect of the life of the individual we have thus sketched, might induce the opinion that we have exhibited him rather in the light of a prominent politician than an American merchant. It is true that his mercantile career, dating back from rather a remote period, is devoid of brilliant achievement or much interesting reminiscence. But it seems to us, the example of such a man is most pregnant of instruction to the merchant of the present day. Here we behold the career of a trader who freighted no rich argosies; whose transactions, unlike those of merchant princes, spreading over the waters of half the globe, were confined to the simple prosaic details of every-day business life. But in the brief history of these private transactions, we behold the man of unimpeachable veracity and scrupulous honesty, whose acquisitiveness was circumscribed by temperance and prudence, so that he could easily determine when that unstable limit of "rich enough" had been reached; who, when the cares of business had been laid aside, did not choose to rust out his life in inglorious ease, but to direct his energy and activity in works of public and private beneficence. How to set bounds to this inordinate greed of gain should be a lesson ever before the merchant, because in his calling the fierce competitions of trade are too apt to afford undue prominence of the baser passions of the mind to the exclusion of the nobler. When years come on apace, more time should be taken for that self-culture, which will exhume the better feelings clogged during the battle of our business life,—feelings which enable us to form a kindlier estimate of humanity,—feelings which prompt us to discard our previous philosophy, which taught us that every man is *prima facie* a rogue, for that which persuades us that "none are not all evil." Arrived at this latter and better state of mind, we can pity the fallibility of humanity; and even when we are badly used by the selfish and dishonest, instead of regretting our misplaced trustfulness, exclaim with the poet—

> "Perhaps the pleasure is as great
> In being cheated as to cheat."

It is, perhaps, proper, before presenting the subject of our memoir in another aspect, that we should record the printed copy of maxims which was found in his pocket when his body was recovered from the waters of the Hudson—a victim of the dire catastrophe on board the ill-fated steamer Henry Clay:

"Keep good company, or none. Never be idle; if your hands cannot be usefully employed, attend to the cultivation of your mind. Always speak the truth. Make few promises. Live up to your engagements. Keep your own secrets, if you have any. When you speak to a person, look him in the face. Good company and good conversation are the very sinews of virtue. Good character is above all things else. Your character cannot be essentially injured except by your own acts. If any one speaks evil of you, let your life be so that none will believe him. Drink no kind of intoxicating liquors. Ever live, misfortune excepted, within your income. When you retire to bed, think over what you have been doing during the day. Make no haste to be rich. Small and steady gains give competency with tranquillity of mind. Never play at any game of chance. Avoid temptation, through fear you may not withstand it. Earn money before you spend it. Never run into debt unless you see a way to get out again. Never borrow unless you cannot possibly avoid it. Do not marry until you are able to support a wife. Never speak evil of any one. Be just before you are generous. Keep yourself innocent, if you would be happy. Save when you are young, to spend when you are old. Read over the above maxims at least once a week."

We have portrayed Stephen Allen as the moral man. We propose now to notice him in his latter days as the Christian. The benign influence of a good mother had so nurtured his religious feelings as to make him a reverential and sincere respecter of religion from his youth upward. He was a constant and uniform church-goer, and a rigid observer of the sanctity of the Sabbath. His early associations were with the sect of Moravians, of which his mother was a member. Subsequently he attended the Presbyterian Church, and finally, a short period before his death, became a member of the Mercer-street Church, under the pastoral care of its present incumbent, Rev. Dr. Prentiss.

Although his formal profession of Christianity had been thus made at the latest period of his life, we are not to conclude that a trivial matter thus induced him to neglect the calls of religion, who was at all times a deep and earnest thinker on such momentous subjects. But he was peculiarly an independent thinker; and, as in every other duty in life, he sincerely thought that it would not do to pin his faith to the sleeve of another, but that he himself must diligently search the Scriptures, and work out his own salvation. His sympathies were all with his fellow-worshipers, and he tried earnestly and faithfully to conform his belief to the dogmas of the Church with which he so anxiously desired to fraternize. But his inflexible honesty would ever interpose between his inclination and his sense of duty. Whether finally he succeeded in his efforts, or whether, on the part of his friends, a point or two not deemed fundamental was by them yielded, is not known; but we have been permitted to inspect a large amount of manuscript left by Mr. Allen, in which he appears prayerfully to have reviewed almost every line of the Holy Scriptures—manuscript sufficient to form a volume of some size.

The Rev. Dr. Styles, who preceded the present incumbent, had anxiously endeavored to clear away his doubts concerning the doctrine of the Trinity, and for that purpose had addressed, near the close of 1850, a letter to Mr. Allen, inclosing remarks on the Trinity, and a letter by him to a young lady on the same doctrine. In answer thereto Mr. Allen writes as follows:

"January 1st, 1851.

"MY DEAR FRIEND:—I have read your remarks on the Trinity, and also your letter to a young lady on the same subject, for the opportunity of perusing which I return you thanks. You conclude your remarks as follows: 'Therefore Jesus Christ is the Supreme God;' and your letter to a lady concludes, 'He who died on Calvary for you and me is the very God who made us.'

"I will not attempt an extended argument on this weighty and important subject, but will barely take the privilege to state a few facts as they have been marked in my Scripture reading, and are now referred to. And I may as well, at the outset, declare that I cannot concur with you in the belief that Christ our Saviour is at the same time the Supreme God.

"I find both in the Old and New Testament the great and leading fact proclaimed, that there is but one Supreme God—'Thou shalt have no other god, before me, for I am the Lord thy God, and am a jealous God. Even I am he, and there is no god with me.' I need not increase these quotations, for you have them in your mind in abundance. You apply all these Scripture declarations as meaning Christ, the promised Messiah. But Christ taught his disciples otherwise, and asked one, 'Why callest thou me good? There is none good but one, that is God.' And to his disciples he said, 'When you pray, say, Our Father who art in heaven:' and his own prayer was uniformly addressed to his Father. The apostles, in all their addresses to the churches they had established, and in their prayer for them, direct their supplication to the Father of our Lord Jesus Christ. The apostle Paul, in addressing the Church at Corinth, says, 'But to us there is but one God, the Father, of whom are all things, and we in him; and one Lord Jesus Christ, by whom are all things, and we by him.' And to Timothy he says, 'There is but one God and one mediator between God and man, the man Jesus Christ.' The Saviour having taught his disciples to pray to God the Father, and uniformly made his own prayer to God the Father but a short time previous to his crucifixion, he says to them, "Hitherto thou askest nothing in my name; but I say unto you, whatsoever you shall ask the Father in my name, he will grant it you.' We accordingly find the prayers and addresses of the apostles ending in these words, 'through Jesus Christ,' or 'for the sake of Jesus Christ.'

"Now, the prayers of Christ being uniformly addressed to God the Father, how can we justify the opinion that Jesus Christ is the Supreme God? For if this were so, then was he praying to himself, as there can be but one Supreme God. Instead of this, Christ is continually assuring his disciples that all his power comes from God. He says, 'I can of myself do nothing.' 'I seek not my own will, but the will of the Father.' 'The words that I speak unto you I speak not of myself, but of the Father that dwelleth in me.' 'He doeth the work, and the words which you hear are not mine, but the Father that sent me.' All these and other sayings of Christ are explained by some, who affirm in all these cases and others, Christ only speaks as man, he being man as well as God; but from whatsoever these conclusions are drawn I know not.

"In the latter part of his stay on earth, the Saviour was

much distressed, and he prays fervently to his Father that he would receive his disciples, and says: 'I have manifested thy name to the men thou hast given me out of the world; thine they were, and thou hast given them to me, and they have kept thy word. Now they have known that all things whatsoever thou hast given me are of *Thee*.'

"It cannot be necessary to augment the instances in which Christ endeavors to impress upon the minds of his disciples a firm belief that all his power came from God his Father. Thus we find one wanting his promise that her children shall sit on his right and on his left in his kingdom; others, when certain events shall come to pass, &c., &c.; in all which cases he declares, 'of such things knoweth no man, not even the angels in heaven, neither the Son, but my Father only.'

"I now beg leave to refer to the first promise of the Messiah, or what I think was the first promise. Moses was filled with the spirit of God when he declares: 'The Lord said unto me, I will raise up a prophet from among thy brethren, like unto thee, and will put my words into his mouth, and he shall speak unto them all that I shall command him. Like unto thee, being filled with power as thou wast to release my people from bondage and proclaim to them my commandments.' So shall he release the world from the penalty of sin, embracing all who believe on him and repent. Thus, as I think, this is the first promise of redemption through Christ.

"Now let us look, for a moment, at the commencement of the Saviour's ministry. We find, at his baptism by John, the power of the Highest coming upon him through the Holy Ghost, or Spirit of God, accompanied with the declaration that he was the Son of God. Then he received power to perform miracles; and the first on record, as I think, is the turning water into wine, at the marriage festival. Now, who made the declaration? A voice from heaven, saying, 'This is my beloved Son, in whom I am well pleased.' Surely it was God who spoke; and to whom was it made? Not to God, but to the Son, as the agent of the Father. Thus, there was but one God, even the Father of our Lord Jesus Christ, and but one Saviour, even Jesus Christ our Saviour.

"I believe the Holy Scriptures were given for the use and benefit of the human race; and admitting this to be a fact, we are directed to read and search them. Thus, every person must read and search for himself, and adopt the common-sense meaning of what he reads; for, otherwise, the reading would be useless. This I consider the true Protestant doctrine, and I have thus read carefully, beseeching God to enlighten my mind, and save me from error.

"Under this reading, I have formed the following belief or creed:

"There is one God, the Creator, by whose power all things and beings, whether in the heavens or on the earth, were brought into existence, and are now and always have been governed and protected by him. I believe in Jesus Christ, the promised Messiah and the Son of God, who was brought into existence by the operation of the Spirit of God. That he only is the Saviour of the human race; for which purpose, and in the fulfilment of the promise, he suffered the pains of death and rose therefrom on the third day, ascended into heaven, where he is the advocate and mediator before the Father, for all those who believe in him and keep his precepts. I believe in the Holy Ghost, word or Spirit of God; these words being used in Scripture synonymously, or as an emanation from God, by which the holy prophets were sanctified, the Saviour filled with the Spirit without measure, and the disciples and apostles of Christ enabled to perform mighty acts in his name.

"Thus, I believe in the Father, in the Son, and in the Holy Ghost, or Spirit of God through his operations; and I believe that all three, in their acts, are operating jointly and severally in promoting the salvation of our race. If I am wrong in this belief, I can only pray that God will enlighten my understanding and mind, and bring it into subjection to his will, which is all-powerful for expelling doubt, and enlightening the understanding of his creatures.

"But, as I have before said, the Bible was undoubtedly given us as a guide to our ways, and this being the fact, if I have not the capacity to understand it, of what use is the information it contains? Now, I believe the Giver of the Bible has also given us common sense—ability to understand its teaching. If there are mysteries above our comprehension—and perhaps there are—they are not for us, but for beings of a higher nature. For us sufficient is revealed, viz., there is but one God, and one Mediator between God and man.

"I am fearful the numerous creeds promulgated by man, and the confusion of ideas on the subject, do much mischief, as many of them were not taught by Christ and his apostles. They taught that the promised Messiah had appeared, and that Jesus Christ was he; and they proclaimed in every place they visited, whosoever believed in him and followed his teaching should be saved. 'This is life eternal, that we should know thee, the only true God, and Jesus Christ whom thou hast sent.' Now here is common sense, that the most illiterate can understand, and for which he is led to render thanks to God, the Father, through Christ the Mediator.

"That the Scriptures were not written for the exclusive use and benefit of learned men and casuists, I think is plainly revealed by the fact, that Christ thanked his Father for revealing his will to the common people, and had hid it from the wise and learned of this world.

"I have extended the foregoing remarks much beyond what I expected when I began to write, and it becomes me to apologize for troubling you with my religious opinions so much in extent, especially as I differ with you in some of your views.

"I have read many of the creeds promulgated by ecclesiastical councils and church assemblies, and from which I have been compelled to differ. I know it is contended that without a creed, no church can be held together in unity; but, it appears to me, the discipline of the church, with the help of reading and explaining the Scriptures, and the preaching repentance and forgiveness of sins through the Saviour Jesus Christ, is sufficient to keep the true disciples of Christ in unity. This, it appears to me, was the sum of the preaching of the apostles, and the plan of the church government was the disowning of such as led lives or committed acts contrary to the law, pronounced by Christ in his teachings.

"But so soon as creeds were established through the councils of the clergy, we find confusion prevailing among the churches, and a separation of the people the consequence. Now I may truly say that my difference of opinion with you and others has not caused me to consider those with whom I differ as heretics, or castaways, from the common salvation by Christ; and I am therefore led to hope, that you and all my fellow-Christians, with whom I join weekly in prayer and praise, worshiping the same God and the same Saviour, will not treat me as an unbeliever in the Gospel of Christ; at least not until they have read and examined for themselves, as I have done, the Bible history, and from such examination drawn their conclusions whether I am so wrong, and if not found materially wrong, to give me the right hand of fellowship.

"With great respect, I am your friend,

"STEPHEN ALLEN."

Since it is known that among the large number of able exponents of the doctrine of the Trinity scarcely any are found to agree in their explanation of its mysteries, it is scarcely to be wondered at that those, like Mr. Allen, who carefully searched the Scriptures must need differ. We have given the above letter in its length, because it was a striking example of that earnest and conscientious spirit which inbred in his very nature compelled him to take nothing for granted, but carefully to weigh and consider for himself every subject of which his mind took cognizance.

The principal characteristics of Stephen Allen were truthfulness, activity, energy, great conscientiousness, a strong sense of justice, self-reliance, and indomitable perseverance. The sole artificer of his own fortunes, emphatically a self-made man, his manners were molded in the age in which he commenced his career, and partook of an earnestness and gravity which, to those who knew him superficially, had the appearance of sternness. But to the many who were the recipients of his bounty, or who had to court his political influence, it was a most agreeable disappointment to find that his performance far exceeded his promises; and that, though they had encountered a plain-spoken man, they had in the end experienced the valued bounty of a true and honest friend. His instructive honesty of disposition had a tendency to make him sometimes slow to truly estimate character; and he was at times misled by the hypocrisy of wicked men, because he ever judged them from his own standard of what all men ought to be. Upon this point he remarks in a letter to a friend, detailing a case of dishonesty, of which he had been a victim: "The deception practiced upon me is of a piece with hundreds of others, which I have since experienced; for even now, after having been deceived for more than the thousandth time by the falsehood of those whom I have placed confidence in, it is the most difficult thing in nature for me to doubt the solemn protestation of a fellow-being; for feeling an utter repugnance to deception myself, I am led to believe that others have the same feelings, until I am too frequently convinced by sad experience of my error."

On the twenty-eighth day of July, 1852, in the eighty-sixth year of his age, Stephen Allen died; a victim of that cruel tragedy which launched into eternity some seventy or eighty human beings. Not long before this, he had been heard to express a horror of a lingering and painful death, and to hope that, when his beneficent Creator should call him hence, it might be by some sudden visitation. His prayer was answered.

MAJOR SAMUEL SHAW.

Among the discordant materials of which our army of the Revolution was composed, those men were not wanting who are commonly the early victims of great popular struggles: men, moderate and firm in the council, prudent and fearless in the field; not selfish in their ambition, not rancorous in their patriotism—in whom a pure conscience and a clear intellect rule with an equal and a harmonious supremacy. Such men, impatient of injustice and of corruption, are usually foremost in those acts of resistance in which every revolution begins; but, as the contest goes on, they are thought to move too slowly. Their virtues are not understood. If they are in the senate, their motives are suspected; if in the army, their courage is questioned. Fiercer and less scrupulous spirits, more nearly akin to the heightened passions of the people, press forward and take their place; and the old scene is again enacted, of a nation, risen in arms against its oppressors, only to be desolated by anarchy and bound anew in servitude.

It was the good fortune of America, or rather—if we may read in the events of this world's history the motives of its Ruler—it was the blessing of God on America, that, in her Revolution, such men as we have described maintained their control to the end. They were the leaders of the army, for it had been the plan of England to shut them out from the high offices of state. They were beloved by the army, for their peculiar virtues found daily exercise in the long train of disaster that makes up the story of the war.

Washington was at their head, and the qualities that distinguished them shone forth in him with a still brighter lustre. They were the interpreters of his spirit to the people; and, doubtless, if ever his wonderful equanimity failed, and he became like other men, he gathered fresh courage and renewed strength from their intelligent sympathy.

Of these men, holding a rank in the army suited to his age and experience, Samuel Shaw was one. Like most men of his time, he acted various parts in the changing drama of life. In his youth, an active and gallant soldier; in his manhood, a sagacious and enterprising merchant; for a short period, filling an office of trust in the Department of War; for several years, representing his country, as consul, abroad; and at all times maintaining a lofty character for talents and integrity, it is not to be doubted that his early death alone prevented him from reaching a station more marked and eminent.

His memoir, before us, is written by one who, in early youth, enjoyed "the privilege of his acquaintance and correspondence;" and who, after the lapse of more than fifty years passed in constant intercourse with mankind, says that he has "never known an individual of a character more elevated and chivalric, acting according to a purer standard of morals, imbued with a higher sense of honor, and uniting more intimately the qualities of the gentleman, the soldier, the scholar, and the Christian." With the memoir are interwoven many letters, written by Major Shaw from the camp to his friends at home. These are so selected and arranged as to indicate the character as well as the passing emotions of the man. Apart from their personal interest, they form a valuable commentary upon those memorials of the times which have been collected with so much zeal and judgment by the historian of Washington.

To the memoir written by Josiah Quincy are appended

the journals of Major Shaw's first two voyages to Canton. "These journals of Major Shaw," says Mr. Quincy, "came, after his death, into the possession of his nephew and legal representative, Robert Gould Shaw, of Boston. Their publication has often been solicited, but has hitherto been withheld; the present proprietor doubting if a work not originally designed for the press could with propriety be given to the public. He has, however, now yielded to the urgency of friends, and to the assurance of judicious merchants long and intimately acquainted with the China trade, that their publication not only will be practically useful, but is due to the memory of their author, will redound to his honor, and will gratify a wise public curiosity concerning the early state and history of this branch of American commerce. Assuming all the expenses, Mr. Shaw has transferred the copyright of the book to the Boston Marine Society, in aid of whose funds he was of opinion its proceeds would be most appropriately applied, and to this object they are devoted."

We hope that a brief sketch of Major Shaw's life, and such extracts from his letters and journals as our limited space will allow, may not be uninteresting to our readers.

Shaw was a Boston boy and a North End boy. He was educated at the common schools, and at the Latin school then under the care of Master Lovell. Of course his heart was full of patriotism, and his mind well grounded in good learning. His father, Francis Shaw, an eminent merchant, designed the lad for his own pursuits, and, at the opening of the war, Samuel had lately entered a counting-house. His mercantile success in after years shows that the occupation was not uncongenial to his tastes; but the quick spirits of the youth perceived something of more interest than money columns in the stirring events of the time. A tradition preserved in the family proves how keenly, at this time, he felt for the honor of his country. Boston being held as a garrison town by the British, the officers of the army were billeted upon the inhabitants. The house of Francis Shaw was assigned for quarters to Major Pitcairn and Lieutenant Wragg. At the table the latter, in the presence of Samuel Shaw, called the Americans "cowards and rebels." Shaw was indignant at the reproach, and immediately challenged the lieutenant. Before the arrangements for the duel were completed, however, Major Pitcairn interfered, and induced Lieutenant Wragg to offer an apology, which, being accepted, the affair was thus happily terminated.

On the 2d of October, 1775, Shaw came of age. With his father's approbation, he immediately prepared to join the army which Washington was then organizing at Cambridge. On the 1st of January, 1776, he received the commission of lieutenant in the train of artillery, and in this branch of the service he remained during the whole of the war.

On joining the army, Lieutenant Shaw was stationed at Prospect Hill, a height overlooking Charlestown and opposite to Boston, which were both in the possession of the British. Nothing of interest occurred here, save now and then an irregular attack upon the outposts of the enemy. A characteristic anecdote of General Putnam is related, in connection with one of these skirmishes:

"A successful attempt had been made on Charlestown, and ten houses were burnt. The expedition was carried on with great secrecy, hardly any person, besides those employed, knowing a syllable of the affair, until they had the pleasure of seeing the blaze. Among the prisoners taken was a woman, who, being something fatigued, was, by Gen. Putnam's order, carried between two men part of the way; but this mode being found inconvenient, the general, with his usual affability, cried out—'Here, hand her to me;' which being done, she put her hand round his waist and made this pious ejaculation as they rode off: 'Jesus bless you, sweet General! May you live forever!'"

For some time Washington had been meditating a plan for dislodging the enemy. Accordingly, on the night of the 4th of March, 1776, a portion of the army, in which was Shaw's company, took possession of Dorchester Heights, a range of hills commanding the harbor of Boston. The movement was successful. On the 17th of March the British troops evacuated the city. From that time the current of the war was turned in other directions.

Lieutenant Shaw went, with the main body of the army, to the westward. In August, 1776, he was intrusted with the command of Fort Washington, an important post on the Hudson. About this time Col. Tupper, a partisan officer, with the galleys under his command, made an attack upon two of the enemy's ships, which, in the month of July, had succeeded in passing the American batteries and ascending the river as far as Tappan Bay. Lieutenant Shaw volunteered on the occasion, and in a letter to his father he gives the following account of the affair:

"It was a hazardous design, the force on our side being so much inferior. We had only six galleys, that could bring but eleven guns in the whole to bear against two ships, one of twenty, the other of forty-four guns, assisted by three tenders, with the advantage of spring-cables, while we were obliged to work our little fleet entirely with oars. Notwithstanding which we engaged them, within reach of their grape-shot, for nearly two hours, when, being much damaged, two men killed and fourteen wounded, we were obliged to retire, which we did without their pursuing, though one of our galleys lay on the careen a whole tide in sight of them. Five of the wounded fell to the share of the Washington, where I was on board, which was hulled thirteen times, besides the grape-shot received in her sails and rigging. You will, perhaps, wonder what business I had on board, it being out of my sphere—which I readily acknowledge; but the desire I had to see an affair of that nature got the better of any other motive, and inclined me to volunteer. It was no small encouragement to me when I saw two other gentlemen come on board in the same capacity—one of whom was a merchant in the city, and the other first aid-de-camp to General Washington. The commodore treated us very politely, and, when the action came on, gave me the command of the two bow-guns, which was sufficient employment for me, while my companions had nothing to do but to look on."

In October, 1776, shortly before the battle of White Plains, Shaw left Fort Washington, the capture of which, in the following month, "formed," says he, "a pretty subject for Howe to write upon. He would, otherwise, have had chagrin enough, since he has done so little towards subduing America."

Between this time and August, 1779, Shaw was successively promoted to the ranks of adjutant and brigade-major in the corps of artillery. By his gallantry in the various actions at Trenton, Princeton, the Brandywine, Germantown, and Monmouth, he gained the confidence and affection of General Knox, who, in August, 1779, made him his aid-de-camp. In this station he remained till after the close of the war. The friendship thus formed between the young officer and his general continued, without interruption, until they were separated by death. In 1792, party spirit commenced its opposition to the administration of Washington by violent assaults upon the character of Gen. Knox and other members of the cabinet. We make a short extract from a letter written at that time by Major Shaw to his early friend, to express his indignation at these attacks. It relates an interesting incident of the war:

"Happy must you feel—thrice happy am I—in the reflection that, so long as the American name shall last, yours will be handed down with distinction in the list of the 'valued file;' and the artillery which, formed under your auspices, equalled every exigence of war, will be regarded as the child of your genius. Well do I remember the honorable testimony of the gallant Lafayette, amidst the thunder of our batteries on the lines at Yorktown. 'We* fire,' exclaimed he, with a charming enthusiasm, 'better than the French' (and faith we did, too). To this I made a suitable objection. His reply was, 'Upon honor, I speak the truth; and the progress of your artillery is regarded by everybody as one of the wonders of the Revolution.'"

In a letter written in June, 1779, Major Shaw gives the following account of the pecuniary situation of an officer, at a time when the depreciation of the continental currency, in itself a sufficient evil, had made the army the prey of every mean vice that avarice breeds and fosters:

"I wish, seriously, that the ensuing campaign may terminate the war. The people of America seem to have lost sight entirely of the noble principle which animated them at the commencement of it. That patriotic ardor which then inspired each breast—that glorious, I had almost said godlike, enthusiasm—has given place to avarice, and every rascally practice which tends to the gratification of that sordid and most disgraceful passion. I don't know as it would be too bold an assertion to say, that its depreciation is equal to that of the currency—*thirty for one.* You may, perhaps, charitably think that I strain the matter, but I do not. I speak *feelingly.* By the arts of monopolizers and extortioners, and the little, the very little, attention by authority to counteract them, our currency is reduced to a mere name. Pernicious soever as this is to the community at large, its baneful effect is more immediately experienced

---

* Lafayette, being in the service of the United States, always spoke as an American.

by the *poor* soldier. I am myself an instance of it. For my services I receive a nominal sum—dollars at *eight* shillings, in a country where they pass, at the utmost, for *fourpence* only. If it did not look too much like self-applause, I might say that I engaged in the cause of my country from the purest motives. However, be this as it may, my continuance in it has brought me to poverty and rags; and, had I a fortune of my own, I should glory in persevering, though it would occasion a sacrifice of the last penny. But, when I consider my situation—my pay inadequate to my support, though within the line of the strictest economy—no private purse of my own—and reflect that the best of parents, who, I am persuaded, have the tenderest affection for their son, and wish to support him in character, have not the means of doing it, and may, perhaps, be pressed themselves—when these considerations occur to my mind, as they frequently do, they make me serious; more so than my natural disposition would lead me to be. The loss of my horse, by any accident whatever (unless he was actually killed in battle, and then I should be entitled only to about one-third of his value), would plunge me in inextricable misfortune; two years' pay and subsistence would not replace him. Yet the nature of my office renders it indispensable that I should keep a horse. These are some of the emoluments annexed to a military station."

In 1781, Major Shaw's younger brother, Nathaniel, decided to enter the army. In a letter, encouraging the plan, Shaw gives a list of the articles necessary for an outfit; which, in deference to its statistical character, we extract. The reader will notice in the advice, "superfine will be cheapest," a touch of the peculiar thrift of New England:

Clothing, etc., necessary for a young campaigner:—

Beaver hat,	15
Coat, faced and lined with scarlet—white vest and breeches—plain yellow buttons—(superfine will be cheapest,)	60

Three white linen vests and breeches,	25
Six ruffled shirts and stocks,	60
Four pairs white cotton or linen hose,	10
Boots,	10
Sword,	20
Total, silver dollars,	200

"If the above sum can be raised on my notes," adds he, "I can spare it without injury to myself, and as much as will bring Nat. on to the camp."

But we must close our extracts from these letters of Major Shaw. We turn, with reluctance, from the vivid story of "the battles, sieges, fortunes, he had passed;" from the glad tidings of victory at Trenton, and Princeton, and Monmouth; from the painful description of the mutiny of the Jersey and Pennsylvania lines; from the sad tale of Arnold's baseness and André's untimely fate; and, especially, from those pages in which he dwells so fondly upon Washington's demeanor in that most perilous hour, when, after their seven years' apprenticeship, in want, and danger, and neglect, officers and soldiers could bear up no longer against the broken faith of Congress and the injustice of their countrymen. We know how feebly we present the picture. We have but borrowed, here a tint and there a line, from the harmonious whole.

On the 19th of April, 1783, just eight years from the first shedding of blood at Lexington, the cessation of hostilities was proclaimed to the army. The disbanding of the troops was assigned to General Knox. As a member of his military family, Major Shaw remained with him during the year, sharing in this delicate and arduous duty.

In the events which accompanied the dissolution of the army, Major Shaw took an active interest. He was chosen secretary of the committee of officers who organized the Society of the Cincinnati, and the original draft of its constitution is said to have been from his hand. With General

Knox, he accompanied Washington upon his entrance into the city of New York after its evacuation by the British; and he was present at that solemn and august scene, when the officers of the American army took their final leave of their great chief, and when manly cheeks paid tribute, in tears, to that affection, passing the love of woman, which his stern virtues commanded in the hearts of those who had suffered and triumphed at his side.

Shaw's military life was now over. He was without occupation, and in debt; and his future fortunes were to be based upon the universal respect which his talents and his integrity had secured, and upon his characteristic energy. With these, and the winning manners which were natural to his generous disposition, and to which the training of the camp had given dignity and polish, he was not likely to fall short of success in any pursuit.

Without delay, he turned his attention to those occupations for which he had been destined in his youth. A company of capitalists had just been formed in the city of New York, for the purpose of carrying on a trade with China. Daniel Parker, Esq., a friend of Major Shaw, and agent for those concerned, offered him the situation of supercargo. He accepted the offer, on condition that Captain Thomas Randall, with whom he had formed an intimate friendship during the war, and who, like himself, was "out of suits with fortune," should accompany him and share the profits of his agency. No one, except Shaw himself, was to sacrifice any thing by this condition. It was readily agreed to; and, on the 22d of February, 1784, the two friends sailed from New York, on the first voyage ever made by an American vessel between this country and China. The ship in which they sailed was the Empress of China, commanded by Captain John Green. Her burden was 360 tons. She was loaded chiefly with ginseng, of which she carried about 440 piculs; the value of a picul

(133⅓ pounds) in China being, at that time, from one hundred and thirty to two hundred dollars.

Having paid due honor to the Old Man of the Tropics, by abundant libations of sea-water and grog; and every greenhorn having sworn faithfully to observe those great laws of morals and manners of which that deity has special cognizance, namely, that no man shall drink small-beer when he can get strong, unless he likes the small better; nor kiss the maid when he can kiss the mistress, save under a similar and not less wise condition, the voyagers arrived at St. Jago, one of the Cape de Verde Islands. Here they stopped several days, to obtain fresh provisions, and for repairs. A French brig, with a cargo of slaves from Senegal, was anchored in the harbor. It seems that not even the sanction of the law was able wholly to clear the escutcheons of persons engaged in this "abominable traffic." When the captain of the brig came on board of the Empress, Captain Green bade his people to beware of the French sailors. "These fellows are Saint Peter's children," says he; "every finger a fish-hook, and each hand a grapnel."

Shaw left St. Jago on the 27th of March, and on the 18th of July he arrived in the Straits of Sunda. Here he found a French man-of-war, the Triton, Captain d'Ordelin, bound to Canton. The gentlemen of the two ships, representing nations so closely united by good offices, met with great cordiality. Captain Green being, of course, unskilled in the passage, took advantage of the experience of Captain d'Ordelin, and sailed, in company with him, from Java. On the 28th of August the Empress arrived at Whampoa, having been at sea one hundred and seventy-four days since leaving New York.

It is pleasing to notice the courtesy with which the Americans were welcomed. On arriving at Whampoa, they were saluted by all the shipping in the harbor. An officer came from the French vessels, with boats, anchors, and cables, to assist them in getting a good berth. The Danish sent an officer, with compliments; the Dutch, a boat; and the English, an officer, "to welcome their flag to that part of the world." Then followed national dinners, and visits of congratulation. The French, surpassing the rest in their kindness, gave them the use of their factory and a part of their banksall (a large building of bamboo, for the storage of water-casks, spars, sails, &c., and for the reception of the sick), during their stay.

"The Chinese themselves," says Major Shaw, "were very indulgent towards us; though, ours being the first American ship that ever visited China, it was some time before they could fully comprehend the distinction between us and Englishmen. They styled us the *New People;* and when, by the map, we conveyed to them an idea of the extent of our country, with its present and increasing population, they were highly pleased at the prospect of so considerable a market for the productions of their own empire."

From Major Shaw's Journal, we take the following account of foreign ships visiting Canton in 1783 and 1784:

Exclusive of the country ships returning to India, there sailed last year from Canton and Macao forty-five ships for Europe, sixteen of which were English. The present season the numbers were as follows (Dec. 27):

English, 9; French, 4; Dutch, 5; Danish, 3; Portuguese, 4.	25 for Europe.
American	1 for America.
English country ships, 8 }	9
Danish snow, 1 }	
In all	35

The amount of tea annually consumed by Great Britain and her dependencies at that time, is here stated to have been 14,000,000 pounds.

Major Shaw's stay was marked by the occurrence of what was called "the Canton war," and by the honorable part which he took on that occasion. We quote his narration of the circumstances from a letter written by him, after his return, to John Jay, who was then Minister of the United States for Foreign Affairs:

"On the 25th of November, an English ship, in saluting some company that had dined on board, killed a Chinese and wounded two others in the mandarin's boat alongside. It is a maxim of the Chinese law that blood must answer for blood; in pursuance of which, they demanded the unfortunate gunner. To give up this poor man was to consign him to certain death. Humanity pleaded powerfully against the measure. After repeated conferences between the English and the Chinese, the latter declared themselves satisfied, and the affair was supposed to be entirely settled. Notwithstanding this, on the morning after the last conference (the 27th), the supercargo of the ship was seized while attending his business, thrown into a sedan chair, hurried into the city, and committed to prison. Such an outrage upon personal liberty spread a general alarm, and the Europeans unanimously agreed to send for their boats with armed men from the shipping, for the security of themselves and their property, until the matter should be brought to a conclusion. The boats accordingly came, and ours among the number; one of which was fired on, and a man wounded. All trade was stopped, and the Chinese men-of-war were drawn up opposite the factories. The Europeans demanded the restoration of the supercargo, Mr. Smith, which the Chinese refused, until the gunner should be given up. In the meanwhile, the troops of the province were collecting in the neighborhood of Canton; the Chinese servants were ordered by the magistrates to leave the factories; the gates of the suburbs were shut; all intercourse was at an end; the naval force was increased; many troops were embarked in boats ready for landing, and every thing wore the appearance of war. To what extremities matters might have been carried, had not a negotiation taken place, no one can say. The Chinese asked a conference with all the nations except the English. A deputation, in which I was included, for America, met the *Fuen*, who is the head magistrate of Canton, with the principal officers of the province. After setting forth, by an interpreter, the power of the emperor, and his own determination to support the laws, he demanded that the gunner should be given up within three days, declaring that he should have an impartial examination before their tribunal, and if it appeared that the affair was accidental, he should be released unhurt. In the mean time, he gave permission for the trade, excepting that of the English, to go on as usual, and dismissed us with a present of two pieces of silk each, as a mark of his friendly disposition. The other nations, one after another, sent away their boats, under protection of a Chinese flag, and pursued their business as before. The English were obliged to submit; the gunner was given up, Mr. Smith was released, and the English, after being forced to ask pardon of the magistracy of Canton, in presence of the other nations, had their commerce restored. On this occasion, I am happy to remark that we were the last who sent off our boat, which was not disgraced with a Chinese flag; nor did she go till the English themselves thanked us for our concurrence with them, and advised to the sending of her away. After peace was restored, the English chief and four other gentlemen visited the several nations, among whom we were included, and thanked them for their assistance during the troubles. The gunner remained with the Chinese, his fate undetermined."

The unfortunate gunner was executed by the Chinese a few months afterwards.

The bankrupt system of the Chinese is peculiar. All payments are required to be made before the close of their calendar year. If, on the last night of the old year, a debtor has left an account unsettled, he is visited at his house by his creditor, who seats himself, and, in unbroken silence, "watches the old year out and the new year in." When midnight is past the creditor rises, congratulates his debtor on the new year, and retires. The insolvent has then "lost his face." There is no credit for him afterwards.

On the 26th of December, 1784,. the business of the voyage being completed, the Empress of China set sail for home. Captain Green deemed it prudent to profit by the sailing of a Dutch ship, and to keep her company through the Chinese seas. The Dutchman, being a dull sailer by right of nationality, this confidence was repaid by a delay of several days and the loss of an anchor. During the sixty years that have elapsed since these occurrences, our ships have learned to go alone.

The Empress stopped at North Island for wood. There Major Shaw met a young man who had left Europe with the intention of spending his days at Pekin. On reaching Canton, however, the impossibility of ever returning, if he should once enter the capital, appalled him, and he refused to proceed. The mandarins were in trouble, for they had mentioned his intention in their dispatches to the court. He gave, as his excuse, that his father had died during his absence from home, and that his mother had written to him conjuring him to return and provide for her support. The mandarins admitted the piety of this excuse; but, deeming it insufficient to satisfy the authorities, they ingeniously settled the matter by reporting him sick in their next dispatches, and afterwards officially apprising the court of his death.

On the 10th of May, 1785, the Empress of China arrived in New York. Shortly after, Major Shaw addressed a letter to John Jay, relating the occurrences of the voyage. This letter was laid before Congress, who directed Jay to announce to Major Shaw, "that Congress feel a peculiar satisfaction in the successful issue of this first effort of the citizens of America to establish a direct trade with China, which does so much honor to its undertakers and conductors."

The profits of this voyage were $30,000, upwards of 25 per cent. on the capital employed. Major Shaw's share of this, however, after being divided with his friend Randall, proved to be but a poor remuneration for his time and services.

The period of Shaw's absence had been one of bereavement. His father, to whom he was devotedly attached, and whose declining years he had hoped to cheer with his presence and society, had died in 1784. A few months afterward his eldest brother died; and Shaw felt it to be his duty to relinquish, for the present, the mercantile plans he had formed, and to remain in America, that he might attend to the settlement of his father's estate.

General Knox was eager to manifest his kindness. He offered Shaw the post of first Secretary of the War Department, a station whose labors were not inconsistent with the performance of the duties he had assumed. Major Shaw accepted the office; and, shortly afterward, accompanied General Knox on a tour, to inspect the magazines in the Southern States.

The success which had attended the voyage of the Empress of China had attracted the notice of merchants; and, toward the close of 1785, it was proposed to Major Shaw, by Isaac Sears, Esq., and other gentlemen in New York, that he should take part with them in another enterprise of the same kind, and, in conjunction with Mr. Sears, should superintend the business of the voyage. The offers were liberal, and Shaw was induced to leave his public station, and to return to a business which promised him much success. In February, 1786, he was honorably discharged from the War Department; and, about the same time, he was appointed by Congress consul for the United States at Canton.

On the 4th of February, 1786, he sailed from New York in the ship Hope, Captain James Magee; his friend, Captain Randall, who, he had arranged, should be concerned with him in this undertaking also, and Mr. Sears, being his companions. In August they arrived at Canton, where Mr. Sears died. Shaw returned to New York in July, 1789, having, during his absence, passed several months in Bengal. Nothing, probably, in the life of Major Shaw, will be more pleasing to the reader than an incident which occurred after his return from his voyage:

"His brother, Francis Shaw, had died in the year 1785, leaving, besides daughters, two sons, who were at this time about seven or eight years old. To the widow of this brother, then residing in Goldsborough, Major Shaw, immediately on his arrival in the United States, wrote: 'I beg you to put your two sons under my care, that I may be to them instead of a father. If you consent, let them accompany, at once, their uncle William to Boston.' The offer was gratefully accepted. They were sent, and from that time were regarded by Major Shaw as his children. One of them was Robert Gould Shaw, one of the most eminent and prosperous merchants of Boston."

At the time of the publication of the Memoir, R. G. Shaw addressed to Mr. Quincy the following graceful letter:

"I am, sir, the oldest of those fatherless boys, and I well remember how affectionately and kindly he received me. He told me, if I would be a good boy, that I should never want a friend. I will not undertake to describe the influence that his kindness had upon my mind. From that day to this, I have, as he promised, never wanted a friend in time of need, nor have I ever forgotten, I trust, those who in such times have been my friends; by whose aid, protected by kind Providence, I have been placed in a position to repay, in part, by kindness to others, the debt that is so justly due from me."

And most amply has the debt been paid. That germ of human kindness, planted in the heart of the child, has borne rich and abundant fruit, in the large beneficence of the man.

During Major Shaw's absence on this voyage, he had ordered a ship to be built, on his own account, at Germantown, in Quincy. This ship was launched in September, 1789, and was named the Massachusetts. She was of 820 tons burden—larger than any merchant vessel previously built in the United States; and her model was pronounced by naval commanders abroad, "as perfect as the then state of the art would permit." In this ship, commanded by Captain Job Prince, Shaw sailed from Boston in March, 1790, on his third voyage to Canton. Before his departure, his commission, as consul, was renewed by President Washington. On his outward passage he stopped at Batavia, to dispose of some merchandise which he had purchased for that market. He was there informed, that, on account of some supposed violations of the revenue laws by the Americans, all commerce with that people had been forbidden by the home government. Shaw immediately made a suitable representation, to the governor-general and council, of the injustice and the impolicy of the measure. What was the result of this step, we are not informed. It seems, however, that the prohibition was regarded with as little favor by the colonists as by the Americans.

Major Shaw returned to this country early in 1792. He immediately procured a ship of his own, and prepared for another voyage. While he remained at home, he paid his addresses to Hannah, the daughter of William Phillips, Esq., "of a family distinguished for its virtues and its prosperity." They were married on the 21st of August, 1792; but, auspicious as their union seemed, their happiness was doomed to be of short duration. In a few months they parted;—the one, to be hurried to an early death; the other, to treasure up the memory of a few sunny hours through a long night of mourning—a night sad and lonely, yet not uncheered by the great rewards that active charity bestows upon the heart from which it springs, and by the glad contentment of a steadfast trust in God.

In February, 1793, Shaw sailed from Bombay for Canton. At Bombay he contracted a disease of the liver, incident to the climate. He pursued his voyage to Canton; but, obtaining no relief there, he sailed for home. On the 30th of May, 1794, he died at sea. The intelligence of his sickness and of his death came to Mrs. Shaw at the same moment.

Immediately after his marriage, Major Shaw had written this passage in his Bible:

"Beneficent Parent of the universe! as in the years that are passed, so in those which are to come, may I rejoice in thy goodness; and whether longer or shorter, may I be satisfied with life, and cheerfully submit myself to the dispensations of thy providence!"

In this temper and spirit he died. "Not long before his death," says his physician, "as I was standing by him (we were alone), he took hold of my hand and pressed it affectionately to his breast. He then sighed heavily, and casting his eyes on the miniature of his wife, that hung at the foot of the berth, sighed again, and said, 'God's will be done.'"

It was the close of a useful and an honorable life. Washington, who seldom erred in his judgment of men, gave him this commendation:

"From the testimony of the superior officers under whom Captain Shaw has served, as well as from my own observation, I am enabled to certify, that, throughout the whole of his service, he has greatly distinguished himself in every thing which could entitle him to the character of an intelligent, active, and brave officer."

Those qualities of heart and mind which formed the intelligence, the activity, and the courage of the soldier, were not less conspicuous in the sagacity, the enterprise, and the integrity of the merchant. The esteem in which he had been held during his life, and the impression produced by his death, are well told in an obituary notice published in the Columbian Centinel of the 20th of August, 1794, from which we take the following:

"His fine natural talents, elegant erudition, and social benevolence, gained him the esteem of a numerous acquaintance, and fitted him for extensive usefulness to society. As an officer in the army, in which he served during the whole of the late war, his merit was conspicuous. Though possessed of much romantic ardor, he supported a dignity and consistency of character; was equally prudent and brave, and ever attentive to the duties of his station.

"In his character of American consul for the port of Canton, he was called to act a part which required much discretion and firmness. On the occasion of 'the Canton war,' as it was called, Mr. Shaw represented the American interest in such a manner as to throw a lustre on his commission, and give him great credit among the European merchants and other eminent characters abroad. At his return, his conduct met the approbation of the representatives of the United States in Congress.

"He was considered as an ornament to his country, for his inflexible integrity, and a greatness of heart which he displayed on every occasion. The virtues which adorn the man, and which he manifested in his youth, became more splendid as he advanced in years, and engaged in public action. In the opinion of some persons, his spirit was too exalted to be successful in the common concerns of life. He did not love property for its own sake, but as the means of making his benevolence more extensive. He disdained many of those arts of traffic, which are daily practiced, and deemed justifiable. His commercial dealings were regulated by the strictest honor, refined by the principles of philosophy and religion.

"The engagements of commercial, and even of military life, did not seduce him from a love of science. Though he had not the advantage of an academical education, yet his classical merit was so conspicuous, that, in 1790, he was presented with the honorary degree of Master of Arts by the University of Cambridge. This was done in his absence, and without his knowledge, at the solicitation of several gentlemen of eminence in literature. About the same time he was elected a Fellow of the American Academy of Arts and Sciences.

"Had he lived a few years longer, his country might have derived much benefit from his abilities, his information, and his virtues. His zeal to make others happy would have endeared him still more to those who enjoyed his friendship, and made those hearts beat with new sensations of pleasure, which are now heavy with grief. The universal regret caused by his death is an evidence of the great esteem in which he was held. All who knew him lament him with expressions of sorrow equally lively and sincere."

Gladly, as we close this imperfect sketch, would we pay our tribute of respect to him, who has given the hours of his well-earned leisure to these grateful labors. But it becomes us to be silent. It is not for us to apportion the measure of praise that is due to one who has borne, with new honor, so illustrious a name. Most pleasing will it be to those, his contemporaries, who saw his great abilities and his untiring industry, in the years when he held a lofty place in the councils of the State; most pleasing to the thousands, still on the threshold of active life, who have learned to love him in that near relation in which he was ever a watchful guide and a zealous friend; to behold him thus filling up the full circle of duty, and, to the many labors in which he has done good service to the living, adding this merited offering to the memory of the dead.*

* The Journals of Major Samuel Shaw, the first American Consul at Canton. With a Life of the Author, by Josiah Quincy. Boston: Wm. Crosby and H. P. Nichols.

C. Harding pinxit. J. Andrews sc.

Truly Yours

Amos Lawrence

AMOS LAWRENCE.

AMOS LAWRENCE was born in Groton (Massachusetts), on the 22d of April, 1786. He came of "good farmer people." The first American Lawrence was John of that name, who was a native of Wissett,* in the county of Suffolk (England), where he was born in the autumn of 1609. The family was originally of the county Palatine of Lancaster, but had long resided in Suffolk at the time of John Lawrence's birth. The exact date of his arrival in America is not known, but it is supposed that he was one of Governor Winthrop's company, which sailed from England in 1630, when Mr. Lawrence was on the verge of completing his majority. That company is described by Grahame as containing "several wealthy and high-born persons, both men

* Wissett is one of those places which time has not favored, according to the ordinary judgment of men. It is a parish in the hundred and union of Blything, and contained in 1841 only eighty-four houses and four hundred and seventy inhabitants. It is one hundred and five miles from London. The nearest town is Halesworth, distant about two miles, and containing, perhaps, 3,500 inhabitants. The founders of America frequently came from hamlets too insignificant to have places even on county maps. Willoughby, where Captain John Smith was born, contained not much above six hundred souls in 1841. Our country is one of the very few nations which cannot borrow the language of the Douglases of Scotland, who were accustomed to trace their lineage to the times of antique fable, and there to lose it, boasting that men had seen their house in the tree, but never in the sapling—in the stream, but never in the fountain. The stream of our history is easily traceable to its fountain-heads, and the American oak can be followed back to the acorn whence it sprung. Though our history is not without its full share of romance, it has, in a national sense, no antiquity, no fabulous period, no time when the vivid hues of fiction blend with the somber colors of truth. If falsehood there be in our early annals, as they have been written, it must be there as the result of deliberate purpose, or of an ignorance as inexcusable as unparalleled.

and women, who expressed their determination to follow truth and liberty into a desert, rather than to enjoy all the pleasures of the world under the dominion of superstition and slavery." The first that is definitely known of Mr. Lawrence is, that he was a resident of Watertown in 1635, and married—though it is not known whether he married in England or in the colony. He was one of the original proprietors of Groton, a town which was founded in 1655. His name occurs in the town-records as early as 1663. From him are descended the numerous Lawrences of that part of Massachusetts, and not a few persons of the same name who are to be found in every quarter of the republic, from New York to San Francisco. If family pride be allowable—and every human being has in his bosom the sentiment out of which that pride grows—the Lawrences can point to an unblemished American descent of six generations, with their English ancestors to the back of that for sixteen more. Cooper's remark, that the American has a better gentility than common, as, besides his own, he may take root in that of Europe, is founded in strict truth. The subject might be pursued, and would not be without interest at a time when genealogical matters are attracting no ordinary care, and employing for their illustration no ordinary amount or degree of talent in the United States.* Nor can the fact that most American families, whose histories are known, belonged through generations to the class of farmers—incorrectly called yeomen, a social and political order that

* An eloquent American advocate and writer, David Paul Brown, in his last work, *The Forum*, complains of the little respect that is paid to the past in America, and of our indifference to our ancestors and their history. We cannot speak as to the justice of his remarks as applied to Pennsylvania, but we are sure that they do not apply to New England, where, just now, a very general interest is felt in genealogical matters, and where ancestors are thought very highly of. Mr. Sears, in the Introduction to his admirable *Pictures of the Olden Time*, mentions that he "became possessed with the very common propensity for antiquarian and genealogical researches." The propensity is very common in New England, and is on the increase.

never, in any just sense, has had an existence in America, and never could have existed here, though we have kept the word and made use of it as a sort of inheritance from the mother-land—be urged as making against the claim of Americans to good descent, using the words in their common acceptation. What were the Roman patricians but farmers, and small farmers, too, in most cases? The farmers of New England at least were the owners of the soil, and the rulers of the land; and possession of landed property and of political power are the very things that are held to raise men above the common lot, and to make of them all that a nobility ever has been or ever can be.

Samuel Lawrence, son of Captain Amos Lawrence, was a young man at the commencement of the war of the American Revolution. He belonged to a company of "minute-men" in Groton. These bodies were in a certain sense *compagnies d'élite*, the flower of the militia, having a respectable acquaintance with military duties, and probably a better knowledge of the uses of the infantry weapon, considering them only as individuals, than any regular troops in the world. They were selected because of their spirit, their personal hardihood, and their patriotic attachment to the common cause. It argues much in any man's favor that he was a "minute-man" in 1775, when all intelligent observers of the political horizon could see that an appeal to arms was soon to be made, though no man could say where the first blow was likely to be struck. At one time it seemed as if the drama was to be opened in a quarter quite different from that which saw its commencement. At length the resolution of the British commander to seize on the stores accumulated by the provincial authorities at Concord, assigned the honor of ushering the American nation into existence to the husbandmen of Middlesex county, of which Groton was then, and is now, one of the principal towns. On the morning of the 19th of April, 1775,

General Prescott—"Prescott of Pepperrell,"—rode up to the house of the Lawrences, and said to the young "minute-man," "Samuel, notify your men; the British are coming." Taking his colonel's horse—Prescott commanded the regiment to which the Groton "minute-men" belonged—Mr. Lawrence notified the men of his circuit, and returned home to make his personal preparations for service, having gone over seven miles in forty minutes, besides warning his associates. In three hours from the time he had received the orders of General Prescott, his company was on its march, and arrived at Cambridge the next day, a distance of about thirty-three miles. The "Siege of Boston" dates from that day. The important part which Prescott's regiment took in the battle of Bunker Hill is well known. It is uncertain whether the whole regiment was present on that memorable field or not. Even Mr. Frothingham, the highest authority on the subject, admits his inability to speak on the matter with the desired precision. "It is impossible," he says, "to ascertain even all the companies that were in the battle, much less the officers. The letter of General Prescott makes it uncertain whether the whole of his own regiment were in it, as only three hundred of it went on with him on the evening of June 16th." The loss of the regiment, and the character of that loss, show that it had the first place in the battle, and that its commander did not spare it. It had forty-two men *killed* and twenty-eight *wounded**—a singular reversal of the ordinary rule, which generally gives four or five wounded to every man slain outright, even in modern battles, where the liberal use of artillery and the tremendous power of improved infantry weapons are calculated largely to increase the number of killed. Stark's regiment, which experienced the next greatest loss to that of Prescott's, had fifteen men killed and forty-five wounded. Besides the actual loss of the regi-

* A brother-in-law of Mr. Lawrence was one of the number.

ment, several incidents occurred which show how hotly it must have been engaged. General Prescott's body and waistcoat were pierced with balls and bayonets in various places, and nothing but his skill as a swordsman saved his life. His nephew, Lieutenant Prescott, after being wounded in the arm, continued to serve on the field, and was about to discharge a musket when he was dashed to pieces by a cannon-ball. Mr. Samuel Lawrence was struck on one of his arms by a spent grape-shot, which inflicted no serious injury; and a musket-ball passed through his cap, cutting "his hair from front to rear." Many members of his company fell, among them being his captain, Henry Farwell, a veteran of the Louisburg expedition. It should be remembered that most of the regiment experienced their "baptism of fire" at Bunker Hill, for though some few of its members had served, the mass of it were new soldiers. If but three hundred of its number were present in the action, the loss it experienced was large indeed, and almost without precedent.

Mr. Lawrence served in the Revolutionary army down to the autumn of 1778, or about three and a half years. He was adjutant under General Sullivan, in the Rhode Island campaign of 1777. As early as 1775, he had been engaged to Miss Susanna Parker, and they were wedded in 1777, the "crisis" year of the war. The circumstances of the marriage can best be given in the language of their son. Writing under date of July 22, 1844, he says:

"Sixty-seven years ago this day, my mother, now living, was married; and, while standing up for the ceremony, the alarm-bell rang, calling all soldiers to their posts. My father left her within the hour, and repaired to Cambridge; but the colonel, in consideration of the circumstances, allowed him to return to Groton to his wife, and to join his regiment within three days at Rhode Island. This he did, spending but a few hours with his wife; and she saw nothing more of him until the last day of the year, when he made her a visit. I have ordered a thousand dollars paid to the Massachusetts General Hospital, to aid in enlarging its wings, and to commemorate this event. The girls of this day know nothing of the privations and trials of their grandmothers."*

The union thus effected was in all respects a happy one, and lasted for more than half a century, Mr. Lawrence dying on the 8th of November, 1827, at the age of seventy-three. Mrs. Lawrence survived him almost eighteen years, her death occurring May 2, 1845, when she had reached the very advanced age of eighty-nine. The importance of the mother in the training of children is one of the few things concerning which all are agreed. Most men who have risen to eminence, have borne ample testimony to the worth of their mothers. Mrs. Lawrence, from all that is known of her, was a woman singularly well endowed with those qualities which tell on the training of a family, and through that training on the State. One who knew her well —Dr. William R. Lawrence, one of her grandsons—bears evidence to her moral worth and intellectual superiority, in language as forcible as it is elegant. "Of his mother," he says, "Mr. Lawrence always spoke in the strongest terms of veneration and love, and in many of his letters are found

---

* Diary and Correspondence of the late Amos Lawrence, p. 184. As this is the first occasion for alluding to this work, we may state that its full title is, "Extracts from the Diary and Correspondence of the late Amos Lawrence, with a Brief Account of some Incidents in his Life. Edited by his son, William R. Lawrence, M. D." Not the least fortunate thing in the history of Mr. Lawrence, is the fact that he should have had a son so competent to the work of doing full justice to his name and memory. The work was not published originally, only one hundred copies being printed, all of which were distributed among the nearest relatives and friends of Mr. Lawrence. The world, however, called for the publication of the work, and, after much hesitation, Dr. Lawrence consented that it should be published. The sales have been very large. We have made great use of the book, and desire in this place to make a general acknowledgment of our obligations to its author. His work evinces taste, discrimination, and scholarship, and can be depended upon for its scrupulous exactness.

messages of affection, such as could have emanated only from a heart overflowing with filial gratitude. Her form bending over their bed in silent prayer, at the hour of twilight, when she was about leaving them for the night, is still among the earliest recollections of her children. * * * She was a woman well fitted to train a family for the troubled times in which she lived. To the kindest affections and sympathies she united energy and decision, and in her household enforced that strict and unhesitating obedience, which she considered as the foundation of all success in the education of children. Her hands were never idle, as may be supposed, when it is remembered that in those days, throughout New England, in addition to the cares of a farming establishment, much of the material for clothing was manufactured by the inmates of the family. Many hours each day she passed at the hand-loom, and the hum of the almost obsolete spinning-wheel even now comes across the memory like the remembrance of a pleasant but half-forgotten melody."* This pleasing picture of New England life, as it was in hundreds of small towns seventy years ago, can scarcely be appreciated by the younger portion of our readers, so great has been the change in the modes of that life. We shall not stop to discuss the point whether that change has also been improvement.

Mrs. Lawrence lived to see all her sons distinguished and opulent, a happiness in which her husband but partially shared. Without egotism, she could lay claim to much of that success as her work, though there is no reason for supposing that she ever gave the subject a thought. As the constitution of Amos Lawrence was feeble, he must have been more than ordinarily under maternal influence. Often kept at home from illness, he was not idle, but read such books as were within his reach, and evinced a genuine

---

* Diary and Correspondence, pp. 18, 19.

Yankee taste for the jack-knife. When past fifty, he dwelt with pleasure on the recollection of the "pop-guns and squirts" which he manufactured from elder-bushes that grew about the ruins of an old fort, built as a defense against the Indians in the colonial times. Even then his mind evinced that mixture of the practical and the elevated in thought for which it was remarkable in his latter years, and, though to a less extent, in the active period of middle life. He saw many of the soldiers of the Revolution,—men who had seen Warren die, and to whom Washington had spoken,—and heard their stories of Brandywine, and Saratoga, and Yorktown. His father having himself served with distinction, being a man of note in that part of the country, and withal of a genial and hospitable disposition, the Lawrence homestead was much frequented by men to whom war in all its phases had for years been one of the most real of things, and something very different from what it is painted by the imaginations of ardent young gentlemen, and romantic young ladies who "adore" "the martial air, the gay cockade, the sword, the shoulder-knot, and plume." In those long-gone times, it was hardly possible for half a dozen men to get together in Massachusetts without half of their number being retired soldiers. That State—counting continental troops, militia, and seamen—furnished nearly one hundred thousand men to the national service in the war of the Revolution; and that vast number was drawn from a population that numbered only 370,000 souls in 1775. Military subjects were the themes of common conversation, nor were they likely to give way to other matters when the great European wars commenced in 1792, and it was the common American impression that the quarrel which had been fought to the utterance here had been renewed in the old world, with a greater stage and mightier actors. An ordinary young man, or rather boy, listening to those bewitching tales that soldiers love so well to tell, would have become filled with a love of adventure, and have left the paternal roof in search of it. Their effect on the mind of Amos Lawrence was lasting, but it was characteristic, and therefore sound. He admired the valor of the heroes of the Revolution, and in after days thoroughly appreciated the worth of their services. His correspondence shows how deep-seated was his reverence for that order of men of whom his father was not one of the least conspicuous. He was proud of the part which his father took in the struggle for American nationality, and his natural vivacity as a writer is always much increased when he speaks of our heroic age; but we find nothing in his writings, or his life, that would leave the impression that he ever thought highly of military distinction merely as such.

Of "schooling," Mr. Lawrence can not be said to have had much, seeing that he entered upon active life some months before he had completed his fourteenth year, and that illness frequently detained him at home when he was nominally a scholar. The means of education were not scarce at Groton, a town which has ever been honorably distinguished for the excellence of its schools. "As we children came forward," he writes in 1849, "we were carefully looked after, but were taught to use the talents intrusted to us; and every nerve was strained to provide for us the academy which is now doing so much there. We *sons* are doing less for education, *for our means*, than our father for his means." He first attended the district-school that was kept hard by his father's house. Changing from that to another district-school, he was finally transferred to Groton Academy, an institution now imperishably connected with his name by the strong bond of great benefits conferred thereon in the interest of letters. His stay at the Academy, however, must have been short, for we find him actively engaged as a clerk in a country store, some months before the close of the year 1799.

The work of education is not confined to the school-house. It goes on at all times, from the day of one's birth until the day of one's death. It is most vigorous in childhood, because *care* does not then habitually ride with us. But the schoolmaster is then literally abroad, and has as many shapes as places. The face of external nature—the great utterances of the forests—the changing aspects of the heavens—the babbling of brooks—the opening of the pond-lilies on those beautiful sheets of water to which they are as pearls on the bosom of beauty—the sighing of the night wind,—these, and a thousand other things that might be named, have as much to do with the formation of character as matters of a more artificial description. It is true that education forms the common mind, and also minds that are not common; but it is education in its broadest and most significant meaning. The story of "The Shepherd Lord," which was so great a favorite with the philosophic poet of our day, shows how comprehensive is the effect of education, in this sense, on the mind of youth, converting, as in that instance it did, the child of one of the fiercest and most cruel of barons into the gentlest of scholars, a votary, not of the star of glory, but of the stars of heaven. The words which Shelley places in the mouth of one of his spiritual characters are of almost universal application:

"The starlight smile of children, the sweet looks
Of women, the fair breast from which I fed,
The murmur of the unreposing brooks,
And the green light, which, shifting overhead,
Some tangled bower of vines around me shed,
The shells on the sea-sand, and the wild flowers,
The lamp-light through the rafters cheerly spread,
And on the twining flax—in life's young hours,
These sights and sounds did nurse my spirit's folded powers."

No place could be better calculated than Groton to have an effect on the mind of a youth predisposed to the influences of nature. It is a town of much beauty, though that is generally of a quiet character, and more calculated to convey dreamy impressions than to rouse thought into activity. But it is right that we should dream in childhood, and the dreams of that period of life are not unfrequently made to become the realities of after days. "Several passages in Mr. Lawrence's letters," says his son, "will show the attachment which he felt toward the place of his birth, connected as it was with so many associations and memories of the past. The old house, with the great elm in front, and its welcome shade; the green meadow, stretching for a mile along a gentle declivity to the river; the range of mountains in the west, just distant enough to afford that tinge of blue which adds an indescribable charm to every landscape; the graceful undulations of the hills on the east, with the quiet village sleeping at their base;—all seemed, in his mind, so associated with the loved inmates of his early home, that he ever contemplated the picture with delight." As his mind was singularly impressionable, the effect of those beautiful scenes by which he was surrounded must have been great, and have ended only with his existence. Throughout life he had that "joy in flowers" which is occasionally found in the hardest natures, and which the man of humane sentiment never lacks. Long after he had won a high place for himself in the regard of men, he spoke of the old homestead as having, in his mind's eye, "all the charms of the most lovely associations of early days, with all the real beauty of those splendid descriptions given by the prophets of the holy city. I would," he adds, "earnestly impress all my children with a deep sense of the beauty and benefit of cherishing and cultivating a respect and affection for this dear spot, and for those more dear objects that have served to make it what it really is to all us children."

The first responsible place held by young Lawrence was in a shop, or "store," in the town of Dunstable, which he took in the autumn of 1799, being too feeble to be employed on his father's farm. Dunstable, though an old town, as antiquity is reckoned in America, is but a small place, containing even now but a few hundred inhabitants, and must have been a mere hamlet* in those times when the elder Adams was president. This was but an humble beginning for one who was to rise so high in the world of commerce, but it was well for him that he should know every phase of business. The child who sails his vessel of shingle and paper on the village brook, is unconsciously taking the first of those lessons which may lead him to undertake and to accomplish the most daring and adventurous of voyages.

After a few months' service at Dunstable, the boy was promoted to a post in a shop kept by a Mr. Brazer, in Groton. This was quite a large concern. Groton was then, and to a certain extent is now, the center of considerable traffic. People could not in those days make a journey to Boston, effect purchases, and return home all on the same day, and at a trifling cost, so far as the journey itself was concerned. It required three days at least for such a jaunt. People generally made their purchases of the nearest well-supplied country trader. To many farmers' families it was a sort of holiday affair to make a trip to the largest town in the vicinity of their homes. That was "going to town" to them, as going to Shrewsbury was to the gentry round the Wrekin in the reign of Charles the Second. Relatively, Groton was, with a much smaller population, a far more important place in 1800 than it is in 1857. Science and the inventive faculties of man had not then been enslaved by the spirit of centralization. The country store which

---

* The population of Dunstable in 1800 was six hundred and three, or about the same that it now is. Like many other Massachusetts towns, it has had its boundaries more than once changed, so that it is impossible to speak of its growth with literal exactness.

had an established reputation was an important establishment, and deserved its name of a " Variety Store." It was not only resorted to by the inhabitants of the town to which it belonged, but by those of other towns not large enough to support a similar concern. Such was Mr. Brazer's shop, where " puncheons of rum and brandy, bales of cloth, kegs of tobacco, with hardware and hosiery, shared attention in common with silks and threads, and all other articles for female use." It seems ludicrous that even medicines formed a part of the Brazer stock in trade, but so it was. Dr. Lawrence assures us that, among other duties, his father " was obliged to dispense medicines, not only to customers, but to all the physicians within twenty miles around, who depended on this establishment for their supply. The confidence in his good judgment was such that he was often consulted in preference to the physician, by those who were suffering from minor ails; and many were the extemporaneous doses which he administered for the weal or woe of the patient."

The place which the youth then held was one in which the important work of education was well continued. It brought him in contact with many varieties of men, and afforded him opportunities for hearing important subjects discussed with much of that plain sense and practical wisdom which belong to New England life. The Brazer store was situated on the great north road that leads from Boston to Canada, and which used to be so thronged before the construction of railways had changed the modes of internal intercourse. The store was a place of general resort, and Groton was one of the stopping-places of the coaches by which men then traveled, as also of travelers by other conveyances. Those were exciting times, and every mail brought accounts of some great military or political event. One can imagine the eagerness with which an intelligent youth, already revolving in his mind schemes of a comprehensive character, must have heard the tidings that came slowly along of the progress of the great European wars. One day he learned that Genoa—around which public interest had concentrated itself, much the same as we have seen it do around Sevastopol in our time—had fallen; and he heard men, old soldiers of the Revolution, whose sympathies were generally with the French, express their regrets that Massena, the hero of Zurich, and before whom the hitherto invincible Suwarrow had been compelled to retreat, should have been conquered by the soldier's sternest foe—famine. Then came news that the First Consul Bonaparte, not much beyond half a year in office, had scaled the Alps, had entered Italy, and had won a decisive victory over the Austrians at a place called Marengo, and so re-established the affairs of France. Months later, and on some bitter winter morning in the early days of 1801, a passenger alights from a Boston stage-coach—which has been wallowing through the deep snow on its way to Keene—and says that on the previous evening "advices from Europe" had been received in town, to the effect that General Moreau had defeated the Archduke John at Hohenlinden, in Bavaria; that the victors were pursuing the vanquished down the valley of the Danube, and that the Archduke Charles had been called to the command of the Austrian army; but the universal opinion was that the next arrival would bring intelligence that the French were in Vienna. Every one knows that Moreau is not only hostile to Bonaparte, but also to the new order of things of which the First Consul is the head; and as Bonaparte's victories had made him the chief of France, might not these brilliant successes of his personal, military, and political rival operate to a change of French rulers? Grand as had been the victories of many of the republican generals, should Moreau take Vienna he would have surpassed them all. What a termination to that war the first object of which was the capture of Paris, the seizure of the capital of the German Empire by the French! In hundreds of gathering-places in New England, that winter, were these interesting themes discussed. No doubt much nonsense was uttered during the discussions, but mixed with it was not a little sense, from which even the actors in the mighty drama could have benefited, had it reached their ears. Such discussions must have had their effect on the mind of the youthful hearer, whom circumstances compelled to hear them, whether he would or not. They enlarged his mind, extended the circle of his ideas, and taught him how dependent were all peoples upon one another. The prices of his employer's merchandise were affected by the movements of the generals and statesmen of Europe, and he began to see how necessary it was to success in mercantile life for men to be acquainted with all the springs and motives of action.

Nor were domestic occurrences then unimportant. The year 1800 was that in which the complexion of American political life was decided for generations. The presidential election of that year was the first battle of the kind in which parties were fairly arrayed against each other; and the closeness of the electoral votes indicates as well the bitterness of the strife as the near approach to equality of the contending factions. The public mind was deeply moved. Politics attracted more attention than they have at any subsequent period; and, to judge from the writings that have come down to us, there was a far more venomous tone of feeling prevalent than has ever been experienced by the existing generation of party-men. What tended to exasperate opinion, and to render men unrelenting toward their opponents, was the fact that each faction had strong feelings concerning the French Revolution, and the European wars that had grown out of that terrible movement. This was inevitable, and it is worse than idle to condemn the conduct of our fathers in this respect, as some writers have done. They acted in accordance with immutable laws; and it would be as reasonable to censure men for moral faults that are the consequences of climate, as to condemn them for their political conduct, it being understood that that conduct was honest, and proceeded from sincere convictions. The *French party* and the *British party* of those times existed only in imagination. They were airy creations. That men whose minds were under the dominion of strong prejudices should have believed the worst of each other, was natural enough; but there can be no excuse for repeating the senseless political scandal of those times. Mr. Lawrence must have had his mind more or less affected by what he heard of political discussions; but he was naturally a federalist, and the admiration which he felt in his youth for Washington and Jay was not more ardent than that which he felt for their principles in his old age.

The young clerk rose rapidly in the confidence of his employer. Mr. Brazer did not give much of personal attention to the business of the store. He had a number of clerks; but Mr. Lawrence, before he had been two years in the establishment, had become the real head of it, through force of character and fitness for the post. "The responsibility thrown upon the young clerk," says Dr. Lawrence, "was very great; and he seems cheerfully to have accepted it, and to have given himself up entirely to the performance of his business duties. His time, from early dawn till evening, was fully taken up; and, although living in the family of his employer, and within a mile of his father's house, a whole week would sometimes pass without his having leisure to pay even a flying visit."* And again, after mentioning the reliance that was placed in his medical knowledge, the same authority adds: "The

---

* Diary and Correspondence, p. 26.

same confidence was extended to him in all other matters: no one doubted his assertion; and the character for probity and fairness which accompanied him through life, was here established."*

It was while employed in this Groton store that Mr. Lawrence gave the first indications of that moral strength of character by which he was through life distinguished, and without which all his talents and industry would probably not have led him to distinguished success. He resisted temptation, and that too in one of its most seductive forms, and was victorious in the conflict. The besetting sin of that time was intemperance, as it continued to be for years afterward, and as it had been throughout all our previous history. It is a little singular that the use of ardent spirit was commenced by our English ancestors about the same time that serious ideas were first entertained by them of colonizing America. England aided Holland to throw off the yoke of the house of Austria, and Holland partially paid the debt by making known to the English the virtues of gin—a liquor so enticing that one of its most devoted consumers has gravely argued that the reason why Mohammed forbade his followers the use of wine was, that they might devote all their energies to the consumption of juniper juice. Rum, a West India liquor, may be said to have come into use not far from the same time. Both facts worked unfavorably for American society in its early days, particularly as there was little moral restraint exercised against drinking; for, though intemperance was then denounced, as it has been in all ages, no man was considered intemperate who did not get drunk quite often. Our ancestors were extensive consumers of all descriptions of intoxicating fluids. The rich drank wine and brandy, and were not altogether neglectful of more common liquors.

* Diary and Correspondence, p. 23.

The bowl of punch was to be found in the house of every man of any "standing," and was free to all comers. It was a point of hospitality to press all visitors to drink, from the parson to the pedler; and the parson took the invitation quite as coolly as the pedler, and was generally the deeper drinker of the two. So far from its being an offense to ask him to take a can of punch, as it would be to the least stringent of clergymen in these days, it would have been regarded as a gross breach of hospitality's laws if punch, or flip, or toddy, or plain grog, had not been placed before the venerable man, whose spiritual comforts were repaid by ample contributions from the spirits of the still. It was an age and a country of "serious drinking." Our progenitors drank everywhere, and on all occasions: before their religious exercises, during their political discussions, and after they had roasted a whole Indian "nation" in its swamp-encircled wigwams. Their faith was strong, and so was their breath. They drank at births, at weddings, and at funerals—but seldom joyously, save at the latter. Hawthorne, who knows what our colonial life was better than any other man, writes with even more than his ordinary force of the practice of the old Puritans in getting drunk at funerals. He is describing the funeral of old Governor Bradstreet, who died in 1697, at the age of 94—one of the founders of the Massachusetts colony, and who died its patriarch. "Many a cask of ale and cider is on tap," he says, "and many a draught of spiced wine and aqua-vitæ has been quaffed;—else why should the bearers stagger, as they tremulously uphold the coffin? and the aged pall-bearers, too, as they strive to walk solemnly beside it? and wherefore do the mourners tread on one another's heels? and why, if we may ask without offense, should the nose of the Rev. Mr. Noyes, through which he has just been delivering the funeral discourse, glow like a ruddy coal of fire? Well, well, old friends! pass on with your burden of mortality, and lay it in the tomb with jolly hearts. People should be permitted to enjoy themselves in their own fashion—every man to his taste; but New England must have been a dismal abode for the man of pleasure, when the only boon-companion was Death!"

At the beginning of the present century, therefore, drinking was as universal in New England as singing was with the Greeks of old. At eleven o'clock, throughout that region, tens of thousands of men were swallowing their worst enemy. Groton was no exception to the rule; and the clerks in the store where Mr. Lawrence was employed were all unconsciously ruining their constitutions by yielding to the seductions of the deadliest of vices. "We five boys," said Mr. Lawrence, many years afterward, "were in the habit, every forenoon, of making a drink compounded of rum, raisins, sugar, nutmegs, &c., with biscuit—all palatable to eat and drink. After being in the store four weeks, I found myself admonished by my appetite of the approach of the hour for indulgence. Thinking the habit might make trouble if allowed to grow stronger, without further apology to my seniors, I declined partaking with them. My first resolution was to abstain for a week, and, when the week was out, for a month, and then for a year. Finally, I resolved to abstain for the rest of my apprenticeship, which was for five years longer. During that whole period, I never drank a spoonful, though I mixed gallons daily for my old master and his customers." Such resolution in a boy of fifteen years is very rare, and shows not merely that he could see the evil of the course which so many were pursuing, but that he had the vigor to apply the only adequate correction to that evil. In these days of temperance, when it would shock the entire population of a country town if a youth were known among its population who took his regular dram, and when opinion is so determined out of all our large places against the use of ardent spirit, it is hard to comprehend how difficult a thing young Lawrence must have found it to form and to adhere to his wise and noble resolution. The contempt that is now bestowed upon the drinker was then the portion of him who would not drink. But this affected him not. "His mind," said Professor Hopkins, when preaching a sermon in commemoration of him, "was soon made up. Understanding perfectly the ridicule he should meet with, and which for a time he did meet with in its fullest measure, he yet took at once the ground of *total abstinence.* Such a stand, taken at such an age, in such circumstances of temptation, before temperance societies had been heard of, or the investigations had been commenced on which they are based, was a practical instance of that judgment and decision which characterized him through life."

At the same time, he resolved not to use tobacco in any form, though not indifferent to the fascinations of the weed which has enslaved whole nations. He loved its odor in youth, and in advanced life he kept in his drawer a fine Havana cigar to smell of. He confesses to a weakness for the "scented rappee," with which our predecessors of 1800 were accustomed to cram their nostrils; yet he never used an ounce of snuff. He chewed but one "quid," and that before he was fifteen, and thus had nothing of the guilt of what amounts to a national reproach. To his abstinence from liquor and tobacco he was accustomed to attribute most of his success in life; and, though he may possibly have overrated the importance of his abstinence in this respect—seeing that men have achieved eminent successes who both drank and "chewed"—his example is one that can not be too strongly commended to the young. Liquor and tobacco never yet caused good to man; and the chances that the use of them will degenerate into abuse, are ten thousand to one. They should be avoided by all who would not be left unto temptation.

Mr. Lawrence's service in Mr. Brazer's establishment terminated on the 22d of April, 1807, on which day he completed his twenty-first year. He had followed the good old custom of serving a seven years' apprenticeship,—a custom now obsolete, though it should have been maintained,—and was honestly "free of his craft." A week later he went to Boston. He had but twenty dollars in his pocket, but many years afterward he said he felt richer on that day than he ever had felt before, or had felt since, adding—"so rich, that I gave the man who came with me two dollars to save him against loss by his spending two days on the journey here and back." It was not his intention to commence business in Boston. He visited that place for the purpose of establishing a credit, his intention being to open a shop in Groton, with a fellow-apprentice for a partner. But he was to have from the beginning a wider field than a country town could afford him for the sphere in which to develop his eminent capacities as a merchant, and his fortunes were so ordered that his Boston life dates from the time that he made the journey which has been mentioned.

The Boston of 1807 was a very different place from the Boston of 1857. Half a century has wrought such changes there as would render it almost unrecognizable by a person who, having left the town in 1807, should revisit it in 1857. The growth of the place was slow for the first two centuries of its existence. It had but sixteen thousand inhabitants at the commencement of the Revolution, when the world was ringing with its people's doings, and American and Bostonian were almost convertible terms. After the Revolution, Boston grew slowly, and the census of 1810 showed her population to be only 33,250 souls. In 1807 it must have been about thirty thousand. For many years the chief town of the State did not increase so rapidly as the rest of the State. The great population which Boston now has could hardly have been anticipated, even in 1820, when it numbered some forty-three thousand, and was of as homogeneous a character as that of any place of the same size in the world. The moral changes that have come over the place are far more striking than that of the numbers of its inhabitants. The striking picture that Bancroft has drawn of Boston as it was in 1768 (vol. vi., pp. 240–3), seven years before the commencement of what is specifically called the American Revolution, though the bloodless stages of that mighty movement had been going forward vigorously for some years, is applicable to the town for a full generation after that date, and perhaps longer. Even the Revolution did not operate to effect either moral or political changes there, for not only did its more violent phases come gradually upon the country, but in all its phases it was of a conservative character, aiming to maintain what was, and not seeking the development of fanciful theories. Our ancestors had no projects for the colonization of Utopia. The revolutionists were all on the other side. As in the long contest that the English constitutionalists waged against the House of Stuart, they contended, not for the establishment of visionary commonwealths, but for the old polity of their country, with only such changes as the progress of intelligence made imperative for the preservation of the spirit of that polity; so did the men who founded the American nation contend only for what they knew were their constitutional rights. Nowhere in the country has the old conservative spirit that animated our ancestors been more maintained than in Boston. This was peculiarly the case half a century ago, when scientific discoveries and inventions had not commenced those effects on business and ordinary life which we have seen them produce of late years.

The commercial position of Boston was relatively greater in 1807 than it now is. Her trade was extensive, and of a various character. Of that immense foreign trade which the United States then had, and which gave employment to seven hundred thousand tons of American shipping alone, she had her full share. Her domestic commerce was important. Her ships were to be found in all parts of the world, and her smaller vessels in all parts of the Union. The course of events in Europe had had much to do with that rapid and early development of American commerce that lifted the country out of the slough of debt and poverty so soon after the adoption of the federal constitution; and Boston was one of the places that took prompt advantage of circumstances which made so much in our favor, and marched rapidly on the road to opulence. In those times were laid the foundations, not only of many great private fortunes, but of that pecuniary power which the country now holds, and which makes it sufficient unto itself so far as it can be desirable that any nation should be merely self-dependent.

The merchants of Boston had then high places in the estimation of the world. The Perkinses, the Sargeants, the Mays, the Cabots, the Higginsons, and others, were known throughout the world for their integrity, their mercantile skill, and the extent and the beneficial character of their operations. These were the golden days of Boston's commerce, and it is not at all probable that they will ever be there surpassed. The standard of integrity was high, and though it would be absurd to suppose that there was not the usual amount of evil in the place, it may be assumed that in no part of the world was the young trader more likely to find severer judges of character and conduct, or to be better treated if he should afford unquestionable proofs of capacity and honesty.

Such was the place in which Mr. Lawrence found himself at the age of twenty-one, and which was destined to be the scene of his own great operations, though nothing could have been further from his thoughts at that time than the idea of commencing business in Boston. But soon after his arrival in town he received the offer of a clerkship from a mercantile house of good standing, which he accepted, as he wished to make himself acquainted with the Boston modes of doing business, and with business men. He gave great satisfaction to his employers, and, after having been a short time with them, they proposed to admit him into partnership. "Without any very definite knowledge of their affairs, he, much to their surprise, declined the offer. He did not consider the principles on which the business was conducted as the true ones. The result showed his sagacity; for, in the course of a few months, the firm became insolvent, and he was appointed by the creditors to settle their affairs. This he did to their satisfaction."*

Finding himself out of employment, Mr. Lawrence, wh had made many acquaintances during the preceding seven months, resolved to commence business on his own account. He rented a shop on Cornhill, which he filled with dry-goods obtained on credit. So favorable had been the impression he had made during his short residence in Bosto that he experienced no difficulty in obtaining merchandis nor would he have experienced any had he asked for ten times the quantity. But then, as all through life, he was of the opinion which he subsequently expressed in one c his writings, namely—"Excessive credit is the rock c which so many business men are broken."

The best account we have of his financial condition at that time is what he left on record himself. "I was then," he says, "in the matter of property, not worth a dollar. My father was comfortably off as a farmer, somewhat in debt, with perhaps four thousand dollars. My brother Luther was in the practice of law, getting forward, but not worth two thousand dollars; William had nothing; Abbott,

---

* Diary and Correspondence, p. 29.

a lad just fifteen years old, at school, and Samuel a child seven years old." Some four months before, Mr. Lawrence's father mortgaged his farm for the sum of one thousand dollars, and placed the proceeds in his son's hands. Although the son was deeply affected by this act, which had been effected without consultation with any human being, he did not the less deeply regret it. He had no desire for aid that might cause others to suffer through their affording it. Writing on this subject forty years later, he said—"My honored father brought to me the one thousand dollars, and asked me to give him my note for it. I told him he did wrong to place himself in a situation to be made unhappy, if I lost the money. He told me he *guessed I wouldn't lose it*, and I gave him my note. The first thing I did was to take four per cent. premium on my Boston bills (the difference then between passable and Boston money), and send a thousand dollars in bills of the Hillsborough Bank to Amherst, New Hampshire, by my father, to my brother L. to carry to the bank and get specie, as he was going there to attend court that week. My brother succeeded in getting specie, principally in silver change, for the bills, and returned it to me in a few days. In the mean time, or shortly after, the bank had been sued, the bills discredited, and, in the end, proved nearly worthless. I determined not to use the money except in the safest way, and therefore loaned it to Messrs. Parkman, in whom I had entire confidence. After I had been in business and had made more than a thousand dollars, I felt that I could repay the money, come what would of it—being insured against fire, and trusting no one for goods. I used it in my business, but took care to pay off the mortgage as soon as it would be received. The whole transaction is deeply interesting, and calls forth humble and devout thanksgiving to that merciful Father who has been to us better than our most sanguine hopes."

On another occasion he wrote—"This incident shows how dangerous it is to the independence and comfort of families for parents to take pecuniary responsibilities for their sons in trade, beyond their power of meeting them without embarrassment. Had my Hillsborough Bank notes not been paid as they were, nearly the whole amount would have been lost, and myself and my family might probably have been ruined. The incident was so striking that I have uniformly discouraged young men who have applied to me for credit, offering their fathers as bondsmen; and by doing so I have, I believe, saved some respectable families from ruin. My advice, however, has been sometimes rejected with anger. A young man who cannot get along without such aid, will not be likely to get along with it."

It was on the 17th of December, 1807, that Mr. Lawrence opened his shop on Cornhill. His clerk was Henry Whiting, who subsequently entered the United States army and rose to the rank of brigadier-general, and to whom Mr. Lawrence wrote, in 1849—"I have just looked into my first sales-book, and there see the entries made by you more than forty-one years ago. Ever since, you have been going up, from the cornet of dragoons to the present station. Abbott, who took your place, is now the representative of his country at the Court of St. James." On the first day of January, 1808, after having been in business for a fortnight, the profits on all his sales amounted to one hundred and seventy-five dollars and eighteen cents, out of which the expenses were to come. He cleared fifteen hundred dollars the first year, and upward of four thousand dollars the second year. It was his opinion that large success at the commencement of business life, is not favorable to permanent prosperity. "Probably," he said, referring to his early experience, "had I made four thousand the first year, I should have failed the second or third year. I practiced a system of rigid economy, and never allowed myself to spend a fourpence for unnecessary objects until I had acquired it." "When I commenced," he subsequently wrote, "the embargo had just been laid, and with such restrictions on trade that many were induced to leave it. But I felt great confidence that, by industry, economy, and integrity, I could get a living; and the experiment showed that I was right. Most of the young men who commenced at that period failed by spending too much money, and using credit too freely." His mode of doing business, and the principles by which he was guided, are set forth in the following extract from his writings:

"I adopted the plan of keeping an accurate account of merchandise bought and sold each day, with the profit, as far as practicable. This plan was pursued for a number of years; and I never found my merchandise fall short in taking an account of stock, which I did as often at least as once in each year. I was thus enabled to form an opinion of my actual state as a business man. I adopted also the rule always to have property, after my second year's business, to represent forty per cent. at least more than I owed—that is, never to be in debt more than two and a half times my capital. This caution saved me from ever getting embarrassed. If it were more generally adopted, we should see fewer failures in business. Excessive credit is the rock on which so many business men are broken."

On the 8th of October, 1808, Mr. Lawrence was joined by one of his younger brothers, destined to rise to great distinction both as a merchant and as a statesman. Abbott Lawrence was but fifteen years old when he became his brother's apprentice. "In 1808," says the elder brother, "he came to me as my apprentice, bringing his bundle under his arm, with less than three dollars in his pocket—and this was his fortune. A first-rate business lad he was, but, like other bright lads, needed the careful eye of a senior to guard him from the pitfalls that he was exposed to." There would be something almost amusing in the gravity with which Mr. Lawrence speaks of his seniority at two-and-twenty—the very heyday of youth—were it not evident that he was grave far beyond his years. As in old age he retained much of the confident spirit and sprightliness of youth, so in early life he was endowed with not a little of that gravity which ordinarily is born only of care and time. His allusion to his brother's small means is deserving of notice, as it was that with which he commenced those operations that were to lead to possession of one of the colossal fortunes of the country, and which would be deemed such even in countries where the standard of wealth is higher than it is in America. And that fortune, it is the merest justice to add, was used in a spirit so enlightened and munificent as to show it had been worthily bestowed.

His attention to his business duties was rigid, and nothing could divert his mind from their exact discharge. "I practiced," he said long after, "upon the maxim, '*Business before friends*,' from the commencement of my course. During the first seven years of my business in this city, I never allowed a bill against me to stand unsettled over the Sabbath. If the purchase of goods was made at auction on Saturday, and delivered to me, I always examined and settled the bill, by note or by crediting it, and leaving it clear; so that, in case I was not on duty on Monday, there would be no trouble for my boys—thus keeping the business *before* me, instead of allowing it to drive me."

The pleasures of town life are to the young almost irresistible as the songs of the Sirens were to navigators—few altogether resisting their allurements. Mr. Lawrence had his temptations, but he fell not before them. Such time as he could spare from his business was devoted to improving studies. "When I first came to this city," he wrote, in 1832, "I took lodgings in the family of a widow, who had commenced keeping boarders for a living. I was one of her first, and, perhaps, had been in the city two months when I went to this place; and she, of course, while I remained, was inclined to adopt any rules for the boarders that I prescribed. The only one I ever made was, that after supper, all the boarders who remained in the public room should remain quiet for at least one hour, to give those who chose to study or read an opportunity of doing so without disturbance. The consequence was, that we had the most quiet and improving set of young men in the town. The few who did not wish to comply with the regulation, went abroad after tea, sometimes to the theater, sometimes to other places—but, to a man, became bankrupt in after life, not only in fortune, but in reputation; while a majority of the other class sustained good characters; and some are now living who are ornaments to society, and fill important stations. The influence of this small measure will, perhaps, be felt throughout generations. It was not less favorable on myself than on others."

He wrote the following paragraph in his "Diary," on the 10th of February, 1847, which gives a glimpse of Boston life as it was half a century ago.

"In the autumn of 1809, I boarded at Granger's coffee-house, opposite Brattle-street church; and, in the same house, Mr. Charles White took up his quarters, to prepare his then new play, called the 'Clergyman's Daughter.' He spent some months in preparing it to secure a *run* for the winter; and used to have Tennett, Canfield, Robert Treat Paine, and a host of others to dine with him very often. I not unfrequently left the party at the dinner-table, and found them there when I returned to tea. Among the boarders was a fair proportion of respectable young men, of different pursuits; and, having got somewhat interested in White, we all agreed to go and help bring out his 'Clergyman's Daughter.' Mrs. Darley was the lady to personate her, and a more beautiful creature could not be found. She and her husband (who sang his songs better than any man I had ever heard then) had all the spirit of parties in interest. We filled the boxes, and encored, and all promised a great run. After three nights, we found few beside the friends, and it was laid aside a failure. In looking back, the picture comes fresh before me; and, among all, I do not recollect one who was the better, and most were ruined. The theater is no better now."

Mr. Lawrence kept up the closest correspondence with his relatives at Groton, absence only making his attachment to home the stronger. He occasionally visited Groton. He would leave Boston at a late hour on Saturday, and sometimes would not reach his father's house until the morning of the Sabbath. After the midnight of that Sabbath, he left Groton for Boston, reaching town some hours before the time for the commencement of business operations. This was somewhat different from the present mode of making the same journey. Now a man can leave Boston after business hours are over, spend the evening and night at Groton, and return to town in season for work the next morning.

Nearly fifty years since New England was visited by a form of pestilence, which had several names, and by some was called the "cold plague." It raged extensively, and many of the sufferers died from its effects. The alarm was very great, greater, perhaps, than was subsequently caused by the appearance of the Asiatic cholera, and not without reason, for the latter rolled steadily toward the West from the remotest East, and men had accustomed themselves to the thought of it, while the "cold plague" or "spotted fever," came upon the country without warning. It was its own herald. Mr. Lawrence was one of the many who were attacked by this disease, which came upon him suddenly, at the close of one of his hard-working days. He suffered long and severely, but through the attentions of an able physician (Dr. George C. Shattuck, who subsequently rose to deserved eminence in the noblest of all professions), seconded by those of relatives and friends, the disease was conquered, and his health restored, though not until after a considerable period had elapsed. His father, in a particular manner, was attentive to him, and evinced a more than ordinary interest in his condition.

We have already mentioned that Mr. Lawrence commenced business at a time when the commerce of this country was about to receive a series of shocks which worked very material changes in its character. From the very commencement of the wars of the French Revolution, American commerce had been assailed, by both France and England, in various ways; until the so-called highway of nations had become as unsafe to vessels sailing under our flag as ever was the Rhine Valley to the merchants of the middle ages, where and when the robber chivalry were used to sally from their "castled crags" upon all who were wealthy and weak, and who were such important agents in carrying on the trade that existed between Northern and Southern Europe. Looking back upon those times, one wonders that our mercantile marine was not then utterly ruined; and still more, that a nation with the incidents of the Revolution fresh in its mind should so cravenly have submitted to depredations, which it would be to flatter to call piratical. Our government inflicted severe chastisement on the Barbary States, because of their piracy, and all but put an end to a system that had troubled the world for centuries; but it cringed before the Christian robbers of Europe, and allowed those whom it taxed to be plundered with impunity by foreigners. That is a page of American history to which no American can turn without blushing. One lesson we ought to draw from it that is rather hard to learn: we should not abuse the strength we have by acting toward the weak as the strong acted toward us in the early part of the present century.

In the year 1807, matters had come to a crisis between America and the European belligerents. What with orders in council, decrees from Berlin and Milan, broken treaties, acts of impressment, and acts of plunder, our merchants were doomed to experience all the evils of a state of war without being able to offset them by having resort to measures not compatible with peace. That year occurred the attack on the Chesapeake by the Leopard, the most insolent proceeding of which even the British navy was guilty in that age of its wantonness. That act was followed on our part by proclamations of exclusion, embargo acts, and acts of non-intercourse, and, at the end of five years, by war. In less than three years, peace was restored ; and how great soever a blessing peace may be, its restoration is ever accompanied with great effects, some of which must necessarily be very injurious, on business.

The eight years that followed Mr. Lawrence's arrival in Boston, were years in which it was not easy for any man, even the most experienced, to pursue a mercantile life with success. The varying conduct of our government, and that of England, was sufficient to disturb any arrangement on a large scale that the merchant might make. It was peace in the morning ; it was war at noon ; and it might be peace again before night. The cowardice of one government, and the unjust spirit of the other, left it impossible for any one to anticipate what even an hour would bring forth. Human wisdom was utterly at fault in those times, in the great majority of cases, in all matters of commerce.

Yet it was during that very time, when even the most successful of merchants were almost led to despair of the return of better days, that Mr. Lawrence laid the foundation, not only of his own fortune, but the foundations of the fortunes of many members of his family. He was endowed with one of those clear and comprehensive minds which pierce right through whole mazes of difficulties, and see the path by which prosperity is secured. It is probable that, if questioned on the subject, he would have been unable to define the mental process by which he arrived at his conclusions. It is probably beyond the power of language to clothe such subtle thoughts, and language has truly been called thought's garment. "His mind," says his son and biographer, "was not of that logical cast which, from patient reasoning, can deduce effects from a succession of causes; but arrived at its conclusions by a kind of intuition, somewhat like those rare instances of mathematicians who solve a difficult problem, and yet can give no account of the mental process by which the solution has been reached." Of one thing we may be sure, and that is, that he was thoroughly well informed respecting the condition of the world, and that he made no movement without taking into account what would be the effect on any large operation of the actions of men whose positions put it in their power to color the lives of millions upon millions of their fellow-creatures. Without a knowledge of the political condition of the world as it then existed, no man could do any thing in commerce. Sometimes, it should seem, men blunder into fortune, but that is not often the case; and "luck" had nothing to do with Mr. Lawrence's success in one of the most perplexing periods in the history of trade.

During the first two years of his mercantile life, Mr. Lawrence's profits amounted to less than six thousand dollars. This brought him down to the close of 1809. In 1810, his illness, which, as we have seen, was long and severe, must have operated to check the work of accumulation. Without being a blank in his life, that year could not have seen the amount of his means largely increased. From about the commencement of 1811 to the close of 1813, his profits must have amounted to some forty thousand dollars, judging from the assertion that he makes in his "Diary," respecting the state of his arrangements on the 1st of January, 1814. "On that day," he says, "I took my brother Abbott into partnership on equal shares, putting fifty thousand dollars, that I had then earned, into the concern. Three days afterward, the 'Bramble News' came, by which the excessive high price of goods was knocked down. Our stock was then large, and had cost a high price. He was in great anguish, considering himself a bankrupt for at least five thousand dollars. I cheered him by offering to cancel our copartnership indentures, give him up his note, and, at the end of the year, pay him five thousand dollars. He declined the offer, saying I should lose that, and more besides; and, as he had enlisted, would do the best he could. This was in character, and it was well for us both. He was called off to do duty as a soldier, through most of the year. I took care of the business, and prepared to retreat with my family into the country, whenever the town seemed liable to fall into the hands of the British, who were very threatening in their demonstrations. We still continue mercantile business under the first set of indentures, and under the same firm, merely adding '& Co.' as new partners have been admitted." This was written five and-thirty years after the events to which it refers.

Mr. Abbott Lawrence's confidence in his brother was what might have been expected in a man who knew that brother so well; and his determination to abide by the consequences of his first act, was in accordance with every thing else that is known of him. His courage was great, and his sense of honor chivalrously high.

All through the war, Mr. Lawrence guided the business of his house with signal judgment and rare skill. He was no speculator. He knew that, while immense sums were made occasionally through hazardous speculations, in which the players staked every thing against the chance of success—present means, the money of friends, character, comfort, and the risk of losing even the privilege to hope, if they should lose—the instances of such success were not more numerous than those of men making money by the purchase of lottery-tickets. He had a just idea of mercantile honor; and the first condition of speculation is, that it shall place that honor in imminent peril. The fair profits of legitimate commerce—the results of intelligence, sagacity, and the skillful use of capital in ministering to the necessities, tastes, and reasonable habits of civilized men—these were all that he desired, and these he won, making of them such use as never would have been thought of by a man whose nature had been corrupted and heart-hardened by gambling transactions on a gigantic scale. It was because in his youth Mr. Lawrence was not led astray by the glittering temptations that beset all men in the business world, that he was brilliantly successful in middle life, and the benefactor of his species in advanced age. "Through the difficult and troubled times in which the United States were engaged in the war with England," his son says, "his efforts were crowned with success. Dark clouds sometimes arose in the horizon, and various causes of discouragement from time to time cast a gloom over the mercantile world: but despondency formed no part of his character, while cool sagacity and unceasing watchfulness and perseverance enabled him to weather a storm which made shipwreck of others around him."

The restoration of peace, in the early days of 1815, found the Lawrences firmly established, and in condition to enter upon that new course of American commercial life which dates from that time. In March—only a few weeks after the news of peace had been received—and in the first ship, the Milo, that sailed from Boston for England, the junior partner embarked for Europe. It was a responsible undertaking for a youth of only two-and twenty, that of assuming an equality with the leading English and French merchants in great transactions; but the event proved that he was fully equal, even at that early age, to the task confided to him by his senior, who rarely was mistaken in his judgment of men.

Mr. Lawrence, on the 11th of March, wrote an admirable letter of counsel and instruction to his brother, from which we make the subjoined extracts:

"My dear Brother: I have thought best, before you go abroad, to suggest a few hints for your benefit in your intercourse with the people among whom you are going. As a first and leading principle, let every transaction be of that pure and honest character that you would not be ashamed to have appear before the whole world as clearly as to yourself. In addition to the advantages arising from an honest course of conduct with your fellow-men, there is the satisfaction of reflecting within yourself that you have endeavored to do your duty; and, however greatly the best may fall short of doing all they ought, they will be sure not to do more than their principles enjoin.

"It is, therefore, of the highest consequence that you should not only cultivate correct principles, but that you should place your standard of action so high as to require great vigilance in living up to it.

"In regard to your business transactions, let every thing be so registered in your books, that any person, without difficulty, can understand the whole of your concerns. You may be cut off in the midst of your pursuits, and it is of no small consequence that your temporal affairs should always be so arranged that you may be in readiness.

"If it is important that you should be well prepared in this point of view, how much more important is it that you should be prepared in that which relates to eternity!

"You are young, and the course of life seems open, and pleasant prospects greet your ardent hopes; but you must remember that the race is not always to the swift, and that, however flattering may be your prospects, and however zealously you may seek pleasure, you can never find it except by cherishing pure principles and practicing right conduct. My heart is full on this subject, my dear brother, and it is the only one on which I feel the least anxiety.

"While here, your conduct has been such as to meet my entire approbation; but the scenes of another land may be more than your principles will stand against. I say *may be*, because young men of as fair promise as yourself have been lost by giving a small latitude (innocent in the first instance) to their propensities. But I pray the Father of all mercies to have you in his keeping, and preserve you amid temptations.

"I can only add my wish to have you write me frequently and particularly, and that you will embrace every opportunity of gaining information.

"Your affectionate brother,

"AMOS LAWRENCE.

"TO ABBOTT LAWRENCE."

The letters written by Mr. Lawrence to his brother, while the latter was in Europe, breathe the same high tone throughout. He appreciated the advantages that his partner had in visiting Europe, and particularly England; for at that time it was not a common thing for Americans, not immediately engaged in maritime pursuits, to cross the ocean. On the 15th of April, he wrote: "By the favor of heaven, I trust ere this you have landed upon the soil from which sprang our forefathers. In the contemplation of that wonderful 'Isle,' on your first arrival, there must be a feeling bordering on devotion." Again: "You are placed in a particularly favorable situation, my dear brother, for improving yourself in the knowledge of such things as will hereafter be useful to you. Let no opportunity pass without making the most of it. There are necessarily many vacant hours in your business which ought not to pass unemployed. I pretend not to suggest particular objects for your attention, but only the habit generally of active employment, which, while making your time useful and agreeable to yourself, will be the best safeguard to your virtue. The American character, I trust, is somewhat respected in England at this time, notwithstanding it was lately at so low an ebb; and I would wish every American to endeavor to do something to improve it. Especially do I wish you, my dear A., who visit that country under circumstances so favorable, to do your part in establishing a character for your country as well as for yourself."

Mr. Abbott Lawrence was remarkably successful in the arrangement of that business which took him to Europe. He acted with great promptitude and decision, and was favored by circumstances which he knew how to turn to account. His brother was much gratified at this success, for various reasons. Writing to his wife, on the 4th of June, he said: "The Milo got in yesterday, and brought letters from Abbott, dated 4th April. He was then in Manchester, and enjoyed the best health. * * * I received from him merchandise, which I hope to get out of the ship and sell this week. I suspect there are few instances of a young man leaving this town, sending out goods, and having them sold within ninety days from the time of his departure. It is eighty-four days this morning since he left home." To his brother himself, he wrote: "By the arrival of the Milo last Saturday, and packet on Monday, I received your several letters, giving an account of your proceedings. You are as famous among your acquaintances here, for the rapidity of your movements, as Bonaparte. Mr. —— thinks that you leave Bonaparte entirely in the background. I really feel a little proud, my dear brother, of your conduct. Few instances of like dispatch are known."

The time of Mr. Abbott Lawrence's first visit to Europe was when the most remarkable events of modern history were there in course of transaction. Napoleon had just returned from Elba, and had been outlawed by the Robber-Congress of Vienna, the members of which ceased to quarrel among themselves on his reappearance, and were directing their immense armed masses upon France. The campaign that followed was brief, and France was laid hopelessly at the feet of her conquerors, but for whose jealousies of one another she would have undergone the fate of Poland. A million of armed foreigners encumbered and disgraced the soil of that nation which had seen its eagles enter every capital from Moscow to Lisbon. At Paris were all the emperors, kings, and kinglets of Europe, with some few exceptions, with field-marshals and generals enough to make an army by themselves, and statesmen in numbers sufficient to misgovern the world forever. After the occupation of Paris, Mr. Abbott Lawrence visited that city, and saw many things that have since become history, and many men whose names then were far more commonly used than those of Pelissier and Todleben are in our time. War had ceased to be waged, but the giants (with one exception, the greatest of all) who had figured in it were yet on the stage. No traveler could visit the continent without realizing the poet's idea on Waterloo: "His tread was everywhere on an empire's dust." We are not aware that the young American committed the thoughts that rose to his mind, and the result of his observations, to paper. If he did, they would, we venture to say, be found well worth reading, and would be particularly interesting when read by the light of recent events in France. Mercantile travelers have always been the best writers of books of travels. "It is, perhaps," says an eminent authority, "to the circumstance that most of our early travelers were men of business—and the missionary or the embassador were, in their respective lines, as much men of business as the merchant—that we owe the vivacity and interest of their narratives, and their great superiority over those writers whom authorship-prepense has conducted from their homes. In the first case, the journey makes the book; but in the last, it is the book which makes the journey. The business-traveler records those matters only which recreated him amidst his toils, or which were so remarkable as to command his attention, possessing a real and native interest; whilst the author-traveler, turning his recreation into a toil, is perpetually on the stretch, striving to give a factitious, facetious, or fictitious interest to things which have none at all."*

The business operations of the firm were conducted with great success, for years, and through those disastrous times which followed the return of peace, when the country was struggling, as it were, with the agonies of a new birth, and business was about to assume new modes. We have but little material from which to write the history of those operations, and shall here insert, from the "Diary and Correspondence," what was written to its editor by an eminent New York merchant, then a clerk in Mr. Lawrence's house. That gentleman says:

"When the business season was over, he would sit down with me, and converse freely and familiarly, and would have something interesting and useful to say. I used to enjoy these sittings; and, while I always feared to do any thing, or leave any thing undone, which would displease him, I at the same time had a very high regard, and I may say love, for him, such as I never felt for any other man besides my own father. He had a remarkable faculty of

* Sir Francis Palgrave, *The Merchant and the Friar*, p. 88.

bringing the sterling money into our currency, with any advance, by a calculation in his mind, and would give the result with great accuracy in one quarter of the time which it took me to do it by figures. I used to try hard to acquire this faculty, but could not, and never saw any other person who possessed it to the degree he did. His mind was remarkably vigorous and accurate; and consequently his business was transacted in a prompt and correct manner. Nothing was left undone until to-morrow which could be done to-day. He was master of and controlled his business, instead of allowing his business to master and control him. When I took charge of the books, they were kept by single entry; and Mr. Lawrence daily examined every entry to detect errors. He was dissatisfied with this loose way of keeping the books; and, at his request, I studied book-keeping by double entry with Mr. Gershom Cobb, who had just introduced the new and shorter method of double entry. I then transferred the accounts into a new set of books on this plan, and well remember his anxiety during the process, and his expression of delight when the work was completed, and I had succeeded in making the first trial-balance come out right. This was the first set of books opened in Boston on the new system. While Mr. Lawrence required all to fulfill their engagements fully and promptly, so long as they were able to do so, he was lenient to those who were unfortunate, and always ready to compromise demands against such. No case occurred, while I was with him, in which I thought he dealt harshly with a debtor who had failed in business."*

Mr. Lawrence's first marriage took place on the 6th of June, 1811, a few weeks after the completion of his twenty-fifth year. The lady with whom he then formed the most important connection of life was Miss Sarah Richards,

---

* Diary and Correspondence, pp. 60–61.

daughter of Mr. Giles Richards, a gentleman of much enterprise and ingenuity, and who, some seventy years since, had a large establishment in Boston for the manufacture of cards for preparing wool, which was visited by President Washington when he made his Northern tour. Mr. Richards was ahead of his time, and the same genius which would have led to fortune in the next generation was probably the cause of his failure in those early days of the nation. He lost all his property, which seems to have been of large amount, and retired from business, with character unstained, and passed the remainder of his life in seclusion.

Miss Sarah Richards, this gentleman's daughter, became a member of the family of Rev. Dr. Chaplin, minister of the church at Groton. She and her future husband were acquainted as children, and she was one of the most intimate friends of his sisters. In 1803, circumstances caused a separation between these parties to happen, and the acquaintance between Mr. Lawrence and Miss Richards was not renewed, and then accidentally, until 1807. Writing to his sister, in the spring of 1811, Mr. Lawrence said—"You will, perhaps, be surprised to learn the extent and importance of my avocations; for, in addition to my usual routine of mercantile affairs, I have lately been engaged in a negotiation of the first importance, and which I have accomplished very much to my own satisfaction. It is no other than having offered myself as a husband to your very good friend, Sarah Richards, which offer she has agreed to accept. So, next fall, you must set your mind on a wedding. Sarah I have long known and esteemed; there is such a reciprocity of feelings, sentiments, and principles, that I have long thought her the most suitable person I have seen for me to be united with. Much of my time, as you may well suppose, is spent in her society; and here I can not but observe the infinite advantage of good sense and good principles over the merely elegant accomplishments of fashionable education. By the latter we may be fascinated for a time; but they will afford no satisfaction on retrospection. The former you are compelled to respect and to love. Such qualities are possessed by Sarah; and, were I to say any thing further in her favor, it would be that she is beloved by you."

Mrs. Lawrence was a woman of great worth, and both parties were eminently happy in the marriage state. But their earthly union was destined to be of brief duration. In the spring of 1818, Mrs. Lawrence fell ill, and it was soon seen that that scourge of New England, consumption, had marked her for one of its victims. Remaining at Groton, for the benefit of country air, she was suddenly summoned to Boston by the severe illness of her husband, whose life was for some time in much danger. While thus discharging the highest of duties, she was seized, one night, with a hemorrhage of the lungs, which caused her no alarm, as she did not wish to survive her husband. Mr. Lawrence recovered, but his wife's health continued to fail, and by the close of the year hope had left the minds of her numerous friends. She bore her illness with the fortitude of a Christian, and with that calm resignation of her sex which puts to shame the boasted heroism of man. A few weeks before her death, her husband wrote to her mother—"It takes much from my distress to see her so calm, and so resigned to the will of the Almighty. Although her attachments to life are as strong and as numerous as are the attachments of most, I believe the principle of resignation is stronger. She is a genuine disciple of Christ; and, if my children walk in her steps, they will all be gathered among the blest, and sing the song of the redeemed. Should it be the will of God that we be separated for a season, there is an animation in the hope that we shall meet again, purified from the grossness of the flesh, and never to be parted. God tempers the wind to the shorn lamb. I shall have, therefore, no more put upon me than I am able to bear; yet I know not how to bring my mind to part with so excellent a friend, and so good a counselor."*

This excellent woman died on the 14th of January, 1819, leaving her husband overwhelmed with grief. She lived ever in his memory. Mr. Lawrence was so seriously affected by his loss, that he fell into a desponding state of mind, and was advised to try a change of scene, in the hope of effecting a restoration to health. He accordingly made a tour through Virginia and the Middle States, and visited Washington, then the scene of interesting events. The Missouri Compromise was then under discussion, in one of its stages, and the debates were listened to by Mr. Lawrence with no ordinary interest. They produced, his son states, "a strong and lasting influence upon his mind respecting the great question then discussed." He was very hospitably entertained by Virginians, and made a pilgrimage to the tomb of Washington at Mount Vernon. In a letter from Baltimore, he says: "I have a high eulogium to pay the Virginians, which I must reserve for another letter."

He was a keen observer of men and things during this short tour, and those of his letters that were written while making it, and have been published, show that he would have been very successful as a traveler, had circumstances ever allowed him to figure in that character. He wrote a letter from Philadelphia to his brother and partner, which abounds with good sense, and contains suggestions that must ever be valuable to business men.

"When I see how people in other places are doing business, I feel that we have reason to thank God that we are not obliged to do as they do, but are following that regular and profitably safe business that allows us to sleep well o' nights, and eat the bread of industry and quietness. The

---

* Diary and Correspondence, p. 64.

more I see of the changes produced by violent speculation, the more satisfied I am that our maxims are the only true ones for a life together. Different maxims may prove successful for a part of life, but will frequently produce disastrous results just at the time we stand most in need—that is, when life is on the wane, and a family is growing around us.

"Two young brokers in ——— have played a dashing game. They have taken nearly one hundred thousand dollars from the bank without the consent of the directors. A clerk discounted for them. They have lost it by United States Bank speculations.

"Look after clerks well, if you wish to keep them honest. *Too good a reputation sometimes tempts men to sin, upon the strength of their reputation.*"

Returning to Boston, he sought to engross his mind with business, so that the "thick-coming fancies" so natural to one in his situation might not obtain the ascendency. He gave up his house, and resided in the family of his brother and partner, finding there the comforts of a home, to which no man could be more sensible. He gradually recovered his peace of mind, and with it bodily health. He devoted his renewed energies to the business of the firm, which was steadily increasing in extent and importance. Of this part of his life there were but few memorials or letters found, save such as relate to his mercantile pursuits. The subjoined extract from his "Diary," under date of February 15th, 1846, will be read with interest:

"Yesterday was one of the most lovely winter-days. Today the snow drives into all the cracks and corners, it being a boisterous easterly snow-storm, which recalls to my mind a similar one which I shall never forget, in February, 1820.

"I went to New York during that month, for the New England Bank, with about one hundred thousand dollars in foreign gold, the value of which, by law, at the mint was soon to be reduced from eighty-seven to eighty-five cents per pennyweight, or about that. I also had orders to buy bills with it, at the best rate I could. Accordingly I invested it, and had to analyze the standing of many who offered bills, as drawers or endorsers.

"Some of the bills were protested for non-acceptance, and were returned at once and damages claimed. This was *new* law in New York, and resisted; but the merchants were convinced by suits, and paid the twenty per cent. damages. The law of damage was altered soon after.

"On my return I took a packet for Providence, and came at the rate of ten knots an hour for the first seven hours of the night. I was alarmed by a crash, which seemed to be breaking in the side of the ship within a few inches of my head. I ran upon deck, and it was a scene to be remembered. Besides the crew on board were the officers of a wrecked vessel from Portsmouth, N. H., and some other old shipmasters, all at work, and giving directions to a coaster which had run foul of us, and had lost its way. By favor and labor we were saved from being wrecked, but were obliged to land at some fifteen miles from Providence, and get there as we could through the snow. I arrived there almost dead with headache and sickness. Madam Dexter and her daughter left the day before, and reached home in perfect safety before the storm. Such are the scenes of human life! Here I am, enjoying my own fireside, while all who were then active with me in the scenes thus recalled are called to their account, excepting Philip Hone, M. Van Schaick, N. Goddard, Chancellor Kent, and his son-in-law, Isaac Hone."*

In the month of April, 1821, Mr. Lawrence made a second marriage. The lady was Mrs. Nancy Ellis, widow of Judge Ellis, of Claremont, N. H., and daughter of Robert

* Diary and Correspondence, pp. 75, 76.

Means, Esq., of Amherst, N. H. This union was a happy one, and Mrs. Lawrence was worthy of her husband. Dr. Lawrence, in a note to his excellent work, pays her the highest tribute that could be bestowed upon a woman in her position. "The editor, in justice to his own feelings," he says, "will here remark, that he believes the continuation of Mr. Lawrence's life, after he became a confirmed invalid, was, under Providence, in a great measure due to the care and faithful attentions of his wife. For more than twenty years, and during his frequent seasons of languor and sickness, she submitted to many sacrifices, and bestowed a degree of care and watchfulness such as affection alone could have enabled her to render."*

On the 23d of December, 1833, Mr. Lawrence wrote to his wife, who had been summoned to the death-bed of a relative:

"Your absence makes a great blank in the family; and I feel that I must be very careful, lest any little accident should make me feel of a *deep blue* while you are away. Confidence is a great matter, not only in curing, but in preventing disease, whether of the body or the mind; and I have somehow got the notion that I am more safe when you are looking after me than when you are not, and that any trouble is sooner cured when you are present than when you are not. This is, I suppose, the true charm which some people have faith in to keep off their ills. I have been forcibly reminded of the passage of time, by reviewing the scenes of the last three years, and am deeply sensible of the mercies that have been extended to me. What little I do is a poor return: may a better spirit prompt and guide my future services! What few I have rendered are estimated by my brethren beyond their value, and of course tend to flatter my self-love. This should not

* Diary and Correspondence, p. 127.

be; and I ought to see myself as I am seen by that Eye that never sleeps. The situation I occupy is one that I would not exchange, if I had the power, with any man living: it is full of agreeable incidents, and free from the toils and anxieties frequently attendant on a high state of prosperity; and is, besides, free from that jealousy, or from any other cause of uneasiness, so common among the ardent and successful in the world's race."

Mr. Lawrence took part in the introduction of manufactures into this country on a large scale, and risked large sums in a business that has been subjected to very disastrous influences. He conscientiously believed that it was the duty of the country and the government to promote the interests of manufacturers in all honest ways. His name is imperishably associated with our manufacturing system. It is commonly supposed that he made immense amounts as a manufacturer, but great exaggeration prevails on this subject. The business has fluctuated so much that it has never been so profitable as other modes, concerning which little is said.

He was of opinion that he gave too much time to business. It monopolized his time, and to this he was determined not to submit. "Property acquired at such sacrifices as I have been obliged to make the past year," he wrote at the commencement of 1826, "costs more than it's worth; and the anxiety in protecting it is the extreme of folly." One year later he wrote: "The principles of business laid down a year ago have been very nearly practiced upon. Our responsibilities and anxieties have greatly diminished, as also have the accustomed profits of business; but there is sufficient remaining for the reward of our labor to impose on us increased responsibilities and duties, as agents who must at last render an account. God grant that mine be found correct!" He had higher ideas of the duty of man than would lead him to work merely for the sordid purpose of converting a million of gold into two millions, or to lay up money for the purpose of dying in the odor of affluence.

Mr. Lawrence was not a political man, according to the ordinary meaning of the word. The offices that he held were few in number, and were not places of emolument. In 1821 he was chosen a member of the Massachusetts House of Representatives by the citizens of Boston. The representative office stood higher then than it now does, though it is quite probable that there was not much more talent in the Massachusetts Legislature in 1821 than there is in 1857, only that we are so accustomed to look at the past through a Claude glass that we see it in a false light, all its disagreeable features smoothed away, while those that are pleasing stand out prominently and command attention. In the present, we see, for the most part, merely what is repulsive—so amiable is our nature. In the last generation people were more discriminating than they now are in their selection of men for legislators, but whether, on the whole, the change has resulted in a gain or a loss to the community, is a question it would be difficult to settle. Probably every man would answer it from his own stand-point, rather than from any careful examination of the facts that bear upon it.

Having assumed, we may suppose against his own wishes, the office of representative, Mr. Lawrence discharged its duties with that exactitude which he brought to all the transactions of life, and in the most conscientious manner. His business was then very extensive, and demanded his entire personal attention; but this he denied to it, in order that the trust reposed in him by his fellow-citizens might be fulfilled. He was always in his seat when the House of Representatives was in session, and acted at other times on committees, where the real work of every session is done. "As a member of the committee of the Legislature, having in charge the subject of erection of wooden buildings in Boston," says his son, "he seems to have had a correspondence with the late Hon. John Lowell, who took strong ground, before the committee, against the multiplication of buildings of this material, and backed his arguments with some very characteristic statements and observations."* But little is known, however, of his legislative experience, as compared with what we know of his action in other matters. It was not much to his taste, and the greater, therefore, was his merit on the score of assiduous attention to its duties. He never repeated the experiment, finding things more to his taste in other spheres.

Though averse to holding office, Mr. Lawrence was far from being indifferent to public affairs. He felt in them a lively interest, but it was the interest of a patriotic citizen, not that of a politician. The expressions of this interest are very frequent in his letters and memoranda, and are tersely and emphatically worded. Referring, in 1845, to John Lowell, whom he knew intimately, Mr. Lawrence wrote: "The *Boston Rebel* was a true man, such as we need more of in these latter days. The open-mouthed lovers of the *dear people* are self-seekers in most instances. Beware of such." Writing to his son, under date of January 16, 1831, he says:

"Our local affairs are very delightful in this State and city. We have no violent political animosities, and the prosperity of the people is very great. In our city, in particular, the people have not had greater prosperity for the last twenty years. There is a general industry and talent in our population, that is calculated to produce striking results upon their character. In your reflections upon your course, you may settle it as a principle, that no man can attain any valuable influence or character among us, who does not labor with whatever talents he has to increase the

---

* Diary and Correspondence, pp. 77–8.

sum of human improvement and happiness. An idler, who feels that he has no responsibilities, but is contriving to get rid of time without being useful to any one, whatever be his fortune, can find no comfort in staying here. We have not enough such to make up a society. We are literally all working-men; and the attempt to get up a 'Working-men's party' is a libel upon the whole population, as it implies that there are among us large numbers who are not working-men. He is a working-man whose mind is employed, whether in making researches into the meaning of hieroglyphics, or in demonstrating any invention in the arts, just as much as he who cuts down the forests, or holds the plow, or swings the sledge-hammer."*

To a gentleman connected with a leading political journal, who wrote to him in 1848, requesting aid, Mr. Lawrence made the following reply:

"In reply to yours, this moment handed me, I state that my income is so reduced, thus far, this year, that I am compelled to use prudence in the expenditure of money, and must therefore decline making the loan. If my vote would make my brother Vice-President, I would not give it, as I think it lowering his good name to accept office of any sort by employing such means as are now needful to get votes."†

---

* Diary and Correspondence, pp. 103–4.

† This allusion to his brother in connection with the Vice-Presidency may require a few words of explanation. When General Taylor was named for the Presidency, some time previously to his formal nomination at Philadelphia, it was generally supposed that Mr. Abbott Lawrence would be placed in nomination for the Vice-Presidency, on the Taylor ticket; and when another eminent man was nominated, considerable surprise was felt, some of which did not lack adequate expression. Why Mr. Lawrence was not nominated it is not our business to explain; but it would be an interesting subject to political speculators, that of the probable consequences of his succession to the Presidency on the death of General Taylor, in 1850, which would have happened, had he been nominated for the second office. He missed the Presidency by only one step; and in a life that was fortunate beyond that of most men, we hold that this apparent failure was the most fortunate incident. It should be added that Mr.

In one of his letters to President Hopkins, dated June 12th, 1848, alluding to the same subject, he says:

"As to my brother's nomination for Vice-President, I am thankful they did not make it in convention. He is in a higher position before the country than he would be if chosen Vice-President. His course has been elevated and magnanimous in this matter; for he might, by his personal influence and efforts, have received the nomination."

The turn of his mind on politics is well illustrated by a passage in a letter to one of his warmest and worthiest friends, Mr. Jonathan Phillips, written shortly before his death. "About forty years ago," he says to Mr. Phillips, "walking past your father's house, with my wife and some of our family friends, on a bright moonlight night, we were led to discuss the character of the owner (your honored father); some of the party wishing they might possess a small part of the property, which would make them happy—others, something else—when my own wish was expressed. It was, that I might use whatever Providence might allow me to possess, as faithfully as your father used his possessions; and that I should esteem such a reputation as his a better inheritance for my children than the highest political honors the country could bestow."*

Abbott Lawrence received, for the Vice-Presidential nomination, votes enough to secure the position lacking *one*, in the Philadelphia convention. So near was he to securing the highest place to which an American can aspire!

* When President Taylor offered the post of Secretary of the Navy to Mr. Abbott Lawrence, on the organization of the administration in 1849, his brother wrote to him: "I have heard, since noon, that you have the invitation of General Taylor to take a seat in his Cabinet, and that you will proceed to Washington forthwith, to answer for yourself. I am not less gratified by the offer than you can be; but I should feel deep anguish if I thought you could be induced to accept it, even for a brief period. Your name and fame as a private citizen is a better inheritance for your children than any distinction you may attain from official station; and the influence you can exercise for your country and friends, as you are, is higher and better than any you can exercise as an official of the government." Yet he was pleased when his brother was appointed Minister to

It must not be inferred, from these extracts, that Mr. Lawrence was either indifferent to politics, or that he did not have distinct opinions on public matters. He felt no such indifference, and no man ever had clearer political opinions, or was more frank in giving them utterance. In youth he was a federalist, of the school of Washington. In his latter days he was a whig. In 1852, he was a member of the Electoral ticket put in nomination by the whigs of Massachusetts, which was chosen, receiving a plurality of several thousand in the popular vote. The College met at the State House, in Boston, in the month of December; and Mr. Lawrence wrote the following words on his commission of Elector:

"*December* 1.—I have attended to the duty, and have given my vote to Winfield Scott for President, and William A. Graham as Vice-President."

The office of Elector does not rank very high; for, though it is evident that the framers of the Constitution intended that the Electoral Colleges should be important and independent bodies—as independent in the discharge of their duties as are members of the United States Senate—the course of events, and the headlong current of party opinion, have rendered them the mere servants of their nominators. Still, the position of an Elector is an honorable one, and to be placed on an Electoral ticket has ever been considered a mark of high respect. Mr. Lawrence probably was led to make the endorsement on his commission

---

England. When that brother declined a seat in the Cabinet, he wrote to him: "I do most heartily rejoice, and say that I never felt as proud before." In July, he wrote to a friend: "Brother A. has received the place of Minister to the Court of St. James, the most flattering testimony of his worth and character that is within the gift of the present administration, and the only office that I would not advise against his accepting." There was no inconsistency in this, as he made a distinction, as every one knows there is a difference, between a political office and a diplomatic post. The ministry to England is a very agreeable position for any American of high character and ample fortune.

above quoted, by the reflection that he was supporting a fallen cause, and which had all the more claims upon him for the reason that its chosen chiefs had just met with a defeat which has scarcely a parallel in political history. He saw in that defeat an additional reason for bearing testimony, clear and unmistakable, to the worth of that which all men saw was about to pass away.

How firm and decided he was in his opinions, and how energetic in expressing them, appear from various portions of his correspondence. Writing to his son, then at school in France, under the date of March 6, 1830, he thus speaks of an event now belonging to history, and which is becoming shadowy from the lapse of time:

"We are all in New England deeply interested by Mr. Webster's late grand speech in the Senate, vindicating New England men and New England measures from reproach heaped upon them by the South. It was his most powerful effort, and you will see the American papers are full of it. You should read the whole debate between him and Mr. Hayne, of South Carolina: you will find much to instruct and interest you, and much that you ought to know. Mr. Webster never stood so high in this country as at this moment; and I doubt if there be any man, either in Europe or America, his superior. The doctrines upon the Constitution in this speech should be read as a text-book by all our youth."

Mr. Lawrence wrote to Mr. Webster a letter on this occasion, expressing his admiration of the manner in which New England had been vindicated, and also his own personal feelings of gratitude for the proud stand thus taken. To this letter he received the following reply:

"WASHINGTON, March 8, 1830.

"DEAR SIR:—I thank you very sincerely for your very kind and friendly letter. The sacrifices made in being here, and the mortifications sometimes experienced, are amply compensated by the consciousness that my friends at home feel that I have done some little service to our New England. I pray you to remember me with very true regard to Mrs. Lawrence; and believe me,

"Very faithfully and gratefully yours,

"DANIEL WEBSTER.

"To AMOS LAWRENCE, Esq."

It will be interesting at this point to quote what Mr. Lawrence said of Mr. Webster just after the death of that extraordinary man. The passage occurs in a letter to Jonathan Phillips, which is dated October 25, 1852:

"The changing scenes of life sometimes recall with peculiar freshness the events and feelings of years long past; and such is the case with me, growing out of the death of our great New England statesman, who has, for a long period of years, been looked up to as preaching and teaching the highest duties of American citizens with a power rarely equalled, never surpassed. He is now suddenly called to the bar of that Judge who sees not as man sees, and where mercy, not merit, will render the cheering 'Well done' to all who have used their trusts as faithful stewards of their Lord—the richest prize to be thought of. Our great man had great virtues, and doubtless some defects; and I pray God that the former may be written in the hearts of his countrymen, the latter in the sea."

The strength of his political opinions, and the consistency with which he adhered to them, are exhibited in a letter to a friend in South Carolina, written on June 12, 1852. "My nephew by marriage, Franklin Pierce," he says, "seems to be a prominent candidate for the White House for the next four years. He is the soul of honor, and an old-fashioned Democrat, born and bred, and to be depended on as such; but as I am an old-fashioned George Washington, John Jay Federalist, from my earliest days, and hope to continue to be, I shall prefer one of this stamp to him." Four months later, writing to a lady in Florida, he said: "I had a charming ride yesterday with my nephew, Frank Pierce, and told him I thought he must occupy the White House the next term, but that I should go for Scott. Pierce is a fine, spirited fellow, and will do his duty wherever placed. Scott will be my choice for President of the United States."

Mr. Lawrence's sympathies in general politics were large and catholic. He saw with deep interest the movements that were made in other countries for the advancement of liberal ideas and the establishment of free institutions. The French revolution of 1830 excited in his mind the same ardent hopes that burned in so many American bosoms, but which soon became but as ashes; the French, with capacities for every thing else, seeming to be but slow scholars in the art of constitutional government. On the 25th of September he wrote as follows to his son, then in France:

"The events of the late French revolution have reached us up to the 17th August. The consideration of them is animating, and speaks in almost more than human language. We are poor, frail, and mortal beings; but there is something elevating in the thought of a whole people acting as with the mind and the aim of one man—a part which allies man to a higher order of beings. I confess it makes me feel a sort of veneration for them; and trust that no extravagance will occur to mar the glory and the dignity of this enterprise. Our beloved old hero, too, acting as the guiding and the presiding genius of this wonderful event! May God prosper them, and make it to the French people what it is capable of being if they make a right use of it! I hope that you have been careful to see and learn every thing, and that you will preserve the information you obtain in such a form as to recall the events to your mind a long time hence."

The following letter to his old friend, General Whiting, of the United States Army, written toward the close of 1849, shows that he had strong opinions concerning the foulest crime of modern days, and was ever ready to sympathize with, and to aid, those who suffered in the cause of freedom:

"MY EARLY FRIEND:—Forty years and more ago we used to talk over together the dismemberment of Poland and the scenes that followed, and to pour out together our feelings for those martyrs of liberty. At the present moment, my feelings are deeply moved by taking by the hand Colonel P. and Major F., just landed here, and driven from their country, martyrs to the same cause. I need only say to you that they are strangers among us, and any attentions from you will be grateful to them, and duly felt by your old friend, A. L."

The sufferings of the Irish people, from famine, in 1846–7, appealed forcibly to the American people, who did not hesitate how to act. In February, 1847, the citizens of Boston were appealed to in behalf of the Irish, and they responded liberally to that appeal, sending both food and clothing to Ireland. Mr. Lawrence took a deep interest in this benevolent enterprise, and not only gave largely of money in aid of it, but by his personal exertions induced others to forward it. The Mather School, at South Boston, had attached to it a body called the "Lawrence Association," composed of pupils of both sexes, and formed for moral and intellectual improvement. As Mr. Lawrence had from the beginning of this Association's existence exhibited an affectionate interest in its welfare, and given to it books and money, it was named from him. To these pupils Mr. Lawrence wrote, suggesting that the value of the offering to suffering Ireland from Boston would be enhanced by the numbers contributing, as the offering would do more good as an expression of sympathy than as a matter of relief. The letter was accompanied by three purses, containing money, the amount of which had not been ascertained by the donor, and all members of the Association, who would, were to take therefrom "a half-dollar each, and all others a quarter each, for their suffering brethren, and children of a common Father." Mr. Lawrence was not content with suggesting to the children that they should give in aid of human beings who were suffering three thousand miles from them; he afforded them the means of giving, and so set them an example of benevolence and liberality that must have had the happiest effect on their minds. "One hundred and two members of the Association, and four hundred and thirty-eight other members of the school, availed themselves of the privilege thus offered them," says Dr. Lawrence, "and contributed the sum of one hundred and sixty dollars toward the object."

Collections in aid of the same great charity were taken up in the churches of Boston. On a twenty-dollar banknote, which he contributed to the collection that was made at the Brattle-street, where he worshiped, Mr. Lawrence wrote—"A ship of war to carry bread to the hungry and suffering, instead of powder and ball to inflict more suffering on our brethren—children of the same Father—is as it should be; and this is in aid of the plan."

It was characteristic of the man that, only a few days before giving so munificently to help the Irish, he entered the following in his "Diary," under date of February 15th, 1847: "T. J. called, and is to embark to-morrow, on his way to the war in Mexico. He asked me to give him money to buy a pistol, which I declined, as I could not wish them success in Mexico; but gave him some books, a Bible, and good counsel."

On the 26th of April, 1847, he wrote to Sir William Colebrooke, then governor of the British Province of New Brunswick, probably in allusion to the pacific settlement of the Oregon dispute, which had been effected the preceding year,—"What reason have we for devout thanksgiving, that our two countries are not at swords' points, and that the true feeling of our common ancestry is now sweeping over our land! We are in deep disgrace on account of this wicked Mexican business."

Mr. Lawrence was on intimate terms with many gentlemen of the South, who held to very different opinions on the subject of manufactures from those which he entertained. He corresponded freely with them, and, as there were integrity and respect on both sides, the correspondence was such as all might have been proud to see published. He had no desire to see the manufacturers of New England monopolists. He wished that other "sections" of the republic, and particularly the South, should turn their attention to the same industrial modes that were so extensively pursued in Massachusetts and Rhode Island. "During seasons of high political excitement and sectional strife," says his son, "he wrote to various friends at the South, urging them to discard all local prejudices, and to enter with the North into manly competition in all those branches of domestic industry which would tend, not only to enrich, but also to improve the moral and intellectual character of their people." A letter which he wrote to Mr. Robert Barnwell Rhett, on the 12th of December, 1849, may be taken as a good example of the correspondence which he had with southern gentlemen, though the introduction of the slavery question into the politics of the country, and the peculiar aspect which that question was assuming in 1849, had their effect on his mind, as they had on the minds of all reflecting men. Mr. Lawrence held to the common northern opinion on the subject of slavery. Like all northern men whose opinions are of any consequence, he had no desire to interfere with the local institutions of any of the States. He looked upon slavery as a local institution, and as being utterly destitute of even the pretense to nationality in its character. Such being his view of this all-engrossing matter, he would neither have consented to the extension of slavery nor to interference with it in the *States*. He was a conservative in the most comprehensive sense of the word. He was, too, a representative of northern sentiment, as it was, and as it still is, in spite of all the aggravating circumstances that have occurred during the last four years. To a man who knows what northern opinion is, nothing can be clearer than that the great mass of the people of the North have never had the slightest wish to make or to meddle with any of the constitutional privileges of the States of the South. It is because this truth is not understood, or has been designedly and pertinaciously questioned, that great evil has been done, the consequences of which are yet to be fully developed, and which promises to be as incalculable as disastrous. It would be foolish to suppose that disunion is to follow from the bitter disputes that have agitated the republic for many years, and which, unhappily, are far from being exhausted. Our country is destined to endure. It is the work of God and nature, and against such work not even the labors for evil of the ablest and wickedest politicians can be of any avail. The troubles which we experience are such as have beset every nation, but have destroyed none. What right have we to claim exemption from the common lot?

The following is Mr. Lawrence's letter to Mr. Rhett:

"BOSTON, December 12, 1849.

"MY DEAR SIR:—Your letter of November 30th reached me in due course, and gave me unfeigned pleasure in seeing my hopes confirmed that the practical common sense of South Carolina was returning, and that the use of their head and hands was getting to be felt among the citizens as necessary to their salvation as common brethren in the great family of States. Without the use of those trusts placed in their hands by our common Father, the State will not be worth the parchment on which to draw the deeds fifty years hence; and I most earnestly pray God to guide, guard, and save the State from their childishness in their fears that our northern agitators can harm them. I spent the winter of 1819 in Washington, and heard the whole of the debate upon admitting Alabama and Missouri into the Union. Alabama was admitted, Missouri rejected; and I made up my mind then that I would never interfere until requested by my brethren of the slaveholding States, which resolution I have carried out from that day to this, and I still hold to it. But I would not have admitted Alabama then or Missouri, on the terms they were admitted. We of the North have windy, frothy politicians, who hope to make capital out of their ultraism; but, in the aggregate, they soon find their level. Now, of the point to which I desire to come, I do earnestly desire your State to carry out your prophecy, that, in ten years, you will spin all your own crop of cotton—for we of Massachusetts will gladly surrender to you the manufacture of coarse fabrics, and turn our industry to making fine articles. In short, we could now, if you are ready, give up to you the coarse fabrics, and turn one half of our machinery into spinning and weaving cotton hose, and nothing will help us all so much as specific duties. The whole kingdom of Saxony is employed at this moment in making cotton hose for the United States from yarns purchased in England, and made of your cotton. How much better would it be for you and for us to save these treble profits and transport, by making up the cotton at home! Think of these matters, and look at them without the prejudice that prevails so extensively in your State. A few years ago I asked our kinsman, Gen. ——, of your State, how the forty-bale theory was esteemed at that time. His answer was—'We all thought it true when it was started, and it had its effect; but nobody is of that mind now.' Still, I believe, when an error gets strong hold of the popular mind, it is much more difficult to eradicate it than it is to supply the truth in its place. If I know myself, I would not mete to you any different measure from what I would ask of you; and I must say to you, that your State and people have placed themselves in a false position, which will be as apparent to them in a few years as the sun is at noonday.—My own family and friends are in usual health, and no man this side heaven enjoys earth better than I do. I do pray you to come and see us. I hope to see your son at Cambridge this week.

"Most respectfully yours,

"AMOS LAWRENCE."

In a letter to another friend in South Carolina, dated June 12th, 1852, occurs the following passage:

"My connection with the people of your State, growing out of my marriage, has brought me into personal intercourse, for more than thirty years past, with a great family connection, embracing in its circle many of your distinguished characters. All the M. family, of whom your present governor is one, came from the same stock; and the various ramifications of that family at the South include, I suppose, a great many thousand souls. I, therefore, take a lively interest in every thing interesting to your people. We have hot-heads, and so have you; but I think your people misjudge, when they think of setting up an independent government. The peculiar institution which is so dear to them will never be interfered with by sober, honest men; but will never be allowed to be carried where it is not now, under the federal government. Politicians, like horse-jockeys, strive to cover up wind-broken constitutions as though in full health; but hard driving reveals the defect, and within thirty years the old slave States will feel compelled to send their chattels away to save themselves from bankruptcy and starvation. I have never countenanced these abolition movements at the North, and have lately lent a hand to the cause of colonization, which is destined to make a greater change in the condition of the blacks than any event since the Christian era."

The regular course of our narrative has been interrupted, in order to afford to the reader a clear idea of Mr. Lawrence's political opinions. We resume the narrative.

"On the 1st of June, 1831," says the editor of the Diary and Correspondence, "the weather being very warm, Mr. Lawrence, while engaged in the business of his counting-room, drank moderately of cold water, and soon after was seized with a violent and alarming illness. The functions of the stomach seem to have been destroyed, and for many days there remained but small hope of his recovery. Much sympathy was expressed by his friends and the public, and in such a manner as to afford gratification to his family as well as surprise to himself when sufficiently recovered to be informed of it. He had not yet learned the place which he had earned in the estimation of those around him, as a merchant and a citizen, and it was, not improbably, a stimulus to merit, by his future course, the high encomiums which were then lavished upon him."

From this illness Mr. Lawrence cannot be said ever to have recovered, though he had intervals of what might have been called, comparatively speaking, health. He would be confined to his house for months, and one consequence was, that he had to withdraw from active business. At other times he could take much exercise, being partial to horse-riding, which he greatly enjoyed, and from which he derived not a little benefit. But it required only a small matter to prostrate him. He was "servile to all the skyey influences," and a slight cold would paralyze his digestive powers. A little mental anxiety would have the same effect. He would amuse himself sometimes, in his chamber, with mechanical pursuits. In 1837 he writes: "I continue to mend in strength, and feel at times the buoyancy of early days. It is now raining in torrents, keeping us all within-doors. I have been at work with gimlet, saw, fore-plane, and hammer, thus securing a good share of exercise without leaving my chamber." He had to pay the utmost attention to his diet, but seems rather to have enjoyed the system he was forced to adopt and pursue. He did not, for sixteen years, take a meal with his family. His food and drink were of the simplest kinds, and the amount of each was regularly weighed, a balance for that purpose always standing before him upon his writing-table. Writing to President Hopkins, he said: "If your young folks want to know the meaning of epicureanism, tell them to take some bits of coarse bread (one ounce, or a little more), soak them in three gills of coarse meal gruel, and make their dinner of them, and nothing else; beginning very hungry, and leaving off more hungry. The food is delicious, and such as no modern epicureanism can equal." We fancy that few people would be inclined to obtain luxury at the price which Mr. Lawrence paid for it. His was not the new pleasure for which an imperial reward was offered.

His correspondence during this period of his life exhibits a Christian resignation to the evils under which he was suffering, and a warm appreciation of the blessings by which they were balanced. Illness did not harden his heart; it had the effect of causing him to regard all who suffered as his brethren, who had claims upon that wealth which he had amassed through diligence, industry, and intelligence, ever guided by the highest honesty; but which he held had been given to him only in trust by Heaven. He had always been a liberal man, giving freely and giving wisely; but it is from the time that circumstances withdrew him from participation in active business operations, that he became one of the greatest benefactors of his species that the world has ever known. His mind had formed and guided the business of the great house of which he was the head, and the impress of that mind was still upon it long after he had retired. Mr. Abbott Lawrence, who had always been a most efficient member of the firm, now had the principal responsibility of it placed upon him, and proved himself fully equal to the post, and rose to deserved eminence, both in the business world and as a statesman.

Mr. Lawrence's beneficent acts are deserving of elaborate mention. He believed that it was his duty to make use of his wealth and his intellectual powers to promote the welfare of his fellow-creatures. Knowing the value of system and method in all things, he proceeded with as rigid exactness in this pursuit as in all the rest of his actions. He commenced, on the first day of the year 1829, the keeping of an exact account of such expenses as come under the denomination of charities, and appropriations for the benefit of others not of his own household, for many of whom, he said, he felt under the same obligation as for his own family. This account was kept for twenty-four years, and the amounts entered in it will hereafter be stated. It is the noblest record of benevolence that ever was penned, and its writer never thought its contents would be laid before the world. Had he believed so, he would probably have destroyed the record, for he was sensitively alive to the thought that he might be suspected of ostentation in his benevolence, though there never lived a man against whom the charge could have been preferred with less justice. It would have been impossible, however, to hide from the world what he was doing. To do the world justice, it has a ready acknowledgment for excellence, and its most sordid members are quite sincere when they praise the liberality which they can appreciate, though to imitate it is beyond their moral nature. There is no hiding good deeds from the world. As well might it be expected that the beneficent operations of sun and light should be hidden from the gaze of men, and be known only from their effects, as that true charity, when employed on a large scale, should not be known to all.

Mr. Lawrence gave much individually and directly. He was active in ascertaining objects of charity, and equally so in endeavoring to put them in positions that should prevent them from being objects of that kind any longer. He gave away clothing, food, books, and so forth, in great quantities, as well as ready money. "Two rooms in his house," Dr. Lawrence states, "and sometimes three, were used principally for the reception of useful articles for distribution. There, when stormy weather or ill health prevented him from taking his usual drive, he was in the habit of passing hours in selecting and packing up articles which he considered suitable to the wants of those whom he wished to aid." Aided by his coachman, on such days, he would spend the time in selecting, and packing, and tying up into what he called "small haycocks," those articles which he wished to send to the poor. "Most of the packages forwarded contained substantial articles for domestic use, and were often accompanied by a note containing from five to fifty dollars in money." They often consisted of materials adapted to the use of poor students, and were sent to some professor of this or that college, to be appropriated as he might think proper. Others were given to poor ministers, or to widows. Children were not forgotten by him on these occasions, nor on any other, and books and toys, and other things calculated to promote their enjoyment, entered bountifully into his gifts. In making up his packages, he would sometimes work so hard and continuously as seriously to endanger his health.

Books he distributed in whole libraries. It afforded him

great pleasure to give this "food for the mind," in large measure, to individuals who lived in remote places, where it is not easily to be had. Collections of books were sent to many literary institutions. When he drove out, his carriage was well filled with books, which he gave away, sometimes to acquaintances, at others to strangers. He was one of the best patrons of the American Tract Society and the Sunday-school Union, purchasing liberally of their numerous publications, for distribution. "A barrel of books," we are told, "is no uncommon item found in his record of articles, almost daily forwarded to one and another of his distant beneficiaries."

Mr. Lawrence gave abundantly in aid of literature. Among the objects of his bounty in this respect was Williams College. To that excellent institution he gave nearly forty thousand dollars. He paid the sum of two thousand dollars to connect Grotón Academy with the college, establishing four scholarships for students who might come from the former institution. He founded the library of the college, gave to the institution a valuable telescope, bestowed upon it all that it had of works of art at the time of his death, and added to its landed property. He was busily engaged, when he was called away, in raising the sum of fifty thousand dollars for the college. In a sermon commemorative of Mr. Lawrence, preached by President Hopkins, at the request of the students, that learned divine said: "The aid which Mr. Lawrence thus gave to the college was great and indispensable; and probably no memorial of him will be more enduring than what he has done here. By this, being dead, he yet speaks, and will continue to speak in all coming time. From him will flow down enjoyment and instruction to those who shall walk these grounds, and look at the heavens through this telescope, and read the books gathered in this library, and hear instruction from teachers sustained, wholly or in part, by his bounty. Probably he could not have spent this money more usefully; and there is reason to believe that he could have spent it in no way to bring to himself more enjoyment. The prosperity of the college was a source of great gratification to him; and he said, more than once, that he had been many times repaid for what he had done here. That he should have thus done what he did, unsolicited, and that he—and, I may add, his family—should have continued to find in it so much of satisfaction, is most grateful to my own feelings, and must be so to every friend of the college. In doing it, he seemed to place himself in the relation, not so much of a patron of the college, as of a sympathizer and a helper in a great and good work." This eloquent eulogium was richly deserved, and will be sincerely responded to by the reader.

He gave sums of money to Wabash College, to Kenyon College, and to the Theological School at Bangor. Mrs. Lawrence gave six thousand dollars to Bowdoin College from her own resources.

A favorite project with Mr. Lawrence was that of establishing a charitable hospital for children in Boston. Such institutions have been very successful in France, of which he had heard much, though they had never been tried in the United States. He believed, says his son, "that a great benefit would be conferred on the poorer classes by caring for their sick children when their own poverty or occupations prevented their giving them that attention which could be secured in an institution of this kind. The great object was to secure the confidence of that class, and to overcome their repugnance to giving up their children to the care of others." He looked upon it, however, as only an experiment, "but considered the results which might be obtained of sufficient magnitude to warrant the large outlays required. He viewed it not only as a mode of relieving sickness and suffering, but as a means of exercising a humanizing effect upon those who should come directly under its influence, as well as upon that class of persons generally for whose benefit it was designed. His heart was ever open to the cry of suffering, and he was equally ready to relieve it, whether it came from native or foreigner, bond or free."*

Accordingly, in the autumn of 1846, Mr. Lawrence purchased the building which had for a long time been used as the Medical School of Harvard College, and which is on Mason-street, for the purpose of converting it into a Children's Infirmary. But the building was found not well adapted to the purpose, the situation being confined, and also the internal arrangements unsuitable. Mr. Lawrence then offered the house to the Boston Society of Natural History at the cost, subscribing five thousand dollars himself toward making up that sum. The society accepted this munificent proposition, and now own and occupy the building. The Children's Infirmary was opened in a house on Washington-street, which was put in admirable order for the purpose, and provided with physicians and nurses, all at Mr. Lawrence's expense. It was calculated for thirty patients.

"The following spring," Dr. Lawrence tells us, "was marked by a great degree of mortality and suffering among the emigrant passengers, and consequently the beds were soon occupied by whole families of children, who arrived in the greatest state of destitution and misery. Many cases of ship-fever were admitted, so that several of the attendants were attacked by it, and the service became one of considerable danger. Many now living in comfort attribute the preservation of their life to the timely succor then furnished; and had no other benefits followed, the good bestowed during the few weeks of spring would have compensated for the labor and cost." But, though the prejudices

---

* Diary and Correspondence, pp. 230–231.

which originally existed against the Infirmary were removed by the success of its managers, and several hundred persons were restored to health within its walls, it was found impossible to keep it up; and, after existing about a year and a half, it was closed. The cost of its maintenance was not only very great, but the good that followed therefrom was out of proportion to the amount expended; that is to say, "the same amount of money could be made to afford relief to much larger numbers of the same class of sufferers applied in some other way." Such was the conclusion to which Mr. Lawrence, in full view of all the facts, came, and on which his action was based. He had closely observed the Infirmary, visiting it constantly, and making himself familiar with the history of many of its inmates. Had the number of patients been larger, the cost of the Infirmary would not have been increased at the same rate, the undertaking being one of those in which large expenditures are necessary to provide for a few persons, which are not proportionately increased with the increase of inmates. It was found, Dr. Lawrence states, from the limited number of beds, that the cost of each patient was much greater than if four times the number had been provided for. It may be doubted if the institution was one altogether adapted to society as it now is in most parts of the United States, though Mr. Lawrence must be allowed to have acted as wisely as benevolently in trying the experiment, which has unquestionably worked admirably in other parts of the world, where circumstances allow of its being practiced on a very large and comprehensive scale. As social evils develop themselves here, it is not unlikely that we shall see institutions of this kind resorted to as one of many modes of lessening the suffering therefrom.

Mr. Lawrence was fond of circulating books of a moral or religious character, particularly if they united practicalness to theoretical worth. In the summer of 1852 appeared

"Uncle Toby's Stories on Tobacco," which so pleased him that he had several thousand copies of it printed for gratuitous distribution. The chief agents employed in the work of circulating it were the boys of the Mather School. He also had some of the works of the Rev. Dr. Hamilton printed for the same purpose, with good effect.

He often sent money to poor clergymen—men who do much work, but who are generally paid with a grudging hand. On one occasion he canceled a note of five hundred dollars against a clergyman. The instances in which he sent sums of one hundred dollars to such men, and larger ones, were very numerous; and the aggregate amounts thus dispensed must have amounted to many thousands of dollars. This was besides what he sent to them in the shape of goods.

Mr. Lawrence had a very prominent part in those measures which ended in the erection of Bunker Hill Monument. The son of an old soldier of the Revolution, who had distinguished himself in the battle of the 17th of June, 1775, and well acquainted with many others who had fought in it, it was natural that he should desire to see something done to express the public sense of that brilliant action, in which the event of the war was virtually decided. Others probably felt as strongly as he on the subject, but they were not ready to act as liberally. It is not too much to say, that, but for Mr. Lawrence's aid, afforded in various ways, the monument never could have been erected. He was in favor of reserving the whole battle-ground for the public forever—a project worthy of his munificent mind. In 1830, in a letter to his son, written on the anniversary of the battle, he says: "To-day completes fifty-five years since the glorious battle of Bunker Hill, and five years since the nation's guest assisted at the laying of the corner-stone of the monument which is to commemorate to all future times the events which followed that battle. If it should please God to remove me before this structure is completed, I hope to remember it in my will, and that my sons will live to see it finished. But what I deem of more consequence is to retain for posterity the battle-field, now in possession of the Bunker Hill Monument Association. The Association is in debt, and a part of the land may pass out of its possession; but I hope, if it do, there will be spirit enough among individuals to purchase it, and restore it again; for I would rather the whole work should not be resumed for twenty years, than resume it by parting with the land. I name this to you now, that you may have a distinct intimation of my wishes to keep the land open for our children's children to the end of time."

In 1825 Mr. Lawrence was chosen one of the building committee of the board of directors for the construction of the monument, his associates being Dr. John C. Warren, Gen. H. A. S. Dearborn, George Blake, and William Sullivan, all men of ability and distinction, and all now dead. He labored indefatigably in this cause for more than fifteen years, and at last had the happiness of seeing the monument completed, though at times he must almost have despaired of success, so great were the difficulties encountered. At the close of the year 1830 he "made provision by his will, in case of his own death, to secure the battle-field, liquidate the debts of the corporation, and complete the monument." In another will, executed in 1833, he said: "I am of opinion that the land owned by the Bunker Hill Monument Association, in Charlestown, will be of great value to posterity if left as public ground. The spot is the most interesting in the country; and it seems to me it is calculated to impress the feelings of those who come after us with gratitude to the people of this generation, if we preserve it to them. The whole field contains about fifteen acres; and in the hope of preserving it entire, either as the property of the State, of this city, or of any other competent body, and with the further view of insuring the completion of the monument, which now stands as a reproach to us, I have set apart a larger share of my property than would be necessary, had not the subject been presented to the public in such a manner as to discourage future attempts at raising the necessary funds by voluntary contribution."

The sum of fifty thousand dollars was thus devised. Nearly two years before, in the autumn of 1831, Mr. Lawrence wrote to Dr. J. C. Warren, proposing to subscribe five thousand dollars, on condition that fifty thousand dollars should be raised in one year, to complete the monument and retain the battle-field. "I think it inexpedient," he said to Dr. Warren, "to allude to the sale of the land on Bunker Hill, as a resource for paying the debt, except in case of extreme necessity; and, at this time, I should personally sooner vote to sell ten acres of the Common, in front of my house, to pay the city debt (of Boston), than vote to sell the ten acres of Bunker Hill, until it shall appear that our citizens will not contribute the means of saving it." Those only who know the force of a Bostonian's feelings concerning the "Common" can fully understand the extent of Mr. Lawrence's readiness to make any sacrifice rather than see alienated a portion of the first of the Revolution's many battle-fields. In his case, the loss of the "Common" would have been a serious evil indeed, as it lay directly in front of his residence, and abounds with those natural beauties to the influence of which no man was more susceptible.

Nothing came of this offer. It was renewed in 1832, before the annual meeting of the Monument Association. This likewise proved a failure. The next year, he "proposed to the Massachusetts Charitable Mechanic Association to attempt the raising of fifty thousand dollars, to be secured within three months, for completing the monument and preserving the field: accompanying the proposition was an offer of five thousand dollars, or ten per cent. on any less sum that might be raised, as a donation to the Association. A public meeting was held in Faneuil Hall in response to this proposition, at which Hon. Edward Everett made a most powerful appeal, which produced so great an effect upon the auditors, that the object was considered as accomplished. The effort was again unsuccessful."*

Seven years later, in 1839, Mr. Lawrence addressed a letter to Mr. Darracott, president of the Mechanic Association, regretting that the state of his health would not allow of his making personal application to his fellow-citizens, and adding:

"The next best thing I can do is to give money. The Monument Association owes a debt. To discharge the debt, finish the monument, surround it with a handsome iron fence, and otherwise ornament the ground as it deserves, will require forty thousand dollars more than it now has. If the Association will collect thirty thousand dollars the present year, and pay off the debt, I will give to the Charitable Mechanic Association ten thousand dollars to enable it to complete the work in a manner which our fathers would have done, had they been here to direct it."

The consequence of this liberal offer was the completion of the work. Mr. Judah Touro gave ten thousand dollars in aid of it. Five thousand dollars were given by others; and at a Fair which was held in Quincy Hall, Boston, in September, 1840, to obtain funds for the same purpose, the profits were thirty thousand dollars. The monument was soon completed, and the celebration in honor of the event took place on the 17th of June, 1843, on the sixty-eighth anniversary of the battle. The President of the United States was present on the occasion, accompanied by several of the distinguished men who were associated with him in

---

* Diary and Correspondence, p. 172.

the government of the nation. Mr. Webster, who had delivered the oration on the laying of the corner-stone, eighteen years before, was the orator on this last day of the great and long-protracted work.

Mr. Lawrence felt more than ordinary satisfaction at the successful termination of this patriotic undertaking. He well might thus feel, for if he had remained idle it is quite probable that the monument would not have been completed even at this day. We have seen that he had provided for the completion of the work by the terms of his will, executed ten years before the last funds for it had been raised, so that he was satisfied that the monument would one day exist: but this decision he wisely kept a secret within his own bosom, and left it for others to do something in the cause. He labored resolutely, and gave munificently, to promote an object that lay near to his heart. "His only regret," says one of his sons, "was that the whole battle-field could not have been preserved, and have remained, to use his own words, 'a field-preacher to posterity.'" Writing to another son, then in Europe, in 1832, he said,—"If we be true to ourselves, our city is destined to be the Athens of America, and the hallowed spots in our neighborhood to be the objects of interest throughout all future time. In this view I would never permit a foot of the battle-field of Bunker Hill to be alienated; but keep it for your great-great-grandchildren, as a legacy of patriotism worth more than their portion of it, if covered with gold by measure. Until you are older, I do not expect you to feel as I do on this subject."

At a celebration which was held in honor of the completion of the monument, the presiding officer remarked that, "among the benefactors to whom the Association had been particularly indebted for the means of completing the work, two, whose names were written on a scroll at the other end of the hall, were Amos Lawrence and Judah Touro, each of whom made a donation of ten thousand dollars. He thought it proper they should be remembered at the festive board, and gave the following:

"'Amos and Judah—venerated names!
Patriarch and prophet press their equal claims:
Like generous coursers, running neck and neck,
Each aids the work by giving it a check.
Christian and Jew, they carry out a plan—
For though of different faith, each is in heart a man.'"

The aid furnished by the Lawrence family to the Academy in Groton, and in which Amos Lawrence largely participated, is among the most agreeable incidents in their history. This institution was founded in 1792, and so has attained to a respectable age, as age is counted in America. Among the founders was Deacon Samuel Lawrence, who was one of the fifteen original trustees when the Legislature granted an act of incorporation, September 25th, 1793.

From the commencement of its existence this Academy proved eminently serviceable to the cause of education. The Lawrences regarded it with much affection, not only because they had enjoyed its benefits, but because their father had labored hard to establish it.

On the 22d of August, 1838, the trustees of the Groton Academy, at their annual meeting, passed a vote of thanks to Mr. Lawrence for his liberal donation of books and philosophical apparatus. A year later they acknowledged, in a similar manner, the donation from him of a new and valuable telescope, and a copy of Dr. Bowditch's translation of the *Mécanique Céleste* of La Place, in four quarto volumes. In 1842, Mr. Lawrence gave to the trustees of the Academy the sum of two thousand dollars, which they expended in enlarging and improving the building, and on the grounds attached to it. He sent to the principal of the Academy, for its use, in 1845, a box of books, containing one hundred and sixty volumes, and subsequently a magnificent copy of the account of Captain Wilkes's Exploring Expedition, in five volumes, with an atlas. He also gave, the same year, two eight-day clocks, one for the upper and the other for the lower room of the Academy. In July, 1846, he purchased the Brazer estate, which adjoins the Academy grounds, paying therefor the sum of $4400, and conveyed it by deed to the trustees of the Academy. "Born and educated in Groton," says the deed of conveyance, "deeply interested in the welfare of that town, and especially of the Lawrence Academy established in it by my honored father and his worthy associates, and grateful for the benefits which his and their descendants have derived from that institution, I am anxious to promote its future prosperity, trusting that those charged with the care and superintendence of it will ever strive zealously and faithfully to maintain it as a nursery of piety and sound learning. Therefore, know ye, that the said Amos Lawrence, in consideration of the premises, and of one dollar," &c. Mr. Lawrence requested the trustees to have all the buildings and fences on the estate completely repaired. This was done, at a cost of upward of twelve hundred dollars, so that the whole value of this donation exceeded five thousand six hundred dollars.

Mr. Lawrence founded several free scholarships in the Academy. In his donation-book, and under date of August 20th, 1847, was found the following: "I have felt a deep interest in Groton Academy for a long time, and while brother L. was living, and its president, he had it in charge to do what should be best to secure its greatest usefulness, and while perfecting these plans, he was suddenly taken from the world. Since then, I have kept on doing for it, which makes my outlay for the school about twenty thousand dollars. I had prepared ten thousand more, which brother William assumed, and has taken the school upon himself, to give it such facilities as will make it a very desirable place for young men to enter to get a good preparation for business or college life."

It would be unjust not to mention the extraordinary liberality of Mr. William Lawrence toward the Academy. On the 6th of April, 1844, that gentleman addressed a letter to the trustees, announcing that, from a deep interest in the prosperity of the Academy, he had given it the sum of ten thousand dollars. The following passage in his letter shows the nature of the endowment, and the objects which the giver had in view. After expressing his especial desire that such compensation should be paid to the instructors of the Academy as should constantly secure for it the services of learned persons perfectly competent to all their duties, he said:

"And this gift is, therefore, upon condition, that the present rate of charge for instruction in said Academy shall not be reduced. But whenever, hereafter, in any year, the whole net income of the present funds and property of said institution, and of the fees received for instruction, added to the net income of said ten thousand dollars, shall be more than sufficient for the payment of liberal salaries to such instructors, so that a balance of said income shall remain unexpended, I request the said trustees, in their discretion, and if they deem it expedient, to pay and distribute such balance, or any of it, to and among such deserving male pupils in such institution, preparing for a collegiate education, as the trustees may think deserving of such aid; but not more than one hundred dollars shall be paid or allowed to any one such pupil in any one year. And in granting such aid, I earnestly request that no regard may be had to any sectarian views entertained by the pupils, on the subject of the Christian religion."

These conditions indicate an enlarged mind, and do honor to the benevolent giver, who was above all small considerations in the ordering of his benefactions. Not satisfied, however, with what he had already done for the Academy, he bestowed upon it the further sum of five thousand dollars, in August, 1846, to be appropriated to various useful purposes. When Mr. William Lawrence died, in 1848, it was found that he had bequeathed to the Academy the sum of twenty thousand dollars. The Academy now has, in the hands of the trustees, more than forty thousand dollars provided by Mr. William Lawrence, for purposes of instruction.

The name of the institution was changed from the Groton Academy to "The Lawrence Academy of Groton," in 1846, leave so to do having been granted by the Legislature of Massachusetts.

A rich man, who is known to give away large sums of money annually, occupies a very unpleasant position, in any community, on some accounts. All wealthy men are in the daily receipt of letters for aid, and are frequently honored with "calls" from persons who would fain be objects of their benevolence; but if, to the known fact of a man's large wealth, there be added a high character for liberality, his situation is likely to become in every way one of a peculiarly disagreeable nature. He is expected to help all who are, or who may suppose that they are, in need of assistance. Some ask him for gifts; others, with more modesty, hint only at loans; and the founders of associations for various objects demand endowments. Young men, who desire "an education," and old men, who have found "education" vanity, are alike ready to afford the benevolent rich man chances for the permanent investment of his surplus capital. Widows, who never knew peace until their "deprivation," are ready to found upon that "deprivation" claims to his assistance. Schemers and inventors pester him with accounts of their doings, solemnly declaring that they "need only a little money" (his money!) to perfect something that shall go far to banish misery from the world. Pious men, who believe that their "mission" is to convert the heathen of the Moluccas or the Lacadives, are forward as sinners in their entreaties for money, and occasionally will say something about Dives and Lazarus if a blank check is not given them on the instant, the filling up to be left to their own indiscretion. Many a rich man, when thus beset, though conscious that he has done all that could even unreasonably have been expected of him in the way of assisting his fellows, has fervently wished for poverty, and has waked with a sigh from a dream in which he has figured in a destitute condition.

One of the evils that follows from this state of things is the difficulty that exists in discriminating between persons who deserve assistance and those who are impostors, mere "sturdy beggars," desirous of living easily at the expense of others. It requires more than mortal intelligence thus to discriminate, so as never to fall into error, never to refuse the meritorious, and always to turn away from the undeserving. Even an approach to such discrimination implies an amount of care, and a keenness of observation, that would soon make many fortunes in business. It is not money alone that the liberal and rich man gives: he gives also time, attention, and labor to the business of advancing the interests of others; and if he did not give them, all his money benefactions would most probably be bestowed in vain.

Mr. Lawrence had his full share of these applications for aid from strangers, of whose claims he must have had more than mere human powers to have been able to form any thing like a correct judgment. The very fact that he gave away forty or fifty thousand dollars every year was enough to make him the subject of applications—compliance with which in all cases would have exhausted his entire fortune in a very short time. Many of the applicants probably never thought that there were others besides themselves who were asking pecuniary favors of him, and so took refusals unkindly, though they would have been puzzled to say on what their own "claims" were founded, had the question been fairly put to them. What Mr. Lawrence himself thought on the subject will appear from the following extract from his "Diary," bearing date April 11, 1849:

"A subscription paper, with an introductory letter from ——, was handed me, on which were seven or eight names for a hundred dollars each, to aid the family of ——, lately deceased. Not having any acquaintance with him or family, I did not subscribe. Applications come in from all quarters, for all objects. The reputation of giving freely is a very bad reputation, so far as my personal comfort is concerned."*

There is some humor, and a great deal of truth—indeed, it is all truth, and truth in "utter nakedness"—in the last sentence. The following extract from the "Diary," dated April 10, 1850, shows the peculiar nature of the annoyances to which he was not unfrequently subjected:

"Mrs. T. called to ask aid for a poor widow, which I declined, by telling her I did not hear or read people's stories from necessity, and I could not inquire this evening. She claims to be acquainted with Rev. Mr. ——, and Rev. Mr. ——. She gave me a severe lecture, and berated me soundly."

This good lady probably lost her temper, and her recollection of the common forms of politeness, through excess of zeal; but there is something whimsical in the thought of her taking Mr. Lawrence to task, and berating him soundly, because he would not look at once into the "claims" of her *protégée*. She seems to have thought that he was a second Providence, and bound to aid all who were in distress. Few men, it is certain, ever did more—it may be doubted, the amount of his fortune considered, if any other man ever

---

* Diary and Correspondence, p. 267.

did as much—toward affording substantial relief to the poor; but there are limits to human means, and in order that a man may at times give, it is necessary that he should sometimes refuse to comply with the demands—for such in fact they are—that are made upon his purse. Many men of liberal dispositions have been prevented from giving freely and systematically because they have learned from the experience of others how hard it is to satisfy even the tithe of human expectations. As to giving in secret, the thing is utterly impossible anywhere. If large sums are given, the world knows it through the noisy gratitude of the receivers; if small ones, through their not less noisy grumblings, which, like the hisses of an angry spectator of some dramatic entertainment, are sure to be heard through the echoes of the loudest popular applause.

Another extract from his "Diary," on this subject, is proper to be made, on various accounts, which will suggest themselves to the reader. The date is August 23, 1848:

"T. G. sent me a paper this morning, having many names on it, with a polite note. The paper I returned without reading; telling him I did not read such, or hear stories, and must be excused. He took the answer in high dudgeon, and sent another note, saying he had mistaken me, and desired that his first note should be returned. I wrote upon it that I lived by the day and hour, an invalid, and for two years had adopted this course, and had treated bishops, clergymen, and laymen with the fewest words; that I intended no disrespect, and begged his pardon if I had done any thing wrong. I also told him this course was urged upon me by my medical adviser; but, with all my care, there is now an average of six applications a day through the year." This would make two thousand one hundred and ninety annual applications!

On the 29th of August, 1846, Mr. Lawrence made the following entry in his "Diary:"

"A woman writes a figuring letter, calling herself S. M.; says she is sixty years old; has lost her sons, and wants help; came from New Hampshire. Also N. T. wants aid to study, or something else. Also, a Mr. F., with a great share of hair on his face, gold ring and chains, wants to travel for his health; has a wife and child. These three cases within twenty-four hours are very forbidding."

Lawyers are often excused for holding low opinions of men because they see mostly only the baser phases of human nature; but the rich man, with a reputation for open-handedness, sees quite as much as the lawyer of the infirmities of humanity. What spectacle could be more calculated to create disgust than that of a whiskered, ringed, and chained beggar? Lazarus sick and in rags is an object that might melt the hardest heart; but Lazarus in purple and fine linen, begging for money, in order that he may make the grand tour, and fare sumptuously every day, is a sight that would justify the conversion of even the good Samaritan's heart into something hard as the nether millstone.

It was a source of serious annoyance to Mr. Lawrence that his name was so frequently to be found in the public journals, in connection with benevolent acts of his doing, but of which he had no wish that any mention should be made. Writing to Mr. Parker, principal of the Johnson School for Girls, in 1846, he says:

"I hope to send a few volumes to help forward the young guides of the mind and heart of the sons of New England, wherever they may be—for it is the mothers who act upon their sons more than all others. I hope to be felt as long as I am able to work, and am quite as vain as I ought to be of my name and fame, but am really afraid I shall wear out my welcome if my little paragraphs are printed so frequently in the newspapers. I gave some books last Monday, and saw them acknowledged yesterday in the newspaper, and since have received the letter from the children. Now, my dear sir, I merely want to say, that I hope you will not put me in the newspaper at present; and, when my work is done here, if you have any thing to say about me that will not hurt my children and grandchildren, *say on.*"

Shortly after the above was written, a letter was sent to him by the parties to whom the books mentioned had been given, asking if he could suggest the name of some benevolent individual to whom they could apply for further aid. "In reply to yours of to-day," he answered, "I know of no one; but must request that my name be not thrust forward, as though I was to be a byword for my vanity. I want to do good, but am sorry to be published, as in the recent case."*

It may be proper to mention here that Mr. Lawrence made at least ten persons Life Directors of the American Bible Society, by the payment of one hundred and fifty dollars each. His reverence for the Bible was deep and unaffected. "The Bible," he said, "is our great charter, and does more than all others, written or unwritten." "What should we do," he asks, in a letter to President Hopkins, "if the Bible were not the foundation of our system of self-government? and what will become of us, when we wilfully and wickedly cast it behind us? We have all more than common reason to pray, in the depths of our sins—God be merciful to us, sinners. The efforts made to lessen respect for it and confidence in it, will bring to its rescue multitudes who otherwise would not have learned how much they owe it."

The whole amount of money given away by Mr. Lawrence for charitable purposes, during the last twenty-four years of his life—from the close of 1828 to the close of 1852—was six hundred and thirty-nine thousand dollars.† This

* Diary and Correspondence, pp. 229, 230.

† Mr. Lawrence made the following entry in his Diary, under the date of January 1, 1852, after remarking that the value of his property was somewhat

statement rests on the most positive evidence. Nearly five-sixths of the amount were given during the last eleven years of his life. From 1842 to 1853 he gave five hundred and twenty-five thousand dollars for such purposes. The preceding thirteen years, from 1828 to 1842, he expended in this way one hundred and fourteen thousand dollars. It is but reasonable to suppose that during the twenty-two years that elapsed between the date of his commencing business in Boston and the close of 1829, the amount of his benefactions was more than the sum necessary to make seven hundred thousand dollars. Were it possible to get at all the facts, it would probably be found that the amount was much larger than has ever been named. But taking it at the sum mentioned, and considering the amount of his fortune, it may be doubted if any thing like equal benevolence can be quoted from the history of men. It is to be recollected, too, that much of the money that he gave for the promotion of benevolent objects was so given as annually to produce good fruits. It was not so bestowed as to be consumed at once, but in a manner that should cause excellent results to flow from excellent deeds for ages. For generations to come, learning will be advanced, pain will be removed, and morality and religion inculcated, because one good man saw fit to lay up treasure where it is beyond the reach of moth and rust. Like the endowments that were made so long ago in the old world, and the value of which have been immensely increased, Mr. Lawrence's donations to colleges and other institutions will exist, and continue to accomplish the ends he had in view in making

greater than it had been a year before, and praying that he might be faithful in the use of it: "The outgoes for all objects since January 1, 1842 (ten years), have been six hundred and four thousand dollars, more than five-sixths of which have been applied in making other people happy, and it is no trouble to find objects for all I have to spare." This shows that he expended more than half a million of dollars in ten years for benevolent purposes, his average income being but little over sixty thousand dollars a year.

them, when all that appertains to the present time shall be almost as dim and shadowy to the men who shall then live as to us is the ordinary life of our English ancestors of the days of the Plantagenets. The mere giving of alms for the relief of present distress, though much to be commended, is but a secondary form of benevolence, and will bear no comparison with that form of it which looks to the future, and which aims permanently to affect the condition of mankind. How far it is given to the race to remove those social evils the existence of which are stumbling-blocks alike to the foolish and the wise, it is impossible to say; but we may assume that if they are ever to be essentially lessened—if they do not form a necessary part of our mortal state—it must be, to no light extent, the consequence of benevolence in individuals, who shall, by their gifts and their labors, aid to place within the reach of all the blessings of education and the means of fighting manfully the great battle of life. Many such persons the world has known, and among their number no one has a higher rank or a purer fame than Amos Lawrence, as the history of his life clearly shows. No man will have a loftier fame, when the world shall have commenced making its judgments in accordance with the principles of strict justice, and shall cease to allow its mental vision to be dazzled by the glare of the fires of strife. Full justice to him, and to men like him, will be done in after days, when "the dead grow visible from the shades of time."

In the year 1847 Mr. Abbott Lawrence gave fifty thousand dollars to Harvard College, to found the Scientific School to which was afterward given his name. This act of wise liberality, and one of proportions so noble, was well calculated to make a strong impression on the mind of the giver's brother, which ever responded to deeds having their origin in enlightened benevolence. The following letter will show how deeply his feelings were moved on this interesting occasion:

"Wednesday Morning, June 9, 1847.

"Dear Brother Abbott:—I hardly dare trust myself to speak what I feel, and therefore write a word to say that I thank God I am spared to this day to see accomplished by one so near and dear to me, this last best work ever done by one of our name, which will prove a better title to true nobility than any from the potentates of the world. It is more honorable, and more to be coveted, than the highest political station in our country, purchased as these stations often are by time-serving. It is to impress on unborn millions the great truth that our talents are trusts committed to us for use, and to be accounted for when the Master calls. This magnificent plan is the great thing that you will see carried out, if your life is spared; and you may well cherish it as the thing nearest your heart. It enriches your descendants in a way that mere money never can do, and is a better investment than any you have ever made.

"Your affectionate brother,

"Amos.

"To Abbott Lawrence."

"This noble plan," he says to a friend, in one of his letters, "is worthy of him; and I can say truly to you, that I feel enlarged by his doing it. Instead of our sons going to France and other foreign lands for instruction, here will be a place, second to no other on earth, for such teaching as our country stands now in absolute need of. Here, at this moment, it is not in the power of the great railroad companies to secure a competent engineer to carry forward their work, so much are the services of such men in demand."*

In the year 1839 Mr. Lawrence had the misfortune to lose his eldest brother very suddenly. Mr. Luther Lawrence, after studying at Harvard College, had selected the law for

* Diary and Correspondence, pp. 244–5.

his profession, and had settled at Groton, which town he represented for twelve years in the Massachusetts Legislature. He was chosen Speaker of the House of Representatives for the session of 1821–22. In 1831 he was induced to remove to Lowell, by the representations of his brothers, and to assume the presidency of a bank which had just been established there. He was elected mayor of Lowell in 1838. On the 17th of April, 1839, "he accompanied an old friend and connection, who was on a visit at Lowell, to inspect the works of the Middlesex Manufacturing Company, recently erected by his brothers. In passing rapidly through one of the rooms, he made a misstep, and was precipitated many feet into a wheel-pit, causing almost instant death." Mr. Lawrence felt this misfortune deeply, though he summoned religion to his aid, and not in vain. In a letter to his sisters he wrote: "Brother L.'s death may, perhaps, be more efficient in instructing us in the path of duty than would have been his life; and the whole community around is admonished by this event in a way that I have rarely seen so marked. The homage to his character is a legacy to his children of more value than all the gold of the mint. Shall we, then, repine at his separation from us? Surely not. He has fulfilled his mission, and is taken home, with all his powers fresh and perfect, and with the character of having used those powers for the best and highest good of all around him. We shall all soon be called away, and should make his departure the signal to be also ready."

In 1844, his daughter, Mrs. Susan Mason, died; and a year later, his youngest son, Robert, a young man of excellent character and much promise, fell a victim to con sumption. In 1847, one of his nephews, Mr. William L. Green, who had just entered upon mercantile life, with talents and knowledge that indicated success as sure to be his, died very suddenly. He lost his brother William in

1848. If it be true, as Bacon says it is, that a man dies as often as he loses a friend, how much must the bitterness of death be increased on every occasion when he loses one who has been far more than a friend to him! It was Mr. Lawrence's fortune to experience a full share of those deaths which men die when others depart.

The opinions of Mr. Lawrence on various subjects show that he was a wise and liberal-minded man, capable of rising above the prejudices of position, and that he thought for himself. The following extract from a letter to one of his sons, then abroad, and written nearly thirty years since, when opinion was not so liberal in New England as it now is, affords a pleasing example of the direction of his mind to liberality of sentiment in religious matters:

"I suppose Christmas is observed with great pomp in France. It is a day which our Puritan forefathers, in their separation from the Church of England, endeavored to blot out from the days of religious festivals; and this because it was observed with so much pomp by the Romish Church. In this, as well as in many other things, they were as unreasonable as though they had said they would not eat bread because the Roman Catholics do. I hope and trust the time is not far distant when Christmas will be observed by the descendants of the Puritans with all suitable respect, as the first and highest holiday of Christians; combining all the feelings and views of New England Thanksgiving with all the other feelings appropriate to it."

The advice which he gave to his sons, and to other young persons, might, we think, be published by itself, for the general good of youth. His letters of this kind frequently remind us, though as much by contrast as by comparison, of the famous "Advices to his Son," by Lord Burleigh. There are wisdom, shrewdness, and terse writing in the one case as in the other; but in liberality, kindliness of heart, and Christian spirit, the American merchant towers above the great English statesman, to whom both Britain and the United States, and the enjoyers of constitutional liberty everywhere, owe so large a debt. The difference, perhaps, is only one of time—the difference that there is between the sixteenth century and the nineteenth century. The following, from a letter to one of his sons, then in Europe, was written by Mr. Lawrence in 1829:

"Bring home no foreign fancies which are inapplicable to our state of society. It is very common for our young men to come home and appear quite ridiculous in attempting to introduce their foreign fashions. It should be always kept in mind that the state of society is widely different here from that in Europe; and our comfort and character require it should long remain so. Those who strive to introduce many of the European habits and fashions, by displacing our own, do a serious injury to the republic, and deserve censure. An idle person, with good powers of mind, becomes torpid and inactive after a few years of indulgence, and is incapable of making any high effort. Highly important it is, then, to avoid this enemy of mental and moral improvement. I have no wish that you pursue trade; I would rather see you on a farm, or studying any profession.

"It should always be your aim so to conduct yourself that those whom you value most in the world would approve your conduct, if your actions were laid bare to their inspection; and thus you will be pretty sure that He who sees the motive of all our actions will accept the good designed, though it fall short in its accomplishment. You are young, and are placed in a situation of great peril, and are, perhaps, sometimes tempted to do things which you would not do if you knew yourself under the eye of your guardian. The blandishments of a beautiful city may lead you to forget that you are always surrounded, supported, and seen by that best Guardian."

The circumstances of position and early education made Mr. Lawrence a merchant, and caused him to be so prominently connected with business for more than forty-four years, the half of which he was one of the most active of men in the leading pursuits of commerce and manufactures. But the native powers of his mind were such that he must have risen to eminence had he adopted some other calling in early life, and adhered to it. Clearness of mental vision and force of character were his leading traits; and these, joined to industry, are sure to command success in any pursuit. He would have excelled as a writer, as his letters show. He had much interest in literature, and was familiar with the works of the best authors. That he was conscious of the deficiencies in one department of letters, is strikingly proved by what he wrote to Mr. Haddock, in 1851, when that distinguished gentleman was Minister of the United States to Portugal. "Your letters to me before leaving the country, and after reaching England," he wrote, "awakened many tender remembrances of times past, and agreeable hopes of time to come. In that, I felt as though I had you by the hand, with that encouraging 'Go forward' in the fear of God, and confidence in his fatherly care and guidance. I know your views have always put this trust at the head of practical duties, and that you will go forward in your present duties, and do better service to the country than any man who could be sent. Portugal is a sealed book, in a great degree, to us. Who so able to unlock and lay open its history as yourself? Now, then, what leisure you have may be most profitably applied to the spreading out the treasures before us; and, my word for it, your reputation as a writer and a thinker will make whatever you may publish of this sort desirable to be read by the great mass of our reading population." This is the suggestion of a well-read man—of a man who has studied history so accurately as to know in what respects it is imperfect.

Portugal *is* a sealed book to the millions who read even the most prominent of the modern languages; and the literature of our language can boast of no work from which a clear and accurate account of Portuguese history can be obtained. Yet that history is singularly rich in things that men delight to read of, and knowledge of which is useful to all. It is reasonable to suppose that Mr. Lawrence, when he wrote to Mr. Haddock, was thinking of the great part which Portugal, four hundred years ago, took in the mighty work of maritime enterprise and discovery, in which she preceded all other nations; and of the patron of her deeds, the enlightened and benevolent Prince Henry. As a merchant, and as a man curious in all that related to those doings that were calculated to have an effect on the condition of great masses of men, the subject was one very likely to be uppermost in his thoughts when writing of the history of a country in which it is the most remarkable chapter. It is to be hoped that his happy suggestion will yet bear fruit, and that his name may be imperishably associated with a work the writing of which was one of the favorite projects of the learned and industrious Southey, but which circumstances prevented him from ever accomplishing. It would be a felicitous combination of circumstances that should enable the world to trace the existence of a good English history of Portugal—a country so prominent in the annals of commerce—to the suggestion of one of the most eminent of American merchants. Several of our distinguished scholars have done much to liquidate the debt that we owe to Spain for the part which she took in the discovery of our continent; and not only was the enterprise of Columbus one of the consequences of what Portugal had effected by her long and steadily-continued course of maritime action, but a Portuguese admiral would have discovered the American continent, and have made its existence known to the world within eight years after the date of the success of the great Italian in revealing the mighty mystery of the ocean-sea, had that Italian never been born, or had he always failed to interest monarchs in his vast conceptions.

Among the subjects which Mr. Lawrence deemed worthy of grave treatment, though most people are inclined to smile when it is mentioned, is that of the existence of the sea-serpent. For years this marine monster has been more or less talked of; and it is a standing jest against New England that he is much more talked of than seen. He occupies, with reference to the animal world, some such position as the Island of St. Brandon occupies in geography—that mysterious island, of which Irving has written so eloquently, and the fairy mountains of which the people of the Canaries fancied they saw rising above the distant horizon of the Atlantic. It is certainly unfair on the part of the disbelievers to treat the existence of the sea-serpent as if there were no arguments to be adduced on the other side, and as if ridicule were the only weapon proper for their use. Why should it be held impossible that there is such an animal in the ocean, when the remains of monstrous animals are often found on land, fragments of a long-perished world? May there not be one survivor of that world in the waste of waters—one whose life has been continued down to our time, and the contemporary of those huge creatures which roamed over the earth long ere man was? In alluding to the state of feeling that prevailed in the Shetland Islands in the last century, Sir Walter Scott mentions that "the kraken, the hugest of living things, was still supposed to cumber the recesses of the Northern Ocean;" and the Shetlanders also had a firm belief in the sea-snake, which had a mane like that of the war-horse, and broad, glittering eyes. Sir Walter, writing in 1831, mentions that, a few years before, there was seen in the Bay of Scalloway an object so much resembling the kraken in common opinion, that the hardy boatmen shuddered to approach it, for fear of being drawn down by the suction supposed to attend its sinking. Yet these men were among the most adventurous and daring of mariners, accustomed to the *haaf*-fishing, and to furnish large numbers of the crews of the British whalers that visited the Northern Seas. The same distinguished writer says that he "heard a mariner of some reputation in his class, vouch for having seen the celebrated sea-serpent. It appeared, as far as could be guessed, to be about a hundred feet long, with the wild mane and fiery eyes which old writers ascribe to the monster." These facts show that those who talk of the belief in the sea-serpent being confined to New England are altogether in the wrong. The belief is a common one, as we could show, were it necessary, by quotations from many writers of established reputation. It is the quality of ignorance to be positive, and those who are most positive that the sea-serpent never existed are those least entitled to have opinions on scientific subjects.

Writing to one of his sons, in 1830, Mr. Lawrence said: "Our old neighbor, the sea-serpent, was more than usually accommodating the day after we left Portsmouth. He exhibited himself to a great number of people who were at Hampton Beach last Saturday. They had a full view of his snakeship from the shore. He was so civil as to raise his head about four feet, and look into a boat, where were three men, who thought it the wisest way to retreat to their cabin. His length is supposed to be about one hundred feet, his head the size of a ten-gallon cask, and his body, in the largest part, about the size of a barrel. I have never had any more doubt respecting the existence of this animal, since he was seen here eleven years ago, than I have had of the existence of Bonaparte. The evidence was as strong to my mind of the one as of the other. I had never seen either; but I was as well satisfied of the existence of both as I should have been had I seen both. And yet the idea of the sea-serpent's existence has been scouted and ridiculed."*

In 1849 he reiterated these sentiments, giving some of the reasons upon which his belief was founded:

"I have never had any doubt of the existence of the *sea-serpent* since the morning he was seen off Nahant by Martial Prince, through his famous mast-head spy-glass; for, within the next two hours, I conversed with Mr. Samuel Cabot, and Mr. Daniel P. Parker, I think, and one or more persons besides, who had spent a part of that morning in witnessing his movements. In addition, Colonel Harris, the commander of Fort Independence, told me that the creature had been seen by a number of his soldiers while standing sentry in the early dawn, some time before this show at Nahant; and Colonel Harris believed it as firmly as though the creature were drawn up before us in State-street, where we then were. I again say, I have never, from that day to this, had a doubt of the *sea-serpent's existence.* The revival of the stories will bring out many facts that will place the matter before our people in such a light as will make them *as much ashamed* to doubt as *they formerly* were to believe in its existence."†

In order to aid toward the removal of those prejudices which exist against dissection, Mr. Lawrence at one time had serious thoughts of imitating the example of Bentham, and leaving his body to the surgeons. This was one of the very few occasions on which he was emphatically wrong. The remains of every man belong to his friends—to those who loved him in life, and who feel a profound, though melancholy, satisfaction in doing the last honors to that which was the tenement of the soul, and the abode of the mind. The idea of rest which is associated with the grave,

---

* Diary and Correspondence, pp. 100–1.　　† *Ib.*, pp. 268–9.

and that goes far to counteract the terrors which false modes of education have connected with it, ought not to be disturbed by the thought that those whom we have loved in life have been mangled in death. We grant that there must be "subjects," and that surgical education must always be very imperfect where they are not to be had; but the matter is one that does not admit of reasoning. The logic of the heart is alone applicable to it, and that is worth all that the head can do to the end of time. Even those very men who have bequeathed their own bodies to the dissecting-table, have never thought of thus disposing of their dead children.

Mr. Lawrence took no little interest in the subject of Prison Discipline, and mentions, in his writings, in affectionate terms, the late Mr. Louis Dwight, who, for so many years, efficiently acted as Secretary of the Massachusetts Prison Discipline Society.

Among the persons whom he aided with money was Mrs. Martha Gray, widow of Captain Robert Gray, who discovered, and first entered, Columbia River, which he named. Mr. Lawrence accompanied his gift with the following note: "As a token of respect to the widow of one whose name and fame make a part of the property of every American who has a true heart, will Mrs. Gray accept the accompanying trifle from one who, though personally unknown, felt her memorial to Congress through every nerve, and will hope to be allowed the pleasure of paying his respects in person when his health permits?" There was something peculiarly appropriate in the most liberal of Boston merchants affording aid to the most adventurous of the early mariners of that town. Captain Gray has become an historical character, and, considering the position which he has in our naval and commercial annals, no man's family is better entitled to the consideration of the government, or of the munificent among the country's merchants.

Mercenary marriages, which are now becoming so common in the United States, he looked upon with abhorrence. "It used to be said," he writes, in one of his letters from Washington, "that Washington and the Springs were the places for matrimonial speculations. I feel a natural dislike to a lady being brought out as an extraordinary affair, having all perfections, and having refused *forty-nine* offers, and still being on the carpet. It shows that she is either very silly herself, or has very silly friends, or both. Good strong common sense is worth more than forty-nine offers, with any quantity of slaves, or bank-notes, or lands, without it." No man had a higher respect for woman, and it moved his indignation to see any one of the sex bearing herself in such a manner as to reflect disgrace upon it. His mind was essentially chivalrous, using the word in its best sense, and as indicating a quality that had no existence in the "age of chivalry," and which it was impossible should then have existed.

"The decline of life," says a thoughtful writer, "is a sort of Calabrian soil, ashy as well as tremulous."* Much, we presume, depends upon the character of a man's past life, as to his state of mind in old age. The person who can look back upon his career with the well-founded conviction that he has not neglected his duties, and that he has used properly the talents given him by God for the improvement of man's estate, should be as happy in the last days of existence as he was in the noon of his life. An eminent philosopher has said, he admits with reluctance, that "two causes—the abbreviation of time, and the failure of hope—will always tinge with a browner shade the evening of life." The philosopher had no hopes or expectations that were not bounded by this "visible world of dust," so that his opinion can not be of much account with those who believe in a life beyond the grave, to which our mortal life is but

* Joseph Downes, in the preface to *The Mountain Decameron.*

a preparatory stage. It is certain that all men admit that youth disappointed them, and that manhood was vanity. May we not infer that, as we do not find in early or middle life all the good that we anticipated, we shall be agreeably disappointed as to old age? May we not find in it sources of comfort, of happiness which we had not looked for? Mr. Lawrence's latter days favor this view of the subject. In spite of his sufferings from illness—illness long continued, and of a nature singularly calculated to irritate the mind and to unsettle the temper—in spite of the loss of relatives and friends, he preserved a happy state of mind, and his last days were not less agreeable than those of his youth and early manhood had been active and successful. He found in the discharge of his duties the best solace of his cares, and consolation for his deprivations. Sorrow, which is said to hold the key to our mortal life, had unfolded treasures to him that he might never have known had his career been one of unmixed prosperity. Virtue, we are assured, "is like precious odors, most fragrant when they are incensed or crushed; for prosperity doth best discover vice, but adversity doth best discover virtue." This was the case with Mr. Lawrence, the most actively benevolent portion of whose life was that which followed the permanent loss of his health—a loss that often sours the temper and hardens the heart.

The life of Mr. Lawrence was now drawing rapidly to a close. His death was sudden, though he had so long been a sufferer, and for many years had abandoned all idea of a restoration to health. On the 1st of January, 1852, he wrote in his "Diary,"—"My life seems now more likely to be spared for a longer season than for many years past; and I never enjoyed myself more highly." He was very active in 1852, as if he believed he was under increased obligations to labor for the benefit of others as his bodily state apparently improved. Yet how complete an invalid he was at that time, and at an age when many men are in the enjoyment of even robust health, will appear from what he wrote to a friend, respecting his system of diet. "My own wants," he says, "are next to nothing, as I live on the most simple food,—crusts and coffee for breakfast; crusts and champagne for dinner, with never more than three ounces of chicken, or two ounces of tender beef, without any vegetable, together eight ounces; coarse wheat-meal crusts, and two or three ounces of meat, in the twenty-four hours,—beginning hungry, and leaving off more hungry. I have not sat at table with my family for fifteen years, nor eaten a full meal during that time, and am now more hale and hearty than during that whole period." This was written a few months before he was to see "the last of earth."

His correspondence in 1852, was large. Some of his most spirited letters were written in the course of that year. Among his correspondents were President Hopkins, Dr. Lowell, Mayor Seaver, Lady Buxton, Mrs. Stowe, Jonathan Phillips, Governor Davis, Professor Packard, and others. Extracts from several of his letters then written have already been given. The following, dated October 14, and written to a lady in Florida, should be read, because it shows the state of his mind at a time when he was soon about to "enter into his rest:"

"Dear Mrs. ——:—Your deeply interesting note reached me within the last half hour, and I feel that no time should be lost in my reply. My life has been protracted beyond all my friends' expectations, and almost beyond even my own hopes; yet I enjoy the days with all the zest of early youth, and feel myself a spare hand to do such work as the Master lays before me. This of aiding you is one of the things for which I am spared; and I therefore forward one hundred dollars, which if you are not willing to accept, you may use for the benefit of some other person or persons, at your discretion. Your precious brother has passed on; and, in God's good time, I hope to see him face to face, and to receive, through the Beloved, the 'well done' promised to such as have used their Lord's trusts as he approves."

Mention has already been made of the interest which he took in the Presidential election of 1852, when he allowed his political friends to place him in nomination for the office of elector, to which he was chosen. A few days after he had given his vote for General Scott and Mr. Graham, he was visited by General Pierce, then President-elect of the United States, and that gentleman's family. The intimacy between Mr. Lawrence and that distinguished statesman had been very close for many years, and was founded on common esteem. Together they visited many interesting places and benevolent institutions, the statesman being a warm-hearted man, to whom such things were far from indifferent. One of the last letters received by Mr. Lawrence was written by General Pierce's son, a boy of twelve years, in acknowledgment of a beautiful pencil which that gentleman had bestowed upon him, accompanied by one of those kind notes which no man knew better how to write to young people. The letter was written on the 27th of December, and in less that ten days both the writer and his correspondent—the boy "in the morn and liquid dew of youth," to whom life appeared so full of joy, and the venerable man of nearly seventy years, who had done life's full work, and done it so well—had passed to the world beyond the grave. The son of the fortunate statesman was instantly killed in one of those railway disasters which are so common in this country. A Greek would have said that this was the sacrifice which Nemesis exacted, that it followed from the *envy of the gods*, ever jealous of human prosperity, and determined upon rebuking it.

The last entries in Mr. Lawrence's "Diary" show that

while death was hovering over him he was active as ever in his labors to make the lives of others happy. They are as follows:

"DEC. 28.—I sent a large bundle of clothing materials, books, and other items, with sixty dollars, by steamer for Bangor, to Professor Pond, of Bangor Theological Seminary, for the students. Also gave a parcel, costing twenty-five dollars, to Mrs. ——, who is a Groton girl, and now having twins, making twenty children; is very poor."

"DEC. 30.—To Professor ——, by dear S., one hundred dollars. Books and items to-day, five dollars."

On the afternoon of the 30th of December, Dr. William R. Lawrence, who has published so excellent an account of his father's life, passed some hours with his father, having been led to do so by one of those unaccountable impulses which sometimes govern human conduct, and cause a departure from all previous arrangements. He had left his home for his usual walk, and was passing by his father's house, intending to call there on his return home. After proceeding a few steps, he resolved to give up his walk, and to spend the time with his father. He did so, and finding that gentleman in health, and very cheerful, considerable conversation took place. "Nearly an hour," he says, "was agreeably spent in discussing the topics of the day. He seemed more than usually communicative; and, although always kind and affectionate, there was, on this occasion, an unusual softness of manner, and tenderness of expression, which can not be forgotten. The last topic touched upon was the character of a prominent statesman, just deceased, and the evidence which he had given of preparation for an exchange of worlds. He spoke somewhat fully upon the nature of such preparation, and expressed a strong hope, that, in the present instance, the exchange had been a happy one."*

* Diary and Correspondence, p. 337.

Professor Packard, of Bowdoin College, was at that time engaged in preparing a history of the Bunker Hill Monument, for the Historical Society of Maine, and had written to Mr. Lawrence for information on the subject. Late in the evening of the 30th of December, he wrote the following reply, which is not only interesting from its details, but particularly so as being the last of his earthly labors. It is singularly clear, lucid, and straightforward, and indicates great powers of memory.

"Boston, December 30, 1852 (evening).

"My Dear Friend:—Your letter of Tuesday reached me just before my morning excursion to Longwood, to see our loved ones there. In reply to your first query, I answer that Mr. E. Everett presented a design of Bunker Hill Monument, which was very classic, and was supported by Col. Perkins and Gen. Dearborn, I believe, and one or two more. Young Greenough (Horatio), then a student of Harvard College, sent in a plan with an essay, that manifested extraordinary talents, and was substantially adopted, although the column was amended by the talents, taste, and influence of Loammi Baldwin, one of our directors. The discussion of the model was very interesting; and, among the whole mass of plans, this of Mr. Everett and Mr. Baldwin, or, as I before said, a modification of Greenough's, were the only ones that were thought of. Mr. Everett, and those who favored his classic plan, were very cordial in their support of the plan of the monument as it is, very soon after its adoption. Mr. Ticknor was very active in support of the plan as adopted; and I have a strong impression that young Greenough's arguments were wholly just, and, abating some assertions which seemed a little strong for a mere college lad, were true and unexceptionable. I write from memory, and not from overlooking the plans carefully since the time they were considered.

Young Greenough I felt a deep interest in, and advanced money to his father to allow him to go abroad to study, which has been repaid since his father's death. Here I have an interesting story to tell you of this debt, which I wished to cancel, that the widow might receive the amount. Mr. Greenough was near his end, and deeply affected; but fully persuaded that, by the provisions of his will, his widow would soon have an ample income, and declined the offer. It has turned out better than he ever anticipated. The books shall go forward, as you requested. All our family, 'kith and kin,' are pretty well. The President-elect has, I think, the hardest time, being overworked; and, as we are now without any one, we shall be rejoiced to see you here. Pray come. I shall write again when I send the 'red book' you request.

"With love to all, N. and I join; and I bid you adieu.

"From your friend,

"AMOS LAWRENCE.

"To PROF. PACKARD, Brunswick, Me."

This letter was folded, directed, and left upon his table, and his son says that it "doubtless contained the last words he ever wrote. After the usual family devotions," that gentleman adds, "he retired at about ten o'clock, and, before his attendant left the room, asked a few questions relating to the situation of a poor family which he had relieved a day or two before. Mrs. Lawrence had been in an adjoining room, and, on returning, found him lying quietly, and apparently engaged in silent prayer. She did not, therefore, disturb him, but retired for the night without speaking. In less than two hours she was awakened by one of his usual attacks. Remedies were applied; but, no rallying symptoms appearing, the physician and family were summoned. All that medical skill could do was in vain; and, at a quarter past twelve, on the last day of the year, he quietly breathed his last, without having awakened to consciousness after his first sleep."*

Thus died one whose death was mourned in many dwellings where his face was unknown, but which he had been the means of filling with happiness, and with a sincerity that is rarely felt when the great pass away. There was a strong sympathy with the bereaved family, and the people of Boston felt as if each of their number had experienced a personal loss, and the whole public one of its surest guides. The amplest tributes to his worth came from all quarters, not in the language of exaggeration, but clothed in words that bespoke its unaffectedness and sincerity. He had for years filled a large place in the public eye, such as is rarely awarded to a man who had no prominent connection with politics or literature, or with any of the leading professions. This was the more remarkable because of his unobtrusiveness, and his not entering much into what is called society. It was the homage that was willingly paid to a man whose good deeds were known, and whose motives were thoroughly appreciated. His death created a vacancy in Boston such as that city had rarely before known, and is not likely soon to know again.

All Mr. Lawrence's worldly affairs were found to be admirably arranged. Recognizing his duty, in this as in all other respects, he had not hesitated for a moment in discharging it. Of that singular superstition, from which some great minds have been not altogether free, which leads to a total neglect of earthly arrangements founded on the possibility of sudden death, he had no knowledge. Twenty years before his death he had made a will. A codicil was added to his will only four days before he died. It had been his intention that the partnership that had existed so long between himself and his brother should end only with

* Diary and Correspondence, pp. 339–40.

his life, but from this intention he had been induced to depart; and had he lived but twenty-four hours longer, an advertisement, which had been drawn up, would have appeared in the public journals, announcing his withdrawal from all business pursuits. Thus prepared in a worldly sense—of his preparation in a higher sense the story of his life affords the best evidence—he passed quickly from the earth, happy in that he had done his task, and without suffering.

The funeral ceremonies were performed on the 4th of January, 1853. After prayer at the house, by the Rev. Dr. Vinton, Rector of St. Paul's Church, public exercises were had in Brattle-street Church, where Mr. Lawrence had worshiped during a large part of his life. They were conducted by three eminent divines, namely, the Rev. Dr. Lathrop, pastor of Brattle-street Church; the Rev. Dr. Hopkins, President of Williams College; and the Rev. Dr. Sharp, pastor of the Baptist Society in Charles-street. "A beautiful and appropriate hymn was sung by the members of the Lawrence Association, from the Mather School, who surrounded the coffin, and at the conclusion of the hymn, covered it with flowers. The body, followed by a large procession of mourning friends, was then conveyed to Mount Auburn, and deposited by the side of the loved ones who had preceded him, and under the shade of the 'old oak,' where may it rest until summoned to the presence of that Saviour whose example and precepts he so much loved on earth, and through whom alone he looked for happiness in heaven!"*

Mr. Lawrence had nearly completed his sixty-seventh year at the date of his death. For almost a third of his life he had been an invalid, and was liable at any moment to be prostrated by attacks from the most harassing form

* Diary and Correspondence, pp. 341–42.

that disease can assume. Yet it was precisely during this time of continued affliction that the excellence of his character shone most conspicuously. Illness, particularly if lasting, is apt to spoil men. It was not so with this gentleman. His was a nervous temperament, and he had in early life to struggle much against the consequences of it. It caused him to be warm, and impatient. This infirmity he finally mastered, and his victory over it was obtained at a time when the peculiarities of his long and wearing illness had come in aid of this foe of his peace. He was not always able to control himself, but no man could make nobler amends when his mind had recovered its usual serene tone.

The sense of justice which had guided all his business operations he carried into the transactions of private life. It was a part of his nature. It characterized his intercourse with all, from the members of his household to the least known of the many applicants for assistance who were induced to wait upon him from his well-founded reputation for practical benevolence.

His affections were strong and enduring. Few men have had more friends, or from among a better class of people, persons distinguished for their moral worth and intellectual excellence. His correspondence shows this, not less than it shows his charity both in thought and in deed.

He was a devout believer in Christianity, and reverenced the whole Bible. He was no sectarian, however, and "had no taste for the discussion of those minor points of doctrine upon which good men so often differ, but embraced with all his heart the revealed truths of the Gospel, which the great body of Christians can unite in upholding. He sought those fields of labor where all can meet, rather than those which are hedged in by the dividing lines of sect and party. . . . . Religion was for him a practical thing for every-day use, consisting not so much in frames and emotions as in the steady and persevering performance of the daily duties of life. His view of duty did not limit him to the common obligations of morality, but included the highest sense of duty toward God. . . . . He was an active helper in all that tended to promote the cause of Christianity among nations, as well as to promote spiritual progress among individuals. The Christian banner, in his view, covered many denominations; and, with this belief, his charities were directed to the building up of institutions under the influence of the various sects differing from that under which he himself was classed."

His mind was a happy mixture of the theoretical and the practical. He seems to have wrought out his whole theory of business when a youth, and to have planned his work so well that it was as easy for him to operate on one stage as on another. President Hopkins said of him, that "he had a fertile and shaping imagination; he built air-castles, and they vanished, and then he built others; but, when he decided to build any thing on the ground, it was well planned and promptly finished. His tastes were natural and simple, his habits plain, and his feelings always fresh, genuine, and youthful. Not even the smell of the fire of prosperity had pressed on him." The same eminent scholar said of him, as a writer,—"His command over the English language, especially in writing, indicated his power. Style is no mechanical product, that can be formed by rules, but is the outgrowth and image of the mind; and his had often great felicity and strength. When he wrote under the impulse of his feelings, he seemed to impregnate the very paper, and make it redolent of them." As a speaker he was not fluent. Like many other men who have achieved eminence, his powers of utterance, even in conversation, were not good. The very excess of ideas seemed to operate as a check to his powers of speech. Perhaps if he had been thrown in early life into a position that required the development of the faculty of "thinking on his legs," he would have been found fully up to his work, the adaptation of himself to circumstances being throughout life one of the strongest points of his character. But his aversion to public life, that is to say, to political life, was calculated to render permanent any natural deficiency in those qualities which that life tends to develop.

The rapid advance of American commerce, and the natural adaptedness of Americans to commercial avocations, must cause many of our countrymen to excel as merchants. Such men can find in the life of AMOS LAWRENCE much matter for profitable contemplation. His energy, his intelligence, his integrity, and his liberality are what every business man should seek to imitate. Thus doing, though they may not always reach to his standard of excellence, they will accomplish much good, win honorable fame, aid in extending the national power and in elevating the national character, and form in their turn brilliant examples to aspiring youth.

ABBOTT LAWRENCE.

Abbott Lawrence was by profession a merchant—a profession which is not often associated with the higher exhibitions of intellect. It is true it is often accompanied with great wealth, and wealth alone carries with it power, and a certain degree of distinction.

The merchant is at the head of the numerous family who live by trade—in the distribution, on a smaller or larger scale, of the commodities which supply the wants and fancies of life. The whole family is actuated immediately and directly by the selfish principle, in its application to property. The sole object of trade is profit—gain to the trader. Other occupations and professions, whilst tied down by the common necessity of providing for the wants of life, are associated with other aims which command the higher places in the world's estimation.

Notwithstanding the eloquent expostulations of the friends of peace, the world continues to assign the foremost rank to the successful warrior, who fights for glory as well as patriotism. A Napoleon or a Wellington always commands the applause of his day and generation. Even Washington won his glory as a warrior before he was known as the statesman. In the learned professions—in the various departments of science—and in the higher walks of art, it is the love of fame which is the spur to excellence, rather than any pecuniary acquisition. The same principle will apply, in a considerable degree, to the mechanic arts. It is true that some modification of the selfish principle may be said to lie at the root of all human action, but nowhere is it so naked and undisguised as in the profession of the merchant, whose direct and avowed object is the getting of gain. At the same time, the world has always given honor to merchants. We are told in Holy Writ, that "the traffickers of Tyre were the honorable of the earth," and the same character has been freely bestowed in all succeeding ages. It is to be taken for granted, however, that it has always been the use made of the wealth acquired in trade, which has been the object of commendation and honor, rather than the success in its accumulation.

The merchant makes no claim to benevolence or patriotism as his ruling motive in trade: all he professes is absolute and undeviating justice. The morals of trade are of the strictest and purest character. It is not an uncommon opinion that there is a laxity in the mercantile code, which looks with indulgence on what are called the tricks of trade. It is not so. Whilst the direct object of all trade is gain, individual benefit, not the slightest prevarication or deviation from truth is allowable. There is no class of men with whom the Christian rule of doing to others what we expect or require in return, is more strictly demanded than amongst merchants. Mercantile honor is as delicate and fragile as that of a woman. It will not bear the slightest stain. The man in trade who has been found to equivocate or falter in his course, becomes a marked man. He is avoided. It is thus found, by experience, that integrity is almost as uniformly the accompaniment of success, as it always is of character. It is true, that in the manifold operations of trade, there are opportunities and temptations to acts of dishonesty, more frequent than in other occupations; and it is not to be denied that, in many instances, poor human nature is found to yield to them. What we insist on is the rigidity of the rule which controls the action of the honorable merchant, and under which alone he can claim that name.

But whilst the selfish principle lies at the foundation of trade, there is no reason why the trader himself should not be active in benevolence and all the Christian virtues. There is no occupation which has a tendency to liberalize the mind more than that of the merchant. His intercourse is wide with men of all opinions and of all countries. He perceives that integrity, virtue, and honor are not confined to a narrow circle, or to one country. We accordingly find a full proportion of men engaged in trade among the patrons and managers of our charitable and benevolent institutions. They are also amongst the most liberal supporters of enterprises undertaken for the public good. It is perhaps natural that men accumulating their own fortunes, should have less hesitation in adventuring property in new enterprises, than those holding property by inheritance. The fact appears to be so. These general views of the mercantile profession may serve as an appropriate introduction to the life of one who was so eminent an ornament of that profession, and whose whole career was an illustration of the integrity, liberality, and public spirit, which are indispensable elements in the character of the great and good merchant.

Abbott Lawrence was born in the town of Groton, Massachusetts, December 16th, 1792. He was the fifth son of Deacon Samuel Lawrence, a respectable farmer, who did good service as a soldier during the Revolutionary war, in which he rose to the rank of major, and was highly esteemed by his fellow-citizens. The ancestor, John Lawrence, one of the early Puritan emigrants, settled at Watertown in 1635, and removed to Groton in 1660. He came from Wissett, in Suffolk, where, and in the neighboring parish of Rumburg, the family had been long settled. It was of great antiquity, Sir Robert Lawrence having been knighted by Richard Cœur de Lion, in 1191, for his bravery in scaling the walls of Acre. The early education of the subject of this memoir was at the district school during the winter, and for a few months at the academy which now bears his name. This was the narrow foundation on which he himself added the superstructure which carried him successfully through the various places which he was destined to fill. With this, the common outfit of every New England boy, he came to Boston, in 1808, as an apprentice to his brother Amos, who was already established in business, and who thus speaks of him in his diary: "In 1808 he came to me, as my apprentice, bringing his bundle under his arm, with less than three dollars in his pocket, and this was his fortune. A first-rate business lad he was, but, like other bright lads, needed the careful eye of a senior to guard him from the pitfalls that he was exposed to." He is reported to have been most assiduous and diligent in his duties, and to have devoted his evenings to supply the deficiencies of his early education. The business of the elder brother was prosperous, and when Abbott came of age, in 1814, a copartnership was formed between them, which continued until terminated by death. Their business was the importation and sale of foreign manufactures, in which the firm stood at the head of that class of merchants —and by their industry and enterprise acquired a large fortune. Under the tariffs of 1816 and 1824 the manufacture of cottons and woolens was extensively introduced, and the house of A. & A. Lawrence entered largely into their sales on commission. It was not until the year 1830 that they became interested in the cotton-mills at Lowell.

On the establishment of the Suffolk, Tremont, and Lawrence Companies, as well as subsequently in other corporations, they became large proprietors. From this time, their business, as selling agents, was on the most extensive scale, and their income from all sources large in proportion. As a man of business, Mr. Lawrence possessed talents of the very first order. Prompt, energetic, with an intuitive insight into the characters of men, with sound judgment, and an openness of character which won favor on the slightest acquaintance, he acquired the confidence of the community in the highest degree. For many of the last years of his life, he was largely interested in the China trade, the source of a good deal of profit. But his mind was not confined to the numerous details and ramifications of his business, extensive as it was. He took a deep interest in all matters of public concern, in politics, political economy, finance. He was among the most zealous advocates of the protective system, before he was himself interested in manufactures, and was one of the delegates from Massachusetts to Harrisburg, in 1827, where he took an active part in the deliberations of that assembly. In 1834 he was elected a member of the twenty-fourth Congress, for the district of Suffolk. He was placed at once on the Committee of Ways and Means, where his acquaintance with mercantile affairs gave him much deserved influence. He won the favor of all parties, by his general intelligence, and by his genial and affable manners. Without making set speeches for display, he spoke well, on proper occasions, on the matters of business before Congress. He declined a re-election at the end of the term, but in 1839, in consequence of a vacancy, he was with difficulty persuaded to allow himself to be a candidate for the twenty-sixth Congress, to which he was triumphantly elected. His usefulness in this position was, however, soon brought to a close, by a severe attack of fever, in March, 1840, on his recovery from which he considered it necessary to resign the office.

In 1842 he was appointed, on the part of Massachusetts, a commissioner on the subject of the Northeastern Boundary, which had become a most dangerous and difficult question, intrusted on the part of the British government to Lord Ashburton. It is the belief of the writer, who was then in Congress and in daily confidential communication with him, that to Mr. Lawrence, more than to any other individual, is due the successful accomplishment of the negotiation, which resulted in the important treaty of Washington. Lord Ashburton was himself a merchant, of an open, straightforward character. He had accepted the office of ambassador with the especial purpose of settling this vexed question. Mr. Lawrence accepted the office of commissioner with much the same feeling. They were both of opinion that any terms of settlement which involved no sacrifice of honor, were better than that this portentous question should remain unsettled, liable at any moment to break out into a regular war. They soon came to an understanding with each other. Lord Ashburton communicated freely to Mr. Lawrence the utmost limits to which his instructions would allow him to go, and Mr. Lawrence was thus enabled to bring his somewhat intractable colleagues to the final happy issue. He was at last, at the close of the negotiation, called in to satisfy the scruples of President Tyler, who had found a difficulty in his own mind with some of the details, which Mr. Webster, the Secretary of State, was unable to remove.

In the presidential campaign of 1840 he took an active part in favor of the election of Gen. Harrison. In September, 1842, he was President of the Whig Convention, which nominated Henry Clay for President, on the part of Massachusetts. He was a delegate to the Whig National Convention in 1844, and, in the same year, one of the electors at large for the State. In the presidential canvass of 1848, the name of Mr. Lawrence was prominently associated for the office of Vice-President with that of General Taylor for President, and at the convention in Philadelphia he wanted but six votes of being nominated for that office. This result was owing to the peculiar and unexpected course of some of the delegates of his own State. He was disappointed, but never allowed his equanimity to be disturbed. He had, with extreme delicacy, foreborne to allow his name to be brought forward by his friends until the last moment, and he did not allow any personal feeling to affect his course. He presided at a ratification meeting, in Faneuil Hall, to sustain the nomination of Taylor and Fillmore. As a presiding officer, on this and similar occasions, he appeared to great advantage. He was, in fact, a self-made, but very successful and forcible public speaker. This was shown effectively, during this campaign, in what are called caucus speeches, in which he was always happy. He was urgently solicited, in various quarters of the country, to address his fellow-citizens, but confined himself to a few of the most important points, in which he was eminently successful.

Immediately after the inauguration of Gen. Taylor, he was summoned to Washington, and urged to take a seat in the cabinet. But the two highest places had been disposed of, and those which remained were not to his taste, and were declined. A higher position was soon after offered him—that of the representative of the United States at the Court of Great Britain. This is a station of the highest honor, which has been filled by some of the most eminent men of the country, requiring sound discretion as the necessary foundation, and in which the highest and the most varied information upon all subjects will find full exercise. This place, after some hesitation, he accepted, and, with Mrs. Lawrence, embarked for England in September, 1849. It is difficult to find greater contrasts in the life of any man, than those presented by his first and last visits to England: the first as a novice, confined to the operations of trade at Manchester and Leeds, and the last introducing him directly to Queen Victoria and the British Court, and giving him free intercourse with the most distinguished statesmen of the land. This position he occupied not merely respectably, but with the highest honor, not only to himself, but to his country. He did not attempt to pass for what he was not, but his general information, especially upon matters relating to trade, commerce, and finance, caused his opinions to be sought in the highest quarters, while his peculiar urbanity and gracious manners made him a favorite with all with whom he came in contact. The possession of an ample fortune enabled him to support a style of hospitality more in accordance with the higher European embassies, than is usual under the somewhat niggardly allowance of our own government. All this, however, he did without overstepping the bounds of the strictest propriety and decorum. On public occasions, and at the numerous festivals which he attended, he acquitted himself in the happiest manner,—and his speeches may well compare with those made by statesmen of the highest education.

Having had an opportunity of examining copies of his diplomatic correspondence, a small portion only of which has been published, the writer has no hesitation in characterizing it as exceedingly able, both in matter and manner, and as comparing well with the best specimens of that species of composition. It is very evident that he inspired the deepest respect in the different functionaries with whom he came in contact.

One of the first objects requiring his attention, was the project of a ship canal from the Caribbean Sea to the Pacific Ocean, which had been brought forward by his predecessor, Mr. Bancroft. The assent and guarantee of both the United States and Great Britain were necessary to effect this object. An obstacle existed in the claim set up by Great Britain to the Protectorate of the Mosquito Territory, on a part of which the eastern terminus of the canal must be made. This subject was one which received his immediate attention, and, as early as December, 1849, he obtained from Lord Palmerston a disavowal, on the part of Great Britain, of any intention "to occupy or colonize Nicaragua, Costa Rica, the Mosquito Coast, or any part of

Central America." His mind was very much occupied with this matter, in the expectation that it would devolve on him to negotiate a treaty with the British government. In a letter of December 14th, 1849, to Lord Palmerston, he presents a view of the important advantages to result from such a canal, and of the obstacle interposed by the claim in behalf of the Mosquito Indians as an independent sovereignty. In the mean time, he set himself to work in collecting information in illustration of the connection of the British government with the Mosquito Indians, out of which their claim to certain peculiar rights as their protectors was founded. In this he was entirely successful. He became possessed of some very important manuscript documents, which had never been published, consisting of the Vernon and Wager manuscripts, which he characterizes as "a collection embodying, in the original, official as well as private letters of the Duke of Newcastle, of Sir Charles Wager, of Admiral Vernon, of Sir William Pulteney, of Governor Trelawney, of Mr. Robert Hodgson, and many others, a mass of authentic information never published, and not existing anywhere else, unless in Her Majesty's State Paper Office."

He was arranging all these matters into a legal argument and historical document, when in April, 1850, he received notice from Mr. Clayton, Secretary of State, that "these negotiations were entirely transferred to Washington, and that he was to cease altogether to press them in London." This was naturally a severe disappointment, but he at once set about changing the character of this document from a letter to Lord Palmerston to a dispatch to our own Secretary of State. It bears date 19th April, 1850. It covers eighty-five folio pages of manuscript. It discusses the question of the title of the Mosquito Indians to the sovereignty of the country claimed for them by Great Britain. It states, very clearly, the law established by the different nations of Europe, in reference to their own rights, and that of the savages inhabiting the continent and islands of America. "The Christian world have agreed in recognizing the Indians as occupants only of the lands, without a right of possession, without domain, the sovereignty being determined by priority of discovery and occupation."

In the historical review of the question, he states that Spain established her rights on the Mosquito territory in the fifteenth century, which were recognized in the treaty of 1672 by Sir William Godolphin. He quotes from the documents, before mentioned, abundant evidence of the tampering of the Governor of Jamaica, and of the admiral on that station, with the Mosquitoes, during the war which broke out with Spain in 1739. The treaty of 1763, as well as that of 1783, would seem to admit the sovereignty of Spain in the fullest degree. The whole question is argued with great ability. It is unfortunate that while this document was on its passage to Washington, a treaty was actually signed by Mr. Clayton and Sir Henry L. Bulwer, out of which a serious misunderstanding has arisen. This could hardly have happened had this document been communicated to the British government, as the American view of the question.

Mr. Lawrence's own view of the subject was, " that whenever the history of the conduct of Great Britain shall be published to the world, it will not stand one hour before the bar of public opinion without universal condemnation."*

A question was left unsettled by Mr. Bancroft, in relation to the postal rates on the transit of letters across England, to which Mr. Lawrence devoted a good deal of time. Not being able to induce the Postmaster-general to adopt rates more reasonable than the existing ones, he recommended to our government to give notice to annul the convention of

* This document was published on a call from the Senate, February 9th, 1853. Senate Doc., 32d Congress, 2d session, No. 27.

1848, as they had a right to do, as the only means of bringing about a more equitable arrangement.

Another matter which Mr. Lawrence pressed upon the British government with earnestness and ability, was the injustice of her lighthouse system, by which foreign tonnage is taxed to support sinecure offices, whilst our own lighthouses are free to all the world, without any tax whatever. These dispatches, which were never satisfactorily answered, were made public by vote of the House of Commons on motion of Mr. Hume.

A delicate and spirited correspondence took place between Mr. Lawrence and Lord Granville in relation to the outrage committed by H. M. ship Express on the steamer Prometheus, for which an ample apology was made.

In August, 1852, England was thrown into intense excitement in consequence of a letter written by Mr. Webster on the subject of the new ground taken by Great Britain in reference to the fisheries. This led to several interviews between Mr. Lawrence and Lord Malmesbury, the result of which was such a modification of the instructions to the vessels on the station as prevented any collision. His attention was unremitted in reference to the very numerous private claims upon the British government which required his care. A joint commission was afterward appointed to decide definitively upon this description of cases.

In September, 1851, Mr. and Mrs. Lawrence made a tour in Ireland, of which he gives an interesting account in a dispatch under date of 2d December. They visited Dublin, Galway, Limerick, Killarney, Cork, &c. In many of these places he was met by deputations, and received the most flattering and respectful attentions. His account of the present state of Ireland, and his remarks upon it, are in the highest degree interesting and instructive.

On the whole, it may be doubted whether, since the mission of Dr. Franklin, any minister of the United States has accomplished a diplomatic success greater than must be awarded to Mr. Lawrence. This was the result of his peculiar endowments, quick apprehension, sagacity, retentive memory, power of reaching the pith of a matter, tact, kindness of heart, and perfect truthfulness.

His residence in London, mingling freely in society, did much in producing a change in public opinion, favorable to his own country. The writer thought he saw good evidence of this at a dinner at which he was present, given by Mr. Westhead, member of Parliament for Knaresborough, at the Clarendon Hotel, to a party of about fifty, consisting equally of English and Americans. This gentleman had met Mr. Lawrence during a visit which he made to Manchester and Liverpool, and was so much pleased with him that he requested permission to give him such a dinner, which it would have been ungracious to refuse. It was a compliment to Mr. Lawrence and his country, graced by the presence of distinguished members of the British cabinet, and such Americans as happened to be in England. It was opened by a neat speech from Mr. Westhead, to which Mr. Lawrence replied in his happiest manner. Speeches followed by Lord Palmerston, Mr. Gladstone, Earl Powis, Mr. Cardwell, and others. They were beautiful specimens of dinner speeches; but what was particularly striking, was the amiable manner in which they tendered the right hand of fellowship to their American brothers. There seemed to be a general desire to express the feeling that Brother Jonathan had proved himself a worthy chip of the old block, and was entitled to their kindest regards. There was an air of sincerity and cordiality on the occasion which could not be mistaken. Unfortunately, reporters were excluded, so that these speeches were never given to the public.

After three years' service, Mr. Lawrence obtained leave to return to his country, which he did in October, 1852.

On this occasion he was invited to a public dinner, but, happening at a period when the whole community were deeply affected by the recent death of Mr. Webster, he declined it;—he arrived, in fact, barely in time to attend the funeral of that lamented statesman.

Mr. Lawrence was always ready and foremost in supporting measures which promised benefit to the public. He was a large subscriber to the various railroads projected for the concentration of trade in Boston, and this from a feeling of patriotism rather than the expectation of profit. His subscriptions for public objects of charity or education were always on the most liberal scale; but the crowning act of this character was the establishment of the Scientific School at Cambridge, connected with Harvard College, for which he gave fifty thousand dollars in 1847, and left a further like sum by his will. His letter to Mr. Eliot, the treasurer of the college, accompanying the donation, was a proof how completely his mind was imbued with the subject, and how fully and accurately he had investigated it. This institution supplied a great want in our system of education, in the application of science to the arts. He left a further sum of fifty thousand dollars for the purpose of erecting model lodging-houses, the income of the rents to be forever applied to certain public charities. He received, in 1854, the honorary degree of Doctor of Laws from Harvard College, and also from that of Williamstown.

Viewing his character phrenologically, it was the symmetry and beauty of the whole organization which constituted its excellence, without the peculiar prominence or exaggeration of particular organs which give the highest power of genius in their manifestation. In other words, his intellectual and moral powers were in due and admirable proportion—with no deficiency and with no excess. In his person, he was at the same time commanding and prepossessing, with a suavity and air of benevolence and sincerity which indicated the perfect gentleman.

In his social relations he was eminently happy. Early in life, he married Katharine, the daughter of the Hon. Timothy Bigelow, long known and distinguished as the Speaker of the House of Representatives of Massachusetts. She aided in his labors with devoted fidelity, and shared in his honors with becoming dignity. He lived to see a numerous family of children well married, and settled in life. His eldest son married the daughter of the eminent historian Prescott.

In June, 1855, he was attacked with alarming symptoms of disease. These continued to increase, and his life was brought to a close on the 18th day of August, in the sixty-third year of his age. He was, in principle and practice, during life, a sincere and pious Christian. He met death as becomes a Christian to die. At this comparatively early age, with every thing about him calculated to make the close of life a period of calm and tranquil enjoyment, in the consciousness of a life well spent, he resigned his spirit to God who gave it, without a murmur or expression of any thing but gratitude for the blessings he had experienced.

There was no circumstance of his life more remarkable than the demonstration of public feeling during his sickness, and after his death. During the last few lingering days of his life, there seemed to be but one topic on the public mind. Was there any hope? Is he to die? Seldom has the death of an individual, holding no public office, called forth such an expression of deep feeling. Faneuil Hall, on a short notice, was spontaneously crowded by our citizens, in order to give vent to their grief. Speeches were made by several of our most distinguished men. It was the loss of a friend, of a general benefactor, of a good man, which called forth this universal expression of sorrow. The government of Harvard College, and a great number of Societies held special meetings, and adopted resolutions to attend his funeral. The Rev. Dr. Lothrop, his pastor, in a funeral discourse did justice to his religious character. He says, "The benevolence of Mr. Lawrence, and all the virtues of his life, had their strong foundation and constant nourishment in religious faith. He believed in his heart on the Lord Jesus Christ, and received him as the promised Messiah and Saviour of the World. He was truly catholic in his feelings, loving all who love our Lord Jesus Christ in sincerity and truth; and extended the helping hand of his charities to the enterprises of various Christian denominations."

In connection with the brief but comprehensive memoir by Mr. Appleton, the following account of the meeting held at Faneuil Hall, which he mentions, and the speeches of Everett, Winthrop, Stevenson, Sturgis, and others, will be read with interest. These were incorporated in an article published in the *Merchants' Magazine* for January, 1856 (vol. xxxiv, pp. 46–53), in which we endeavored to offer an adequate tribute to the personal, and what seemed to us the less appreciated qualities of Mr. Lawrence's character.

It is not often during the life, it is not always immediately after death, that the character even of a great man—one deemed to be well known and fully appreciated—becomes fully understood. The complaint of unappreciated excellence, of unrecognized genius and virtue, is not the only one which has just foundation. A man known and appreciated for one class of virtues, for merit of a certain kind, may still—and perhaps in consequence of the very prominence of those qualities which first gained him distinction—fail to receive due credit for equal excellence of another, it may be a higher order.

This was the case, to some extent, with Abbott Lawrence.

Something like justice has been done to his talents as a business man; his services as a diplomatist and statesman are less adequately, but still quite generally appreciated. His public charities, from the nature of the case, have become widely known. It is the personal excellence of the man, the genial temperament, the expansive sympathies, the ready charity, which did a thousand good deeds that no one heard of—it is these which the very extent of his public benefactions has caused to be overlooked, so that some people have been led to say that Abbott Lawrence's liberality was of the ostentatious, not of the wholly disinterested character, which marked that of his lamented brother.

His personal excellences, best known at home during his life, should now be known to the world, not merely for example, not merely for incitement, but for the sake of *justice.*

His genial nature and courteous manners were carried with him into the marts of trade. His unselfishness exhibited itself in his readiness to share with his contemporaries in trade the benefits of honorable enterprise. An anecdote in point, which we have from a most reliable source, and hundreds such might be told. We heard it from one who had intimately known him for more than thirty years. A merchant called at his counting-room one day, and told him that flannels were selling low, very low. "Buy, then," said Mr. L. "I am afraid to; besides, I have not the means," said the other. "Go buy them—I will back you and share with you in the speculation." How different this from the narrow-minded capitalists, who, taking advantage of the information, would have gone into the market, made the purchase, and pocketed the profits.

A contemporary, in an obituary notice, at the time of his death, remarked in effect that his charities were fewer in number and more ostentatious than were those of his brother Amos. Such we have the best testimony for knowing was not the fact. It is true Abbott Lawrence made a few munificent donations in his life-time; such, for instance, as the fifty thousand dollars to found the Scientific School of Harvard College, Cambridge, donations which could not, and should not, be "hid under a bushel."

But if the veil could be lifted, we are satisfied it would be found that his private charities were neither few nor far between. AMOS LAWRENCE was an invalid for thirty years, and noted down all he gave away—not to blazon it abroad—still many of his gifts were known in the community in which he lived. ABBOTT LAWRENCE was in active life, attending to the multiform pursuits of trade, to say nothing of the various trusts committed to his charge by the circle, public and private, in which he moved. He kept no note of his charities—his right hand did not know what his left hand had done.

The writer of this enjoyed the personal acquaintance of Mr. L.; experienced his cordial kindness, if not his friendship, and though differing with him on some subjects, we never could discover that difference of opinion ever narrowed the large sympathies, or contracted the liberal views of ABBOTT LAWRENCE. The last time we met him—a few months before his death—we solicited his advice on a subject connected with our literary labors. "Write," said Mr. Lawrence, to ———, "and use my name, if you please."

On the 20th August, 1855, the Monday following Mr. Lawrence's death, a public meeting was held in Faneuil Hall, Boston, of the citizens of that city and vicinity, and of all others "desirous to consult together and determine upon a proper testimonial of their appreciation of the distinguished character and services of the Honorable Abbott Lawrence, and of their profound sense of bereavement at his lamented death."

"Among the distinguished men present," says the Boston *Courier* of August 21, 1855, "we recognized the Hon. Edward Everett, Hon. R. C. Winthrop, Hon. Rufus Choate,

Hon. Peleg Sprague, of the United States District Court, Hon. Nathan Appleton, Hon. William Appleton, James W. Paige, Esq., Hon. Samuel A. Eliot, Hon. J. Thomas Stevenson, Hon. Nathan Hale, Hon. William Sturgis, Hon. Benjamin Seaver, Moses Grant, Esq., Frederick W. Lincoln, Esq., Thomas Motley, Esq., and many other leading merchants and gentlemen of Boston and vicinity."

The meeting was called to order at ten minutes past twelve o'clock by Mayor Smith, who said:

FELLOW-CITIZENS:—A melancholy interest attaches to this meeting. We have been called together to make preparations for showing respect to the memory of a distinguished citizen. The Honorable Abbott Lawrence is now numbered with the dead. His efforts and his character are eminently connected with the history and character of this city, in which he has breathed his last. This meeting was originally proposed by the Board of Trade, as it was necessary that some preliminary steps should be taken. But Mr. Lawrence belonged to the city, and therefore every class of citizens should participate in awarding proper honors to the memory of the man who has been the benefactor of the city of Boston. His enterprise, his public spirit, his goodness of heart, his patriotism, have eminently contributed to the good name and fame of Boston; and whatever we can do to show how much we respect his memory, will contribute I am sure, to the gratification of all within the limits of my voice. And with these observations, it is proper that this meeting proceed to some fitting action, with a view to carry out the object for which it was called.

The meeting was then organized by the choice of Hon. WILLIAM STURGIS, as Chairman; and of J. W. EDMANDS, ADAM W. THAXTER, JR., and F. W. LINCOLN, JR., as Secretaries.

SPEECH OF HON. WILLIAM STURGIS.

We are called together, fellow-citizens, by an event that has cast a shade of sadness and gloom over the whole community. The great Controller of all has, in his wisdom, taken from among us one distinguished alike for the extent and value of his public services, and for the purity and usefulness of his private life. Few, if any, were more widely known than Mr. Lawrence—few, if any, were held in higher estimation.

It is not for me, however, to attempt his eulogy; that must be left for those far more able to do justice to his memory. He has passed away after a life devoted to duty, and to promoting the happiness of his fellow-men, and we, his immediate friends, associates, and fellow-citizens, who witnessed his useful and honorable career, and appreciate his worth, are met to consult how we can best manifest the sentiments of warm esteem and unfeigned respect with which we regarded him while living, and shall ever cherish for his unsullied memory.

The meeting is now opened for any suggestions that may be offered.

SPEECH OF HON. J. THOMAS STEVENSON.

Mr. Chairman:—I have been requested by the Hon. Nathan Appleton, for many years the intimate and confidential friend of the deceased, to offer to this meeting the preamble and resolutions which I hold, and which, with your permission, I will read. This sad privilege is accorded to me solely for the reason that that gentleman, who is present, feels that his voice would hardly fill this hall.

This spontaneous assemblage is evidence of the deep sensibility with which this community has learned the death of the Hon. Abbott Lawrence.

While we mourn this severe dispensation of Providence, which has deprived us of one of our most honored citizens, we bow in submission with no other feeling but that of gratitude for the benefits which his life has conferred upon us.

As a merchant, he was upright and honorable in the highest degree.

As a statesman, able, intelligent, and patriotic, he filled high public stations in a manner most creditable to himself, and most useful to his country.

As a citizen of Boston, he was prominent in every public enterprise which promised to promote the general prosperity.

His truth, and kindness, and courtesy, made his private life a blessing to those who were brought within its influences; his public labors extended the resources of his country, strengthened its political relations, and multiplied its means of learning. He poured out his wealth with a public spirit, which attested at once his just discrimination and his unfailing liberality.

Endowed by nature with a strong mind, he improved it by cultivation to a degree which made him the delight of his friends, and which, in all his public duties, especially in his mission abroad, did high honor to his country.

It is proper we should honor his memory; therefore,

Resolved, That we request the owners and masters of vessels in the harbor to display their colors at half-mast on the day appointed for the funeral.

Resolved, That we will, on that day, close our places of business, and that, as a sad duty, we will attend the funeral services.

Resolved, That the officers of this assembly be requested to communicate these proceedings to the family of the deceased, with the assurances of the public recognition of his virtues, and of the public sympathy in the days of their bereavement.

Mr. Stevenson laid the resolutions on the table, and proceeded thus:

Mr. Chairman and Gentlemen:—We are here at Death's summons.

A public benefactor has yielded his spirit to his God.

A distinguished citizen has finished an honorable career.

A good man has gone to his reward.

The arrow, that is sent from an unseen bow, has struck a conspicuous mark.

Abbott Lawrence rests from his labors on earth.

This concourse of men, assembled here upon so short a notice, proves the public appreciation of his many virtues, and of the great loss which this community has sustained in his death.

We may not invade the sanctuary of private grief.

We may not trespass upon the home just made desolate.

We may not attempt to sound the depth of that sorrow, which broken ties only can fathom.

But the public heart prompts an expression of the public sympathy; and may that sympathy tend to remind those who have lost for a season their dearest companion and their safest guide, how much reason they have to rejoice that they have had so much to mourn for.

Mr. Lawrence possessed all the qualities which, in this community, make a merchant a prince.

He was a wise counselor and an honorable man.

Deliberate in judgment, prompt in action, understanding the details as well as comprehending the principles of trade, liberal-minded, far-seeing, transparent in his frankness, he stood in the front rank among men, with an integrity as fixed as the rock, and an honor as unsullied as the stars.

His private trusts were almost public duties, so widely were his interests intertwined with those of many others; and those trusts were always faithfully executed.

He was allured by no success, he was diverted by no obstacles, from the straight path of mercantile honor.

Truth was at home upon his lips, and the kindliest feelings nestled in his heart.

Those older than himself were happy to lean upon him; those younger than himself were wise to follow him.

He was a safe adviser; and he pointed out to no one any path which he was not prepared to tread himself.

The fullness of his heart overflowed in the amenity of his manners. We shall all miss his cordial greeting.

Those who communed with him loved him; and those who knew him through his more public acts respected him.

Sincere in his friendships, honorable in his antagonism, he never descended to animosities, for he knew how to respect the convictions of those he differed from.

He indulged a well-directed generosity.

His large contributions for the promotion of science and the useful arts was tendered by a living hand.

He did not leave it; he gave it; and he remained with us to see the useful institution which he so founded firmly established.

He must, indeed, have been a remarkable man, whose name deservedly rests upon the highest scientific school in the country, and upon one of the busiest cities in the State.

He was a public-spirited man. He loved the city which was the scene of his enterprise and of his success.

Every worthy object was sure of his heart and his hand.

The same intelligence and energy which achieved success in his profession, carried him beyond it to the duties and the dignities of public station; and few persons have enjoyed, through an active life, the uninterrupted confidence of so many men.

He filled and adorned every place which he occupied.

Whether he represented this community at home, or the whole country abroad, he always did it in a manner alike honorable to himself, and satisfactory to those who intrusted him with large public interests.

The corner-stone of his character was a firm religious belief. He was a devout Christian, and an unshaken faith supported him, after the hope of a longer life here was gone.

His life has been a practical benefit to his age.

He is fit for an example. We will cherish his memory while we mourn his loss.

SPEECH OF THE HON. ROBERT C. WINTHROP.

I am sensible, Mr. President and fellow-citizens, how little can be said, and how little can be listened to, with any satisfaction, at an hour of so much general sorrow as the present. But I could not resist the impulse to be here with you this morning, and, being here, I trust I may be pardoned, as one of those who have had the privilege of being associated with Mr. Lawrence in many public and private relations, as well as in immediate compliance with the request of those by whom this meeting has been arranged, for adding a very few words to what has been already so well said.

The protracted illness of Mr. Lawrence has in some measure prepared us all for the blow which has at last fallen. But I can not help feeling to-day, as I felt many weeks ago—when it was first announced to us that he had been struck down by a sudden and serious illness—that Boston has hardly another life of equal value to lose. I might say, *not another*. Yes, strange as it might seem, when we reflect that within the remembrance of yourself, Mr. President, and of others whom I see around me, he entered Boston a poor lad from the country, "bringing his bundle under his arm, with less than three dollars in his pocket, and that was his fortune" (I use the words of his late excellent and lamented brother), strange as it may seem, it is not too much to say now, that take him in all his relations—commercial, political, and social, together—he had become, at the hour of his death, the most important person in our community.

His enterprise, his liberality, his wealth, his influence, his public and private example, his Christian character, all conspired to render him a peculiar signal blessing to our city, and one which could not have been taken away from us at any time—and now especially, when so many years of usefulness might still have been hoped and expected for him—without exciting the deepest emotions of sorrow. No, I do not misinterpret this throng of quivering lips and moistened eyes. We all experience to-day, sir, a sense of personal bereavement. We all feel that we have lost a friend—a friend never wanting to any occasion where good words, good deeds, where a warm heart or an open hand could be of service. Not the merchants and manufacturers only are called to mourn one of their best advisers and most valued associates. The moral, the religious, the charitable, the literary and scientific institutions of our city and State, the neighboring university and our own public schools, have lost one of their noblest benefactors. The whole country has lost a citizen of earnest, eminent, intelligent, and comprehensive patriotism, who has rendered her no ordinary service in the national councils at home—(I followed him there, sir, and know how difficult it was for anybody to fill his place)—who represented her worthily and admirably as an ambassador abroad—and to whom she might still have looked in the thick-coming exigencies of the future, for filling the very highest places in her gift.

His name was a tower of strength to every good cause, and it was never given to a bad one. His noble bearing and genial presence seemed the very embodiment of an enlarged and enlightened public spirit. If some one of the gifted artists of our land should desire hereafter to personify, on the breathing canvas or in the living marble, the mingled dignity and energy, the blended benevolence, generosity, and enterprise which have characterized the good Boston merchant for so many generations past, I know not how he could ever do so more successfully than by portraying the very form which has just been laid low, and by molding the very lineaments upon which death has now set its seal. I can not think of him as he was among us but yesterday, without recalling the beautiful words of Edmund Burke in reference to his friend Sir George Saville:—"When an act of great and signal humanity was to be done, and done with all the weight and authority that belonged to it, this community could cast its eyes on none but him."

Let us rejoice, fellow-citizens, even in this hour of affliction, that he was ours so long. Let us thank God, as we bend over his honored dust, for having given us such a man, and let us not murmur that in His own good time He has taken him back to Himself. Such a man can never be wholly lost to us. His example remains. His noble acts survive him. His memory will be among the cherished treasures of all our hearts. Of such as him we may say with the poet—

"The dead are like the stars by day,
Withdrawn from mortal eye;
But not extinct—they hold their sway
In glory through the sky."

SPEECH OF THE HON. EDWARD EVERETT.

Mr. Chairman and Gentlemen:—I have come a considerable distance this morning (from Newport) at the request of the committee having charge of the arrangements for this meeting, with scarce any preparations to address you but what consists in a most heartfelt participation in the feeling which calls you together. I come to tell you that already, at a distance from home, the news of Mr. Lawrence's decease excites the same deep sympathy as here. With ample opportunities to witness the great and excellent qualities which made him so respected and valued a member of the community, acting with him confidentially on many important occasions, public and private, I need scarcely add that I have cherished for him feelings of the warmest personal regard—the fruit of a friendly intercourse, commencing with my entrance upon life, and continued without a moment's interruption or chill to the close of his. He was, sir, but one or two years my senior, and I should be wanting in common sensibility if on this occasion I did not associate with that sorrowful regret, which is common to us all, the more solemn reflection that, having walked side by side with him for forty years—having accompanied him to the brink of the "narrow sea" which "divides that happy land from ours"—in a few years only at most, in the course of nature, that narrow sea will cease to divide us.

It would be an unseasonable and superfluous, though a grateful task, before this assembly—composed of the neighbors, the associates, the fellow-citizens of our deceased friend—to attempt minutely to relate his career or delineate his character. You are acquainted with them from personal observation, and they have already gone forth, on the wings of the press, to the four quarters of the land. You have been accustomed to hold them up and to speak of them as a most happy specimen of the life and qualities, which, without early advantages over the rest of the community, are naturally produced by that equality of condition which prevails in New England, and by those means of common school education, and the facilities which attend a virtuous, energetic, and industrious young man upon his entrance on the world. You habitually point to him, as a bright example of the highest social position, of commanding influence over others, of overflowing abundance of this world's goods, attained by the calm and steady exercise of home-bred virtues and practical qualities, by the energetic and unostentatious pursuit of an industrious career, which are the common birthright of the country; and the greater his praise, who out of these familiar elements of prosperity was able to rear such a rare and noble fabric of success.

Mr. Lawrence, sir, as you well know, belonged to that class of merchants who raise Commerce far above the level of the selfish pursuit of private gain. He contemplated it as a great calling of humanity, having high duties and generous aims; one of the noblest developments of our modern civilization. I know these were his views. I had a conversation with him many years ago, which I shall never forget. I was to deliver an address before one of our local associations, and I went to him and asked him what I should say to the young men. "Tell them," said he, "that Commerce is not a mercenary pursuit, but an honorable calling. Tell them that the hand of God has spread out these mighty oceans, not to separate, but to unite the nations of the earth; that the winds that fill the sail are the breath of heaven; that the various climates of the earth and their different products are designed by Providence to be the foundation of a mutually beneficial intercourse between distant regions." Mr. Lawrence was justly proud of the character of a Boston merchant, and that character suffered nothing at his hands. His business life extended over two or three of those terrible convulsions, which shake the pillars of the commercial world, but they disturbed in no degree the solid foundations of his prosperity. He built upon the adamantine basis of probity; beyond reproach, beyond suspicion. His life gave a lofty meaning to the familiar line, and you felt, in his presence, that

"An honest man *is* the noblest work of God."

Far from being ashamed of his humble beginnings, he was proud of them; as the merchant princes of Florence, at the height of their power, and when they were giving the law to Italy, preserved upon their palaces the cranes by which bales of merchandise were raised to their attics. A young gentleman told me yesterday, at Newport, that two or three months ago Mr. Lawrence took from his waistcoat pocket, and exhibited in his presence, a pair of blunt scissors, which had served him for daily use at the humble commencement of his business life. As for his personal integrity, Mr. Chairman, to which you alluded, I am persuaded that if the dome of the State House, which towers over his residence in Park-street, had been coined into a diamond, and laid at his feet, as the bribe of a dishonest transaction, he would have spurned it like the dust he trod on. His promise was a sacrament.

Although in early life brought up in a limited sphere, and in the strictness of the old school, which prescribed a somewhat rigid perseverance in one track, Mr. Lawrence was not afraid of bold and novel projects; he rather liked them. He was an early and an efficient friend of the two great business conceptions—creations I may call them—of his day and generation. As much as any one man, more than most, he contributed to realize them, to the inappreciable benefit of the country. When he came forward into life, India cottons, of a coarser and flimsier texture than any thing that has ever been seen in this country by any man under thirty-five years of age, were sold in this market at retail for a quarter of a dollar a yard. Every attempt to manufacture a better article was crushed by foreign competition, acting upon imperfect machinery, want of skill incident to a novel enterprise, and the reluctance of capital to seek new and experimental investments. Mr. Lawrence felt that this was an unnatural state of things. He believed, if our infant arts could be sustained through the first difficulties, that they would assuredly prosper. He believed the American Union to be eminently calculated for a comprehensive manufacturing system. He saw, in no distant perspective, the great agricultural staple of the South enjoying the advantage of a second and that a home market, by being brought into connection with the mechanical skill and the capital of the North. He saw the vast benefit of multiplying the pursuits of a community, and thus giving play to the infinite variety of native talent. He heard in advance the voice of a hundred streams now running to waste over barren rock, but which was to be brought into accord with the music of the power-loom. He contemplated a home consumption at the farmer's door, for the products of his cornfield, his vegetable garden, and his dairy. These were the views and the principles which led him, in common with Mr. Jackson, Mr. F. C. Lowell, Mr. Appleton, and their associates, to labor for the establishment of the manufactures of the United States. These surely were large and generous views. At the time when his own pursuits and interests were deeply engaged in commerce, entertaining the opinions I have so briefly indicated, he threw himself with characteristic ardor into the new pursuit, and the country is largely indebted to Mr. Lawrence for the noble result. We are now, without any diminution of our agriculture and navigation, but on the contrary with a large increase of both, the second manufacturing country in the world. The rising city which bears his name, on the beautiful banks of the Merrimack, will carry down to posterity no unworthy memorial of his participation in this auspicious work.

The other great conception, or creation, to which I had reference, was the railroad system of the country. For this also the community is largely indebted to Mr. Lawrence. With respect to the first considerable work of this kind in New England, the Worcester Railroad, I can not speak with so much confidence (I mean of Mr. Lawrence's connection with it) as my friend behind me (Hon. N. Hale), but with regard to the extension of that road westward, I am able to speak from my own information. Mr. Lawrence was one of its earliest and most efficient friends. It is twenty years ago this summer since we had a most enthusiastic and successful meeting in this hall in furtherance of that great enterprise. Mr. Lawrence contributed efficiently to get up that meeting, and took a very active part in the measures proposed by it. It was my fortune to take some part in the proceedings. At the end of my speech, for which he had furnished me valuable materials and suggestions, he said to me, with that beaming smile which we all remember so well, "Mr. Everett, we shall live to see the banks of the Upper Mississippi connected with iron bands with State-street." He has passed away too soon for all but his own pure fame; but he lived to see that prophecy fulfilled. I need not tell you, Mr. Chairman, that to these two causes—the manufactures and the net-work of railroads strewn over the country—New England is greatly indebted for her present prosperity.

There is another cause to which she owes still more than to any thing that begins and ends in material influences—the cause of education. Of this also, Mr. Lawrence was an efficient friend. Besides all that he did for the academies and schools of the country, in answer to applications for aid continually made, and as constantly granted in proportion to their merits, he has left that enduring monument of his enlightened liberality, the Scientific School at Cambridge. My friend and former associate in the Corporation of Harvard College (Hon. S. A. Eliot) can vouch for the accuracy of what I say on this head. Mr. Lawrence felt that our collegiate seminaries, from the nature of those institutions, made but inadequate provision for scientific education as a preparation for the industrial career. He determined, as far as possible, to remedy the defect. He had felt himself the want of superior education, and resolved that, as far as he was able to prevent it, the rising generation of his young countrymen should not suffer the same privation. I had the honor at that time to be connected with the University at Cambridge. I conferred with him on this subject, from the time it first assumed distinct shape in his mind to that of its full development. He saw the necessity of systematic training in the principles of science, in order to meet the growing demands of the country and the age. He saw that it was a period of intense action. He wished our agriculturists, our engineers, our chemists, our architects, our miners, our machinists—in a word, all classes engaged in handling the natural elements, to lay a solid foundation on the eternal basis of science. But his views were not limited to a narrow utilitarianism. He knew the priceless worth of pure truth. He wished that his endowment should contribute to promote its discovery by original researches into the mysteries of nature, and he especially rejoiced in being able to engage for his infant establishment the services of the great naturalist of the day. These were the objects of the Scientific School—this the manner in which he labored for their promotion. What nobler object for the appropriation of the fruit of his hardly-earned affluence could be devised? For material prosperity, and all the establishments by which it is augmented and secured, may flee away; commerce may pass into new channels; populous cities, in the lapse of ages, may be destroyed; and strong governments be overturned in the convulsions of empires; but science and truth are as eternal as the heavens, and the memory of him who has contributed to their discovery or diffusion, shall abide till the heavens themselves have departed as a scroll.

In these and other ways, of which I have not time to speak, Mr. Lawrence rendered noble service to the community, but always as a private man. He wished to serve it in no other capacity. He resisted, as much as possible, all solicitations to enter public life. He served a little while in our municipal councils and in our State Legislature, but escaped as soon as possible. He served two terms in Congress, with honor and good repute. He brought to that market articles with which it is not overstocked—sound, reliable, practical knowledge, and freedom from electioneering projects. He was a forcible and persuasive though not a frequent speaker, and always listened to, because he never spoke except when he had something to say pertinent to the matter in hand and worth hearing. He rendered the most important aid as one of the commissioners on behalf of Massachusetts in the negotiation of the Northeastern Boundary question.

He was offered a seat in General Taylor's cabinet, which was promptly declined; and when the mission to London was placed at his disposal, he held it long under advisement. While he was deliberating whether to accept the place, he did me the honor to consult me, naturally supposing I could give him particular information as to the duties of the office, and remarking that it would depend in a considerable degree on my report whether he accepted it. Among many other questions, he asked me "whether there was any real foundation in truth for the ancient epigrammatic jest, that 'an ambassador is a person sent to a foreign government to tell lies for his own,'" adding that, "if that was the case, his mind was made up; he had never yet told a lie, and was not going to begin at the age of fifty-six."

I told him "I could answer for myself as a foreign minister, that I had never said a word or written a line which, as far as my own character or that of my government was concerned, I should have been unwilling to see in the newspapers the next day;" and this explanation, he said, removed one of his scruples. I encouraged him, of course, to accept the mission; and his brilliant success is known to the country and to Europe—success equal to that of any of his predecessors, living or dead, however distinguished. His genial disposition, his affable manner, his princely hospitality, his appropriate speeches at public meetings and entertainments—not studied harangues, not labored disquisitions—but brief, animated, cordial appeals to the good feelings of the audience—the topics pertinent to the occasion, the tone cheerful and radiant with good-humor, lively touches on the heart-strings of international sympathy—these were the manly and honest wiles with which he won the English heart. His own government—first duty of a foreign minister—was faithfully served. The government to which he was accredited was conciliated. The business confided to him (and it is at all times immense) was ably transacted. The convenience of a host of traveling countrymen promoted. The public in England gratified. What more could be done or desired? His success, as I have said, was fully equal to that of any of his predecessors—perhaps I ought to use a stronger term.

He came home and returned to private life the same man. He resumed his place in his happy home, in his counting-house, in the circle of friends, and wherever duty was to be performed or good done. To the sacred domain of private life I will not follow him, except to say a word on that trait of his character to which the gentlemen who have preceded me have so feelingly alluded. I mean his beneficence—a topic never to be omitted in speaking of Mr. Lawrence.

And here I will say of him what I heard President John Quincy Adams say of another merchant prince of Boston (Col. Perkins), in the hall of the House of Representatives, that "he had the fortune of a prince, and a heart as much larger than his fortune, as that was than a beggar's." I will say of him what was said of his lamented brother Amos, that "every day of his life was a blessing to somebody." Sir, he gave constantly, by wholesale and retail; and as I venture to affirm without certainly knowing the fact, every day of his life.

His bounty sometimes descended in copious showers, and sometimes distilled in gentle dews. He gave munificent sums publicly where it was proper to do so, by way of setting an example to others; and far oftener his benefactions followed humble want to her retreat, and solaced the misery known only to God and the earthly steward of his bounty. Vast sums were given by him while he lived, which evinced, but, if I mistake not, did not exhaust his liberality.

Such he was; so kind, so noble, so complete in all the relations of life—the son, the husband, the parent, the brother, the citizen—in a word, in all that makes a man; and the ultimate source of all this goodness, its vital principle, that which brought all his qualities into harmonious relation, was religious belief—the faith and hope of the gospel.

This is no theme for a place like this; other lips and another occasion will do it justice. But this it was which gave full tone to his character, and which bore him through the last great trial. This it is which must console us under his irreparable loss, and administer comfort to those with whose sorrow the stranger intermeddleth not.

C Harding Pt. H. Wright Smith Engr.

WILLIAM LAWRENCE.

WILLIAM LAWRENCE.

WANT teaches us value. They know best how to prize a thing, who are deprived of it, or have never been blest with its possession. This explains the fact, that education, for its wider diffusion and its enlarged instrumentalities, is greatly indebted to the benefactions of many, who, in their youth, had themselves but slight participation in its advantages.

If the facilities of commerce have been multiplied, and her gains increased by the discoveries of science and the inventions of art, commerce has repaid the debt, by her rich gifts to schools and colleges, her noble endowment of institutions of learning, at which science can be studied and art promoted, and where many successive generations can have the benefit of the highest intellectual and moral culture.

The history of education, in all ages and countries, bears some testimony to this fact; New England especially abounds with evidences and illustrations of it. The sneer about "The Almighty Dollar," in connection with American character, is as false as it is silly, and as ungenerous as it is untrue. Our people are undoubtedly frugal, industrious, enterprising. Like all the rest of the world, they love money, they strive to get it, and commonly succeed in obtaining it. But they know how to use and enjoy it. They love money, not for its own sake simply, but for what it enables them to do, and, as a general remark, it may be said that they do well with it. They have devoted large portions of it, in every generation, to objects of public benefit and blessing.

New England, as regards the Anglo-Saxon occupation of her soil, is but little over two hundred years old. She is not without spot or blemish, either in her present condition or her past history; but if we recollect the statistics of her beneficence, if we take an inventory of her schools, colleges, hospitals, asylums, the various institutions of learning or philanthropy, which that beneficence has established, endowed, made strong and efficient, the result is honorable alike to human nature and the New England character. It teaches that wealth does not always beget a hard-hearted selfishness; that many rich in this world's goods have also been rich in good deeds, and, as faithful stewards of the Lord's bounty, have used their wealth for wise and noble purposes.

Among those entitled to this eulogy, is the late WILLIAM LAWRENCE, who, in common with his brothers, Amos and Abbott, was a noble specimen of a New England merchant, and a Christian citizen and patriot. He was born at Groton, September 7, 1783, and was the third son and child of Samuel and Susan Parker Lawrence, some account of whom may be interesting, as indicating the source of the strongly marked character of their sons. The name of Lawrence dates far back in English history, and has gathered to itself honors in many successive generations. The common ancestor of the New England Lawrences was John Lawrence, of Great St. Albans, Hertfordshire, who came to this country in 1635, and settled at Watertown, where he resided many years, became the father of a numerous family, and the possessor, as the town records show, of many valuable parcels of land. In 1660, he removed to Groton, then recently erected into a plantation or township by order of the General Court, on the petition, with others, of Dean Winthrop, son of Governor Winthrop. It received its name, probably, from Winthrop, who came from Groton, Suffolk County, England. Here John Lawrence soon became an honored, trusted, and influential citizen, and here some one or more families of his descendants have ever since resided, identifying the name of Lawrence with the history and character of the town.

Samuel Lawrence was the fifth generation in descent from the above-mentioned John Lawrence. He was born in Groton, April 24, 1754, and was, therefore, in his early manhood, when our revolutionary struggles commenced. In common with all the hardy, intelligent, liberty-loving yeomanry of New England, he espoused the cause of the Colonies, and devoted himself to it with a courage that never failed, a constancy that never faltered till his country had passed "from impending servitude to acknowledged independence." At work in the field, plowing his paternal acres, when the news of the attack upon Concord reached Groton, he immediately unloosed a horse from his team, and mounting, rode rapidly through Groton and some of the adjoining towns, spreading the alarm, and summoning the militia to assemble. He returned in season to join his own company at the church at Groton, at twelve o'clock, where, after prayer offered by the pastor of the town, they started for Concord, helped to swell that impetuous tide of resistance which drove back the invaders, and slept that night on Cambridge Common, after a forced march of thirty miles, and hot skirmishes with the retreating foe. From that time to the peace of 1783, he was "a soldier of the Revolution," and, with the exception of one or two brief visits to his family and friends at Groton, he was in actual service throughout the whole war. He rose to the rank of major, and for a considerable period was attached to General Sullivan's staff, as adjutant; an office for which his powerful lungs and sonorous voice, which could be heard throughout a long line of troops, peculiarly fitted him. He was in many of the severest battles of the Revolution. At Bunker Hill, where he was slightly wounded, his coat and hat were pierced with the balls of the enemy, and were preserved in the family for many years. At one time, he commanded a company, whose rank and file were all negroes, of whose courage, military discipline, and fidelity, he always spoke with respect. On one occasion, being out reconnoitering with this company, he got so far in advance of his command, that he was surrounded, and on the point of being made prisoner by the enemy. The men soon discovering his peril, rushed to his rescue, and fought with the most determined bravery till that rescue was effectually secured. He never forgot this circumstance; and ever after took especial pains to show kindness and hospitality to any individual of the colored race who came near his dwelling.

Mr. Lawrence was married during the war, in the year 1777, to Susanna Parker; and, while the marriage ceremony was in progress, the tolling of the bell summoned the minute-men to assemble at the church for instant service. The moment the rite was concluded, he parted from his bride and friends, and hastened to Rhode Island. He was permitted to return, however, on a brief furlough of two or three days, at the expiration of which he entered again upon active service, from which he had no respite till late in the autumn of 1778, when he visited Groton, rejoicing to find himself a father as well as a husband.

At the close of the war, Major Lawrence settled in Groton, on a beautiful farm on the outskirts of the village, where he passed the remainder of his life, honored and esteemed by his townsmen, who gladly elected him to such offices and honors as he was willing to accept. A man of strong sense, of clear judgment, of stern integrity, of ardent patriotism, and devout piety, his influence was felt, his energies exerted in every thing that concerned the social, moral, and religious improvement of the town. He was deacon of the First Congregational Church in Groton for more than forty years. He was one of the original founders, and for thirty-three years a trustee of Groton Academy, an institution which his sons have since munificently endowed. In Shay's rebellion, and during all the troubles of 1786–87, he stood firm for the government, and was foremost in advocating the supremacy of the laws. A devout man, strict in all religious observances, firm, almost rigid in the discipline of his family, he was cheerful, joyous, benignant, "given to hospitality," and never so happy as when making happy those around him. The young loved him, and the reverence with which they gathered around him was tempered by the most confiding affection.

He lived to be present at the laying of the corner-stone of the Bunker Hill Monument, in 1825; an occasion in which, as one of the survivors of that most memorable and important battle of the Revolution, he felt a deep personal interest. The excitements of that week, passed in Boston, brought on a paralytic attack, from which he never entirely recovered. He died November 8, 1827, aged seventy-three.

Susanna Parker Lawrence was born in Groton, where her father, William Parker, cultivated a farm, now owned by the town. He subsequently removed to Concord, where he resided several years. Susanna, his youngest daughter, was distinguished for quiet and gentle manners, a loving spirit, a truly feminine grace and dignity of character; with these qualities were united a nobility of soul, a lofty and indomitable energy, that made honor and reverence to mingle largely in the love borne to her by her husband and children. In illustration of her own energy, as well as of the customs of that period, it may be mentioned that, while her father lived at Concord, it was no unusual thing for her to mount a horse, ride to the ferry at Charlestown, a distance of seventeen miles, go over to Boston "shopping," and return to Concord on the same day. From a hill in the rear of her father's residence, in the easterly part of the village of Concord, she saw the British troops enter that town on the morning of the 19th of April, 1776, and remained there till she saw them pass out a retreating and discomfited foe. Like most of the women of that day, she was an ardent patriot, espousing the cause of the colonies with an intense devotion, ready to endure all the trials and make all sacrifices which the interest of that cause demanded; and it may be, that not a little of the courage, the perseverance and fidelity displayed by her lover and husband, amid the perils and hardships of that long struggle for liberty and independence, is to be ascribed to her inspiring influence.

To an extraordinary energy of character, and excellent habits of industry and frugality, which enabled her to manage successfully, in the absence of her husband, both the affairs of the farm and of the household, she added the power of religious faith, and the winning graces of an elevated Christian character. She was eminently a religious woman, governing herself by religious principles in the discipline of her family and the education of her children; and thus exercising over them, in the forming period of character, a winning and persuasive religious influence. In the earliest recollection of all of them, there distinctly abides her hallowed image, kneeling at their bedside, and breathing a devout, earnest prayer, for the divine protection and blessing upon their young hearts. Her faith, which had ever adorned her life and character, which made her active, open, honorable, and useful, shed a halo of moral beauty and glory around her declining years. Serenely cheerful, still young in her affections and sympathies, devoutly submissive, ready to "abide, or to depart and be with Christ," she presented a most attractive picture of lovely and venerable old age. She survived her husband eighteen years, and died May 2, 1845, aged eighty-nine years.

Such were the parents of "the Lawrences;" intelligent, virtuous, high principled, devout, ordering their family in the fear of God, and sanctifying all social affections and sympathies, all domestic duty and intercourse, by Christian faith and daily prayer. A family thus ordered and pervaded by the spirit of religion, is a miniature of heaven; it is a nursery of virtue to the State, the Church, the world. Incalculable blessings and holy influences go forth from it. Here is the point at which to begin the reform of the world, —the family, which is a divine institution; and every scheme of philanthropy, every enterprise of social or civil reform that overlooks or disregards this, will fail. They who are faithful here, are benefactors of the community to an extent which can not be calculated; negligent in this, they have no claim to be benefactors, though their names stand first among the contributors to every public charity in the land.

Samuel and Susanna Lawrence did not fail in this great duty. They made their home eminently a Christian home; and to the influences of this home and of those parents, may be traced all the marked and prominent features in the character of their sons.

Of these sons, William, the subject of this memoir, originally intended to be a farmer. A strong constitution, robust health, and a vigorous physical frame, united with a natural love of agricultural pursuits, with which he had been familiar from his childhood, had their influence in producing this determination. But this physical strength was under the direction of an earnest, enthusiastic spirit, that might easily be lead to task it beyond what it could bear; and it was so tasked. In the autumn of 1809, after three or four years of very hard work on the farm, his health failed, and there was so much danger that his strength and constitution would break down entirely, that it was thought best that he should relinquish for a season all laborious occupations, and, leaving home, pass the winter quietly with his brother Amos, who had then recently established himself in business in Boston. He accordingly repaired to Boston in October, and during the winter remained with his brother, more as a companion than a clerk or an apprentice; occasionally helping him, and doing so more and more as he became interested and competent in the sale of goods at the store, and in making purchases at auctions.

When the spring opened, he found himself much improved in health, but not strong enough to resume the severe labors that would devolve upon him in the care and culture of his father's farm. He found also that the winter's experience had developed a tact and taste for commercial pursuits, and he determined to change his plan of life and become a merchant. He passed the remainder of the year, therefore, with his brother, adding to his experience and knowledge; and in 1810, commenced business for himself, in a small store near that of his brother Amos, with no capital but his own energies and talent, and the credit which these could procure for him. The fact, that at twenty-six years of age, with only the limited experience of a few months in his brother's store, he passed at once from agricultural to commercial pursuits, and prosecuted the latter from the beginning with an uninterrupted and constantly widening success, is a sufficient evidence both of the energy of his character and the force and capacity of his intellect.

The incidents of his commercial life are few and simple. He continued in business by himself, gradually enlarging his operations as his means increased, till 1822, when he formed a partnership with his brother Samuel, under the style of W. & S. Lawrence. This union of his own experience and judgment with the fresh energy and talent of his younger brother, made a strong commercial house, whose operations soon became extensive and prosperous. In 1825, W. & S. Lawrence, who had hitherto been chiefly importers, became interested in domestic manufactures. It was through their agency and influence that the first incorporated company for the manufacture of woolen goods was formed at Lowell, —the Middlesex Company. This enlargement of their operations required an addition to the strength and means of the firm, which was accordingly made. Mr. William W. Stone became a partner of the house in 1826, and the business was transacted under the firm of W. & S. Lawrence & Stone. In this connection, Mr. Lawrence continued in active business, principally the domestic commission business, for the manufacture and sale of American woolens, till 1842, when he retired with an ample fortune, partly acquired by his own industry and enterprise, and partly received as his wife's patrimony from her father, William Bordman, of Boston, whose daughter Susan, Mr. Lawrence had married in 1813, and who still survives him, together with four children, one son and three daughters, all of whom are married.

In addition to the wise forethought and patriotic enterprise with which he and others encouraged the introduction of domestic manufactures, two events in his commercial career may be briefly noticed. In the movement made by Messrs. Greenough & Cotting, by which Cornhill, leading from Dock Square to Court-street, was opened, Mr. William Lawrence took an active and hearty interest, and was one of the first to occupy one of the stores in the lower part of the new street. This was at that time one of the most important enterprises, and a greater change affecting the convenience of intercourse in the heart of the city, than any that had been attempted. Mr. Lawrence was interested in it, through that feeling which prompted him always to encourage, by his influence and means, every enterprise that promised to promote the prosperity and progress of the community.

But as a merchant and a business man, the most signal point in his career—that which proves his clear discernment, not only of the importance to all the interests of trade of an equalized circulating medium, but of the best method of producing such equality of value in the circulating medium of New England, and which entitles him, therefore, to the gratitude of the merchants and business men of Boston and the New England States—was his persevering efforts to introduce what is now familiarly known as "The Suffolk Bank System." This bank was chartered in 1818. Mr. Lawrence was a member of the Board of Directors, from its organization up to the time of his death, a period of thirty years. It is not necessary that we should explain this system in detail. It is sufficient for us to say, that the bills of every bank entering into it are current, at par value, at Boston, and all over New England. If a trader in the country has a demand to meet in Boston, he can send or bring down the bills of the local bank in his neighborhood; the Boston merchant can receive them without discount, because he can immediately deposit them at the Suffolk Bank, and receive in return Suffolk Bank bills or specie. The effect is obvious; but the value and importance of the arrangement, in facilitating all the exchanges of business, or the difficulty of introducing it, can only be justly appreciated by those who are old enough to remember the state of things that existed before it was put in force. Then the merchants and traders of Boston—formerly the central market of the New England States more than now—were in the habit of selling the bills of country banks to brokers at a discount, which depended upon the distance of the bank from Boston, the difficulty of sending the bills for redemption to the towns where they were payable, a want of knowledge of their responsibility, and other like considerations. There was an inequality and irregularity in the currency, causing great embarrassments and delays in pecuniary transactions. These operated as a great restriction upon trade. To remove it was the object of the arrangement introduced and carried to a successful issue by the Suffolk Bank. The undertaking was a bold one, and indomitable energy and perseverance were necessary to success. It naturally met with opposition at first, from the sensitiveness of the several States in regard to their currency, and from the prejudices of the smaller and jealousy of the larger towns in the Commonwealth. The earnest advocacy of its friends, and the practical working of the plan as fast and as far as it prevailed, gradually overcame this opposition; and the "system" now embraces all, or nearly all the banks in the New England States, giving to these States a sound and uniform currency, the comforts and advantages of which can not be too highly appreciated.

It is not intended to detract in the least from the credit due to other early and earnest advocates of the system—some of whom are still connected with the Suffolk Bank, and take a deep interest in its prosperity and usefulness—when we say, that its success is to be attributed in no small degree to the wise, various, and persevering efforts of Mr. William Lawrence.

For these efforts, were there no other cause, he is entitled to the grateful remembrance of the mercantile community.

On retiring from active business, in 1842, Mr. Lawrence turned with fresh relish to agricultural pursuits, and the old homestead and the paternal acres at Groton became objects of deep interest. He continued to reside in Boston, but the improvement of the farm at Groton occupied much of his thought, and gave a zest and pleasure to the closing years of his life. His health, which had been failing for some time, broke down entirely in the autumn of 1847; and after a lingering illness of ten months, which he bore with Christian fortitude and resignation, he expired on the 14th of October, 1848.

As a citizen and merchant of Boston, Mr. Lawrence was always a cheerful and prominent contributor to every enterprise of Christian benevolence, and to any object that an enlightened patriotism and a broad and generous humanity approved. In common with many of the wealthy merchants of this country, he felt deeply the importance and value of a good education; and his claims to the grateful remembrance of the community as a benefactor to this noble cause, are worthy of particular attention. These claims are substantiated not simply by the munificence of his gifts to the Lawrence Academy, but also by the wisdom of the manner in which they were bestowed, and the good sense which marked the conditions annexed. The Groton Academy dates its origin from a joint-stock organization formed for the purpose, on the 27th of April, 1793. Five pounds constituted a share of this stock. Three hundred and twenty-five pounds were raised by subscriptions, or shares taken by forty-four individuals, all of whom were inhabitants of Groton, except four, who were citizens of Pepperrell. The town of Groton subscribed forty shares, on which, however, interest only was to be paid from year to year. Application was made to the General Court for an act of incorporation, which was granted, bearing date September 25, 1793. Under this act, organization was duly effected on the 17th of October, 1793, and fifteen persons chosen to constitute the Board of Trustees. In November of that year, the school opened in the academy building, which had been erected for the purpose, and which "stands yet on the same spot where it was originally placed, though at present it is not to be recognized in the pile of improvements which have been built up around it."

Thus, small in its beginnings and slender in its means, was this academy, which is now one of the most flourishing and best endowed institutions of its class in New England. For some years, the only resources of the school were the tuition fees of the pupils and the interest on the forty shares subscribed by the town of Groton. In 1797, on petition of the Trustees, the General Court made them a grant of one half of a township of land in Maine, about eleven thousand five hundred and twenty acres, which was subsequently sold for fifty cents per acre. In 1825, the widow of James

Brazer, Esq., one of the original subscribers to the joint stock for the establishment of the school, by her will, made the Trustees residuary legatees of one half of her estate, besides leaving them specific legacies of five hundred dollars in money, payable on the death of each of five relations. In 1838 and 1839, Mr. Amos Lawrence made liberal donations of books and philosophical apparatus; and, in 1842, he placed in the hands of the Trustees the sum of two thousand dollars, to be expended according to their judgment, in enlarging and improving the academy building. But these things added but little to the cash fund of the academy, and, while they enlarged its instrumentalities, they did little to place it upon a firm and permanent foundation. This it was left for William Lawrence to do, in 1844, by a donation of Ten Thousand Dollars. This donation was communicated to the Trustees in the following letter:

"Boston, April 6, 1844.

To the Trustees of Groton Academy:

Gentlemen,—Born and educated in Groton, I feel a deep interest in its prosperity, and especially in your academy; an institution which my honored father labored so hard to bring into existence more than half a century ago, and to which I am indebted for what little education I possess.

Having been highly blest in my temporal concerns, I have thought I could not better dispose of a portion of my abundance than to give to the academy over which you preside, a sum of money for the advancement of education for all coming time.

I, therefore, hereby give to Groton Academy the sum of ten thousand dollars, and direct that the same shall be invested in such manner, for the benefit of said corporation, as the Trustees thereof shall, from time to time, deem safe and expedient, and that the net income thereof shall be applied in their discretion. I am especially desirous that such compensation shall be paid to the instructors of said academy, as shall secure for it constantly the services of learned persons, perfectly competent to all their duties.

And this gift is, therefore, upon condition that the present rate of charge for instruction in said academy shall not be reduced. But whenever hereafter, in any year, the whole net income of the present funds and property of said institution, and of the fees received for instruction, added to the net income of said ten thousand dollars, shall be more than sufficient for the payment of liberal salaries to such instructors, so that a balance of said income shall remain unexpended, I request the said Trustees in their discretion, and if they deem it expedient, to pay and distribute such balance, or any of it, to and among such deserving male pupils in such institution, preparing for a collegiate education, as the Trustees may think deserving such aid; but not more than one hundred dollars shall be paid or allowed to any one such pupil in any one year. And, in granting such aid, I earnestly request that no regard may be had to any sectarian views entertained by the pupils on the subject of the Christian religion.

You will please draw on Lawrence & Stone, Boston, for said sum of ten thousand dollars, in such sums and at such times as will suit your convenience.

Your obedient servant,

WILLIAM LAWRENCE.

This letter is an honorable testimony to the noble and generous feelings of the writer; and, at the same time, the three conditions annexed to the donation,—that there should be no diminution of the tuition fees, but that the income of the ten thousand dollars should be used in procuring the best and most competent teachers; that, in case after paying liberal salaries to such, from the other resources of the academy, and the income of this fund, there should remain an unexpended balance, it was to be distributed at the discretion of the trustees among meritorious students preparing for a collegiate education; and that, in such distribution, no regard should be had to any sectarian views entertained by the pupils on the subject of the Christian religion,—are alike indications of Mr. Lawrence's practical wisdom, his sound judgment, and his comprehensive charity. A special meeting of the Trustees was called to acknowledge this, the largest and most generous donation which they had at that time received; and on their petition to the General Court, the next winter, at the session of 1845, the corporate name was changed from "Groton Academy," to the "Lawrence Academy at Groton."

In 1846, Mr. William Lawrence made to this institution another donation of five thousand dollars, to be expended under the direction of the Trustees in enlarging and improving the academy building, procuring a bell, ornamenting the grounds, &c., &c.; and, during the same year, Mr. Amos Lawrence purchased the residence of the late James Brazer, Esq., adjoining the academy lot, and presented it to the Trustees for the use of the successive preceptors of the academy.

Thus furnished with an enlarged and improved academy building, valuable additions to its library and philosophical apparatus, an elegant and commodious residence for the preceptor, and ten thousand dollars in funds, the institution was placed upon a secure and permanent foundation. Public attention was naturally directed to it, its scholars increased in number, its standard of education was elevated, its usefulness enlarged and extended, and had nothing further been done, the propriety of the appellation, "The Lawrence Academy at Groton," would have been justified, and all who bore that family name might have felt a deep satisfaction in its past history, and its present and prospective usefulness.

Whether Mr. William Lawrence originally determined to give something more to this institution at his death, or whether that determination was produced by an observation of the good effected by his former donations, can not be clearly ascertained. Probably the purpose of further endowment was entertained, but left contingent upon the result of that observation. Always Mr. Lawrence exhibited one of the sure evidences of a pure heart, uncontaminated by those evil influences of wealth, which beget pride, haughtiness, a selfish and worldly spirit. He delighted in the memories and associations of his childhood and youth. The old homestead was a hallowed spot in his affections, of which nothing could take precedence. The friends of his early days, the people and the interests of his native town, were never forgotten. There was something holy and reverent in his feelings toward Groton; and this feeling, always fresh and strong, increased both in tenderness and strength, as life waned, and he felt its end approaching. It was this feeling, united with the clear observation of the good already done, that produced the munificent donation contained in the following codicil to his will:

"Desirous to increase the usefulness of the Lawrence Academy in Groton, and to place its prosperity (as far as I can do so) on a secure foundation, I have, at different times heretofore, made donations for its benefit, and have also made provision for it in my will. But, upon reflection, I am induced to apprehend that what I have thus done may not be sufficient to accomplish the objects I have in view. Therefore, I hereby revoke the bequest contained in my said will, of ten thousand dollars to the Trustees of the Lawrence Academy at Groton, and I hereby give to the Trustees of the Lawrence Academy at Groton, aforesaid, their successors and assigns forever, the sum of TWENTY THOUSAND DOLLARS, to be paid to the said corporation within one year after my decease, without interest, to be held by them, as a permanent public corporate body, specially charged with the care and superintendence of education, upon the following trusts; that is to say, carefully to manage and invest the said sum of twenty thousand dollars as they shall deem most safe and advantageous, having more regard to the safety of the principal than the amount of income; to collect and receive the interest and income thereof; to deduct therefrom, and pay all such necessary and proper charges as may be incurred in the management of the said trust fund; and to apply the net interest and income of said twenty thousand dollars, or of the property in which it may be vested, to and for the following purposes, viz., to add one thousand dollars of said net income annually to the said principal sum (so that it shall become part thereof), until the whole principal fund held under this codicil shall amount to thirty thousand dollars; which shall forever afterward be taken and deemed to be the principal trust fund; to apply the residue of the net interest and income of said twenty thousand dollars, until said trust fund shall amount to thirty thousand dollars, and afterward to apply the whole net income and interest of said trust fund of thirty thousand dollars to the payment of the expense of keeping the buildings of said corporation at all times sufficiently insured by some safe Insurance Company or Companies in said commonwealth, to the payment in whole or in part (in their discretion) of the salaries and compensation of any instructor or instructors at said academy; to aid in the maintenance and education at said academy of any such meritorious persons as may resort thither for instruction, who may, in the opinion of said Trustees, deserve and need such assistance, by advances as gifts or loans (in the discretion of said Trustees), not exceeding one hundred dollars to any one such student in any one year; and to apply such portion of said net income, as said Trustees may from time to time deem expedient, to the purchase of books for the library of said academy, and philosophical and other instruments for the use of the pupils.

"Whenever, and as often as from losses or other causes, the said principal fund shall be less than thirty thousand dollars, I direct that one thousand dollars of the net income of the residue of said fund shall be added annually to the principal, until the whole fund shall amount to thirty thousand dollars, and whenever the capital fund shall sustain a loss or diminution of less than one thousand dollars, then and in every such case, and within one year afterward, sufficient of said net income shall be taken and added to the principal to make the sum thirty thousand dollars. I earnestly enforce it on all those who may have the care and management of the funds and property, given by me for the benefit of said academy, to invest the same with the utmost caution and prudence; to appropriate the net income as herein directed, and in applying portions of it to the benefit of deserving students, as herein provided, to do so without favor or partiality, and without regard to the religious sect to which any such student may belong, provided he be a Christian and a Protestant."

We lay the whole codicil before our readers, because we wish to do justice not simply to the benevolence of Mr. Lawrence, but to his wisdom, his practical good sense, and sound judgment. These are strikingly manifest in this codicil. Every thing that ought to be left to the discretion of the Trustees is intrusted to their decision from year to year, while every provision, condition, and restriction introduced is marked by a wise forethought, a large, comprehensive prudence. The fund is charged with the expense incident to its proper care and management, with an insurance to be constantly had on the building belonging to the academy, and provision is made that the income shall be used to keep the capital sum up to the amount of thirty thousand dollars, in case it should at any time, through bad investments or other causes, be diminished. The wisdom of this last provision is obvious. Unless the whole should be at once and irretrievably lost, which is altogether improbable, it secures to the academy, for all coming time, a capital of thirty thousand dollars, a sum sufficient to insure a perpetual prosperity and usefulness. Meeting these conditions, the Trustees are at liberty to use the income in paying the salaries of teachers either in whole or in part, in aiding indigent students, either by an outright gift or by a loan for such term of time as they see fit, the amount in each case not to exceed one hundred dollars, or in purchasing books, philosophical and other instruments for the use of the pupils. Here all the great interests of the institution, its buildings, its teachers, its students, its library and philosophical apparatus, are covered and secured by this codicil; and a large liberty is given to the Trustees to determine, from year to year, to which of these objects and in what proportions they will appropriate the income of the fund intrusted to them.

In this codicil, as well as in his other gifts to the academy at Groton, Mr. Lawrence showed himself to be a wise and enlightened, as well as generous benefactor of the great cause of education, and as such his name deserves to be held in remembrance and honor.

The importance resulting from the permanent character of his donations to Lawrence Academy, is justly described by the Rev. Mr. Means, in his discourse delivered before the Alumni of the school, at the jubilee held July 12, 1854. Speaking of Messrs. William and Amos Lawrence, as the benefactors of Groton Academy, he says: "There was a singular difference in the character of these two brothers, and there is a singular difference in the results of their benefactions. I have reason personally to know that they conferred frequently and earnestly respecting the parts which they should severally perform in upbuilding this school. There was an emulation, but there was no selfishness, there was no difference of opinion; both loved the academy, wished to bless it and to make it a blessing; each desired to accommodate the feelings of the other; each was unwilling to interfere with the other; each was ready to do what the other declined. Mr. William Lawrence was older in years, but he was later in commercial experience. He was firmer in health, and had less occasion, in the experience of bodily pain and dangerous illness than his brother, to lay to heart the injunction, 'Make unto yourselves friends of the unrighteous mammon, that when ye fail, they may receive you into everlasting habitations.' But though he began later, in respect to the amount bestowed upon this school, he was not behind his brother. On the contrary, he was before him. He gave more; and more of what he gave remains to this day in a productive form. Out of more than forty-five thousand dollars, provided for the academy by Mr. William Lawrence, forty thousand will remain in the hands of the Trustees, for purposes of instruction; while out of all that was given by Mr. Amos Lawrence, not one single cent was designed to be or now remains among the cash funds of the academy."

To William Lawrence, then, belongs the credit of the endowment of the Lawrence Academy at Groton, with a cash fund of forty thousand dollars, guarded by wise provisions, which secure thirty thousand in perpetuity, while in the distribution of the income they leave a large liberty of choice and discrimination to the Trustees. The wisdom and benevolence of his conduct in this noble benefaction to the cause of education, indicate the two simple elements of his character. He was a man of sound judgment, of strong practical common sense, and of a large and kindly heart; and one source of his wise and sound judgment was his pure heart. He had no selfish or sinister ends to accomplish, the desire to accomplish which so often darkens the conscience, bewilders and misleads the judgment. Undoubtedly he had that desire of success and accumulation, which naturally accompanies every man in the enterprises of trade and commerce, but this success was to be accomplished by an open, manly, straight-forward honesty. "There were no disguises, concealments, subterfuges, pretenses, or pretensions about him; all was plain, simple, frank, open as the day to all the world." Not eaten up with an intense *personal* anxiety, accustomed to look at all matters in the light of their broad relations to the interests of the whole community, his mind was clear to discern that which was wise, right, best, and his heart free to love and pursue it. The profound declaration of Scripture, "Out of the heart are the issues of life," found its fulfillment and illustration in him. A good heart, kind, tender, sympathizing, benevolent, strong in its affections, generous in its impulses, devout in its emotions, quickened and sanctified by a deep sentiment of religious faith, reverence, and responsibleness, this was the inspiring and controlling element of his character. A good heart gave him a clear head, a sound judgment, a wise discrimination. A good heart, deeply conscious of its responsibleness to its Maker, filled with a love of God that unfolded itself in love and good-will to man, this made him pure as well as wise, his career honorable as well as successful, his life useful, his death peaceful, his memory to be revered and honored—that "memory of the just which is blessed."

"Go thou and do likewise," is the voice of instruction with which his example speaks to many a wealthy son of New England.

JOHN JACOB ASTOR.

THE German critic and historian, Wolfgang Menzel, in his History of the Germans, says: "One of the most distinguished Germans in America was John Jacob Astor, the son of a Justice in the village of Waldorf, near Heidelberg (in the Duchy of Baden). He emigrated to America, and gradually became the richest fur-trader there. He founded at his own expense the colony of Astoria, on the northwest coast of America, so charmingly described by Washington Irving; and created the Astor fund, formed with the object to save the German emigrants, on their arrival in New York, from cheating speculators who might abuse their inexperience. He resided at New York, possessed of immense wealth, and esteemed for the noblest philanthropy."

Thus, with just national pride, Menzel claims for Germany the honor of Astor's brilliant mercantile career; Americans are disposed to claim the credit of his success for the merchants of America. Probably both are right; for if to America belongs Astor's career, it may be admitted that his character belongs to Germany. It is, in truth, a noteworthy fact, that while the faculty of money-making is believed to be, and doubtless is, pre-eminently an American trait, the two wealthiest merchants of America were of foreign birth and breeding—Girard of Bordeaux, and Astor of Waldorf, in Baden. The truth is, making money is one thing, making a fortune quite a different thing. To the one, the dashing spirit of American enterprise and the indulgent spirit of American law are highly favorable, but to the making of a fortune, getting is even less essential than saving. And saving and prudence, spite of what is thought to be the universal influence of the Poor Richard spirit of Franklin's maxims, in America, are not the prevailing spirit of American business. To save, is a lesson, we are inclined to believe better taught in the cottage of the German farmer than in the log hut of an American settler. The career of Astor, however, although he was carefully taught and faithfully learned this lesson, is not to be selected as a special illustration of it, for there have been few merchants so early, so rapidly, so uniformly successful as he; few who have been less called upon to practice the more plodding and sober mercantile virtues, or were animated by wider and more comprehensive views, and by more of what may be termed, in the best sense, the spirit of speculation.

John Jacob Astor was the youngest of four sons, and was born on the 17th of July, 1763, the year which brought to a close the Seven Years War, and by the treaties of Paris and Hubertsburg, gave to England the control of nearly all the fur-yielding regions of North America, from the Gulf of Mexico to the Arctic Circle.

Astor's father was a farmer, and his boyhood was passed amid the strengthening toils and healthful influences of a farmer's life. The family belonged to that large class in Germany, who, with but humble fortunes, and leading toilsome lives, are taught in childhood to read Luther's Bible and the Prayer-book—a class furnishing in all Protestant countries the elements and basis of a true republican and civilized state, and compared with whom the peasantry of France and Spain and Italy are children and serfs. Astor was trained from childhood in the practice of rising early and giving a portion of his first waking hours to the Bible and Prayer-book, a practice kept up in after life, and, as he often declared, the source of unfailing comfort and pleasure. A class thus educated by toil and the Bible is equal to all the best offices of ordinary life; and when to such preparation are added great intellect and a high aim, there is nothing in active life and business beyond the reach of one so prepared.

Such an intellect and aim were Astor's. While yet a boy, he looked beyond the horizon of youth to a great career of manhood before him; he looked beyond the Black Forest and the Rhine, which shut him in on the east and west, beyond the farmer's life he was leading, to a new and triumphant life in the great world. This confidence and ardent assurance of success ever went with him from boyhood up, and are strikingly illustrated by an anecdote which belongs to a later period of his life. "While yet almost a stranger in the city" of New York (the statement is from the lips of Mr. Astor himself), "and in very narrow circumstances, he passed by where a row of houses had just been erected in Broadway, and which, from the superior style of their architecture, were the talk and boast of the city. 'I'll build, one day or other, a greater house than any of these, in this very street,' said he to himself."* He accomplished the prediction.

The time and tide, without which the best powers and the strongest purposes are of no avail, but which they somehow are very apt to find, soon came for Astor. The oldest son of the family, by eleven years his senior, had established himself as a maker of musical instruments in London, and so successfully, that when young Astor was about sixteen years of age, he invited one of his brothers to join him in business. It is evident that business spirit and business talent were in the family, and not confined to one member of it. In fact, another of the brothers had already settled in America, or very soon after went thither. The invitation from London, declined by an older brother, was accepted by the youngest, who, with adventurous spirit, waited

* Irving's Astoria, p. 28.

for no outfit, bade adieu to his parents with affection, but doubtless without lingering, and set off for Manheim. From there he walked nearly all the way to the coast of Holland, whence a Dutch smack took him safely to London. Here, certainly, were courage and determination in the young Swabian; although the way had been somewhat opened before him by the brother, whose skill and success enabled him to offer the new-comer a house and business at once. With steady German purpose he entered upon his new life. As the clock struck four—and they lived within the sound of Bow-bells, that *will* be heard—he rose and dressed, then read his Bible and Prayer-book, and by five was ready for work. His brother was well pleased with his young assistant; but the spirit of Astor, while too conscientious and well disciplined to neglect or slight the duty before him, was too bold not to long for a wider field of duty.

The year of his birth, we have seen, was the date of a great historical event, the peace which secured to England nearly all North America; the next marked epoch of his life was the year in which the best part of North America, apparently destined by Providence to be held by England in trust, only until ready for a community better able to use it, was transferred to the United States.

The American Revolution was not so much a liberation from political, as from commercial thraldom. The chains of which our fathers complained, were rather figurative; there was substantial protection of the life and property of the highest and lowest. The Revolution, was, in great part, a commercial movement, favored by the merchant, producer, and manufacturer, or rather those ready to produce and manufacture, if permitted access to foreign or even home markets; by men conscious of the immense resources in the soil beneath them, in the oceans and lakes around them, in the enterprising courage of the sea-faring men of New England, and the backwoodsmen of Virginia, and who groaned under restrictions dictated by the spirit that declared the Colonies were not to be allowed to manufacture so much as a nail for themselves. Independence lifted a weight from energies kept down for a hundred years; and for seventy years past the world has been gazing in wonder at a growth in power, population, and wealth, which certainly is wonderful, but whose rapidity and suddenness are explained by the fact that it is the expansion following a long and unnatural compression. It is a growth which, in the natural course of things, would have gone on more moderately and evenly for two hundred years.

One of the most striking features of this growth, in fact one of the most remarkable events of the age, is the great migration, we may almost say, of whole nations and races, of which it has been both the cause and the effect. Hither, ever since the Revolution, have been flowing with constantly swelling volume, two streams, the German and the Celtic, to strengthen both elements of our Anglo-Saxon blood, and fill the ranks of toil and skill—the Irish, to dig canals and throw up railroad embankments; the German, with his thorough training as a mechanic, his steady industry as a farmer, his prudence as a merchant.

It looks like one of the strange cross-purposes of history, the "revenges" which the "whirligig of time" brings with it, that the two nations and the two races, which the perversity of their rulers sought to make instruments in subduing American freedom, are the very nations which have profited most by the opening that American independence has made for them. Ever since the war ended, they have been flocking over from Germany, which sent the Yägers of Cassel to fight at Saratoga, and from Ireland, whose parliament, at the request of the British ministry, voted four thousand troops for service against America. And it is difficult to say which has been most benefited by this migration, the emigrants themselves or the governments whom it has relieved of their presence. Europe, which for the last seventy years has so often prophesied the failure of freedom in America, has doubtless been itself saved from disastrous revolution by the safety-valve of American emigration. Perhaps the cause of liberty has suffered there, while the growth of the United States has been promoted. That it is one of the chief causes of the immense rapidity of this growth, is everywhere apparent, North, East, and West.

Among the pioneers of the great migration there is no more striking figure than John Jacob Astor. He is now twenty years of age, just maturing into that noble and manly person and presence which were among his few gifts from fortune, and which he owed to a fine head, an intellectual forehead, a look of high intelligence, and an address by turns commanding and persuasive. Such at least he is described to have been in maturer years. The young man stands on the shore of the sea. The child has "seen London." He sees "more beyond." He is ready to launch upon the top wave of that swelling prosperity in the New World which is destined to rise all the higher for being hemmed in so long.

A brother is already in the United States. Thus again a way is opened. And he is ready for the time and tide that will not wait for any man, and need not wait for him. The Treaty of Versailles was signed September 3d, 1783; Astor sailed for Baltimore in the following November, taking with him a few hundred dollars' worth of musical instruments to be disposed of on his brother's account, and prepared to face the dangers of a wintry voyage and the uncertainties of a new life in a new land. Detained by the rough weather of a very severe winter, the vessel did not reach Chesapeake Bay until the end of January, and there it was beset with floating ice and remained at anchor until March. This wintry quarantine might chill the spirit even of a young man. But he could wait. There was deliberation as well as ardor. There was the spirit that could make the best of possibilities and endure the inevitable. During a storm at this time, which filled the passengers with alarm for their safety and drove all other thoughts from their minds, Astor appeared on deck, arrayed in his best. Some one asked him why he selected such a time to discard the clothes he had worn during the voyage, and thus array himself. He replied, that if he escaped with his life it would be with his best clothes; if he perished, no matter what became of them.

This disheartening delay was the first check at the threshold, yet precisely this delay it was, or rather the use he made of it, that gave shape and direction to all his future life. Other ships and emigrants were likewise detained; the passengers would pass from ship to ship; acquaintances were made under the influence of the feeling which binds countrymen together in a strange land, and all men together under strange circumstances, and much useful information was given, many useful suggestions made. Among the German emigrants in the other ships was a furrier, very clever in his business, very shrewd, and willing to communicate. Astor made his acquaintance. His attention had been previously directed to the fur-trade, and he accordingly addressed numerous inquiries to his new friend, in relation to the various kinds and qualities of furs, and the mode of transacting business. In this way he obtained suggestions of the greatest value. The furrier advised him to go to New York, and ultimately accompanied him thither. The proceeds of the musical instruments were by his advice invested in furs. With these he hastened back to London, where they were disposed of to great advantage. He at once prepared again to cross the Atlantic, and devote himself systematically to the fur-trade, as the business of his life. To do this it was necessary to study the markets of Leipsic and London, and the other fur marts of Europe, and to make himself thoroughly familiar with the different varieties of the article. To these studies and inquiries he devoted his time in London.

There are many noticeable and striking things about the fur-trade and the use of furs. Of all traffics it is the most cosmopolitan. Sought for in the remotest recesses of one continent, they find their market at the most distant points of another. The otter and beaver of North America clothe the Chinese. They are obtained by the savage, amidst the wildest scenes of nature, to be worn in cities, where they are the most luxurious ornaments of civilization. Articles of the sheerest necessity in Arctic regions, they are deemed indispensable beneath the suns of Egypt, where of course they are the merest luxury; equally sought for and valued in Syria and Siberia. There are nations like the Poles and Armenians who wear them from a sort of hereditary habit; and heraldry once marked its distinctions by the ermine and sable.

But the ermine and sable are unknown in North America. The chief fur-bearing animals on this continent are the bear, the fox, the wolf, the beaver, the otter, the marten, the raccoon, the mink, the muskrat, the seal.*

A glance at the state of the fur-trade at this period will show at once over what a wide field the eye of Astor was already ranging, on what a wide field he was now entering.

Before the peace of 1763, the fur-bearing regions of America were divided between the English and the French. The British Possessions, extending north from Canada as far as exploration had gone, were under the exclusive control of the Hudson's Bay Company, acting under a charter granted by Charles II. to Prince Rupert and his associates, in 1670. This charter will expire in 1859, and it is becoming an interesting question in the Colonial politics

* Silliman's Journal, January, 1834.

and policy of England, whether that charter shall be renewed. The furs obtained throughout this vast region were collected at York Factory, on Hudson's Bay, and thence shipped to England.

South of the British Possessions, the forests and rivers of Canada were ransacked by the French and half-breed boatmen and rangers. At this time the French were the most successful fur-traders. At first they obtained their peltries by purchase from the Indians of different tribes, the Hurons, the Ottawas, who brought them down to Montreal in their light birch canoes. Gradually the Frenchmen learned the arts of the trapper; they lived among the Indians, intermarried with them. A race of half-breeds thus grew up, who proved the most daring and enduring of rangers and boatmen. But the peace of 1763 proved a sad check for a time to the French fur-trade. A few Englishmen became interested in the business, however, and the French trappers and their Indian allies gradually became reconciled to the new-comers.

The irregular trading by individuals with the Indians led to great abuses, the most serious of which was the unchecked sale of spirituous liquors, an abuse scarcely known under the French rule. To put an end to these abuses and bring about system in the fur-trade, a company was established in 1785, the year after Mr. Astor returned to New York, named the Northwest Company, which was managed by partners, several of whom resided as agents at Montreal, while the others were stationed at the interior trading-posts. The chief trading-post was at Fort William, on Lake Superior. Here, from time to time, there would be gatherings of the motley and mongrel retainers when the agents came up from Montreal, and held feudal court among the French and Indian trappers, boatmen, and traders.

A few years later a third company was formed, whose headquarters were at Michilimackinac, near Lake Huron;

hence called the Mackinaw Company. The field of its operations was the Lake Superior region, and the country extending westward from the Mississippi to the Rocky Mountains. It seems to have been considered no obstacle to their designs, that the region to which the company looked for their furs had become the territory of the United States. But, although peace had been concluded, the frontier forts had not been given up. Oswego, Niagara, Detroit, Michilimackinac, and other posts, were still in the hands of the English. The Indian tribes continued hostile, being under English influence. No company had as yet been formed in the United States. Several French houses at St. Louis traded with the Indians, but it was not until 1807 that an association of twelve partners, with a capital of forty thousand dollars, was formed at St. Louis under the name of the Missouri Company.

The trade, it will thus be seen, was almost wholly in the hands of the English companies—the Hudson's Bay Company in the North, the Northwest Company in the Canadas, the Mackinaw Company in the territories of the United States; and the few American traders in the field had to rely on their individual resources, with no aid from a government too feeble in its infancy to do more than establish a few Indian agencies, and without constitutional power to confer charter privileges.

A new branch of the fur-trade was unexpectedly opened by the discovery made by Captain Cook, during his last voyage, of the immense numbers of sea-otter to be found on the northwest coast of America. The fur of this animal, which was first introduced into commerce in 1725, is described as a beautiful, soft, close jet black. The excitement produced by Cook's discovery was something like that which followed the news from the American fork of the Sacramento in 1849. Adventurers from many countries flocked to the Pacific, and in 1792 there were twenty-one vessels, under different flags, principally American, and owned in Boston, on the coast. Among these was the Columbia, Captain Gray, of Boston, who, while coasting along the Pacific shore, discovered the river to which he gave the name of his ship, and the first settlement on whose shores was destined to bear the name of Astor.

Such was the broad field of enterprise upon which Astor now entered, and in which he labored for years with an assurance of success from the start, which was never falsified. It is not to be supposed that he hoped or expected at once, and without untiring effort, to make head against such formidable competitors. But he was certainly endowed to a remarkable degree with a fore-seeing and far-seeing spirit, that anticipates the future, grasps the details of the widest combinations, and was prepared for the turns of fortune. He foresaw the time when the American posts would be given up, and "then," said he, "when the frontiers are surrendered, I will make my fortune in the fur-trade."

On returning to America, Mr. Astor established himself in New York, where he always continued to reside. He at once applied himself with all the vigor of his mind and his trained business habits to the fur-trade, and to that almost exclusively. From his brother in London, it is true, he frequently received valuable consignments, and the profits derived from them were doubtless of advantage; but otherwise he was unaided in the struggle for fortune, unaided except by those qualities of mind, character, and habit, which are the best of capital. He occasionally went to London, and frequently visited Montreal and distant trading-posts in Canada, collecting furs wherever he could find them, in large or in small quantities.

The treaty negotiated by Mr. Jay in 1794, was of two-fold advantage to Mr. Astor. The posts at the West were given up, and the restrictions upon commerce were relaxed.

It was now no longer necessary to export from Canada the furs designed for foreign markets. The time to which he had looked forward had now come, and no man was better prepared for the opportunity to make a fortune. The trade which had been gradually and surely growing under his patient labors now expanded with sudden rapidity. Among the boatmen, the trappers and traders of Canada, and the Hudson's Bay territories, in the Lake Superior region, on either side of the Rocky Mountains, and from York Factory to Oregon, his name was known and respected. The furs brought together at New York were shipped to Europe and the East in his own ships, which brought back cargoes that thus secured a double profit. The ships which carried furs to France, England, or Germany, or peltries and dollars to China, brought back wines, silks, Indian goods, and teas. He made himself minutely acquainted with the markets of Europe, and he was thus enabled to guide the action of his supercargoes and captains with the most precise instructions. His business required the minutest acquaintance with four different markets in different quarters of the globe—the Oriental, the Indian, the European, and the American—as well as that of all the great fur marts. He became, by the natural course of his business operations, a ship-owner and importer as well as fur-trader. The mind that could hold in its grasp, and master, and not be overwhelmed by the details of all these combinations, must needs have been one of no ordinary power. But his intellect, aided by an iron memory, worked quick, as well as strong. Some one has said, the secret of success in business is to be beforehand with your affairs. No man was better able to fulfill this condition than Astor. Always an early riser, he generally left business at 2 o'clock P. M. He was never at rest, but he was seldom in haste. His forces, his resources, were always marshaled and in order. An enthusiastic admirer of this great business genius declared that Mr.

Astor could command an army of five hundred thousand men.

His unresting industry was not hampered by false pride. He could work with his own hands, and he was not ashamed of workman's garb. He knew that the master's example must guide, that the master's eye must be on the work if it is to be well done. If his furs required sorting and beating, he could do it himself with the best of his men, and was as ready to work when worth millions as when struggling for success. No humble disciple of Poor Richard was ever more ploddingly diligent in the practice of the virtues of frugality and thrift, which the spirit of speculation is prone to overlook, than he, and yet no one was ever more highly endowed with the genius for speculation in the highest sense, or earlier free from the necessity of practicing a narrow economy. It was in fact this combination of the lower and higher qualities of the business man, the plodding industry with the soaring genius, which gave Astor his peculiar power and great success.

A false view of the comparative dignity and value of the different pursuits of life will lead one to regret that abilities like Astor's were not devoted to some higher pursuit than business. Why was he not a general, a statesman? If the only aim of the merchant were indeed money-making, the regret would be reasonable. But we underrate the dignity of the mercantile calling and do injustice to the motive of the merchant, when we call the one money-making, or rank the other beneath war. War can destroy, war can defend, but it can not create. It is the pursuits of peace alone that create wealth and build up States. We date the rise of a great nation from the close of some successful war. We say the United States owe their existence to the Revolution. But the Revolution created neither the political order and principles of liberty, nor the social order and industrious habits of the American people. It only protected these, which had been maturing and growing for one hundred and fifty years, from the first approaches of oppression. It was the farmers and merchants of the Colonies who built up their material greatness.

It is not necessary to deny that the merchant has a selfish motive, that his aim is to make money. It is equally undeniable that the soldier fights for fame. But do these motives exclude other and higher aims and purposes? Nor is that love of money which impels the merchant merely the miserly greed of lucre. There must be an excitement and a pleasure in erecting the fabric of a great fortune, such as the architect feels in building a great house or a great ship. Add to this the necessity for activity which exists in all strong minds, which the long habit of years of business renders irresistible. Making these deductions for what may be considered the lower motives of the mercantile career, we have a right to claim for the great merchant aims and purposes of public good, as high and disinterested as those of the soldier or statesman.

We shall now see Astor, after securing a fortune large enough to satisfy any reasonable love of wealth, still pressing on with ceaseless activity, and entering upon schemes that took in the continent—schemes of trade, colonization, and settlement—schemes not only for buying furs and supplying the marts of Europe, of Asia, and America, but for planting towns and spreading civilization across the continent. He wanted to make more money, you say, to erect a colossal fortune. Be it so. But can any one doubt that he felt and was animated by that high delight and satisfaction which all genius, whether in art, or war, or affairs, feels in all creative efforts?

By the beginning of the century, Mr. Astor, it is said, was worth a quarter of a million of dollars, the result of only sixteen years of business life. He was then but thirty-seven years of age, twenty-one of which had been passed in

England and America. Large fortunes have often been more suddenly made, and in these Californian times we have been witnesses of many such instances, instances too where the luck has gone as quickly as it came. Astor's was the result of systematic effort, and was but the basis for higher and larger results.

Within the next ten years he took his place among the first of American merchants and financiers. He had wealth, name, and influence. He was in frequent communication with government, in relation to the fur-trade and Indian affairs, and his opinion commanded the highest respect. By adopting his suggestions, with regard to supplies to the Indians, many heavy expenditures were avoided, and through his influence a law was passed excluding British fur-traders from American territories.

It was frequently a subject of complaint of the Russian government, that American vessels on the northwest coast supplied the Indians of that region with fire-arms. Mr. Astor proposed to send supplies by regular ships to the Russian establishment. This proposition was approved at Washington, and by Count Pahlen, the Russian minister. Desirous of obtaining the sanction of the Russian government, Mr. Astor sent a special agent in March, 1811, to whom a passage was given on board the John Adams, a government armed vessel.

This plan of sending regular supply-ships to the Pacific coast was but one feature of the great scheme which, though unsuccessful, fills a prominent place in Astor's life, and is marked in every part of it with the stamp of high ability and the power to organize and combine.

While his plans grew with his means, and his views widened as the field widened before him, two great obstacles hitherto stood in his way. He was but an individual, while against him was the rivalry of great and wealthy corporations. They had the support of a powerful government, and held the same controlling influence over the Indians which the French had enjoyed before, and which was inherited from them. The frontier posts were indeed surrendered, but from 1794 to 1797 the government of the United States was engaged in Indian wars; and although the territories of both countries were, by the terms of Jay's treaty, equally open for trade with the Indians to the citizens of each, the reciprocity was but nominal. The trade among them was carried on by Americans with risks to life and property which the English traders were free from, and which they did nothing to diminish or remove.* We have seen that the Mackinaw Company was formed in Canada for the express purpose of trading within the American territories, and the Northwest Company were beginning to push their operations into the Pacific regions lying between the possessions of Russia and the United States.

Mr. Astor's first step was to seek the aid of government authority; its countenance and good wishes he received, but there was no power to confer corporate privileges such as the English companies enjoyed. In 1809 he obtained an act of the Legislature of New York incorporating the American Fur Company, with a capital of one million of dollars, which he furnished himself; and he was, in fact, the company, for the board of directors was only nominal. Subsequently, Mr. Astor bought out the Mackinaw Company, and merged it and the American Company in a new association called the Southwest Company. In this he had the sanction of the authorities at Washington. In this way he acquired the control of half the Indian posts held by the Mackinaw Company in the United States, with the understanding that the remainder were to be surrendered within five years.

He thus prepared the way for the great enterprise he

---

* Letter from Albert Gallatin to J. J. Astor, August 5th, 1835.

was now maturing in his own mind. His design was to organize and control the fur-trade from the Lakes to the Pacific, by establishing trading-posts along the Missouri, and Columbia to its mouth. He designed establishing a central depot and post at the mouth of the Columbia. He proposed sending regular supply-ships to the Pacific posts, around the Horn. By these, stores were to be sent also to the Russian establishments. It was part of his plan, if possible, to obtain possession of one of the Sandwich Islands as a station, for from the Pacific coast he knew that the Chinese market for his peltries could be most conveniently reached, and thus the necessity for a long and circuitous voyage be avoided. Instead of bringing the furs intended for China to New York, they could be sent from the Pacific. By the supply-ships, too, the stock of goods suitable for the Indian trade would be kept up there, and the cargoes purchased with the proceeds of furs sold in China, brought back to New York. The line of posts across the continent would become a line of towns, emigration would follow, and civilization would belt the continent.

In this grand scheme, Mr. Astor was only anticipating the course of events which, fifty years later, we are beginning to witness. When he laid his plans before the government, Mr. Jefferson, who was then president, "considered as a great acquisition," as he afterward expressed himself in a letter to Mr. Astor, "the commencement of a settlement on the western coast of America, and looked forward with gratification to the time when its descendants should have spread themselves through the whole length of that coast, covering it with free and independent Americans, unconnected with us but by the ties of blood and interest, and enjoying, like us, the rights of self-government." Even Jefferson's mind, wide as it was, could not take in the idea of a national unity embracing both ends of the continent; but not so thought Astor. The merchant saw farther than the statesman. It was precisely this political unity which gave him hope and chance of success in his world-wide schemes. When the constitution was adopted, the chief source of apprehension for its permanence, with men like Patrick Henry and other wise statesmen, was the extent of our territory. The Alleghanies, it was thought, had put asunder communities whom no paper constitution could unite. But at that early day, when Ohio was the far west, and no steamboat had yet gone up the Mississippi, Astor looked beyond the Ohio, beyond the Mississippi and the Rocky Mountains, and saw the whole American territory, from ocean to ocean, the domain of one united nation, the seat of trade and industry. He saw lines of trading-posts uniting the western settlements with the Pacific; following this line of posts he saw the columns of a peaceful emigration crossing the plains, crossing the mountains, descending the Columbia, and towns and villages taking the places of the solitary posts, and cultivated fields instead of hunting-grounds of the Indian and the trapper.

No enterprise, unless it be the Atlantic telegraph, engages more deeply the public attention than a railroad communication with the Pacific coast. The rapid settlement of California and Oregon, the constant communication by steam with the Pacific coast, render it easy now to feel the nearness of that region, and the oneness of the nationality which covers the continent. But to Astor's eye the thing was as palpable then as now. And yet but two or three attempts had then been made to explore the overland routes.

The expedition proposed by Jonathan Carver, an officer in the colonial army, to explore the continent between the forty-third and forty-sixth degrees of latitude, with a view to ascertaining its greatest breadth, establishing a communication between Hudson's Bay and the Pacific, and perhaps discovering a northwest passage, was defeated by the breaking out of the Revolution.

In 1793, Sir Alexander McKenzie crossed the continent to the Pacific, which he reached in latitude 52° 20′ north. In his account of the expedition, he proposed establishing a communication by means of a line of posts. He showed that almost the entire command of the fur-trade of North America, including the territory of the United States, in part, might be secured; as, by a well-organized system, the rivalry of the American traders could be overcome without difficulty.

The famous expedition of Lewis and Clarke, in 1805, was the first attempt on the part of the United States to explore the overland route to the Pacific. They descended the Columbia to the Pacific, and in their celebrated Report, which excited a deep public interest, they pointed out the most practicable routes discovered by them to the Pacific.

Such were the feeble and ineffectual attempts made by official authority toward accomplishing an enterprise which Astor now undertook almost on his individual responsibility. He had been no careless student of the results of these explorers; his frequent intercourse with the northern fur-traders had made him familiar with the field to be explored; and he now set about boldly realizing what, with others, had remained but faint and timid suggestion.

At the start, however, he endeavored to disarm the rivalry and secure the aid of the Northwest Company, by offering them a one-third interest in the enterprise. They took time, ostensibly to consider, in reality to steal a march upon him, and by dispatching a party to the Pacific, to secure the mouth of the Columbia. After much delay, they declined the proposition.

Mr. Astor then invited several gentlemen who had acquired much experience in the fur-trade and Indian life, in the service of the Northwest Company, to join him. Alexander McKay, one of these, had accompanied McKenzie in his expedition; the other two, Duncan M'Dougal and

Donald M'Kenzie, were supposed to be skillful and reliable.

As his chief agent, Mr. Astor selected Mr. Wilson Price Hunt, a native of Trenton, N. J., who, he intended, should have charge as superintendent of the post at the mouth of the Columbia. Mr. Hunt, although not a fur-trader, had acquired much experience in the Indian trade at St. Louis.

These gentlemen and Mr. Astor associated themselves together as the "Pacific Fur Company," on the 23d of June, 1810.

The general tenor of their agreement is briefly stated by Mr. Irving in his Astoria.

"Mr. Astor was to be at the head of the company, and to manage its affairs in New York. He was to furnish vessels, goods, provisions, arms, ammunition, and all other requisites for the enterprise, at first cost and charges, provided, that they did not at any time involve an advance of more than four hundred thousand dollars.

"The stock of the company was to be divided into a hundred equal shares, with the profits accruing thereon. Fifty shares were to be at the disposition of Mr. Astor, and the other fifty to be divided among the partners and their associates.

"Mr. Astor was to have the privilege of introducing other persons into the connection as partners, two of whom, at least, should be conversant with the Indian trade, and none of them entitled to more than three shares.

"A general meeting of the company was to be held annually at Columbia River, for the investigation and regulation of its affairs; at which absent members might be represented, and might vote by proxy under certain specified conditions.

"The association, if successful, was to continue for twenty years; but the parties had full power to abandon and dissolve it within the first five years, should it be found unprofitable. For this term, Mr. Astor covenanted to bear all the loss that might be incurred; after which it was to be borne by all the partners in proportion to their respective shares.

"The parties of the second part were to execute faithfully such duties as might be assigned to them by a majority of the company on the northwest coast, and to repair to such place or places as the majority might direct.

"An agent, appointed for the term of five years, was to reside at the principal establishment on the northwest coast, and Wilson Price Hunt was the one chosen for the first term. Should the interests of the concern require his absence, a person was to be appointed, in general meeting, to take his place."*

It is clear that in undertaking to pay all the expenses of the enterprise for five years, Mr. Astor can have had no expectation of immediate profit. In fact, it has been stated on what is probably good authority, that he looked forward to nothing but outlay during the first ten years of the enterprise, and did not anticipate very profitable returns until the expiration of the next ten. After that he looked forward, it is said, to a nett annual result of something like one million of dollars per annum.

In prosecuting this grand scheme of fur-trade, oriental traffic, and colonization, Mr. Astor determined to send out two expeditions, one by sea, around Cape Horn, and the other overland. In fact, the leading idea, the pivot of his plan, was the facility of communication and supply, by sea, which his position as a great ship-owner and merchant at New York afforded him. His annual supply-ship not only could keep his depot at the mouth of the Columbia well stocked with a larger variety of goods than his rivals could carry across the wilderness, which could be sold at a

* Astoria, by W. Irving, p. 43.

cheaper rate than they could afford; but, arrived at the Columbia, it was already half-way on its voyage to China, and had only to take in the skins accumulated on the Pacific coast, and convey them to Canton.

The company which went by sea was to establish the post on the Pacific, and consisted of four of the partners, M'Kay, M'Dougal, David Stuart, and Robert Stuart, eleven clerks and thirteen boatmen, nearly all from Canada, a ship-carpenter, cooper, rigger, and blacksmith. For the voyage, the ship Tonquin, of two hundred and ninety tons burden, was selected, and the command confided to Captain Jonathan Thorn, a first-lieutenant in the navy, on furlough for the occasion.

The overland party was headed by Mr. Hunt, and consisted principally of boatmen and trappers, whom he hired at Mackinaw and St. Louis. He was joined also by Mr. Ramsay Crooks, destined to play a distinguished part as a fur-trader, in connection with the American Fur Company, and by Messrs. Nutall and Bradbury, two English naturalists.

The Canadian party for the Tonquin came down the Hudson in one of their canoes, and as they swept past the city, in true *voyageur* style, created no little surprise among the inhabitants of the then quiet city. The Tonquin sailed on the 8th September, 1810. Mr. Hunt, after spending some time at Montreal, Mackinaw, and St. Louis, in completing his arrangements, left St. Louis with his party, on the 20th January, 1811. At Charette, one of the old French villages, they met Daniel Boone, then eighty-five years old, but still active and alive to the delights of hunting life. He had just returned from a trapping expedition, bringing with him sixty beaver-skins. The old pioneer, who had always kept in advance of settlement, standing there on the very edge of civilization, doubtless felt a longing which age alone could check, to plunge with this bold band into the wilderness, in an adventure far exceeding his bravest deeds of pioneer daring.

When about sailing, the partners received a letter of instructions from Mr. Astor, in which he earnestly inculcated harmony, and recommended that differences should be settled by the vote of the majority. He was particularly minute in his directions and warnings as to their intercourse with the Indians. "If you find them kind," he wrote, "as I hope you will, be so to them. If otherwise, act with caution and forbearance, and convince them that you come as friends." To Captain Thorn, he wrote: "I must recommend you to be particularly careful on the coast, and not to rely too much on the friendly disposition of the natives. All accidents which have as yet happened there arose from too much confidence in the Indians." Subsequent events brought out in terrible relief, the wisdom and foresight of these remarks. The ship was to touch at the Sandwich Islands, between which and the future settlement it was part of his plan to establish trade, with a view ultimately of obtaining one of them for a station. After leaving the partners and their company at the Columbia, it was to visit the Russian posts, in pursuance of the arrangements Mr. Astor was then making with the Russian government.

Thus, from his counting-house in New York, this American merchant was dispatching his expeditions at the same time by sea and land, one to sail some twelve thousand miles, the other to travel thirty-five hundred miles, to meet at a point on the Pacific coast, where civilized man had never set foot, with purpose of abiding.

Were it proposed to give any thing more than a sketch of Mr. Astor's life, it would be interesting to follow the fortunes of these two parties, pursuing one purpose, aiming for the same destination by such widely divergent routes. Nothing more can here be done than briefly to give a few facts and dates. It seems more than useless too, to glean the field over which the sharp edge of Irving's genius has passed. In his Astoria the whole of this part of Astor's life is so told that it never need be told again. Among the clerks on board the Tonquin was a young Canadian, Gabriel Franchère, who seems to have traveled with a view to publication as well as the fur-trade. His narrative, written in French, is an artless and authentic account of what he saw, and was part of, in the history of Astoria. It has been praised by Mr. Benton, and admirably translated by Mr. J. V. Huntington.

Before following the adventurers, let us remain with Astor at New York, and see that active spirit, after foreseeing every thing and arranging every thing, quietly wait for results with that patience and serenity which only the loftiest activities know; for it is they who know best how to labor, who know how best to wait. From September 10, 1810, when the Tonquin sailed, until October 1811, no news had been received from either party, nor was any expected. On the tenth of that month he dispatched his first annual supply-ship, the Beaver, Captain Sowle. The Beaver carried out Mr. John Clarke, a partner, five clerks, fifteen American laborers, and six boatmen; it being Mr. Astor's design to replace the English, whom he was obliged at first to employ, so far as possible, with Americans. The Beaver was to touch at the Sandwich Islands, take on board as many of the natives for boatmen as he could carry, proceed to the Columbia, thence to New Archangel, the Russian post, obtain a cargo of peltries, and after touching again at the Columbia, sail for Canton.

Months again passed bringing no news from either the Tonquin, the Beaver, or the overland party. Finally came the fearful news that Captain Thorn, Mr. M'Kay, and the crew of the Tonquin had been murdered by the Indians of Vancouver's Island, after a desperate conflict. Captain Thorn, unmindful of his employer's warnings, had allowed large numbers of the Indians to come on board. The murderous act was bloodily avenged, for as the ship was crowded with the savages, ship and savages were blown together into the air, one of the unhappy crew, concealed below, having probably fired the magazine.

Mr. Astor deeply felt the blow. He spoke of it as "a calamity, the length of which he could not foresee." "He indulged, however," says Mr. Irving, "in no weak and vain lamentations, but sought a prompt and efficient remedy." The very same evening he appeared at the theatre with his usual serenity of countenance. A friend who knew the disastrous intelligence he had received, expressed his astonishment that he could have calmness of spirit sufficient for such a scene of light amusement. "What would you have me do," was his characteristic reply; "would you have me stay at home and weep for what I can not help?"

Again months, a year elapsed, without news from the Columbia. The year 1813 came, and with it war with England. The risks of his enterprise were now multiplied; there was the danger of blockade at New York, keeping back his supply-ships; there was the danger of seizure of his Pacific post, danger from the Indians, and uncertainty as to the fidelity of his partners and clerks, who were nearly all British subjects. To increase his anxiety, the news came that the Northwest Company were about sending out the Isaac Todd, a ship of twenty guns, to establish a post at the mouth of the Columbia.

Mr. Astor applied to Mr. Monroe, then Secretary of State, requesting a garrison of forty or fifty men, and representing its importance in a political as well as commercial point of view. No notice was taken by the statesmen at Washington of the suggestion of the New York merchant.

It was then that he determined to dispatch still another ship to the Pacific, and on the 6th March, 1813, the Lark put to sea. With her went Mr. Nicholas G. Ogden, as supercargo. Taking it for granted that Mr. Hunt had reached the mouth of the Columbia, and was established there as the head of the post, Mr. Astor wrote to him by the Lark. "I always think you well," such was the tenor of his letter, "and that I shall see you again, which Heaven I hope will grant." He cautioned him against the plottings of the Northwest Company, complained indignantly of their treatment, and warned him against surprise. "Were I on the spot, and had the management of affairs, I would defy them all; but as it is, every thing depends upon you and your friends about you. Our enterprise is grand, and deserves success, and I hope in God it will meet it. *If my object was merely gain of money*, I should say, think whether it is best to save what we can, and abandon the place; *but the very idea is like a dagger to my heart.*"

At length there came news from over the mountains. He was sitting sadly one evening, thinking of the fate of the Tonquin, when the evening newspaper was brought to him. It brought the news of the arrival of Mr. Stuart, at St. Louis, with intelligence from Mr. Hunt. In June, 1813, he received a letter from Mr. Stuart, dated at St. Louis, May 1st, announcing the arrival of Mr. Hunt and his party at the mouth of the Columbia, and giving encouraging accounts of their success.

Mr. Astor had not waited for this ray of light, the first, and unfortunately the last, to cheer him in his undertaking; he had already determined to send out a fourth ship, the Enterprise, with supplies and men for the post. Learning that the British government were about sending the frigate Phœbe, as convoy for the Isaac Todd, with a view to seizing and destroying the post on the Columbia, he made a second appeal to the Secretary of State. The government determined to dispatch the frigate Adams, Captain Crane. But no sooner were the Adams and the Enterprise ready for sea, than word came from Commodore Chauncey, on Lake Ontario, urgently calling for a reinforcement of seamen. The occasion brooked no delay, and the crew of the Adams had to be at once transferred to another field of action, and the Adams was laid up. Still undismayed, Mr. Astor determined to send the Enterprise, without convoy, when suddenly a British force appeared off New York, and the port was blockaded.

It was while the preparations for dispatching the Enterprise were going briskly forward, that the news from Mr. Hunt was received. "I felt ready," Mr. Astor said, "to fall upon my knees in a transport of gratitude." The adventures of Mr. Hunt's party must be briefly told. They crossed in safety the treeless plains which stretch westward to the foot of the Rocky Mountains, spite of the hostility of Blackfeet and of Sioux, and of the rivalries of Manuel Siza and his party of trappers, belonging to the Missouri Company, who endeavored to stir up the enmity of the Indians against them. The adventures of Dorion and his exploring party; of Carson and his trapping party, who undertook to trap for beaver in the upper region of Mad River; the wanderings of Miller and Robinson; the perilous navigation of Mad River; the mishaps of Mr. Crooks, whose canoe was dashed to pieces in the angry currents of the Caldron Linn, while his companion perished; the perplexity of the explorers, who, after leaving the Caldron Linn of Mad River, completely lost their way, and finally sent out three parties, to set off in different directions—one of Mr. Lillan and three men, one of Crooks and five others, and a third of five men under M'Kenzie; the wanderings of Crooks, and the sufferings from starvation and thirst and cold of all the party, until at last, on the 31st January, 1812, they reached the falls of the Columbia, and descending it in canoes, on the afternoon of the 15th February came in sight of its mouth,—these and many other incidents of the perilous journey, render the story of Hunt's exploration deeply and painfully interesting.

At the mouth of the Columbia he found a post already established. The party which came by the Tonquin had taken possession of a site for their factory and fort at Point George, fifteen miles distant from Cape Disappointment, on the south side of the river. This cape is the northern, and Point Adams, a long tongue of land, is the southern side of the entrance to the Columbia, which is about half a mile wide. Here, on the 12th April, 1811, the Tonquin party had landed, and proceeded to erect their warehouse, residence, and magazine. Here they had been established ten months when Mr. Hunt arrived.

A few words must suffice to tell the adventures of the partners and company who sailed in the Tonquin. It is a picture of perils and hardships, not without touches of the ludicrous under the pencil of Irving, which no one would suspect in the earnest and serious narrative of Franchère.

Never was a motlier or more ill-assorted company got together than were crowded into the narrow quarters of the Tonquin. Captain Thorn was a huffy and high-tempered officer of the old school, had distinguished himself before Tripoli, and did not like nonsense. The partners were argumentative and irascible Scotch Canadians. The clerks were mostly French Canadians, young and intelligent; one or two of them of a decidedly literary as well as mercantile turn. They had a habit of taking notes, which excited the ire of Captain Thorn and was duly reported to Mr. Astor. Soon after starting, a quarrel broke out about an order he issued for extinguishing the lights at 8 o'clock, and the quarrels were endless, growing out of the conflict of his authority as captain, and their supposed authority as partners. At the Falkland Islands, M'Dougal and Stuart went ashore and wandered off after penguins.

Meanwhile some of the clerks found the tombstones of two English sailors, with inscriptions that were beginning to be effaced. The young French "Old Mortalities" set to work at once to piously restore them. Soon after, they saw a signal from the ship, which presently got under way, spread all sail, and put to sea. When M'Dougal and Stuart returned from their penguin hunt, they all started in their boat for the ship, which was now under full sail. Nothing could induce the captain to put back, and for three hours and a half they labored at the oar in vain. Luckily the wind shifted, and they succeeded in reaching the ship. Twice before they had disregarded the captain's orders about returning from shore, and he seems to have been serious in his threats of leaving them on this the third transgression.

The Tonquin doubled Cape Horn on the 25th December, and reached the Sandwich Islands on the 11th February, 1811. Here they negotiated successfully with Tamehameha for a supply of hogs, sheep, and vegetables, and what was still more important, engaged twelve of the islanders as boatmen for service on the Pacific coast. The Canadians admitted their superiority in swimming, diving, and the management of light craft, to the boatmen of the Northwest. The Tonquin left the Islands on the 28th February, and reached the mouth of the Columbia on the 22d of March. Here the first mate, Mr. Fox, an old seaman, and two Canadians were lost in attempting to cross the bar in a whale-boat. The next day, however, the ship drifted to an anchorage near Cape Disappointment, on the north side of the entrance. Again five men were sent out in a pinnace to take soundings, and three of them were lost in the currents and breakers of this dangerous harbor. The Tonquin finally found safe anchorage in what is called Baker's Bay, behind Cape Disappointment. And, as we have seen, on the 12th April following, a party of sixteen proceeded in a launch from the ship to Point George, on the south side of the harbor, and commenced the necessary buildings for a fort and trading-post, to which they gave the only name it could appropriately receive—Astoria.

Mr. Hunt, as has been stated, reached Astoria, February 15th, 1812. On the 6th of May following, the Beaver arrived. She remained at Astoria until the 4th of August, 1812, when, in pursuance of Mr. Astor's instructions, she proceeded north to New-Archangel, the central Russian trading-post, for the purpose of carrying supplies and procuring a cargo of furs for Canton. Mr. Hunt went with her,—an unfortunate step for the superintendent of the post to take, at this critical period in the enterprise. Still more unfortunate was his determination, instead of returning in the Beaver to Astoria (and Mr. Astor's instructions were that the Beaver should touch there on her way to Canton), to proceed in her directly to the Sandwich Islands. Mr. Hunt never saw Astoria again until the 20th of August, 1813, when he arrived there from the Sandwich Islands, in the Albatross, a vessel he had been obliged to charter expressly for the voyage, after waiting for months in vain for the annual supply-ship.

Let us now see what had been going on at Astoria during the absence of the American superintendent. The loss of the Tonquin had proved a damper to the spirits of some of the company, and especially M'Dougal, who became very much disheartened. McKenzie, too, returned from the trading-post he had established on the Shahaptan, quite disgusted with his want of success in trading for beaver-skins. On the other hand, Clarke, the American partner, and Stuart, had met with the most encouraging success at their posts, which were in good beaver regions.

M'Kenzie, on his return from his abandoned post, paid a visit to Mr. Clarke on the river Spokan, and there learned that hostilities had begun between England and America. The President's proclamation to that effect had been brought to them by Mr. John G. M'Tavish, one of the members of the Northwest Company.

The dismay the news created among the company at Astoria, who were nearly all British subjects, may be imagined. "When we learned this news," says Franchère, with all his own simplicity, "all of us at Astoria who were British subjects and Canadians, wished ourselves in Canada; but we could not entertain even the thought of transporting ourselves thither, at least immediately. We were separated from our country by an immense space, and the difficulties of the journey at this season were insuperable. Besides, Mr. Astor's interests had to be consulted first. We held therefore a sort of council of war, to which the clerks of the factory were invited *pro formâ*, as they had no voice in the deliberation. Having maturely weighed our situation; after having seriously considered that being almost to a man British subjects, we were trading notwithstanding under the American flag; and foreseeing the improbability, or rather, to cut the matter short, the impossibility that Mr. Astor could send us further supplies or reinforcements while the war lasted, as most of the ports of the United States would inevitably be blockaded by the British, we concluded to abandon the establishment in the ensuing spring, or at latest in the beginning of the summer. We did not communicate these resolutions to the men, lest they should in consequence abandon their labor, but we discontinued, from that moment, our trade with the natives, except for provisions, as well because we had no longer a large stock of goods on hand, as for the reason that we had already more furs than we could carry away overland."

This may be taken as a pretty fair statement of the reasonings of these Canadian traders. So would not have reasoned a company of Americans; at least, no such hasty and sudden action would have been taken as was now resolved upon.

It is true their supplies were running low; but Franchère

himself, he tells us, succeeded in supplying the post with sturgeon. The Willamette Valley, Messrs. Reed and Seton reported, was a charming country, abounding in game, and a dwelling and trading house had been erected there. As to danger of capture by the Phœbe and Isaac Todd, Franchère truly says that to escape it, all that was necessary was to "remove the effects of the company up the river upon some small stream, and await the result. The sloop-of-war would then have found nothing; she would have left after setting fire to our deserted houses. None of their boats would have dared follow us, even if the Indians had betrayed to them our lurking-places. Those at the head of affairs had their own fortunes to seek, and thought it more for their interest, doubtless, to act as they did; but that will not clear them in the eyes of the world, and the charge of treason to Mr. Astor's interests will always be attached to their characters."*

M'Dougal was the unfaithful partner to whom the last sentence points, as the events which immediately followed too plainly showed. On the return of Clarke, Stuart, and McKenzie, in June, 1813, they found M'Dougal pushing forward his preparations for abandoning the post on the 1st of July. For this sudden movement they were wholly unprepared, having no horses nor provisions for crossing the mountains. They finally, however, agreed to leave the country the ensuing year. On the 1st of July the four partners signed a manifesto, setting forth the failure of supplies and the dangers menacing them, reciting the sixteenth article of the agreement, by which they were authorized to abandon the concern if found unprofitable within five years, and announcing their intention to do so on the 1st day of June, 1814, unless in the mean time supplies should be received from Mr. Astor, with orders to continue.

---

* Franchère, p. 203.

Seven weeks after, on the 20th of August, Mr. Hunt arrived in the Albatross from the Sandwich Islands, to learn with dismay the step taken by the partners. He was induced to acquiesce, but resolved to save as much from the wreck as possible, by securing a market for the rich stock of furs already accumulated at Astoria. He therefore left in the Albatross for the Marquesas, in quest of a ship in which to convey them, intending to return with supplies in January. A few days after he reached the Marpuesas, Commodore Porter arrived in the Essex, with several English whale-ships as prizes, and bringing news of the approach of the Phœbe, frigate, and the sloops-of-war Cherub and Raccoon. Hunt endeavored to buy one of the commodore's whalers, but was unable to give his price, twenty-five thousand dollars, nor would Porter consent, "from want of authority," "to go to Astoria and bring off the property of American citizens there."

There was but one hope left—reliance upon Mr. Astor's punctuality in sending the supply-ship. That supply-ship had been sent; but the Lark was fated never to reach Astoria. She was wrecked in the Pacific, near the Sandwich Islands, on one of which she was finally thrown. Here Mr. Ogden was obliged to abandon her to his majesty the king, in return for clothing and food for himself and companions. On the 20th of December, 1813, Mr. Hunt arrived at the islands from the Marquesas, and at last secured a brig, the Pedler, for ten thousand dollars. He placed Captain Northrop, of the Lark, in command, and they sailed for Astoria on the 22d of January, 1814, their intention being to carry the property at Astoria to the Russian Possessions. Such were Mr. Astor's orders sent out by the Lark.

They came too late. On the 7th of October, 1813, three canoes were seen rounding Tongue Point, above the fort, and approaching Astoria,—two bearing English flags, the other the American. They brought an English party, under Mr.

J. G. M'Tavish, of the Northwest Company, whom Mr. McKenzie had met on his return to the interior posts, and accompanied back to the fort. Mr. M'Tavish was followed by a flotilla of eight boats, loaded with furs, and by seventy-five men. He brought a letter from Mr. Angus Shaw to M'Dougal, announcing the sailing of the Phœbe and John Todd in March, with letters of marque and orders to seize the factory. The party encamped in a little cove, near the factory, and hoisted the British colors. Their numbers, the news they brought, and their attitude were too plain for mistake; yet, when the Americans in the fort proposed to raise the American flag, M'Dougal would not permit it! The Americans had every advantage of position, although inferior in numbers. The new-comers were without supplies or ammunition, unsheltered, and under the guns of the fort, and the season was advancing. The Indians looked upon them with suspicion. The Phœbe did not make her appearance. Had M'Dougal been true, hunger and approaching winter would have driven off the intruders without firing a gun from the fort. If force were necessary, they could easily have been overpowered, as Franchère admits.* But M'Dougal was a traitor. It was subsequently ascertained that he made copies of all Mr. Astor's business letters; and on joining the Northwest Company, which he did in the following December, gave them to his new associates, and also divulged all Mr. Astor's plans.

Their incessant applications at the fort for food were met with supplies from M'Dougal. Finally, from offering to buy food, they proceeded to making an offer for the whole establishment. The shrewdness of this proposition is apparent when it is considered that had the British force arrived and found the fort and its contents in the hands of the Americans, the rich stock of furs would have become their lawful prize,

---

* Franchère, p. 203.

and a total loss to both parties. But M'Dougal had another alternative. He had sixty men, arms, ammunition, boats. The furs could have been removed to the interior posts. The Northwest party could have been starved out or driven out. But instead of making his own terms, he listened to their insolent demands, negotiated and bargained until late in October; and finally, on the twenty-third of that month, an agreement was signed, by which Astoria was transferred to the Northwest Company, and the goods and furs sold to them at their own price, being about one-third of their value. About $40,000 were paid for furs worth more than $100,000. Beaver, worth five dollars, was put down at two dollars per skin; land-otter, worth five dollars, at fifty cents; sea-otter, worth forty-five to sixty dollars, at twelve; and nothing was allowed for several kinds of furs. The goods for Indian trade were sold for one-third the value at Astoria.

The clerks, and several of the Pacific Company, were to receive the arrears of their wages, and a free passage to Canada, overland. The American flag was then hauled down and British colors raised, in token of this virtual surrender of Astoria.

M'Dougal always asserted the fairness of his own intention, pleading the danger of capture and the uncertainty of Hunt's return; but Mr. Astor was not deceived. "Had our place and our property," he wrote to Mr. Hunt, "been fairly captured, I should have preferred it; I should not feel as if I were disgraced."

The British force did not make its appearance until the 30th November, 1813. Instead of the Phœbe, the Isaac Todd, and two sloops, came only the Raccoon, a sloop-of-war of twenty-six guns. M'Tavish, who was almost as much afraid of the English sailors, hungry for prize-money, as if they were enemies, now had recourse to an expedient, in his zeal for the interests of the Northwest Company, which shows how much might have been done by an honest purpose on the part of M'Dougal to serve those of Mr. Astor. He hastily loaded two barges with all the furs, and went up the river to Tongue Point. This was done before it was certainly ascertained that the vessel approaching was English. If it proved American, he intended to carry his furs into the interior, which was precisely what M'Dougal might have done.

The rage of the British officers may be imagined on finding that the rich prize had slipped their fingers. On the 12th December, 1813, Captain Black, of the Raccoon, formally took possession of Astòria, in the name of the king, breaking a bottle of wine on the occasion, and changing the name to that of Fort George. On the 28th of February Mr. Hunt arrived in the Pedler, to transfer the furs to the Russian posts. His disappointment, which was as great as that of the English sailors, was not soothed by a hint from M'Dougal that they might perhaps be purchased back at an advance of fifty per cent., an offer made on behalf of the Northwest Company, of which he had become a partner in December. But this he kept secret, retaining the papers of the Pacific Company in his possession. Hunt's first care was to obtain these papers, in which he succeeded with difficulty, and the bills and drafts for the purchase-money which were readily delivered. These he remitted overland to Mr. Astor, and then on the 3d April, 1814, embarked on the Pedler.

Mr. Astor was not yet quite discouraged. "After their treatment of me," he wrote to Mr. Hunt, "I have no idea of remaining idle." The treaty of Ghent restored Astoria to the United States, and Mr. Astor proposed to the government to renew the enterprise, under the protection of a garrison. The proposition was favored by Mr. Gallatin, and other statesmen, but no action followed. The Northwest Company remained in possession of the ground.

Thus ended the first great enterprise of trade and colonization on the Pacific. The gold of California has effected what the peltries of Oregon could not. The stream of population flowing into California is making its way northward along the whole Pacific coast, and now nothing is wanting but a railroad to the Pacific, to realize, on the grandest scale, his plan of inland communication.

Had his enterprise succeeded, the way would long since have been prepared, the most feasible route long since ascertained, trading-posts and settlements would have dotted the line of travel across the continent. Had the Pacific Company secured possession of the hunting-grounds of Oregon, and been in possession of them when the boundary question arose in 1844, the American government could have presented the strongest of arguments for their claim to the line of 54° 40′, in an actual occupancy for thirty years. As it was, the administration of Mr. Polk was content to accept the line of 49° north, abating, with what grace it might, the pretensions to the whole of Oregon, with which it went into office.

Mr. Greenhow, in his work on Oregon, finds fault with Mr. Astor for employing too few Americans. But it must be remembered that it was difficult to find men experienced in the fur-trade elsewhere than in Canada. It was his intention, moreover, to replace them by Americans as fast as possible. It was his intention too, that the chief charge and direction should be exercised by Mr. Hunt. It was a fatal mistake when that gentleman failed to return to Astoria, after his visit to the Russian posts, at the most critical period in the fortunes of Astoria. In this instance, as in the case of almost every disaster which happened, it is traceable to a disregard of Mr. Astor's instructions, or seems, at least, to have been foreseen by him. The loss of the Tonquin would not have happened, had Captain Thorn been mindful of his warning letter, nor would Astoria have been sacrificed had the American government been able or willing to afford the protection he asked. Had the furs been removed, as he directed, this loss also would have been avoided.

While the Astoria experiment was in progress, Mr. Astor's ordinary operations in the fur-trade in connection with the American Company, and his foreign trade, were going on with uniformly increasing success. While this trade, however, must be considered the leading pursuit of his life, as it was the foundation of his fortune, he early gave his attention to another line of operations, and it would be difficult to say whether the greater part of his immense fortune were derived from his mercantile dealings or his investments in real estate. His foresight early anticipated the rapid growth and future commercial greatness of the city of New York. He early began, and systematically followed up the policy of investing largely, not only in the inhabited parts of the city, where immediate income could be realized, but in unoccupied lots, or acres rather, of fields out of town, which he saw, in anticipation, covered by the spreading city. Many others have invested in the same manner, upon like calculation; few so systematically as he. A glance at the rapid growth of the city, even at that early day, might make the most prudent venturesome. The population of the city of New York was, in

1773......	21,876	1800......	60,489	1816......	100,619
1786......	23,614	1805......	75,770	1825......	166,086
1790......	33,031	1815......	83,530	1845......	371,223

These figures cover the whole period of Mr. Astor's active life. They might prove to one of less insight than he, that there was something in the very dust beneath his feet more precious than ermine and sable. He was not, however, merely prudent; he had the means and spirit to enter into operations covering long periods, and to wait patiently the results of years. He was under no necessity of mortgaging one property for the purchase of another, under no temptation to dangerously expand. Thus he was enabled to make investments which it has been said, no doubt with literal truth, centupled on his hands.

Besides the City Hotel, the Park Theatre, the Astor House, which he built, and which in its day was certainly one of the finest hotels in America, and blocks of houses in Broadway near Broome and Prince streets, in Lafayette Place, in Hammond and Varick streets and elsewhere, so numerous indeed, that it would be hard to point out a part of the *improved* districts of the city where there are not buildings belonging to the Astor estate, he was the owner of large tracts on the Eighth avenue, on the Hudson River between Forty-second and Fifty-first streets, and on the East River at Hell-gate, in the upper part of New York Island. At one time, it is stated, he was in the habit of investing two-thirds of his net annual receipts in land, and in the course of all his vast operations, with a large part of his fortune sometimes literally afloat on the ocean, he is said never to have mortgaged a lot.

As it is interesting to know the height of the highest mountain, and the length of the longest river, so, much curiosity has been indulged as to the amount of the largest fortune ever accumulated in America. It has been said, that to rate it at $20,000,000 would be making a moderate estimate.

Mr. Astor continued in active business fifty years, and during that long period he hardly made a mistake or misstep through defect of his own judgment. Sagacity, strength, activity, rapidity of action, industry, punctuality, integrity—such was the extraordinary combination of the qualities of a great merchant which met in him. He had an iron memory. He could recall the minute details of a transaction in Canada, ten years before. He rose early, and until fifty-five years of age was at his office before seven o'clock. He was a great horseman, and in the constant habit of riding out for pleasure and exercise. In the strength of his general grasp of a great subject, he did not allow himself to be too much disturbed by the consideration of details. His mind worked so actively that he soon got through the business of a day, and could leave his office earlier than many busier men who did less. Troubled and annoyed by petty trials, he was calm and self-possessed under great ones. "Keep quiet, keep cool," was the constant and familiar admonition from his lips. When the great trials came, his spirit rose with the emergency, and he was equal to the hour.

It was the rare felicity of Mr. Astor's most fortunate life, that he lived to a good old age to enjoy his extraordinary success. Many a man toils with all his might through the best years of his life for fortune, looking forward to the reasonable enjoyment of it in old age, qualified for the enjoyment of it by keeping his mind clear and his body free from disease, and not, like the fool in Scripture, bent merely upon taking his ease; yet like him, in the moment of fruition, he gets his summons to surrender all.

Mr. Astor lived nearly a quarter of a century of happy life in retirement among his children and grandchildren, and the society of practical and literary men, which he loved. Halleck was connected with his business for many years. Irving was his friend, executor of his will, and should be his biographer. He enjoyed the society of such men; they doubtless relished with high zest the wide experiences of the merchant. It has been said, the most interesting conversation is that of an enlightened lawyer of large practice; we should make an exception in favor of the great merchant. His closing years have been pictured by one who knew him well, and the reader will prefer these beautiful and fitting words to any other narrative.

"Mr. Astor lived to the good old age of fourscore and

four years and eight months. For some years previous to his death, which happened March 29th, 1848, his manly form was bowed down by age, and his bodily strength greatly enfeebled, but his mind retained much of its original vigor and brightness. Considering his extraordinary activity until a late period of his life, he submitted to the helplessness of age with uncommon resignation. When his impaired eyesight no longer permitted him to read, his principal relief from the wearisomeness of unoccupied time was in the society of his friends and near relatives. All who knew him well were strongly attached to him, and none but those who were ignorant of his true character believed him unamiable and repulsive. His smile was peculiarly benignant and expressive of genuine kindness of heart, and his whole manner cordial and courteous to every one entitled to his respect. There was something so impressive in his appearance, no one could stand before him without feeling that he was in the presence of a superior intelligence. His deep, sunken eye, beneath his overarched brow, denoted the prophetic—it might almost be said the inspired mind within. Although he lived many years beyond the age when 'the grasshopper is a burden,' and was the victim of much suffering, he did not murmur, nor did he become unreasonable and peevish. He was not wont to talk much on the subject of religion, or freely communicate his views in relation to the life beyond the grave; but it can not be doubted that such tranquillity as he exhibited in his near approach to it, must have been derived from 'that peace which the world can neither give nor take away.'"

This is the tribute and the testimony of one who knew Mr. Astor well, and enjoyed his confidence and friendship, Dr. Joseph G. Cogswell. With regard to his religious views, it may be stated that he was a member of the German Reformed Congregation in New York.

Mr. Astor was liberal, if not very charitable, in a certain

narrow and special sense of the word. If to be very rich, places one under the necessity of giving whatever is asked, whenever asked, to whoever asks it, the most colossal fortune would quickly melt under the heat of importunity. The man of system and business-habits would no more give away money without knowing what is to become of it, than he would buy without inquiring the price, or sell without knowing the market. When he gave, he gave liberally, but disliked little indiscriminate charities.

Mr. Astor made many large donations and subscriptions to public institutions during his lifetime, among others to the German Society of the city of New York, and to the Association for the Relief of Respectable Aged Indigent Females.

But his will furnishes ample, and the best proof that he was not unmindful of the justice, the obligation, the duty of liberality, on the part of every rich man, to the community in which he has lived and erected the fabric of his fortune. Owe as much as he may to his own merits—and no man was more indebted than Mr. Astor for the fortune he made, to his own industry, genius, and integrity—there is not a rich man of acquired wealth in the world, who does not owe still more to the institutions and influences of civilized society by which he is surrounded. And of all countries this is especially true of America. The rich man is indebted to society for the fixed and certain laws which define the rights of property and regulate and facilitate its transfer, for the means of safe intercourse, for the armies of laborers it organizes to do his work, and for the mechanic arts. But in America, especially, what does not the rich man owe to the institutions and influences around him?—to the Revolution, in the first place, which unshackled the industry of the country; to equal laws and common-school education; and, as a consequence of all these, to that marvelous growth which, in our cities especially, has been a source of wealth to thousands? Let it not be said that the facilities the rich man enjoys are offered to all alike, and that there is no special obligation incurred by him who improves them best. True, fate offers the chance to all, but not the intellect to improve it. Fate has not a fortune of millions for more than one in a million. But the fortunate and deserving one is as much indebted to the facilities society affords for its acquisition, as if afforded to him alone.

Nor let it be said that the immense accumulations and the tremendous inequalities allowed or facilitated by existing arrangements of society, do not produce evils calling for all the mitigations of a wise liberality. These immense accumulations in the hands of individuals, are the extreme result of the present commercial system, fraught with evils, certainly, although with less evil, than rash attempts to disarrange and rearrange are likely to produce, in which active bad men would stand the best chance of seizing the fortunes which now often fall to active good men. We are told that a millionaire can not eat more meals, wear more clothes, occupy more houses than a poor man. This argument shuts the eye to quality and kind of enjoyment; but waiving that, does it follow that because a rich man may not use, he may not keep others from using the wealth which might otherwise relieve the excessiveness of their toil? He may hoard if he will, and for every dollar he hoards, derived from human toil, as every dollar is, some one has toiled thus much in vain. Or perhaps he invests it in active enterprises, and gives employment, gives labor to the poor, in building railroads, building houses. Is there not something the laboring classes need more, have less of, than labor? It is as certain as that every man needs to work and ought to work, that excessive and incessant physical labor in a measure brutifies and degrades. Can a Christianity according to the higher ideal, exist in a class that toils like our hod-carriers and farm-laborers? The aim and tendency of modern society in its educational and other reforms, and of modern science and invention, by labor-saving machinery, are to reduce the amount of necessary toil, thus to create leisure, and then to furnish means for the use of that leisure in gaining a higher culture.

It is believed that Mr. Astor had at heart the culture and elevation of the laboring class. Many provisions of his will indicate this. It was executed July 4, 1836, and he added to it, from time to time, eight codicils. By one of these he gave to the Society for the Relief of Aged Females the sum of $20,000, and to the German Society $25,000 in trust, to invest and apply the income to establishing an office in the city of New York, and employing proper persons to attend the same who could speak the German language, and were otherwise qualified, whose duty it should be to give "advice and information, without charge, to all immigrants arriving here, touching their establishment here and their course of life, and for the purpose of protecting them against impositions, to which strangers, without knowledge of the country or its language, may be exposed."

For the use of the poor of Waldorf, his native village, he gave fifty thousand dollars. The Grand Duke of Baden has taken great interest in the application of this fund. A fine and appropriate building has been put up, in which instruction is provided for the class whose welfare the donor had in view, and that welfare, it was believed, could not be otherwise more surely promoted.

The crown of Mr. Astor's beneficence is the Astor Library, in the city of New York. Ten years before his death he had announced to some of his friends his intention to bequeath a large sum for a public object, and consulted them as to what it should be. They all, without consultation, fixed upon a public library. He first set apart three hundred and fifty thousand dollars for the purpose, and during the last years of his life the Library became a matter of great interest with him.

"He had plans drawn," we are informed, "of a library edifice, and made repeated efforts to decide upon the one to be adopted, preparatory to beginning the erection of it; but he found every effort of the kind too exhausting to be continued, and he was at length obliged wholly to abandon the attempt. Some small beginnings, however, were made in collecting books, and more would have been done in the same way, but for the want of some convenient and safe place of storing them. It may not be uninteresting to know that the first purchase for the library was made at the sale of part of Major Douglass's books, March 15th, 1839, when about forty volumes were bought; among them Britton's Architectural Antiquities of Great Britain, Young's Recent Discoveries in Hieroglyphical Literature, White's Gradations in Man, and Churchill's Voyages. These were the nucleus of the Astor Library, and may fairly be considered as a type of the whole collection. In the course of the same year, a very valuable library which had been collected by Count Boutourlin, and left at his death in Florence, where he had resided, was offered to Mr. Astor for about fifty-four thousand dollars. He decided to buy it, and furnished a friend (Mr. Cogswell), who was about visiting Europe, with the credit necessary to effect the purchase. But it was too late; when he arrived he found the library had been removed to Paris, to be sold by auction, and a part of it already dispersed. It may help to correct the general false impression, that the value of a library can be estimated by the number of volumes, to know that the Boutourlin Library did not contain more than twelve thousand volumes, and would have cost between fifty and sixty thousand dollars; that is, it would have absorbed nearly one-half of the whole sum to be expended by the Astor Library for books, and it would not have filled more than one-eighth of its shelves. The twelve thousand volumes of the Boutourlin would have been preferred by the *Biblio-*

mane; the forty or fifty thousand which the same sum has procured for the Astor Library, will be found vastly better adapted to the wants of those who use it. The only work bought by Mr. Astor himself for his Library, was a copy of Audubon's Birds of America, and the whole number of volumes bought for it during his lifetime was not above a thousand."

The codicil establishing the library is as follows:

"I, John Jacob Astor, do make this additional codicil to my last will, bearing date the fourth day of July, in the year of our Lord eighteen hundred and thirty-six.

"Desiring to render a public benefit to the city of New York, and to contribute to the advancement of useful knowledge, and the general good of society, I do, by this codicil, appropriate four hundred thousand dollars out of my residuary estate, to the establishment of a Public Library in the city of New York. For this purpose I give to my executors four hundred thousand dollars, to be taken from my personal estate, or raised by the sale of parts of my real estate, to be made by my executors with the assent of my son William B. Astor, upon condition and to the intent that the said amount be settled, applied, and disposed of as follows: namely—First, In the erecting of a suitable building for a public library. Second, In furnishing and supplying the same from time to time with books, maps, charts, models, drawings, paintings, engravings, casts, statues, furniture, and other things appertaining to a library for general use, upon the most ample scale, and liberal character. Third, In maintaining and upholding the buildings and other property, and in defraying the necessary expenses of taking care of the property and of the accommodation of persons consulting the Library. The said sum shall be payable, one-third in one year after my decease, one-third in the year following, and the residue in equal sums in the fourth and fifth years after my decease. The said Library is to be accessible at all reasonable hours and times for general use, free of expense to persons resorting thereto, subject only to such control and regulations as the trustees may from time to time exercise and establish for general convenience.

"The affairs of the institution shall be conducted and directed by eleven trustees, to be from time to time selected from the different liberal professions and employments in life and the classes of educated men. The Mayor of the city of New York, during his continuance in office, and the Chancellor of the State of New York, during his continuance in office, shall always be trustees. The vacancies in the number of trustees occurring by death, resignation, incapacity, or removal from the State, shall be filled by persons appointed by the remaining trustees. The acts of a majority of the trustees, at a meeting reasonably notified, shall be valid. All the property and effects of the institution shall be vested in the said trustees. They shall have power to direct the expenditure of the funds, the investment, safe-keeping, and management thereof, and of the property and effects of the institution; also to make such ordinances and regulations, from time to time, as they may think proper for the good order and convenience of those who may resort to the Library or use the same. Also to appoint, direct, control, and remove the superintendent of the Library, and all librarians and others employed about the institution. And also they shall have and use all powers and authority for promoting the expressed objects of this institution, not contrary to what is herein expressed. They shall not receive any compensation for their services, except that if any one of their number shall at any time be appointed superintendent, he may receive compensation as such. The trustees shall be subject to the visitation of the proper courts of justice, for the purpose of preventing and redressing all mismanagement, waste, or breach of trust.

And I direct that the said Public Library be established on my land, at the corner of Lafayette Place and Arch-street, on the westerly side of Lafayette Place, in the city of New York: beginning on the westerly line of Lafayette Place, eighty-one feet from the corner of the house in which my daughter Dorothea Langdon now resides, and running thence, perpendicular to Lafayette Place, one hundred and thirty-seven feet six inches, to the alley-way in the rear; thence, along the alley-way to Arch-street; thence, along Arch-street to Lafayette Place, and thence to the place of beginning—with the right and benefit of way in the alley. Which land I direct my executors to convey to the said trustees in fee-simple, by such proper assurances as shall secure the land for the purpose of the Library, and on condition to be applied and used therefor. And inasmuch as one of the lots so to be conveyed is devised to the children of Mrs. Langdon, I order that twelve thousand five hundred dollars be paid to the said devisees as a compensation for the lot. And I direct that all the said land hereby appropriated, be valued at forty thousand dollars, and form a part of the said four hundred thousand dollars. I further direct that a sum not exceeding thousand dollars may be expended in the erection of the building for the Library; one hundred and twenty thousand dollars may be expended in the purchase of books and other objects, for the establishing of the Library, and the residue shall be invested as a fund for the maintaining and gradually increasing of the Library. All investment of the funds of the institution shall be made in the public debt of the United States of America, or of the States of the Union, or of the city of New York, as long as such subjects of investment may be had, giving a preference according to the order in which they are named; and in case the income of the fund shall at any time exceed the amount which the trustees may find useful to expend for the purposes above mentioned and particularized, they may expend such surplus in procuring public lectures, to be delivered in connection with the Library, upon useful subjects of literature, philosophy, science, history, and the fine arts, or in promoting in any other mode the objects of the institution, as above expressed. I direct my executors to cause and procure the necessary legal assurances to be made for establishing and securing the application of the funds and property hereby appropriated for the purposes of these presents, and in the mode herein pointed out; and it is my request that the trustees would apply to the Legislature of this State for such acts as may fully secure, establish, and perpetuate this institution, and render its management easy, convenient, and safe, both to themselves and the public. And as this property is devoted wholly to public purposes, I trust that the Legislature will so far favor the institution as to exempt its property from taxation. And as a mark of my respect for the following gentlemen, I name them to be the first trustees, that is to say, the Mayor of the city of New York, and the Chancellor of the State, for the time being, in respect to their offices, Washington Irving, William B. Astor, Daniel Lord, Junior, James G. King, Joseph G. Cogswell, Fitz-Greene Halleck, Henry Brevoort, Junior, Samuel B. Ruggles, and Samuel Ward, Junior. In witness whereof, I have set my hand and seal to this codicil, and publish the same as a codicil to my will, this twenty-second day of August, in the year of our Lord one thousand eight hundred and thirty-nine.

"John Jacob Astor."

By a subsequent codicil, Mr. Charles Astor Bristed, his grandson, was appointed a trustee.

A different site for the Library from that pointed out in

the codicil was afterward selected, on the easterly side of Lafayette Place near Astor Place.

On the 18th of January, 1849, the trustees named by Mr. Astor were incorporated by act of the Legislature of New York, and authorized to receive from his executors the sum of four hundred thousand dollars; to expend not more than seventy-five thousand dollars of the sum in erecting a building for the Library; to expend a further sum of $120,000 in the purchase of books, maps, charts, models, drawings, paintings, engravings, casts, statues, furniture, and other things appertaining to a library for general use; "to invest the residue as a fund for paying for the site of the building, for maintaining and gradually increasing the Library, to provide for public lectures, to make regulations for the good order and convenience of those visiting the Library, and to appoint a superintendent and librarian." They are authorized to take and hold any additional donations, grants, devises, and bequests, which may be made for the support of the Library, or the lectures, or scientific objects connected therewith.

The wish expressed by the founder was heeded by the Legislature, and the property of the Library exempted from taxation.

The trustees had previously met in May, 1848, given to it the name of the Astor Library, and appointed Dr. Joseph G. Cogswell its Superintendent, an appointment amply justified by his fine scholarship and peculiar qualifications, had not the wishes of the founder made it almost imperative. In March, 1849, Dr. Cogswell returned from a four months' visit to Europe, during which he purchased twenty thousand volumes. The time was peculiarly favorable, as the political convulsions of 1848 had thrown many valuable libraries into the market.

In March, 1850, the Library building was commenced, and completed in July, 1853, after the plans of Mr. A.

Saeltzer. On the 9th of January, 1854, it was opened for inspection, and it then displayed upon its shelves a larger number of volumes than any one library in America had ever before contained. These prompt results were due to the diligence of the Superintendent, who had made two other visits to Europe, visited every book-mart from Rome to Stockholm, and purchased in all, about fifty thousand additional volumes.

It has been said, "the true university of these days is a collection of books." If so, the Astor Library, with its hundred thousand volumes, is one of the few universities in America. It is organized, we are informed, "upon the plan of a library of reference, and does not lend out its books." It is open during the daytime only, from 10, A. M., until half an hour before sunset. That the Astor Library should become a Circulating Library can be the desire of no one, but may we not hope that the trustees, whose sole desire, of course, is to so administer the affairs of the Library as to carry out the intention of the founder, and promote the largest public good, may find it advisable to bring its rich treasures within reach of those who can not profit by them during the day? The more strictly its character, as a library of reference only, is maintained, the larger should be the facilities and opportunities of using it as such. One of the largest libraries of Paris, that of Sainte Geneviève, is open in the evening. In this country the class of literary men by profession is small. The class of professional men is large, and among them there are many who have some special and favorite study, outside their profession, which during the evening's leisure they would gladly pursue. During the day it is out of the question, and it is not to be presumed that mechanics have much more leisure. The hours of the Astor Library are precisely those when no business or professional man or mechanic *can* attend. Thousands pass near it day after day for years, who would gladly use it, but to whom it is as if it were not. If the Library Hall may not be itself thrown open, might not its contents, or a portion of them, be made in some way accessible? A book unread is as if it were not. Its meaning is in the mind of him who reads; otherwise, it is as a brick from Nimroud, senseless, a curiosity; and a great library unused becomes a spiritual *mortmain.*

The Library building is a fine structure of brick, resting on a lower story of brown stone, with deeply recessed doors, and mouldings and mullions also of stone. The main or Library Hall is a beautiful room, one hundred feet long, sixty-four feet wide, and fifty feet high. By an economical arrangement of the shelving, it is made to contain one hundred thousand volumes.

It would be an unpardonable omission, even in this imperfect sketch of the Astor Library, not to state that Mr. William B. Astor cherishes with the fondness and interest of a son, the noble institution his father has established. At a cost of sixteen thousand five hundred dollars, he furnished the Library with a complete collection of works on the mechanical and industrial arts, and the applied sciences. He has just erected, at his own expense, a building adjoining the Library, precisely like it in size and style, to be devoted to the same public purpose. The two buildings show but one front, which has now the breadth of effect which it before lacked, and presents a fine façade of 130 feet on Lafayette Place. But the two edifices are really distinct, and should remain distinct—the one to attest the generosity of the founder, the other, the true filial piety with which his son seeks to carry out, giving full scope and wider development to his plans.

It is something to give liberally by will, but a liberal gift during life has the additional, the Christian grace of self-denial.

On either shore of America there stands a memorial of

Astor—the Library in New York, and Astoria on the Columbia; they speak more eloquently than any inscription on monumental brass or stone,—the one, of the genius of the merchant, which won him wealth, the other of the wisdom with which he used it.

JUDAH TOURO.

THE great commercial emporium of the Mississippi Valley is a very peculiar and unique city. Though for the last twenty years the largest exporting town in the Union, and the arena of immense commercial transactions, where many colossal fortunes have been accumulated, New Orleans, owing to the frequent visitations of desolating epidemics, has progressed very slowly, compared with other American cities, in that principal element of a large and flourishing community—a regular, increasing, permanent population.

The busy and struggling crowds that give such life and stir to the streets, and to the magnificent levee, or quay, that stretches for miles along the Crescent Port, in the winter season, are of the class of temporary residents, birds of passage, adventurers, merely sojourning until they realize a satisfactory competency, or some irretrievable disaster. New Orleans is, in fact, among cities, what Turkey has been described among the states of Europe, an encampment, a mart of trade rather than a regular and permanent city. The population of one year vanishes in the next. The residents of a few years soon find themselves overwhelmed by the influx of strangers. Thus the small class of early settlers, who have clung to the city through all its various fortunes, stalk about in the throng of new and strange faces with feelings akin to those of the Chinese prisoner, who, in his dungeon, had outlived his generation, and being restored in his old age to freedom, found that boon a burden heavier than captivity, as he moved, unknown and unnoticed, among the busy millions of his old home. The old resident of New Orleans has indeed survived many generations,—more than the citizen of any other community. Besides the constant changes and fluctuations of the population, to which we have referred, there are the generations that moulder in the vast cemeteries, the victims of the ghastly pestilence which has so long cursed the city of Bienville. It is sad to pass through these populous chambers of the dead, and observe the period of life at which the large majority of the tenants of those unsightly and revolting ovens, have been gathered in the harvest of death.

Ninety out of every hundred have been snatched from the scenes of active life in the very bloom of manhood, between the ages of twenty and forty. Unlike the cemeteries of other towns, you will find here but few of those tender memorials of affection which are usually graven on the tombs of infancy and old age. Those roughly bricked and plastered vaults present only the simple record, in coarse characters, written by some unsympathizing hand, of some unknown young adventurer, who has fallen, far away from his friends, "unwept, unhonored, and unsung." Such is the character of that mortality which has, for the last fifty years, afflicted this city with its annual visits. This circumstance excites a peculiar interest and veneration toward that small and declining class of old men, who have escaped all the perils and trials which have scourged New Orleans during nearly the whole period of its existence. They stand before the present population, relicts of an age which, measuring by generations and the rapid march of events, may justly be regarded one of antiquity. Of such there still linger a small band, who have witnessed the growth of the city from a Spanish post to a great American city. They are of the class of the first American settlers, who were attracted to New Orleans, in the beginning of the present century, when a large and increasing trade sprung up between the northern Atlantic seaports, and this then center of the trade of the rich Spanish colonies lying along the Gulf coast. Having emigrated in early manhood, the last half of the nineteenth century found these pioneers of American settlement in Louisiana, far advanced toward the ordinary limit which the Psalmist assigns to human life,—of threescore and ten. It was, therefore, quite natural, when this turning-point was reached and passed, that one by one of these venerable actors of an age long past should quietly glide from the stage of action, without being missed by the busy company engaged in the stirring drama around them. It would be better for them and the world, if these actors could pause for awhile in their too often wild and reckless career of adventure and speculation, to contemplate the lives and character of those honest, faithful, punctual, and prudent merchants of the old school, who, alas, are rapidly disappearing before the more dashing and ostentatious class of speculators, operators in stocks, luxurious, high-living, "Merchant Princes," as they are called in fashionable parlance, who too often owe much of their prosperity and wealth to the kindly interposition of the Bankrupt Law. These true merchants formed their principles in the good old times of legitimate trade, before the credit system was invented, and when a tradesman who passed beyond his proper sphere was regarded with distrust and suspicion.

Of this class of old-fashioned merchants in New Orleans, who established such a high reputation for the first American settlers in that then foreign town, and who by steadily pursuing the straightforward, honorable path of legitimate trade, attained great wealth, without the sacrifice which too often attends that acquisition,—of the good will and kindly regards of the whole community,—not one was mourned as he whose death excited so profound a sensation, in the winter of 1854, in this usually volatile community.

It was the death of a man who had won a renown nobler, higher, and more enduring than that which the most successful merchant, the most daring warrior, or the most gifted author ever earned. Who that saw him in life, would have anticipated such fervent demonstrations of popular affection and grief at his death? How little of the hero or great man was there, in the simple, humble aspect of that timid, shrinking old man, who was wont to glide so silently and diffidently through the streets, with his hands behind him, his eyes fixed on the pavement, and his homely old face, wrinkled with age, but replete with the expression of genial kindness and benevolence. He was, too, a man of no great deeds, or public services, or brilliant qualities. And yet, when the tidings of his decease go forth, a whole people, a reckless, frivolous, and cynical people, turn aside from their various pursuits of pleasure or ambition, to bewail with heartfelt sorrow his departure. And he died a millionaire. The people do not usually sorrow over the death of the rich man. There is divine authority for this popular repugnance to those who have heaped up the treasures of this world. It is rare, indeed, that the man who does his duty by his fellow-men in life, accumulates large wealth.

Not many months before the death which has suggested these remarks, there had departed this life another millionaire, a contemporary of the lamented subject of this sketch. He was a man of enormous possessions, all of which, it was known, he had bequeathed to public charities. And yet he was not mourned. The people, indeed, reckoned his death a timely event, and hardly respected the immunity from uncharitable comment which death claims for his victim. He has been a brilliant and successful merchant, a man of prominent characteristics, of high intelligence and resolute courage, and a fearless and remorseless litigant. His gains were the result of masterly combinations and heroic tenacity. And yet he was attended to the grave only by a small number of his dependents and employees. So dreary were his last hours, that it was rumored that his death was hastened by the want of proper attendance in sickness. And this was a man whose life had been one of unceasing devotion to Mammon,—to the entire exclusion of all kindly and charitable acts and feelings,—whose career had been along a hard, stony, sterile path, where not a flower bloomed, or blade of verdure relieved the dreary prospect.

How different had been the life of the subject of this sketch! Wealth seemed to flow into his coffers, as the reward of a boundless and incessant benevolence and beneficence—an ever-active philanthropy. His career was a splendid illustration of the Divine injunction and promise, "Cast thy bread on the waters, and after many days it shall return to thee." Avarice, the love of money for its own sake, were as foreign to his nature as dishonesty and falsehood. He deprived himself of all other luxuries in order to enjoy and gratify with keener relish and greater intensity his single passion and appetite—to do good to his fellow-men. He was a miser only in the exercise of his charity and benevolence, from which he jealously excluded others. His only art and stealth were displayed in the concealment of his benefactions, and his chief vexation and trouble were to avoid the ostentation and display which are too often the main incentives to liberal and benevolent deeds.

Such was the character of Judah Touro, "the Israelite without guile," whose decease in the city of New Orleans, in January, 1854, excited so profound a sensation in the community which he had so long blessed and cheered by his numerous benefactions. It is not within our power to do justice to a character which approaches so near to the Godlike,—to the perfection of virtue, goodness, gentleness, and benevolence,—but even a few mementoes, a brief and skeleton sketch of a life so full of goodness, and of attractions to the lovers of the noble and unselfish traits of humanity, may interest not a few readers.

Judah Touro was born in Newport, Rhode Island, in the year 1776. His birth was contemporaneous with that of the liberty of the republic, of which he was ever a worthy, devoted, and patriotic son. In his old age, he was wont to display no little pride—the only occasion on which that weakness was ever manifested by him—in referring to the fact, that his entrance into the world was greeted by the thunders of artillery fired in honor of the Declaration of Independence issued by the Continental Congress. His father, Isaac Touro, was a native of Holland, a learned, accomplished, and excellent man, who emigrated first to the West Indies, where he spent some years. Thence he removed to Newport. Being a strict Hebrew, of all the requisite attainments and qualifications, he was soon chosen as the priest of the synagogue Yeshuat Israel, which was erected in Newport in 1762. He performed the sacred duties of his office to the great satisfaction of a congregation which embraced several of the leading merchants and professional men in this then important commercial town. He had not resided long in Newport before he married the sister of Michael Moses Hays, a distinguished merchant of Boston, the intimate friend of the late Harrison Gray Otis and of Thomas H. Perkins. When the war of the Revolution commenced, Newport was one of the first of our seaport towns which was occupied by the British army. The congregation of the synagogue, in which the Rev. Isaac Touro officiated, embracing many prominent patriots, was dispersed, and the worthy and patriotic priest betook himself and family to Kingston, Jamaica. There he died in 1783, leaving a widow and three children in very destitute circumstances. They returned to the United States, where Mrs. Touro's brother received them into his family, and acted a father's part by the orphans. There were two boys, Abraham and Judah, and a girl, who afterward became Mrs. Lopez. Their mother dying in 1787, they were left entirely to the care and tutelage of their affectionate and faithful uncle, who gave them a good education, rearing the boys in his own counting-room, and imbuing them with the strictest ideas of morality and integrity, and with habits of mercantile promptitude, industry, and sobriety. Their after-life justified and rewarded the interest and care which their excellent uncle bestowed on their education. Abraham remained in Boston, and became a successful merchant, accumulating a large fortune, which at his death, in 1822, he bequeathed to certain charitable institutions in Boston and Newport,—providing the fund called the Touro Fund, out of which the old synagogue in which his father had officiated, the cemetery attached, and the street on which they front, are kept in repair. Abraham died a bachelor. Mrs. Lopez, the sister, died in 1833, and Judah was then left the last of his family.

Having by his good conduct in the counting-room secured the confidence of his uncle, Judah was selected by him as supercargo of a valuable shipment for the Mediterranean. This was in 1798, when hostilities existed on the sea between France and the United States. The ship on which Judah Touro sailed became involved in a desperate conflict with a French privateer, from which the Yankee ship came off victorious, and returned in safety, after a prosperous voyage.

On his return to Boston, there is a tradition that Mr. Touro, for the first and only time in his long life, became involved in the meshes of love. The story runs that his aspirations were thwarted by that too often grim disturber of the affections and hopes of young people—poverty. Whether this is an invention of some imaginative friend who conceived a bit of romance essential to give variety and additional interest to a life remarkable for its monotonous simplicity, we are unable to say.

In October, 1801, Mr. Touro sailed from Boston for New Orleans, in which city, then rising in importance as a commercial mart, he determined to try his fortune. The voyage was a long and tempestuous one, so that Mr. Touro did not reach New Orleans until February, 1802. His sufferings on this voyage induced Mr. Touro to resolve never again to trust himself on the treacherous deep. He faithfully observed this resolution, never after going beyond the limits of the city, except during the war, when he performed the duties of a patriot and soldier on the plains of Chalmette.

At the time Mr. Touro landed in New Orleans, it was a Spanish town of eight or ten thousand inhabitants. It was a great field for the enterprise of young American merchants. The ship in which Mr. Touro came was loaded with "Boston notions," belonging to various shippers, consigned to Mr. Touro. He immediately opened a small store on St. Louis-street, near the Levee, where he began a brisk and profitable trade in soap, candles, codfish, and other exports of New England, making prompt returns to his friends in Boston. His fidelity, integrity, and good management soon secured him a large New England trade, every vessel from that section bringing him large consignments, and many ships being placed at his disposal, as agent, to obtain cargoes and collect freight. His business was prosperous, his funds accumulated. He invested his surplus judiciously in ships and in real estate, which rapidly advanced in value. His career as a merchant was one of honest, methodical labor, and stern fidelity to the principles of legitimate trade, never embarking in any hazardous ventures or speculations, never turning aside from his line of business, and adhering rigidly to the cash system. Such a career presents but few incidents of interest. There was one circumstance, however, in his life which is worthy of remark, as a beautiful example of pure and constant friendship. Shortly after his settlement in New Orleans, Mr. Touro formed the acquaintance of two enterprising young merchants from Virginia—the Messrs. J. H. and R. D. Shepherd. This intimacy and friendship continued during the lives of the parties. The death of Mr. J. H. Shepherd, some years ago, concentrated the affectionate intimacy and friendly devotion of Mr. Touro on the surviving brother, Rezin D. Shepherd, a gentleman worthy of the high regard and devoted friendship of a man like Judah Touro. Besides the ties of early intimacy and mutual respect, Mr. Shepherd derived an additional claim upon the gratitude and affection of Mr. Touro from an incident, which was the most prominent in the history of the modest, gentle, and benevolent old man. We can not present this occurrence in a stronger light, or in a more authentic form, than in the language of the author of Jackson and New Orleans, an authentic narrative of the memorable defense of New Orleans by Andrew Jackson, in 1814–15:

"Among those who were thus engaged, was one whose memory is cherished with pious devotion by thousands in the community, which he so long blessed with his inexhaustible benevolence. The 1st of January, 1815, witnessed the only scene of contention and bloodshed in the long, peaceable and virtuous life of that pure-minded philanthropist,—Judah Touro,—whose fame is coeval with the boundaries of this Republic, and has extended to distant and foreign lands, which he has brightened and comforted by his beneficence.

"After performing other severe labors as a common soldier in the ranks, Mr. Touro, on the 1st of January, volunteered his services to aid in carrying shot and shell from the magazine to Humphrey's battery. In this humble but perilous duty he was seen actively engaged during the terrible cannonade with which the British opened the day, regardless of the cloud of iron missiles which flew around him, when many of the stoutest-hearted clung closely to the embankment, or sought some shelter. But in the discharge of duty, this good man knew no fear and perceived no danger. It was whilst thus engaged, that he was struck on the thigh by a twelve-pound shot, which produced a ghastly and dangerous wound, tearing off a large mass of flesh. Mr. Touro long survived this event, leading a life of unostentatious piety and charity, and setting an example of active philanthropy, which justly merited the fervent gratitude and warm affection in which he was held by the community of which he was justly regarded as the Patriarch, —the 'Israelite without guile.'

"No charitable appeal was ever made to him in vain. His contributions to philanthropic and pious enterprises exceed those of any other citizen. The same patriotism which prompted him to expose his life on the plains of Chalmette, dictated the handsome donation of ten thousand dollars for the completion of the Bunker Hill Monument, and has characterized a thousand other deeds of like liberality, performed 'by stealth,' which were no less commendable for their generosity than their entire freedom from sectarian feeling or selfish aim. An incident, illustrative of the beauty of friendship and gratitude, of the noble and gentle traits of humanity, may serve as an agreeable relief in this narrative of strife and bloodshed.

"Judah Touro and Rezin D. Shepherd, two enterprising merchants, the one from Boston and the other from Virginia, had settled in New Orleans at the commencement of the present century. They were intimate, devoted friends, who lived under the same roof, and were scarcely ever separated. When the State was invaded, both volunteered their services, and were enrolled among its defenders. Mr. Touro was attached to the regiment of Louisiana

Militia, and Mr. Shepherd to Captain Ogden's Horse Troop.

"Commodore Patterson, who was an intimate friend of Mr. Shepherd, solicited General Jackson to detach him, as his aid, to assist the commodore in the erection of his battery on the right bank of the river, and in the defense of that position.

"It was whilst acting as Patterson's aid, that Mr. Shepherd came across the river, on the 1st of January, with orders to procure two masons to execute some work on the commodore's battery. The first person Mr. Shepherd saw, on reaching the left bank, was Reuben Kemper, who informed him that his old friend Touro was dead. Forgetting his urgent and important mission, Mr. Shepherd eagerly inquired whither they had taken his friend. He was directed to a wall of an old building, which had been demolished by the British battery in the rear of Jackson's headquarters, and, on reaching it, found Mr. Touro in an apparently dying condition. He was in charge of Dr. Kerr, who had dressed his wound, but who, shaking his head, declared that there was no hope for him. Mr. Shepherd, with the devotion of true friendship, determined to make every effort to save his old companion. He procured a cart, and lifting the wounded man into it, drove to the city. He administered brandy very freely to his fainting and prostrate friend, and thus in a great degree kept him alive. On reaching the city, Mr. Shepherd carried Touro into his house, and there obtaining the services, as nurses, of some of those noble ladies of the city, who devoted themselves with so much ardor to the care and attendance of the sick and wounded of Jackson's army, and seeing that he was supported with every comfort and need, he hastened to discharge the important duty which had been confided to him, and which he had nearly pretermitted, in responding to the still more sacred calls of friendship and affection.

"It was late in the day before Shepherd, having performed his mission, returned to Patterson's battery.

"The cloud of anger was gathering on the brow of the commodore, when he met the delinquent or dilatory aid, but it soon dispersed when the latter frankly and promptly exclaimed—

"'Commodore, you can hang or shoot me, and it will be all right; but my best friend needed my assistance, and nothing on earth could have induced me to neglect him.' He then stated the circumstances of Mr. Touro's misfortune, and the causes of his dilatory execution of the duty assigned to him. Commodore Patterson was a man,—he appreciated the feelings of his aid, and thought more of him after this incident than before. They continued warm friends throughout the campaign, and ever afterward.

"Shepherd and Touro, with a friendship thus tested and cemented, were ever afterward inseparable in this world. Death alone could sever them, and then only in a material sense. Such fidelity deserved the rich reward which fortune showered on them. They became millionaires, and, as the most valuable of their possessions, retained the esteem and regard of the community of which they were the patriarchs. On the 18th of January, 1854, the venerable philanthropist, Judah Touro, was 'gathered unto his fathers,' amid the lamentation of the whole population of New Orleans. Public journals in their columns, and divines in their pulpits, offered eloquent and just tributes to his virtues. No man ever died in the city, who was more universally regretted, or whose memory will be more gratefully preserved. A few days before his death,—to wit, on 6th of January, 1854,—Mr. Touro made a will, disposing of his immense property. That will is an eternal monument of his goodness and philanthropy. It is not less remarkable for its liberal and discriminating charity, than for the earnest affection and gratitude which the good old man cherished for all who had been kind to him in life. After distributing one-half of his estate among various charitable and religious institutions, including a splendid legacy of $80,000 to that much-needed institution, an Almshouse in New Orleans, and handsome endowments to all Hebrew congregations in the country, as well as a large legacy in favor of the project of restoring the scattered tribes of Israel to Jerusalem, with numerous private legacies to individual friends, Mr. Touro thus nobly embodies and expresses the gratitude and friendship which, for nearly forty years, had warmed his heart toward his old friend and constant associate for half a century:

"'As regards my other designated executor, say my dear, old, and devoted friend, Rezin Davis Shepherd, to whom, under Divine Providence, I am greatly indebted for the preservation of my life when I was wounded on the 1st of January, 1815, I hereby appoint and institute him, the said Rezin Davis Shepherd, after payment of my particular legacies, and the debts of my succession, the universal legatee of the rest and residue of my estates, movable and immovable.'"

The death of Mr. Touro occurred in New Orleans in January, 1854. It was a gradual and dignified decline into the grave, with but little pain or suffering, and with his faculties and his affections unimpaired by age or sickness. A few days before his death, he sent for a notary public, and dictated the remarkable will in which he made so noble and philanthropic a distribution of his large wealth. The bequests were all conveyed in such clear and specific terms, and were so entirely free from all conditions or saving clauses, that there could not be the slightest prospect of any dispute or litigation growing out of them. Of all things, he disliked most lawsuits and controversies of every kind.

We have alluded to the profound sensation which his death produced in New Orleans, where he had resided for over a half century. This feeling extended to other places, which contained the evidences of his generous benevolence. He had provided in his will that his mortal remains should be deposited by the side of the other members of his family in the Jewish cemetery at Newport.

Almost in his last moments he renewed this injunction, and said to those around his dying couch, "When I am dead, carry me to the spot of my birth, and bury me by the side of my mother." How this request and injunction were performed by his friends, is graphically related in a letter from Newport, published in the Providence Journal, from which we quote the following:

"The steamer Empire City, which arrived at New York on Sunday, brought his remains, and they reached here this morning by the Fall River boat. They were conveyed to the Synagogue, and placed before the altar, at which the father of the deceased ministered more than eighty years ago. Upon the coffin stood two lighted candles. The religious services were commenced by Rev. Mr. Goodheim, of New Orleans, the minister of the congregation with whom Mr. Touro worshiped. After reading from the Psalms, both in Hebrew and in English, he pronounced a beautiful and eloquent eulogium upon the character of the deceased, and closed by prayer. Mr. Goodheim is a German, and has been only twelve years in our country. He spoke English, however, with such freedom, accuracy, and elegance, as led all unacquainted with him to believe that he was either of British or American birth. His elocution was most admirable. There was so much euphony in the reading of the Hebrew Scriptures, that even the uninstructed in that ancient tongue were delighted. But when he read in the vernacular, that sublime psalm upon the frailty of human life, beginning, 'Lord, thou hast been our dwelling-place in all generations,' each one present seemed almost voluntarily to exclaim, 'How beautiful! how eloquent!'

"The body was then borne out, followed by a procession consisting of the strangers present, the city government, members of the Redwood Library corporation, other societies, and citizens. The cortege was very long. It has not been equaled since the reinterment of Commodore Perry, 1826. During the process of the procession, the bells of the various churches were tolled, and all the places of business were closed. The whole population of the city came out, and every possible mark of respect was paid to the memory of the honored dead.

"On reaching the cemetery, the body was placed upon a bier by the side of the grave. Rev. Mr. Leeser, of Philadelphia, a personal friend of Mr. Touro, and remembered by him in his will, then pronounced a discourse alike pertinent, felicitous, and enthusiastic. After the coffin was lowered into the grave, Rev. Mr. Isaacs, of New York, said that a quantity of earth had been forwarded from the Holy Land by a Mr. Duncan, to be used on this occasion, and he sprinkled it upon the coffin, accompanying this interesting ceremony with some very appropriate remarks. Each rabbi and many of the laity then threw earth into the grave three times. The rabbis then withdrew toward the cemetery gate, and chanted in Hebrew, which closed the solemnities of the day. When the grave closed upon Judah Touro, it closed upon the last of his family, and his name is now extinct.

"Every thing was auspicious for the performance of these solemn rites. The day was delightfully pleasant; the south wind blandly soft. The ground in which the deceased was interred, is adorned with trees, odorous shrubs, and flowers. The birds of the air have there made their nests, and during the whole of the services mingled their melodious notes with the voices of prayer and praise. On a tree which extended its branches over the grave of the revered mother of the good man now borne to his burial, a robin had made her home. She sat protecting her young, and looking with almost intelligent interest upon this unwonted intrusion of man upon a retreat where, from year to year, quiet and repose reign unbroken and undisturbed. It was peculiarly fitting that all these outward circumstances should so harmonize with the sacredness of the occasion. For, so long as each returning spring shall delight the world with its beauty, and the sweet music of the warbling of birds shall gladden the heart of man, so long shall the name of Judah Touro be held in the most grateful recollection, and the fragrant memory of his virtues and his charities

'Smell sweet and blossom in the dust.'"

The discourses referred to by this correspondent are not only beautiful and just tributes to the virtues and character of the excellent philanthropist, but they are worthy specimens of the eloquence and of the spirit, tone, and style of the sermons of the Jewish priesthood. The following extracts therefore will be found interesting.

The Rev. Mr. Goodheim in his address thus faithfully and eloquently portrays the life and character of his deceased friend and brother Israelite:

"Full seventy-nine years have elapsed—two generations have since passed away—when, within the precincts of this town, Judah Touro was ushered into life. Like his ancestor Jacob, he took the pilgrim-staff in hand—from the north he traveled to the then distant south; like the patriarch, the Lord was with him and prospered his ways; like the patriarch, it was his last injunction, 'When I shall sleep with my fathers, then carry me away and bury me in their burying-place.' To-day, therefore, we are gathered around the bier of the departed, and are about to conduct his earthly remains to their final resting-place, that they may sleep side by side with the ashes of long-departed kindred.

"The life of Judah Touro is marked by none of those brilliant achievements, by none of those dazzlingly striking incidents, which are generally considered to constitute human greatness. His word never marshaled into battle-array and led to victory the hosts of his countrymen; his voice resounded not in the halls of legislation, nor had he the gift 'the applause of listening senates to command.' But in all that is truly honorable, and generous, and noble, he was foremost among the foremost. His heart was instinct with that true benevolence which forces the tear of sympathy into the eye, and opens the hand to succor and to relieve. A sublime goodness characterized his actions, an exalted virtue adorned his life. The warm impulses of a generous heart gushed forth from nature's purest fountain.

"His charity, like his friendship, knew of neither sectional nor sectarian boundaries. The catholicity of the one was equaled by the constancy of the other. Modest and unpretending, meek and humble, even to a fault, he delighted in doing good in secret, and felt happy in the consciousness of being the unknown cause of the happiness of others.

"And to these virtues and principles he remained true to the end of his days. Years will roll on—another generation will succeed us—many a name now shining in the meridian of its glory will be forgotten and unknown; yet the name and memory of Judah Touro will ever live in the hearts of posterity. Through the length and breadth of this country, the name of this philanthropist will ever be coupled with the beautiful words of Scripture—'The memory of the just will be for a blessing.'

"Yes, my friends! the memory of the deceased will ever be blessed. Whether we consider his character as a man, as a citizen, or as an Israelite, it equally claims our admiration, our affectionate regard. Through his munificent bequests, so liberally and so judiciously distributed, he has erected to himself numerous monuments more durable than moulded bronze or chiseled marble, which the gratitude of others may raise. The religious and educational seminaries, the asylums for the poor and the suffering—which he has either established or endowed—for the ennobling of the heart, the improvement of the mind, and the alleviation of distress, are bright evidences of the deep interest he felt for all that tends to ameliorate the moral and physical condition of man. The Touro Infirmary, the Touro Almshouse, the Synagogue, founded by the deceased in that Southern metropolis which had been his constant residence for more than half a century; the Touro Tablets, which will docorate the walls of many a hospital, asylum, school, and sacred place of worship throughout this country, will ever bear witness to those heavenly feelings of benevolence and philanthropy, which animated his good and pious soul.

"'The fruit of the just is a tree of life.' Such a tree of life, affording shade and shelter to many a weary pilgrim, has been planted by the deceased.

"Are we, then, met, to grieve at his death? Not certainly for the sake of the departed. He had passed the ordinary goal; he had fulfilled his great mission, and was waiting for his recall. Sensible of the approach of his end, convinced of a happy immortality, death was to him the commencement of a higher life—an admission to the awful presence of his Father, who is also our Father—of his God, who is also our God.

"Shall we mourn the loss we have sustained! Time mellows and corrects our feelings. The predominant emotion of my bosom is, profound gratitude to heaven for giving us such a man, and sparing him so long. I lose my regret that he is dead, in my deep joy that he has lived; and this I believe to be the general sentiment of his brethren and friends, of trustees and the recipients of his bounty.

The priceless value of such a man is thus best appreciated. In the contemplation of his life we should become profoundly and solemnly impressed with a conviction of the infinite importance which may be given to the life of man on earth, by a beautiful and conscientious devotion of all the means at command, to the nurture and development of the soul's highest faculties, to the culture and manifestation of the soul's highest affections.

"This occasion, then, is not one of exclusive mourning, for the sake of either the dead or the living, but rather one for the expression of fervent gratitude, for the precious example of such a life and death, for the lessons of true wisdom it is designed to teach, and for the devout and lofty aspirations which it should excite. In this spirit let it be improved by us; in this spirit let us raise our hearts to our Creator and heavenly Protector."

The discourse of the Rev. Mr. Leeser presents the religious, as well as the common-day life of the deceased, in a very graphic and forcible style. He said:

"He amassed wealth by honest frugality; treasures flowed into his coffers in the pursuit of his mercantile enterprises. He had no one near him who was bound to him by the ties of blood and kindred, yet he squandered not his acquisitions in extravagance and intemperance, in boisterous wassail or secret debauchery; but he relieved distress when it presented itself to his benevolent eye; when he saw the naked, he clothed them; and those that needed food, obtained it at his hands, whether they belonged to his faith or country, or whether they worshiped at other shrines, and had first seen the light of day in foreign lands. And if you had seen him in his daily walks, you would not have suspected him to be the man of wealth and the honored protector of the poor, as he was: the exterior of our brother betrayed not the man within. But when he gave you his hand, when he expressed in his simple manner that you were welcome, you could not doubt his sincerity; you felt convinced that he was emphatically a man of truth, of sincere benevolence. And thus he lived for many years, unknown to the masses, but felt within the circle where his character could display itself without ostentation and obtrusiveness, at a period when but few of his faith were residents of the same city with him. But when they began to multiply around him, his love for the people of his belief was awakened anew within him, and he looked about himself for the means of supplying a home for his religion in the vicinity where he resided. And if you have ever been in New Orleans, where Mr. Touro lived for full half a century, you will have seen an elegant structure, with the necessary out-buildings attached, which he presented somewhat more than four years ago to the congregated 'dispersed of Judah,' the minister and president of which are now present to join with us in entombing the benefactor of their institutions. And if you have ever been present during the hours of worship, in the house bestowed as a free-gift, without solicitation, on his fellow Israelites, you may have observed a plainly-dressed old man, seated in a corner in the upper portion of the synagogue, devoutly engaged in prayers, not throwing about his eyes to the right or the left, but feeling, as far as a man might judge from the manner he exhibited, as an humble mortal in the presence of his Creator; and all the honor he ever received, was the office of opening the ark where the testimony is deposited before the reading of the law."

The distribution of his wealth, and the motives and considerations which influenced his various bequests, are thus eloquently and truthfully portrayed:

"He thought of the poor in his own city, and endowed a home of refuge to receive them in the day of their distress. He thought of those of his own persuasion who suffered from the heavy hand of disease, and supplied the means to afford them relief, in several cities. He thought of the new and weak congregations in various towns, and afforded them the means to carry on their holy religion in dispensing the blessings which our faith is so well calculated to bestow. He thought of the necessity of diffusing religious education to the children of Israel; and with wise discrimination selected those institutions best calculated to further this end, to make Jewish religion and Jewish literature accessible to the greatest numbers. He thought of those heavenly societies whose mission it is to glide gently into the abodes of the poor, to leave there the traces of benevolence—to cheer spirits which, without this, would droop in despair and gloom. He thought of the afflicted in the land of Israel, to provide for them assistance in their distress, and protection against the arm of violence;—he, the merchant in the far West, who had lived for years separated from his people, almost a solitary worshiper of the one God, amid those who acknowledged him not alone, forgot not those who still linger on the soil consecrated by so many wonderful events which marked our early history, to cheer them on in the deprivations to which they are subjected. And at last he forgot not cherished friendships, some of which were formed late in life, and left them tokens of remembrance, in terms of affection and endearment. But more than all, he clung, with an attachment which nothing could sever, to the man who had stood by him in the hour of trial, on the field where the demon of war made sad havoc among the assailants and the assailed of the place of his residence, and bore him away to a place of safety, beyond the reach of deadly missiles; and he felt a pleasure in bestowing on him the residue of his earthly possessions, after satisfying the demands of benevolence; not because he needed this gift, but to show that the friendship which had endured so many years—which had been cemented amid peace and war, security and danger—deserved to be proved in a manner which few have the means to do. And let me say here, in praise of the living, that the gift has been well bestowed, if for no other cause, for the beautiful manner in which the residuary legatee has discharged all the trusts confided to him by his deceased friend; no delay which the law permits has been suffered to intervene in the bestowal of the benefactions; and what Mr. Touro had willed, his friend discharged to the extent he was able to do it."

These full and graphic delineations of this admirable man, leave us but little to add. In connection, however, with the last observation of the Rev. Mr. Leeser, we can not refrain from uniting in the tribute to that faithful friend of Mr. Touro, who, though far advanced in life, and possessed of more than enough of the riches of this world to satisfy every ambition and desire, devoted himself with so much ardor, zeal, and activity to the execution of all the trusts confided to him by his old friend. R. D. Shepherd has proved worthy of the confidence, the affection, and the generous fidelity which for half a century bound him to Judah Touro, as with "hooks of steel," and the expression of which was the last utterance of the good old man. After the decease of all his relatives, his affectionate regards and thoughts centered in the companion of his manhood, his true friend in the time of need, the comforter and stay of his old age. And when, in his last will, he had provided liberally for all his friends, and for all the institutions and objects which appealed to his charity and his affections, there still remained a considerable sum of his large possessions, which he bequeathed to his friend, not only as a tribute of his regard and remembrance, but in the confidence that his faithful friend would supply any omissions in his benevolent dispositions, and apply the large residue of his estate to objects of an enlightened philanthropy. Mr. Shepherd, though more a man of the world—of habits more practical, active, and stirring than his old friend—entered fully into all his views, and into that spirit of unostentatious benevolence which was the characteristic of Mr. Touro's life. As an evidence of the fidelity and activity with which Mr. Shepherd discharged his duties as principal executor of Mr. Touro, we may state the fact, which is a very remarkable one in New Orleans, that in one year after the will was opened, the succession was settled up, the legacies all paid, and the remaining property placed in such condition as to render it applicable to the unexecuted trusts, and to such other objects as Mr. Shepherd may regard worthy. One of the executors has made a visit to London and to Jerusalem for the purpose of ascertaining the most effective mode of distributing the fund bequeathed to the poor of Jerusalem. The fund left by Mr. Touro to establish an almshouse in New Orleans, is being applied to the important object contemplated; the land, in a very eligible locality near the city, having been purchased, and the designs of the buildings accepted.

One of the personal legacies in Mr. Touro's will, is of the sum of three thousand dollars to the Rev. Dr. Theodore Clapp, the eminent Universalist divine who so long officiated in the first and only church of that denomination in the State of Louisiana. The relations of Dr. Clapp and Mr. Touro were of a very interesting character, and strikingly illustrate the liberal and expansive character of Mr. Touro's benevolence and religion. The church erected many years ago for Mr. Clapp became involved in debt, and was sold by the sheriff. The rapid growth of the second municipality, in the most central part of which this church stood, had rendered this a very desirable site for stores. It was apprehended by Mr. Clapp's friends that the church would be bought by parties inimical to him, and that this then small congregation would be left without a suitable place in which to hold their worship. Great sympathy and interest were excited in behalf of the popular divine, but the great value of the property placed it beyond the power of his friends to save it from passing out of the hands of the worthy pastor and congregation. Mr. Touro, having received a hint of the state of affairs, appeared at the sale, in his usually quiet, modest manner, and, without intimating to any person his intention, bid off the church. He then informed Mr. Clapp that he could continue to worship God in his own way, as long as the edifice stood, "with none to make him afraid." And so for twenty years the Universalists of New Orleans, with their learned, popular, eloquent, and generous minister, were indebted to the kindness and liberality of a strict Israelite for a temple in which to perform, in a becoming and appropriate manner, their religious duties. All this time the property occupied by this church was of the value of fifty or eighty thousand dollars. Not a cent of rent was ever demanded by Mr. Touro for the use of the property, and the pastor was allowed to receive the pew-rents for his remuneration. The great fire in 1849, which originated in the St. Charles Hotel, communicated to this church and destroyed it. In the mean time the congregation of Mr. Clapp had become large and wealthy, and yet on the subscription-list for rebuilding the church, we believe that Mr. Touro's subscription exceeded all others.

We remember another instance of the catholic character of Mr. Touro's benevolence and religion. Some poor wan dering Orientals, professing to be agents to collect funds for the relief of the persecuted Christians in Jerusalem, had applied in vain to several rich men in New Orleans. At last, a gentleman, of rather a frivolous turn of mind, suggested, as a joke, that the poor Christians, who desired to raise funds to build up their church in Jerusalem, should seek the aid of Mr. Touro (who was known to be a strict Jew). The missionaries acted upon the suggestion, and soon returned to thank the gentleman who had directed them to so "liberal a Christian." Mr. Touro had subscribed two hundred dollars to their cause!

But if we were to narrate a tithe of his benevolent and charitable deeds, we should extend this sketch to an unreasonable length. We can therefore allude to only a few instances, as illustrative of the general character of his benefactions. Allusion has already been made to his donation to the Bunker Hill Monument. This was in consequence of reading in some newspaper that Mr. Amos Lawrence had pledged himself to give $10,000 to complete the monument, if any other person could be found to give a like sum. Mr. Touro immediately sent a check for the amount. At a dinner given at Faneuil Hall, at the celebration of the completion of the monument, the following toast was given:

> "Lawrence and Touro, united names,
> Patriarch and prophet, press their equal claims;
> Christian and Jew, they carry out one plan,
> For though of different faith, each in heart a man."

On one occasion a poor widow called on Mr. Touro and opened to him a very moving budget of griefs. She had several children, her rent was due, and her landlord threatened to eject her—she had not a cent to buy food or clothes. Long before she had concluded her affecting jeremiad, Mr. Touro had filled up a check and begged her to go and draw it at once. The poor woman proceeded accordingly to the bank, and eagerly presented the check at the counter. The teller carefully examined the check, and then surveying the poor, badly dressed, woe-begone looking woman, shook his head, and informed her that the check could not be paid. With a heavy heart, and a sense of mingled shame and indignation, that she should have been thus cruelly trifled with, she returned to Mr. Touro's store, and handing him the check, remarked that it ill became a rich man to subject a poor widow to insult and mockery. "My dear madam," exclaimed the astonished old philanthropist, "it is all I can give you to-day: it is, I know, a small sum, but it is all I can spare now." "But the bank officer refuses to give me any thing for it," replied the distressed widow. "Oh, yes! I see it all: he requires proof of your identity. Here," turning to his clerk, "go down to the bank with this lady, and tell them to pay that check." No wonder the teller hesitated to pay the check for *fifteen hundred* dollars to so poor and forlorn a looking holder!

Mr. Touro never forgot a service or kindness, how small soever it might be. The negroes who waited on him in the house of the Shepherds, with whom he lived for forty years, were all emancipated by his aid, and supplied with the means of establishing themselves very respectably in the world. He never owned but one slave himself, and after training him to business, he gave him his freedom and a handsome sum of money, with which he bought a place, upon which he now lives with his family very comfortably and independently.

The personal habits of this excellent man may be easily imagined from the foregoing general sketch of his life. He was as methodical and regular as a clock. His neighbors were in the habit of judging of the time of day by his movements. In his business he rarely employed more than one clerk, and he was generally a lad. It was his custom to open his store himself at sunrise and close it at sunset. He attended to all his affairs himself, and had them so well arranged that there was no possibility of any misunderstanding. We never heard of his being engaged in a lawsuit, and he lived in one of the most litigious communities in the world. He could not bear a disputation, or even a very earnest discussion. On one occasion his friend Dr. Clapp became involved in a very warm discussion on a theological question with some clergyman of the city. Mr. Touro was greatly annoyed at the warfare of words and logic, and begged Mr. Clapp to desist from a controversy which was so unpleasant to him.

Mr. Touro's hard experience of the discomforts of voyages by sea, though it determined him to remain on land for the remainder of his life, could not eradicate that natural passion of the New Englander to own ships. He had invested largely in this business, and owned some of the largest ships that came into the port of New Orleans. It was a rather amusing peculiarity of his, that though he took great pleasure and pride in walking along the wharves and surveying the grand and symmetrical proportions of his noble ships, he could never be persuaded to go aboard and examine and admire their interior.

To sum up, in brief, the characteristics of this good man, we will conclude this imperfect and hastily written sketch with the observation, that he was one of that smallest of all the classes into which mankind can be divided—of men who accumulate wealth without ever doing a wrong, taking an advantage, or making an enemy; who become rich without being avaricious; who deny themselves the comforts and enjoyments of life, that they may acquire the means of promoting the comfort and elevating the condition of their fellow-men.

JOHN BROMFIELD

WAS the last representative in America of the male line of a family distinguished, for more than a century among the citizens of Boston, for integrity and benevolence. It had its origin in Wales, where, in the reign of Edward the Second, it had extensive possessions. William Bromfield removed to England, was appointed by Queen Elizabeth Lieutenant of the Ordnance in the Tower, and purchased a great estate in the vicinity of London. His descendant, Edward Bromfield, was born at Haywood House, the seat of the family, in the New Forest, Hampshire, in 1648, and emigrated to Boston, Massachusetts, in 1675, where he became a merchant, eminent for activity, judgment, and integrity. His mansion-house stood in the street which now bears his name, on the site of the present Bromfield House, then "surrounded by fields and shady groves." He married Mary, the daughter of the Rev. Samuel Danforth, of Roxbury, and granddaughter of the Rev. John Wilson, of Boston. Their son, Edward Bromfield, born in 1696, married Elizabeth Coney in 1722, became a merchant of character and influence, and died in 1756. The youngest of the sons of his numerous family was John Bromfield, the father of the subject of this Memoir He married Ann Roberts, the youngest daughter of Robert Roberts, who emigrated to this country from Wales, and became a much respected inhabitant of Newburyport. The character of Mr. Roberts was marked by "uncommon decision and energy;" he was "stern, self-sustained, thinking for himself, with a never-wavering resolution to do what he deemed right, irrespective of the opinions and practice of others;" and the same spirit was so strikingly developed in his grandson, that it was said of him that the same Cambrian blood flowed in his veins as did in those of his maternal grandfather. Having been educated at one of the English universities, he bestowed on his daughter great advantages of education, of which she had the disposition and power to avail herself.

The current of her husband's affairs became troubled, and at last seriously embarrassed, by circumstances of which the War of the Revolution was one of the causes. Their son, JOHN BROMFIELD, the subject of this Memoir, was born in Newburyport, April 11th, 1779. His early years were passed with his brothers and sisters, under the pressure of misfortunes involving the necessity of great pecuniary restraint, and with no refuge or support except in the elevated spirit of their mother, who was, in all respects, entitled to the epithet of "admirable." Beloved by all, by her children she was little less than adored. Such were the impressions made deeply on the mind of the writer of this Memoir, during many years of intimate friendship with this lady; whose virtues and character are accurately portrayed in the following touching tribute from her surviving daughter.

"In all the more trying exigencies of her life, her conduct was noble and magnanimous; nor was it less so, while pursuing the even tenor of her daily lifelong course, unnoticed and unknown. Retired from the world, and needing not its stimulus of praise or applause, she was never happier than when surrounded by her nursery flock, to whose early training she devoted her almost undivided attention; and for this she was eminently qualified. Her own home school-education, under the supervision of her father, was the best that could be obtained. Her intelligent and highly cultivated mind, good judgment, modesty, sweetness of temper, together with a dignity of manners, commanding, yet strictly feminine, formed a charm that bound her children to her irresistibly, her life being to them *a living commentary* upon the truth and grandeur of what were to them her oracular teachings."

Mr. Bromfield, after receiving his early education from his mother, became, in 1792, a pupil of Dummer Academy, in Byfield, where his habits were so studious and his scholarship was so satisfactory, that his friends were advised to send him to the University; the means for which were kindly proffered by his father's sisters. With that decision and firm spirit of independence which subsequently marked his character, he refused with grateful acknowledgments this kind offer, saying that he was resolved to make his own way to fortune, as a merchant; and accordingly at the age of fourteen he entered the counting-house of Messrs. Larkin & Hurd, of Charlestown, and afterward, during the period of his apprenticeship, that of Messrs. Soley & Stearns. The failure of this house, just as he became of age, was the first cloud upon his prospects as a man of business; but with characteristic kindness he assumed, as far as was in his power, the settlement of their concerns, and devoted himself to their service, without reward, or the hope of it. Mr. Bromfield thus entered upon life without patronage, and without prospects, other than such as his own talents and enterprise might open for him. The times were difficult. Several months elapsed, and every attempt to obtain mercantile employment failed. His desire of activity, and his earnest anxiety to begin the work which might lead him to independence, became at last insupportable, when he said to his sister, "I have made up my mind, I will no longer remain idle. I have spoken to a master-carpenter; I have made arrangements with him to teach me his trade; and, if for three weeks I continue unable to find mercantile employment, I will change my profession and become a mechanic." With those who knew the firmness of his character, it was unquestionable that he would have kept his resolution. Happily an opening occurred within the prescribed period, and he was enabled to enter the path he had prepared himself to pursue.

The confidence which his conduct in relation to the concerns of Messrs. Soley & Stearns had created, as well as his known talents and urbanity of manners, soon opened to him opportunities for employment; but in whose service, or for what objects, is not at this day to be ascertained. By letters from him, preserved in the family, it is known that on the 16th March, 1806, he was at Rotterdam, as factor, or agent, for some mercantile house, and that success had not attended the enterprise, of which he had the superintendence. "I have been pursued," he writes to his mother at that date, "by the most untoward and sinister events. Forty days on my passage to Nantes,—fifty-three days embargoed,—I could not arrive in Holland until the first of March. Fortune has pursued me, undeviatingly, with ill luck; I can not charge her with inconstancy. Existence is not worth possessing unaccompanied by independence of mind."

It appears that in April, 1808, he was again in Europe, in like service, with a similar result. On the 18th of that month he wrote to his mother from London: "My fears of a bad voyage are completely realized. I have been obliged to land my cargo, and make a ruinous voyage for the gentlemen who were good enough to give me employ. My own loss will be total, of all that I have earned during my past life. The decrees of France and England are ruinous to American commerce; which is a whip-top, scourged by both parties. Though a neutral, it is attacked by all the belligerents." In the spring of 1809, he was intrusted with large funds by Mr. Theodore Lyman, senior, upon an agreement to remain in Canton for a year, as his factor; and for this purpose he was associated, as supercargo, with William Sturgis, who was appointed to the command of the ship Atahualpa, owned by Mr. Lyman, with joint control of the destined funds. At the request of the writer of this memoir, Mr. Sturgis has favored him with the subjoined letter, conveying his impressions of the character of Mr. Bromfield.

"Hon. Josiah Quincy—My dear Sir: When you asked for reminiscences of our late friend, Mr. Bromfield, I readily promised to give them, and was gratified at having an opportunity to express and record the high estimation in which I have long held him. But, when I sat down to perform this promise, I found that I had undertaken a task not easily executed, and became conscious of my inability to convey to those not acquainted with Mr. Bromfield the impressions of his character and qualities, that are indelibly stamped on my own mind. He was one who can be appreciated only by those who knew him intimately; and of such the number is small, for he was by no means lavish of his confidence, and, though courteous to all, was intimate with few.

"My own acquaintance with him began under the following circumstances. In the spring of 1809 I was in command of the ship Atahualpa, belonging to the late Mr. Theodore Lyman, senior, preparing for a voyage to China. When nearly ready, Mr. Lyman decided to add another hundred thousand dollars to the large funds already provided, which sum might be left at Canton for investment out of the regular business season, in the expectation that it could be then done on the most favorable terms. This arrangement made it necessary that some one should be associated with me who could remain a year at Canton; and Mr. Bromfield, who had previously been in the service of Mr. Lyman, was selected. We met for the first time only the day before sailing, and were wholly ignorant of each other's views, habits, and tastes.

"The relation in which we were placed, does not always tend to harmony and mutual good feelings. On shore we were upon a footing of equality; but at sea I was vested with exclusive and almost despotic power, to which he, in common with all on board, was bound to submit. In two voyages previously made to Europe, he had unfortunately been associated with shipmasters whose narrow prejudices made them foolishly jealous of their authority, and disposed to regard as interference with it any inquiries or comments (however natural and unobjectionable they may be) made by the supercargo, relative to occurrences and passing events on shipboard. This induced Mr. Bromfield to practice extreme caution at the outset of our voyage; and he afterward declared, that for the first week he scarcely knew whether the foretopsail was set or furled, for, when walking the deck, he avoided raising his eyes above the direct line of vision lest he should be suspected of prying into matters that did not concern him, as had happened to him on previous occasions. We soon, however, came to a full understanding; and I doubt if two individuals ever did, or could, make a four months' passage together more harmoniously and pleasantly. He was full of information on a great variety of subjects, and there was a dry humor and a piquancy in his unreserved colloquial intercourse that were perfectly fascinating; and I have never known a man whom I should prefer as a companion through the usual tediousness of a long passage at sea. There was even then, at times, a slight reserve and peculiarity in his manner, which became somewhat more apparent in after life; but these I was careful never to notice, and left him altogether free to act himself in every respect, so that our pleasant intercourse was never for a moment interrupted.

"His habits on shipboard were very regular. He usually appeared on deck an hour before breakfast-time, and, after a formal exchange of morning salutations, would walk rapidly fore and aft the weather-side of the main-deck for some ten minutes, then join me on the quarter-deck and break forth in his usual style, with remarks that never failed to interest and delight me. After breakfast he would occupy himself with his books, while I was engaged in the usual avocations of a shipmaster, which in my case were not very onerous; for, soon after getting to sea, I became satisfied that I was particularly fortunate in having selected a first officer (Mr. Daniel C. Bacon, then a very young man, scarcely more than twenty years of age, now one of our most estimable and successful merchants) so devoted to his duties and competent to perform them, that I might safely intrust all details to his care and management. This left me at leisure to pass much time in social intercourse with Mr. Bromfield; and having the mild climate and fine weather which the voyager usually finds on a passage to China in the regular season, every thing went on so smoothly and pleasantly, that when we anchored in Macao Roads, on the evening of the 21st of August, we could scarcely forbear regretting that our passage was so nearly finished.

"The next morning a very unlooked-for change came over us. At an early hour I dispatched my first officer, Mr. Bacon, with a boat's crew, for Macao, about seven miles distant, to procure a pilot for the Canton River. Soon after, a fleet of armed vessels, apparently Chinese men-of-war, were discovered a few miles distant, standing directly for us. On the outward passage we had passed through the Straits of Banca, and near the spot where a brother of Mr. Bromfield had been attacked and cut off by Malays some years before. The fate of his brother very naturally led him to regard with more than usual suspicion and apprehension every native-armed vessel; but I thought that he sometimes manifested these feelings in a greater degree than the occasion seemed to warrant, and did not always regard them so much, perhaps, as I ought to have done.

"When the Chinese vessels were within a mile or two of us, Mr. Bromfield came on deck, and I pointed them out to him, remarking, inconsiderately, 'If those fellows should chance to be Ladrones (pirates), and knew that we have three hundred thousand Spanish dollars on board, they would be tempted to pay us attention in a way that might not be agreeable this warm morning.' I instantly perceived that the suggestion alarmed him; and though I did not at the moment participate in the alarm, yet, regardful of his feelings, I promptly took measures for defense and escape, that ultimately saved us; but, had they been delayed till my own apprehensions were awakened, it might very likely have been too late, and our destruction inevitable. Had those who witnessed the whole transaction been disposed at first to ascribe Mr. Bromfield's alarm to timidity, the cool self-possession and firm intrepidity with which he aided in defense of the ship when the danger became imminent and an attack was actually made, would have fully satisfied them that he was by no means deficient in personal courage, but was actuated solely by a prudent desire to avoid danger when nothing but disaster could result from useless exposure.

"Associated as we were in transactions at Canton, I could judge from personal observation of his capacity as a practical 'business man;' and such was the opinion I then formed, confirmed by the experience of after years, of his talents, qualifications, and sound judgment, that I could not select a man whom I should have preferred as an agent for the management of commercial business in any quarter of the globe. I left him at Canton, where he remained a year; and this voyage laid the foundation of the fortune he subsequently acquired, which was slowly but surely accumulated by persevering industry in the safest manner; for I doubt if he ever engaged in a transaction that the most fastidious prudence would have pronounced hazardous. He never commenced an adventure without a careful estimate of probabilities, or closed one without looking thoroughly into details and results. He often remarked, that 'many men were ruined by omitting to make figures.'

"His knowledge of commerce was extensive and accurate, and whatever he undertook to do was sure to be done in the very best manner. He frequently commented upon the loose and careless manner in which business is done in this country, and contrasted it with the European practice. 'Here,' said he, in his familiar way, 'if a purchaser is about to buy a cargo of box sugars, he will bore into one box, look at a second, kick a third, and take the lot; but in Europe they thrust an iron searcher through and through every box, and carefully examine every layer.' He admitted that a system of credit is indispensable in this country, but denounced in no measured terms the extent to which we have carried it, as a fruitful source of commercial embarrassments and financial convulsions. To this dangerous extension and indiscriminate granting of credit he mainly ascribed the failure of three-fourths of those who engage in trade and commerce.

"As his property increased, a portion of it was invested in various manufacturing companies; and, had some of his views in relation to this great branch of industry been adopted and carried out, the interest of those engaged in it would have been greatly promoted. He asserted that the manufacturers themselves were their own worst enemies, and maintained that all the injury they sustained from the unwise and vacillating policy of government, and the hostility of 'free trade' advocates, was trifling compared with the injury they inflicted upon themselves by premature and almost reckless increase of producing power. 'Why, my friend,' he would say to me, 'we manufacturers may clamor for protection, and rail at the government for its hostility to the manufacturing interest till we make ourselves hoarse, and it will do no good. The truth is, government has little power in this matter for weal or woe, and can only aggravate or mitigate, in a degree, the evils we bring upon ourselves *by competing with ourselves.* It is not the government, it is Messieurs A, and B, and C, and D' (enumerating those who usually take the lead in getting up new manufacturing establishments), 'with their associates, who do the mischief by keeping production too far ahead of consumption; and, if the rapid growth of this country chance to bring demand up with supply, these gentlemen seem to strain every nerve to give supply the lead again, as if they dreaded that our occasional periods of prosperity would last too long. It is the eagerness to sell water-power, and find employment for their machine-shops, that prostrates the manufacturing business; and we can only hope, that, as all these concerns are principally owned by the same individuals, they will by and by discover, that, where one dollar is gained by getting up new establishments, five are often lost by the consequent depression in price of the productions of those already in operation.' He was not alone in these views.

"Mr. Bromfield was familiar with matters of finance and currency. He perceived the adaptation of a mixed currency to the business and wants of this country, but was never free from apprehension that the paper element would predominate, and the country be flooded with irredeemable paper. He was proud of the financial position maintained by New England during the war with Great Britain from 1812 to 1815, at a time when all south and west of her borders failed to fulfill their engagements and suffered dishonor; but he was sadly troubled and deeply mortified at the course taken in 1837, when, in a time of profound peace and apparent prosperity, all the moneyed institutions in the country suspended payment, not (as they alleged) for want of means, but because they chose to consider it for *the public good* that they should violate their engagements and refuse to pay their debts. He deplored the circumstance as a national calamity, and seemed to feel it little less than a stain upon every solvent man's personal honor. 'It is not,' said he, 'so much the immediate effect that I deprecate, but I dread the consequences hereafter. If individuals who have once violated faith can never be relied upon afterward, how can you expect that soulless corporations, if once permitted to disregard all laws with impunity, will refrain from doing so again whenever their interest can be thereby promoted. Corporations,' he added, 'are convenient and useful, but there is no safety in them unless regulated by stringent laws, and these laws strictly enforced.'

"When discussing 'usury laws,' Mr. Bromfield admitted the necessity of establishing by law a uniform rate of interest to govern all cases in which no rate was stipulated; but he scouted the idea, that legislation could practically restrict the price to be paid for the use of money to a uniform rate at all times and under all circumstances. 'The value of the use of money,' he said, 'like the price of commodities, is governed by the great law of supply and demand; and this can not be controlled by legislation. Usury laws, as they are called, are doubtless designed to protect borrowers and debtors. Do they effect this? Let us look at the practical working of them. We must assume that the borrower will always be disposed to obtain money at the lowest rate of interest. If he can not obtain it at six per cent., it must be because it will command more. Then, if his prospects or necessities induce a willingness, or compel him, to pay more, the law steps in and forbids its being lent to him, directly, at a higher rate. How then is the borrower or debtor situated? He *must* have money;—he can not borrow it at six per cent.;—the law forbids a *direct* loan to him at a higher rate, and he is compelled either to raise it by a sacrifice of property, or obtain it on loan in an *indirect* way, which every one knows is invariably attended with additional expense, that must be borne by the unfortunate borrower. If no other use could be made of money in times of scarcity, but to lend it, the owner might be driven to let it go at six per cent., by the prohibition to take more; but at such times the current value of the use of money may be realized in many other ways than by lending it. In fact, it may be *legally* lent at any rate of interest agreed upon, provided it be *indirectly* done. If these views are correct,' he added, 'it is evident that usury laws put no effectual restriction upon lenders, but are onerous and injurious to borrowers; and this is confirmed by the fact that applications to the legislature for the repeal or modification of such laws come usually from borrowers, for lenders are little incommoded by them.' As a question of morals, Mr. Bromfield did not recognize a difference between getting the current rate for the use of money and getting the market price for a bushel of potatoes or a barrel of flour; and although habitual respect for the laws deterred him from violating them, yet he did not scruple to take the current rate for the use of money in a legal manner.

"Mr. Bromfield read much and thought more. The tendency of his mind was to investigation, but not speculation. He deemed it a waste of time, however, to investigate subjects upon which even an approximation to certainty could not be reached, and which promised no compensating results for labor thus bestowed. 'There are,' said he, 'enough practical and useful matters to be looked into to occupy the longest life.' He bowed to no authority in matters that admitted of difference of opinion, but chose to examine and collate the views of others, and then to form his own. I have never known one less disposed to adopt opinions, however high the source whence they emanated, without passing them through the alembic of his own mind. He often, therefore, rejected those prevalent at the moment, and was seldom carried away by the current of popular feeling. He was, if I may be allowed the expression, thoroughly *anti-humbug*, and regarded most of the exciting topics of the day with philosophic calmness, or with a feeling bordering upon disgust. You, sir, can readily call to mind the excited state of political feeling in 1808 and 1809, upon questions of embargo, non-intercourse, &c., and will, I think, agree with me, that though too much bitterness is mingled with politics at the present time, yet this bitterness is mild compared with the rancor and hatred of political partisans in former days. Now ultra Whigs and violent Locofocos occasionally meet, in sweet communion, on 'free soil;'—then Federalists and Democrats only came together quietly in the burying-ground, and even there with reluctance. It was scarcely to be expected that Mr. Bromfield and myself should escape participation in feelings that pervaded the community at the time we left the United States; but, once beyond the reach of the exciting influences that surrounded us at home, things soon began to assume a different aspect; and, ere the passage was half over, we could discuss matters more impartially, and smile at the delusion that led to an undue appreciation of events ephemeral in their character, and temporary in their consequences. 'Ah!' Mr. Bromfield would exclaim, 'if those who take but a one-sided view of affairs at home could only look at them as we do, from the latitude of forty, South, how differently they would appear!'

"And in after years, when at any time undue excitement was got up upon any subject,—when politicians (self-styled patriots) were clamoring for the election of some favorite individual, or the adoption of some particular measure, as indispensable to the salvation of the country, he would touch me upon the arm with, 'Ah, my friend, if people could only view these matters from forty, South, wouldn't they wonder at their own delusion and folly?' His opinions, being deliberately and carefully formed, were adhered to somewhat tenaciously; but, though well prepared to defend them, he generally shunned controversy, and it was only with intimate friends that he would willingly engage in dispute. Whenever he did so, his manner was invariably courteous and considerate. He was a firm believer in the great truths of Christianity, and in its adaptation to the condition and wants of humanity, but had no sectarian prejudices, and scarcely a preference. He attached little importance to forms, and was willing that every man should worship after his own fashion. He held that man was accountable to God alone for his belief, and to society only for his actions. I have more than once heard him quote approvingly the sentiment of the poet:

'For modes of faith let zealous bigots fight;
His can't be wrong, whose life is in the right.'

With these liberal views he could, of course, tolerate the great diversity of opinion on such subjects; and he extended this spirit even to what he deemed ill-judged or useless efforts to proselytize. He was willing that Jews should cling to the faith of their fathers and remain Jews, and equally willing that visionary enthusiasts should associate for their conversion. He concurred heartily in the sentiment of Lord Bacon, that the great object in life, and the highest duty of man, are the 'multiplication of human enjoyments and the mitigation of human sufferings.'

"Mr. Bromfield never married. It was a subject seldom touched upon by his friends, as they knew it rather annoyed him. Occasionally, however, it would be brought up; and, when questioned as to his motive for remaining in a state of 'single blessedness,' he would treat it pleasantly, and reply, in substance, that he regarded the other sex too highly to inflict upon any one of them such a husband as he should make. 'No woman,' he would say, 'who has a grain of discretion, would consent to bind herself to such a nervous old bachelor as I am, and a woman without discretion would be—not to my taste.' The truth, doubtless, is, that Mr. Bromfield's characteristic prudence deterred him from changing his condition until he had acquired a competency; and this he did not accomplish until he was so far advanced in life, that the same prudence prevented his venturing upon the change at all. He was temperate even to abstemiousness; and solicitude to preserve health led him to try experiments in diet, exercise, and exposure, that I fear impaired his constitution and shortened his life. The manner of his death was just what he often expressed a wish that it might be,—sudden and without suffering. 'I doubt,' said he, 'if I shall be better prepared at one time than another; and therefore, when the "grim tyrant" comes, I hope he will make short work of it.' Were I to sum up his most prominent traits, I should say they were unwavering devotion to whatever he deemed duty; unwearied industry and unfaltering perseverance in whatever he undertook; but, above all, unswerving integrity and uncompromising self-respect. Pope took a contracted view of the glorious works of the Creator, when he wrote the oft-quoted line,—

'An honest man's the noblest work of God.'

But honesty, in the broadest sense of the term, though not of itself sufficient to constitute the *noblest* work of creation, is an indispensable element in every character worthy of respect; and Mr. Bromfield had this element in perfection. Wiser and more talented men have lived, but an honester man never died.

"I am, dear sir, respectfully and faithfully,

"Your friend and servant,

"Wm. Sturgis."

During his residence in Canton, Mr. Bromfield received repeated and valuable consignments of property from Henry Lee, Esq., either on his own account, or from persons for whose confidence he was indebted to Mr. Lee's recommendation. His grateful feelings on these occasions were repeatedly shown in his letters to his mother and sisters. Thus, in March, 1810, he wrote:—"I am much obliged to Mr. Henry Lee for his attentions. Without the smallest claim on my part to the smallest portion of his time and pains, he has not failed to use both to my advantage." And again, in the following November, "I am deeply indebted to Henry Lee for unremitting marks of friendship, and for seconding my interests on every occasion."

Mr. Lee having been applied to for his reminiscences of Mr. Bromfield, and his views concerning his character, the following graphic delineation of them was received, of which he has kindly authorized the publication.

"BOSTON, April 4, 1850.

"HON. JOSIAH QUINCY—Sir: I am gratified that a memoir of the late John Bromfield is about to be prepared. He was a man worthy to be held up to praise and imitation for his private virtues, not less than for his public benefactions.

"I can give but little aid in writing the history of his life. Our acquaintance commenced in 1806, and our friendly intercourse has been often interrupted by long intervals, during the residence of both of us in Europe and Asia.

"Nature had bestowed on Mr. Bromfield an extreme sensibility. His temperament was ardent, and his family affections intense. His mother, who was one of the most admirable women of her time, was beloved and venerated by all, and by her son with an attachment bordering on devotion. From her precepts and example Mr. Bromfield derived many of the most valued traits of his character; and the desire to secure an independent provision for her and for his brothers and sisters, whom he also ardently loved, gave probably the first bias of his mind to that determined spirit of independence which formed the groundwork of his efforts. In his early life, and during many years of his manhood, he was tried by adversity; and from this discipline he derived many of his peculiar habits, and also many of those admirable traits of character for which he was distinguished. His life was not eventful. It had no striking incident to make it particularly interesting. In this respect it was not, perhaps, much distinguished from that of the most of our merchants and seamen, who seek in distant seas the profits of a commerce peculiarly exposed to danger from the lawless character of the nations with whom, or in the vicinity of whom, it is carried on. There is, however, one incident of Mr. Bromfield's life, in which he had an opportunity to display his personal courage, presence of mind, and force of character, which was highly applauded at the time, and which ought not to be omitted in any memoir of him. It occurred in the year 1809, on board the ship Atahualpa, of which William Sturgis, Esq., was commander, and on board of which Mr. Bromfield was passenger, and was exhibited in defense of that ship when attacked by pirates in the China Seas. You will probably receive from Mr. Sturgis a fuller account of this affair than any I can give. But, as the successful defense and escape of the ship from imminent peril were chiefly attributable to the prowess and skill of Mr. Sturgis, he may possibly feel a delicacy in dwelling on the facts with so much particularity as they deserve, highly creditable as they were to all concerned.

"Mr. Bromfield was joint supercago with Mr. Sturgis, the commander of the ship; they having intrusted to their management a large amount of specie, then on board.

While at anchor in Macao Roads, and beyond the protection of its fort, a large fleet was, early one morning, perceived bearing down toward the Atahualpa. The ships, full of people, were some of them of great size, and were disguised as Chinamen; but in fact they belonged to Ladrones, residents of the neighboring coasts and islands, who make robbery and murder their means of subsistence. They are bold, reckless, and efficient. The Chinese authorities acknowledge their inability to restrain their depredations. Many foreigners, as well as natives, have fallen victims to that treachery and cruelty for which the Malay race are proverbial. It is, perhaps, impossible to be attacked by a more fierce and savage class of men, or one more qualified to fill the stoutest heart with dread. A brother of Mr. Bromfield had been a few years before assassinated by them, in the same seas, under very tragical circumstances; and the sight of the coming enemy naturally excited in his mind sad reminiscences of his brother's fate. Other circumstances, probably, tended to fill his mind with apprehension. The chief officer (Daniel C. Bacon) of the Atahualpa, with a great part of the ship's crew, was absent, having been sent away that morning, on duty, to Macao; and what remained of the ship's company were scarcely sufficient at once to manage the ship and defend her. Captain Sturgis was, however, equal to the exigency. Cutting his cables, he at the same time hoisted his sails, in order, if possible, to get within the protection of the fort, and gave battle to the enemy; and, after a serious engagement, in which some of their balls penetrated to the cabin, and the combustible materials they discharged had well-nigh set the ship on fire, he succeeded in placing her under the protection of the fort at Macao.

"In this defense, Mr. Bromfield was second only to the commander in courage and activity. He took command of a gun, and responded to the orders of the captain with a self-possession and heroism which, with the other qualities of his head and heart, endeared him to Mr. Sturgis forever afterward.

"In the early periods of Mr. Bromfield's career, he was chiefly employed as a supercargo in foreign voyages, having very valuable interests intrusted to his management. The times, however, were those of embargo, non-intercourse, and war; and the circumstances by which his agency was surrounded were unpropitious. But, although much of the property which was committed to him was lost, no shadow of reproach was ever cast either upon his judgment, conduct, or fidelity; and he enjoyed to the last the entire confidence of all those who had constituted him their agent.

"After the restoration of peace, in 1815, Mr. Bromfield employed the small property he had then accumulated in adventures abroad, particularly in eastern commerce, from whence he drew large profits, in consequence of his thorough acquaintance with oriental customs and trade. When, however, through the increase of competition, this employment of his capital became less profitable, he withdrew it, and subsequently devoted himself to its increase by investments, which the course of the exchange offered, and which he made with great prudence, avoiding all risks, and seeking safe rather than extravagant gains.

"His rules of action were fixed, such as he deemed it the imperious duty of a merchant habitually to observe; and these he applied to the management as well of his own property as of that intrusted to him. To put any thing important in jeopardy for the sake of great profits,—to engage in hazardous enterprises on borrowed capital, and, for the sake of gain to ourselves, to risk the property of others,—were frequent topics of his reproof and reprobation; the delicacy and firmness of his principle in this respect are, in this '*go-ahead* community,' so uncommon, that they may well be enumerated as among his '*peculiarities*.' His tastes and habits in the latter periods of his life had indeed the aspect of singularity. Though he shunned society, he did not seek solitude. He lived in the retirement of his own lodgings, yet at proper seasons was on the exchange, where he attended to his own business, but troubled himself not at all with that of others. He had a morbid dislike of notoriety, so that, beyond a very circumscribed circle of old friends and acquaintance, his worth was unknown and unappreciated. This aversion to notoriety led him always to avoid all conversation relative to himself or his own purposes. Being once questioned concerning the engagement with the Ladrones in the China Seas, with a design to draw him into an account of it, he kindly and characteristically replied: 'That affair has been a little exaggerated, and too much praised. I will only say, I am incapable of wishing that even an enemy of mine should be ever placed in so *disagreeable a predicament*.'

"Although Mr. Bromfield avoided frequent intercourse even with those toward whom he stood in intimate and friendly relations, yet this did not arise from any disrespect or want of affection for his fellow-men; still less could it be referred to any mental or moral inaptitude to appreciate the pleasures and advantages of social intercourse, and its elevating and civilizing tendencies. For no one, who enjoyed the pleasure and advantage of his society, could fail to perceive the cordial and respectful spirit in which he sustained his part. His conversation was replete with information, entertaining, and instructive. His mind, naturally strong, had been improved by careful cultivation, and his observations indicated great meditation and research. His opinions were characterized by originality and independence; frequently differing from those generally entertained, and often from those of the persons with whom he conversed; yet he listened with attention and respect to the arguments of those who differed from him, and yielded the same right of independence to the judgment of others which he claimed for his own.

"Mr. Bromfield's manners, on the first approach, were somewhat formal, even to his friends and acquaintance, but in nothing were they austere or repulsive. There was in his demeanor so much of dignity, refinement, and gentleness, that even a transient acquaintance could not fail to perceive that he possessed all the qualities which characterize a gentlemen.

"His systematic avoidance of general society, and of all the amusements which occupy the time and thoughts of most men, and his love of seclusion, were indeed striking peculiarities in his character, and were the result, unquestionably, of habits which, acquired first from a sense of duty, and being continued for many years by the events of his early life, became at last fixed and inveterate. He was also constitutionally liable to physical infirmities, which subjected him to great self-denial. He was, therefore, temperate from principle, and often abstemious from necessity. The exact fulfillment of his moral and social obligations became, in time, the absorbing principle of his conduct, and guided every action of his life. Economy in expenditure, also, which was commenced at first from necessity and duty, resulted ultimately in an unremitting habit. It was the effect neither of selfishness nor of avarice. For, although he scrupulously avoided all ostentatious charities, he was habitually in the custom of contributing to the wants and the comforts of those whose necessities came within his knowledge. As his wealth increased, his desire to be extensively useful increased with it. Having effected his own independence, and also acquired what he deemed sufficient for that of the relatives he loved, he extended his views, and embraced within their sphere more general charities, to which he determined that, either during his life or at his death, they should be appropriated; his design to accumulate being ever associated with the intention to accomplish some wise and benevolent object. To this end he repressed every temptation to self-indulgence, and sought every occasion of self-sacrifice. The spirit which actuated him is not only strikingly manifested in his munificent bequests to the public, but still more by his private legacies.

"In conclusion, I cordially respond to the tribute paid to his memory by the trustees of the Massachusetts General Hospital, in their recent report. 'Notwithstanding the many acts of liberality of Mr. Bromfield, he was not a seeker of notoriety or praise. He was remarkable for integrity, sound judgment, quiet resolution, and public benefactions. What he believed to be his duty, he did. He is remembered for his public bounty. But he deserves as much respect for his private virtues. Those who knew him best, esteemed him the most.'

"I am yours with great respect,

"HENRY LEE."

To these letters of Mr. Sturgis and Mr. Lee, are here subjoined two others, from Messrs. Augustine Heard and Daniel C. Bacon, gentlemen, like the former, of high mercantile standing, and also, like them, universally appreciated in this community for the soundness of their judgment, and for their capacity to estimate justly the qualities of mind and heart which constitute character. The concurrent opinions of such men, the uniformity of their affection for Mr. Bromfield, and their similar testimony to the elevated principles and motives by which he guided his life, form a tribute to his memory, beyond which nothing can be hoped for or desired.

BOSTON, April 18, 1850.

"HON. JOSIAH QUINCY—Dear Sir: You have expressed a wish that I should communicate to you any thing that may occur to me, that would be useful to you in writing a memoir of our late friend, Mr. Bromfield; and I have a sincere wish to do so, but am doubtful if any thing that I can say will aid you.

"My first acquaintance with Mr. Bromfield was in China, in, I think, 1809, where he was joint supercargo of the Atahualpa with Mr. William Sturgis. He remained after the departure of the ship, as Mr. Lyman's agent in China, where he was considered a model man, not only by his countrymen, but by the Chinese with whom he had dealings. In all his transactions he was scrupulously just and accurate, which gave him the entire confidence of all who knew him; and through life he always sustained the character of a man of sterling principles, pure mind, and kind dispositions, never for a moment forgetting the claims of those around him. He was constitutionally a gentleman, and could not, if he would, have been otherwise,—possessing an unusual degree of refinement, combined with great intelligence and sound judgment. His knowledge was always at command, and always at the service of his friends. In speaking upon any subject in which he felt an interest, the ease and flow of his language kept pace with the vigor and rapidity of his thoughts, and his conversation at such times was most interesting. In his habits he was exact and uniform, and to his industry and punctuality may be attributed his remarkable acquisition of information on so many topics. He was always careful of his personal expenditures, from a sense that extravagance would not conduce to his happiness; this, combined with his business talent, enabled him to exhibit during his lifetime a degree of liberality that few men can bring themselves to do.

"In a conversation that I had with him the day before the attack that carried him from among us, when he was unusually cheerful, he spoke very freely of leaving the world, and of the desirableness of being taken away upon a short summons, and named a number of instances of those whom he had known, who had departed without suffering, or giving trouble to their friends (which was always a consideration with him), and without the painful sense of a gradual wasting of the powers and strength of manhood, which is usually attendant upon protracted illness. This comparatively happy exit, however desirable, he observed, could not be secured; we must submit to our destiny. Upon this occasion, he remarked, quoting some ancient authority, that death, as it was the fate of all the living, should not be considered an evil; that leaving this world was part of a great plan unnecessary for us to understand.

"Mr. Bromfield's character was not marked by points which served to make him popular with the world; yet, if it can be said of any one, it may of him, that 'he was a man without guile,' and full of excellent qualities.

"I can hardly suppose that the foregoing will be of any service to you; yet I shall be glad if it should be so. All Mr. Bromfield's friends must rejoice that a remembrance of him is to come from *your* hands.

"I am, dear sir, very respectfully,

"Your obedient servant,

"AUGUSTINE HEARD."

BOSTON, March 28, 1850.

"HON. JOSIAH QUINCY,—My dear Sir: Your favor under date of the 27th instant, requesting me to give you any reminiscences I may have concerning the late Mr. John Bromfield, or any opinion or facts I possess illustrative of his character, is before me. I am aware that I am totally incompetent to do justice to the character of such a man as Mr. Bromfield. I was acquainted with him from 1808 to the time of his death, and can truly say I have always had and still retain the greatest respect for him as a high-minded, moral man, of the strictest integrity, and one of the most agreeable and pleasant companions, both on board ship and on shore, that it was ever my good fortune to be acquainted with. I made a passage with him in the ship Atahualpa, in 1809, to China. During that voyage the ship was attacked off Macao, by twenty-two large Ladrone junks, some of them twice the tonnage of the ship; and it was entirely owing to the courage and good judgment of Capt. William Sturgis, and the great exertions of the others on board at the time, only two-thirds of a crew (myself and four men being absent at the time), that saved the ship from capture, and the lives of all on board; Mr. Bromfield having performed all that lay in his power during the engagement, with the same unflinching discharge of duty, however arduous, which marked his whole life. Mr. Sturgis's conduct for courage and good judgment in that engagement received the highest praise from all those who saw and were capable of judging of the manner in which the ship was worked, and his great exertions to save the ship and crew from the pirates.

"I am, sir, very respectfully,

"Your obedient servant,

"Daniel C. Bacon."

These testimonies from men of highly intelligent and independent minds, to whom different opportunities for observation gave an intimate knowledge of Mr. Bromfield's principles and motives, and the causes of his peculiarities, present a striking delineation of his character.

The high reputation for ability and integrity he thus attained among his immediate associates, and the small capital he acquired during his agency in Canton, laid the foundation of his fortune. After his return to the United States he employed himself in the management of his own funds, and in again superintending agencies in foreign countries, intrusted to him by his friends, in which his knowledge of commerce and his known judgment gave great promise of success. Fortune, however, resumed her former unpropitious aspect. "I have been captured," he writes to his sister, from Cadiz, in January, 1813, "and detained ten weeks in Gibraltar. The consequence is ruin to the business I had undertaken. I regret that I have never been able to impart to you a single instance of my success. But it is a melancholy truth, that in the whole course of my life I have never arrived at a good market."

Mr. Bromfield was now about thirty-four years of age, and the want of success attendant on his foreign voyages induced him to place beyond the reach of such vicissitudes that attainment of independence which was the object of his efforts.

Fixing his residence in Boston, or its vicinity, he watched, with a practiced eye and a skillful foresight, the ebb and flow of the exchange. Sometimes in connection with the house of Bryant and Sturgis, or of Henry Lee, he engaged in adventures abroad, well conceived and carefully insured; at others, he availed himself of the phases of the money market, which he diligently observed and well understood.

Thus, by the vigilant and careful investment of his small capital, by the rigid practice of economy, in seclusion from general society and from the temptations of vanity and amusement, by deducting scarcely any thing from his acquisitions beyond what was necessary to his own subsistence, and to that charity to others which he habitually practiced, he gradually executed his plan of life, attained independence for himself, and the power of conferring important benefits on others and on the public. His books show that his kind acts and charitable contributions, though secret, were constant. The bounty of his spirit to his friends and relatives was uninterrupted, discriminating, and most liberal. To the general claims of pauperism he listened dubiously, and often with disregard, being of opinion, that indiscriminate charity was one of the fruitful causes of the state it pretends to relieve. To public solicitations he seldom yielded. Although the care of his property and its gradual accumulation made the chief employment of Mr. Bromfield, his time was not exclusively devoted to affairs of business. His knowledge of life and acquaintance with the world opened to him never-failing sources of thought and reflection, which were readily placed at the service of all who had recourse to him. In contributing to the instruction of others, his language was easy and eloquent; and in what he uttered there were ever displayed research, meditation, various information, and deep wisdom. Books were to him a constant source of occupation and amusement. In their company he felt not the want of general society. Self sustained, and with an ever-pervading sense of his responsibility to Heaven, he valued but little, and courted not at all, the common opinion of mankind.

As his property increased, his desire of usefulness increased with it. The objects to which his acquisitions should ultimately be applied were, probably, never out of his mind. The right of selecting them was maintained and vindicated with a pertinaciousness belonging to that spirit of independence for which he was distinguished.

In December, 1845, Mr. Bromfield communicated to the writer of this memoir the liberal design which occupied his thoughts, in language at once characteristic, and indicative of a fixed purpose. "My property," said he, "has increased beyond my hopes and even my desires. I now feel myself at liberty to gratify a prevailing wish of my heart, and to do something permanent and useful for a city, in which a great part of my life has been passed. Circumstances have made it my duty to accumulate. But I see no value in wealth, and have little regard for it, except for its ultimate use; but in respect to this I feel a sense of great responsibility. Hitherto my view, as to that ultimate use, has been limited to the provisions of my last will. But, as my property has increased, I begin to doubt whether an application of a part of it to an earlier object of usefulness be not most wise. By will, a man bestows only what he can no longer keep. It is a fund of generosity, formed out of the expectations and rights of relatives and heirs. Nothing can be strictly called a gift, except that which a man executes in his lifetime. For this I am prepared and desirous. But I must be unknown. I have extreme repugnance to notoriety." The conversation then turned upon the amount he proposed to give, and to the objects to which it should be applied. He observed, that he felt justified in giving away *fifty thousand dollars*, but after great deliberation he had resolved to restrict his gift at present to *twenty-five thousand*. As to the object of his bounty, the wants of the Boston Athenæum were known to him, and he had concluded to come to its aid. His pleasure in literary pursuits made a chief part of his enjoyment, and probably decided the direction of his liberality. Mr. Bromfield's repugnance to be known as the author of this gift to the Athenæum was with great difficulty surmounted. But, when it was urged that its origin could not long be concealed in an inquisitive community,—that he might be subjected to inquiries, which his strict regard to veracity would render it impossible to evade,—and also that it was as much a man's duty to be true to himself, as to be just to others, he finally acceded; and reluctantly consented, that if the proposal of his gift and its terms were accepted by the proprietors of the Athenæum, his name should not be withheld.

The friends of Mr. Bromfield were aware that the peculiarities of his life and the delicacy of his sensibility had prevented many of his contemporaries from forming a just estimate of his worth and his generosity; the publicity thus given to his bounty was, therefore, to them, highly gratifying; and it was apparent that the satisfaction derived from perceiving that his character and liberal views were appreciated and understood, added much to the happiness of the few remaining years of his life, and more than compensated for the annoyances arising from the constant application for charity and patronage, which this public donation immediately occasioned.

His death, an event which he had accustomed himself to contemplate and be prepared for, was granted him in a manner for which he had often expressed a hope. On the morning of the 8th day of December, 1849, after an early walk, he returned to his apartment; and, when called to breakfast, he was found insensible from a stroke of apoplexy. Although he was apparently aware of the presence of his sister and her husband, and of other friends, who were immediately summoned to his residence, and who watched over his last hours, distinct consciousness never returned; and on the following day his life, which he had endeavored to lead under a sense of being "ever in his great Task-master's eye," was terminated without gradual decay or protracted suffering.

His property was found after his death considerably to exceed two hundred thousand dollars, invested with great judgment and care, and was distributed by his last will with a wisdom and precision altogether in unison with the principles and habits of his life. Having fulfilled to the utmost the duties of affinity, affection, and friendship, he devoted his remaining ample resources to the service of the public, giving—

To the Massachusetts General Hospital, and to the McLean Asylum, in equal shares	$40,000
" " Massachusetts Eye and Ear Infirmary	10,000
" " Boston Female Asylum	10,000

For the Asylum for Indigent Boys	$10,000
" " Farm School at Thompson's Island	10,000
" " Asylum for the Blind	10,000
" " Seamen's Aid Society	10,000
" " Town of Newburyport, for its improvement and ornament*	10,000
	$110,000

By these noble and generous benefactions to the public, Mr. Bromfield erected an enduring memorial to his own virtues, and to a name of which he was the last representative. And this sketch of his life may be appropriately closed in the words of his nearest surviving relative:

"The distinguishing trait of my brother's character was his quick discernment of the true and the real, appertaining to our human existence, and his power of separating them with almost equal sagacity from their apparent and nominal value. At no period of his life did he look forward to being made happy—hardly to being made happier—by the attainment of that honorable competency for which he struggled nobly and labored unremittingly. Yet this insight, and superiority to the usual incitement to activity, united with a nervous temperament and a delicate constitution, never led him to seek refuge in repose. With systematic, unflinching, personal self-denial, he strained every nerve, and exerted every faculty, to procure for others, not

* The following are the provisions of Mr. Bromfield's will in relation to this subject:

"I order the sum of ten thousand dollars to be invested, at interest, in the Hospital Life Insurance Company, in the city of Boston, so and in such manner as that the selectmen or other duly authorized agents of the town of Newburyport, for the time being, may annually receive the interest which shall accrue or become payable for or in respect of said deposit; and I direct, that, by or in behalf of said town, the interest so received shall be annually expended—one-half in keeping the sidewalks in the public streets of said town in good order, and the other half in the planting and preserving trees in said streets, for the embellishing and ornamenting of said streets for the pleasure and comfort of the inhabitants."

merely the means of alleviating the ills of life, but of gratifying every rational indulgence and merited enjoyment. One portion especially of his mercantile experience strongly tested the self-reliance, decision, and indomitable courage of his character. The grand basis of religious principle laid by his mother, combined with intellectual strength, and power of will, and moral energy, enabled him to sustain himself through a long life, to the accomplishment of his plans of usefulness, and the fulfillment of his destiny."

Engd by A. H. Ritchie

HARRY R. W. HILL.

Throughout every portion of the southern and southwestern region of the United States, the name of the late H. R. W. Hill is known and honored. Mr. Hill commenced life at a very early age, a poor boy, unassisted by adventitious aid, and by his individual energy and enterprise alone he achieved for himself a prominent name, a high social position, and a large estate.

The incidents of Mr. Hill's career are briefly but graphically given in the following sketch which appeared in Cohen's New Orleans Directory:

"One of the wealthiest and most popular citizens of the Southwest is the subject of this notice. Harry R. W. Hill combined some of the rarest qualities of character that were ever found united in the same man. Fortune and Mammon consented to ally themselves with a generous heart and an unbounded beneficence of nature. But the rare combination of virtues in this worthy citizen did not end here. Besides being charitable and liberal to a fault, he was of that frank, confiding, friendly, and sociable nature that rarely achieves pecuniary fortune, if it does augment that wealth which gives greater peace of mind, and a higher order of enjoyment, than any material riches,—the wealth of a contented heart, full of kindly emotions and social virtues. This composite character of Mr. Hill's mind, displayed itself even in the nature of his occupation. He was engaged to an equal extent in mercantile and planting avocations, and in both his operations were, perhaps, on a more extended scale than those of any other citizen in the South.

His planting interest was vast, embracing some seven sugar and cotton plantations, which were cultivated by over a thousand slaves. As a merchant, he was for many years at the head of the largest cotton factorage business in the United States. The history of a citizen thus prominent, and combining such rare virtues of mind and heart, can not but interest all readers, and afford the rising generation many useful lessons to guide them in the path of life and duty.

"Harry R. W. Hill was born in Halifax county, North Carolina, in the year 1797. His parents were of English extraction; were in moderate circumstances, and plain, hard-working people. His father died when he was but five years old, and his mother marrying again, removed to Williamson county, Tennessee, then a frontier county, adjoining the Indian nation (the Chickasaws).

"Here Harry had his first schooling, at an Old Field school; but from the character of the country, and the circumstances of the family, his education was necessarily limited in time, and quite defective in quality. He attended this school for two years, which was all the tuition ever received by the largest merchant and planter in the South, and the Grand Master of the time-honored and powerful order of Free Masons. At the expiration of this time, Harry being frequently sent by his mother to a neighboring store for the little articles required in the family, attracted the attention and interest of the store-keeper by his lively wit, good-nature, and active character. When the inquiry was made, whether he would like to be a store-keeper, his ready and shrewd reply showed a hearty good-will and natural taste for the business, which induced the store-keeper to propose to his mother to allow him to come and try his hand in merchandising. She consented, and Harry commenced to keep store for Nicholas McAlister, in Franklin.

"In 1818, his employer dying, Harry being then a very

young man, undertook the settlement of his estate; which he did so much to the satisfaction of the friends and neighbors of the deceased, that they united in assisting him to set up in business on his own account, and to go to Philadelphia to buy goods. In this business he continued for seven years, realizing in that time a handsome fortune.

"In 1827 he married, and in the year following removed from Franklin, after a residence there of eighteen years; but finding the field rather too contracted for his views, ambition, and means, selected Nashville as a larger arena, and, entering into partnership with William Nichols, embarked very extensively in commercial and steamboating business. Fortune smiled on him at every step, and he in turn smiled on everybody else. The popularity of Mr. Hill followed him in every position of his active and eventful life.

"In 1832 he took another step higher in the ladder of commercial eminence and enterprise, and made his first appearance as a merchant at New Orleans, in connection with those experienced and respected citizens the late N. & J. Dick. The business of the firm of N. & J. Dick & Co. was vast, extending through the Southwest, and involving an enormous amount of capital, of liabilities, and responsibilities. It could not be expected that the revulsions of 1837 would leave such a house unscathed. The numerous failures of individuals, for whom the house had made advances, necessarily involved them, and they were consequently compelled to suspend. The greater part of the ensuing seven years was devoted by Mr. Hill to the settlement of the country business of the firm. They were years of ceaseless toil and application. But the object he had in view—the noble one of retrieving the credit and character of the house—buoyed him up under all the harassments, vexations, and fatigues of his business campaign. He was at last rewarded for all these sacrifices, by seeing the credit of his house restored, all its liabilities, amounting to several millions of dollars, paid off in full, and a sufficient capital saved to be enabled to resume business on a scale almost equal to that in which they had experienced so severe a check.

"Mr. Hill continued the business with Mr. James Dick, until 1847, when the latter retired with a large fortune. J. L. McLean was then taken into partnership by Mr. Hill, under the new firm of Hill, McLean & Co. They were very successful for three years. Two other partners were then taken in, and the business of the house was still further extended. In 1851, the firm of Hill, McLean & Co., having experienced many great losses, was compelled temporarily to suspend. This event was regarded as a public calamity, and created a profound sensation in the community of New Orleans, approaching nearly to a panic. The failure of so extensive and well-established a house, would scatter gloom and despair throughout the Valley of the Mississippi—it would involve thousands in its fall. No man, engaged in business, felt secure when Hill, McLean & Co. were under protest. To increase their embarrassments, the money market was very stringent at that time. Under these circumstances, Mr. Hill came forward with all his large private means, assumed all the liabilities of the firm, pledging his property, and releasing his partners, and in the course of five months paid off all claims, and restored the credit of the house, which he afterward directed entirely on his own account, and under his own name.

"We have thus briefly sketched the personal and mercantile career of Harry Hill. But the task of his biographer does not end here. Mr. Hill, unlike the greater number of our citizens who are engaged in commercial pursuits, and involved in extensive pecuniary transactions, was an active promoter of public works, and had important agencies and influences in public affairs of great moment. He was able to serve his country in many ways besides those in which such service is usually rendered, and to which he always had an invincible repugnance, namely, holding any political office. At an early period, he took a prominent part in furthering public improvements in Tennessee, having been elected the first president of the first macadamized road made in that State. This was the road from Nashville to Franklin, which he personally superintended.

"Called before the Internal Improvement Committee, in the Legislature of Tennessee, in 1829, and invited to give his opinion of the best course for the State in regard to public works, he promptly urged the adoption of the railroad system, as the most democratic in its effects and tendencies, in enabling them to break down the monopoly of the rivers; an idea no less sagacious in its truth, than quaint in its expression. It was on that occasion he made the prophecy, which has been nearly realized, that they would all live to see the time when rivers would only be used for stock-water and to fish in. From that time Mr. Hill was a constant friend of internal improvements; he always contributed handsomely to their furtherance, as well in Louisiana as in Tennessee and Mississippi. His great sagacity, comprehensive views, talent, and extensive experience rendered him a most useful citizen in all enterprises of a useful and practical character. In other and important positions, Mr. Hill was highly useful and efficient as a public man. Always patriotic, devoted to liberty and republicanism, he ever manifested a lively interest in the struggles of all nations that have sought to achieve their independence.

"When the Texan revolution occurred, Mr. Hill, who was then residing at Nashville, presently came forward with his sympathies and substantial aid in behalf of that great movement. When Messrs. Austin, Archer, and Wharton visited Tennessee, they were very kindly entertained and aided in many ways by Mr. Hill, to whom, when they departed, they committed the agency of the Texan revolutionists in Nashville. From his own purse Mr. Hill dispatched $5000 to Texas, which afforded great relief to the Texans, and supplied them with the munitions with which they fought and gained the memorable battle of San Jacinto. This was a freewill donation, and not a speculative venture. He had further made arrangements to send a full battalion to Texas, which he had already organized in camp, when the glorious news of the victory of San Jacinto arrived. He then dismissed the men to their homes.

"When General Lopez was indicted for a violation of the neutrality laws after the Cardenas expedition, Mr. Hill was summoned as a juror. Interrogated on his *voire dire*, he remarked that he should always do his duty as a good citizen, but that, if a strong feeling in favor of all movements to establish and extend republican principles all over the world would incapacitate him to do his duty in that case, he would advise the District Attorney to dispense with him.

"In his political relations and opinions, Mr. Hill was never a partisan. He usually pursued his own ideas, avoiding the extremes of both parties. When General Jackson was first brought forward in Tennessee, Mr. Hill was his most ardent and efficient friend. He subscribed most liberally to forward his election, and when the old general was about to go to the Capitol, and was in straitened pecuniary circumstances, he was enabled to afford the old hero facilities which that great old man never failed to remember and speak of with gratitude. On Mr. Hill's visit to the Capital with his family, he was entertained by General Jackson at the White House in a style of the most splendid hospitality, which attentions were reciprocated by Mr. Hill when the general visited his old home in Tennessee, in one of the grandest fêtes ever given in that State, which was attended by everybody in the neighborhood. But beyond these and many similar deeds of public spirit and patriotic duty, Mr. Hill never permitted himself to embark on the tempestuous sea of politics. He preferred to occupy his mind with schemes for the promotion of peace, harmony, and good-will among men.

"His charity and beneficence were unbounded. He expended more than three hundred thousand dollars in benevolent enterprises. No charitable undertaking was ever presented to him that he did not cheerfully aid. To the Methodist Church in the South he was most bountiful in his liberality and contributions. As a Mason of the highest grade—having been in 1851 elected Grand Master of Louisiana—he found a large field for his benevolence and charity.

"During the life of the late venerable James Dick, there existed between him and Mr. Hill a friendship as cordial, warm, and sincere, as that which bound together Damon and Pythias, Jonathan and David. When Mr. Dick was about to make his will, he consulted his lawyer, Levi Pierce, in regard to it, and stated that it was his intention to leave his large property to his old friend and partner, Harry Hill. The latter, hearing of his intention, remonstrated so warmly and earnestly against such a disposition, that Mr. Dick was induced to forego his darling desire, and bestow his property on others."

In April, 1853, Mr. Hill was called upon to support the deepest sorrow of his life—his wife, to whom he was tenderly attached, was separated from him by the hand of death. She was a lady universally loved and respected, of surpassing goodness and gentleness, of unobtrusive modesty and simplicity, of large affections and unbounded charity. To be in misery and sorrow was all-sufficient to open her purse and enlist her sympathies; she cared not in her charities to ask the nation or creed of her petitioners, enough for her that a human being, in need and suffering, claimed her pity; her wealth was unstintingly applied to relieve distress, and from the fullness of her heart her mouth spoke kind and gentle words of consolation and hope to all who sought her in trouble. She was a sincere and devout Christian—warmly attached to the Methodist Church, to which she belonged, but held in abhorrence all sectarian and bigoted views. A meek worshiper at the shrine of the gentle Jesus, she was content that each should arrange between his conscience and his God the manner of his adoration.

A rich man's wife, she was all simplicity, the most unassuming of the unassuming. Frequently at receptions at her house, when surrounded by the wealth, the high in social position, and the talent of the country, she would, with true delicacy, single out from among her guests some less fortunately circumstanced, as to riches and honors, upon whom to bestow her attention.

In works of true benevolence, in constant thoughtfulness for the happiness and comfort of her husband, in tender care and solicitude for her only son, in intimate and affectionate communion with her slaves, this excellent lady passed her useful life. And when acute and painful disease, preceding dissolution, prostrated her, she bore it with the heroism of a true Christian. A ministering angel was Margaretta E. McAllister, the wife of H. R. W. Hill, and she was mourned by her husband, her son, her slaves, the poor, and a large circle of friends and acquaintances, with a deep and abiding sorrow.

Mr. Hill did not long survive his much-loved wife. In September of the same year, he fell a victim to the yellow fever, which so dreadfully scourged New Orleans in the summer and autumn of 1853. The sickness of some of his black servants retained him in Louisiana. He was earnestly intreated to avoid the epidemic by passing to a northern latitude, but he firmly refused to leave while one slave remained sick to claim his care. In this heroic exercise of true philanthropy, watching over the sick-bed of his slaves, he took the fatal disease, which terminated, at the age of fifty-six years, his noble life. An eloquent writer of New Orleans thus beautifully characterized him: "One of the best men that ever lived—one pure in heart, philanthropic in conception, and liberal in execution, has died of the dread disease that has carried off thousands; and when the body of Harry R. W. Hill was deposited in the tomb, the largest bank of charity forever closed."

The press of New Orleans and the South generally abounded with affectionate tributes to his memory. From every State into which his father's name had passed, words of regard and respect for the dead, coupled with expressions of condolence, reached his son, his sole surviving heir; and the most valuable legacy he left his son, incomparably greater than the large wealth he devised him, was, that he bequeathed him a name that was enshrined in the hearts of the great and good, of the rich and poor, of his fellow-citizens of the South.

Mr. Hill filled a large space in the commercial annals of the South. He possessed, in an eminent degree, the qualities necessary for forming a great and successful merchant. He had a devout reliance upon the great Creator of the universe, and never failed morning and night to invoke his aid and counsel in the direction of his life. He was by nature endowed with a quick and brilliant conception, and was vigorous in execution. His energy displayed itself at a very early age. A mere boy, he performed on foot the journey from North Carolina to Tennessee, walking by the side of the horse that carried his mother. His gun and his activity in the chase supplied them with food upon the road. His mind was most happily framed, a ready imagination being balanced by a calm, clear judgment. He was indefatigable in his attention to his business, and was systematic in the number of hours that he daily devoted to his mercantile occupation. He had fixed principles to guide him in his professional career, the great basis being an unswerving probity.

His planting operations evinced the same practical wisdom and energy. His large estates, worked by an aggregate of more than a thousand slaves, were all under an intelligent system of culture and improvement. Mr. Hill was a humane and kind master, anxious that his slaves should be well used and justly treated. He held an intimate communication with his negroes, lending a ready ear to their troubles, and sympathizing with them in their joys. He gave a constant and personal care to their physical comforts and their spiritual welfare. He kept in his employ, at annual salaries, ministers of the gospel to perform divine service, officiate in the ceremonies of baptism, marriage, and burial, and to instruct his people in religious knowledge. The Sabbath morn would find him in the log-cabin, or seated on a bench beneath the canopy of heaven, worshiping in humility, side by side with his slaves, their common heavenly Father.

By Mr. Hill's orders, his slaves received daily plentiful and wholesome rations. With punctual regularity, at the appointed hour each negro had served out to him his allowance, consisting of a pound of meat, and as much corn bread, milk, and vegetables as he could consume. Each had a patch of ground allotted to him, and time given to cultivate it; and the corn, chickens, and eggs they produced, Mr. Hill bought from them at the current market price. In order to protect them, in their trading, from being taken advantage of, Mr. Hill established stores on his plantations, where the articles they required were sold to them at the cost price. Mr. Hill exerted himself actively to excite a laudable emulation in his slaves. He instituted prizes, which were awarded for good conduct, cleanliness, and attention to work. Bandannas, dresses, objects of ornament and utility, were distributed by him yearly in large quantities in carrying out his philanthropic ideas.

Mr. Hill's claim to popularity was not alone based upon his success as an eminent merchant, and upon his large operations as an extensive and a humane planter. Far and wide, in the rich man's dwelling and the poor man's cabin, his name was a household word, associated with acts of disinterested, generous friendship, and munificent benefaction. The largeness of his liberalities was equaled only by the delicacy with which he proffered his assistance. He derived such pure pleasure from acts of benevolence that he determined to do his charities in his own lifetime, and not leave for others the putting in execution his philanthropy after his death. He kept a book, as carefully posted as any other in his commercial establishment, denominated his Charity Ledger, and the perusal of this book was to him a source of unadulterated gratification.

Mr. Hill was justly proud of the elevated position he held as Grand Master of the Ancient Order of Free and Accepted Masons. Between himself and the fraternity the most intimate relations existed. He was one of the most devoted champions and zealous members of the Order. The sublime dogmas, the ancient traditions, and the varied literature of Free Masonry, had a deep hold upon his reason and his affections. He was proud of his connection with an institution whose self-imposed province it is to visit the sick, clothe the naked, and feed the hungry; whose active benevolence and teachings are vital with the command of the Divine Legislator.

The decease of Mr. Hill called forth from the Masonic fraternity of Louisiana a universal expression of sorrow. His personal worth and merits, and the exalted opinion that was entertained of him by the Order as their Grand Master, were recorded in resolutions which will be handed down by his son as an heirloom, the most precious that he can transmit.

We shall now terminate this imperfect sketch of the life and history of this notable and excellent citizen, by the following eloquent tribute taken from the New Orleans Delta of the 19th September, 1853:

"Solemn and impressive funeral ceremonies evinced the public sorrow and affliction for the loss of Harry R. W. Hill. Yesterday was a day of mourning in New Orleans; and well it might be, for few communities have ever suffered so heavy a loss, as few indeed have stood more in need of such men, as Harry Hill.

"It has been the misfortune and drawback of New Orleans, that her wealthy men, those who have accumulated their fortunes here, have either withdrawn themselves to other parts of the country to expend their wealth, or, remaining here, have stood aloof in their sympathies and feelings from the mass of the people. But Harry Hill was a man of the people—not in the disgusting political sense of the demagogue and placeman—but as one who knew the wants, the virtues, and the failings of humanity, who could perceive the merits of men, through all the repulsive externals of poverty and misfortune, as quick as he could discern selfishness and meanness through the gilded trappings of wealth.

"In his case, an admirable judgment, practical sense, and sagacity, combined with an overflowing charity and benevolence. This is the combination for the truly good and useful man. Your miser, who passes his whole life in one absorbing, cold, selfish pursuit of wealth, indifferent to the claims of the present, to all the suffering and misery around him, merely to hand his name down to posterity associated with some doubtful or impracticable charity, and with an utter disregard of all the claims of family and relationship, is a character too common in our country,—in contrast with which that of Harry Hill stands out nobly conspicuous and honorable.

"He lived to do good; he sought wealth to diffuse happiness and enjoyment around him. His chief pleasure was in witnessing the cheering results of his own liberal but always judicious beneficence. He begrudged his executors that enjoyment; herein alone he was selfish. He reveled in the luxury of doing good. Though even his brilliant mercantile career was often darkened by clouds and the most trying perils, he never permitted any misfortune to affect his charity, or reduce his donations to the poor, and to pious and benevolent associations. They proved good investments, for the Lord smiled upon all his exertions to redeem his losses and conquer his adversity. In his case, the bread cast upon the wates returned tenfold.

"He gave, during his life, more than three hundred thousand dollars to charities, and died worth largely more than a million. Nor was that million accumulated by any other means than the legitimate enterprise of an honorable, liberal, just, and energetic merchant.

"The remains of Mr. Hill, having been brought to this city, were taken to his residence on Canal-street, whence they were borne by a very large concourse of the Masonic body to the Methodist Church, where an eloquent discourse was delivered by the Rev. Mr. Keener.

"The congregation of this church evinced that deep grief which they must feel for the loss of one who has been the most liberal benefactor of the Methodist Church in the South. From the church, the cortége, led by the Masons, of whom Mr. Hill was the Grand Master, and composed of an immense concourse of citizens, proceeded to the Girod-street cemetery, where, after religious and masonic ceremonies, the coffin was placed in a vault. The service was read in a most eloquent and impressive manner by Grand Secretary Samuel G. Risk. A few remarks commemorative of the virtues and usefulness of the deceased Grand Master were then made by Acting Grand Master John H. Holland. The craft deposited their right-hand glove and the sprig of acacia in the grave, and bid a last farewell to him who had so often directed their councils, and the procession again returned to their lodge-room."

James Brown

JAMES BROWN.

James Brown was born in Acton, in Massachusetts, May 19, 1800. He sprang from that class from which so much of the moral worth and intellectual distinction of the country has proceeded,—the rural population of New England,—made up of men who cultivate their own farms with their own hands, whose characters are strengthened by the daily exercise of economy and self-denial, but whose spirits are rarely darkened by hopeless poverty, and never crushed by the consciousness of inability to rise. His father, Joseph Brown, born in Stow, in Massachusetts, about 1751, was the youngest son of a numerous family that came from Rhode Island some years before the date of his son's birth. He was one of the first to offer his services to his country at the breaking out of the Revolution; and at the battle of Bunker Hill he was wounded by a bullet, which passed through one of his legs and lodged in the other. When the lead was extracted, he put it into his pocket, saying that they should have it again. He rejoined the army as soon as his wound was healed, and served till the end of the war, rising to the rank of captain. He was with the northern division of the army, and took part in the operations which led to the capture of Burgoyne; and there, and on other occasions, gave proof of courage and conduct.

When the war was over, he settled upon a small farm in Acton, and resided there till his death, in 1813. He held for many years the offices of constable and collector of taxes. His life was the common life of a New England farmer and householder; he worked upon his farm, read the newspapers, discussed the political men and measures of his time, took part in town and parish affairs, faithfully performed the modest duties of the offices which he held; and thus his days were usefully and happily filled.

Capt. Brown was twice married. By his first wife, whose name was Dorothy Barker, he had five children, none of whom are now living.

His second wife was Abigail Putnam, daughter of Deacon Samuel Putnam of Danvers, in Massachusetts. She was a woman of an excellent understanding, and had been well educated for that period. She had been employed for some time previous to her marriage as a teacher of youth; a good preparation, it may be remarked, for household trusts and the care of a family. She was also a woman of much moral worth, a good wife and mother, and faithful to all the duties devolved upon her. She brought up her children in virtuous habits, and was especially earnest in imbuing them with a love of truth. She was accustomed to devote a part of every Sunday to the moral and religious teaching of her household—a good old New England custom which it is to be feared the establishment of Sunday schools has caused somewhat to decline. If so, these schools have proved to be by no means an unmixed good.

The children of the second marriage were eight in number. Of these, two only now survive; namely, Luke, born in 1795, now residing in the western part of Massachusetts; and Eunice, born in 1802, the wife of Mr. J. G. Lyon, residing at Rockton, in Illinois.

James Brown was the fourth son and sixth child of the second marriage. Unlike his elder brothers,—unlike what would have been supposed by those who knew him in his robust and vigorous manhood,—he was a delicate and sickly child; and on this account he was the object of peculiar care to an affectionate mother, and was in some degree exempted from the rougher labors of the farm. From his earliest years he showed a love of knowledge and a love of books; and those of his friends who believe that "the child is father of the man," and who remember the pleasure he took in his well-chosen library, may deem it not unworthy of record that the first great grief of his childhood arose from the loss, in his third year, of a little picture-book, his solitary possession of the kind. He could only be comforted by the gift of a new book, then not easily or readily procured.

His early years were by no means destitute of the means of intellectual improvement. Besides such instruction as he could pick up at the district school, taught in the winter by a male, and in the summer by a female teacher, he had access to a good circulating library, which was kept at the minister's house; and he was a diligent reader of such books as were suited to his age. There was also the society of an intelligent and well-educated mother, who had among her own possessions a closet full of books; among which those who are conversant with the literary tastes of the last century will not be surprised to hear were Young's Night Thoughts and Hervey's Meditations.

Nor should we overlook, in summing up the influences which acted upon his mind and character, those elements which grow out of the very constitution of New England society, and were found, in a greater or less degree, in every New England town. Life was more quiet and monotonous fifty years ago than it now is; there were fewer books and fewer newspapers; the means of communication were far inferior; but everywhere there was the pulse of vitality and the consciousness of belonging to a growing and progressive community. The newspaper arrived two or three times a week, and the stage-coach kept up a regular communication with the metropolis. State and national politics were discussed with partisan zeal, and town affairs were often fruitful in matters which led to controversy and debate. Though books were fewer, and newspapers more meager than now, they were both read and re-read with a patient deliberation which is now becoming obsolete. All these things would act upon the mind and character of an intelligent and observing boy, who had eyes to see, and ears to hear, what was going on around him—who would listen to the discussions in town and parish meetings, and hear his elders talking about the movements of Bonaparte and the policy of Jefferson, and gunboats, and the embargo, and the orders in council, and the Berlin and Milan decrees; and though all that fell upon the ear was not comprehended, it was none the less calculated to quicken the faculties and keep the life-blood of the mind in circulation.

James Brown was a diligent reader of such books as he could procure; and he read them understandingly. His sister, Mrs. Lyon, remembers his having, when only eight or nine years old, prepared a full abstract of Rollin's account of the seven wonders of the world, and of adding to it a description of all the other remarkable objects he had read of, which seemed to him worthy of being placed in the same class. This was read aloud to the family circle in the evening, and received with great favor.

A gentleman, now living in Boston, a native of Acton, and a school-fellow of James Brown, has given me some recollections of him in his boyhood. He describes him as having been a general favorite from his amiable disposition and the sweetness of his temper. At school, he was a good though not a brilliant scholar; and was especially remarkable for the correctness of his deportment; never having been punished, and rarely reproved. He had a vein of grave drollery, and was a good mimic; frequently entertaining the boys by the exercise of this power. His sense and enjoyment of the ludicrous went with him to the end of life, but in his maturer years he laid aside the habit of mimicry.

My informant also remembers him as a boy of rather slender and loosely compacted frame—not possessed of much bodily activity—and never taking a leading part in the athletic sports of early life. Although of a cheerful spirit, he was rather grave and contemplative, but never dependent upon others for happiness or occupation.

From his farm, and the proceeds of the town offices which he held, Capt. Brown was able to maintain his family in comfort and respectability; but upon his death, in 1813, the widow's means were not enough to enable her to keep all her household together; and the younger sons were obliged to go from home in search of employment and subsistence. James went to live with a farmer in Acton, and remained with him for some time; taking part in such farm labors as were suited to his years and strength. It was while living with Mr. Noyes that his first visit to Boston was made;—an event which was looked forward to with great interest, and long remembered from the distinctness of the impressions which it left. Some time in the year 1815, he went to Cambridge, in search of employment; probably attracted to that place by his love of books, and a sort of undefined feeling that it was something to breathe even the air of learning; and perhaps by a faint hope that some of the crumbs of knowledge which fell from that ample board might drop into his lap.

Immediately upon arriving in Cambridge, he found a situation as a domestic in the family of the late Professor Hedge. The fastidious spirit of our times and our country shrinks from the contemplation of a position like this, as if there were something in it of humiliation and pain; but such a feeling flows from the weakness, and not the strength, of our nature. The relation of master and servant is one which the world is not likely to outgrow; and like every other relation between man and man, it may be elevated and dignified by the spirit which animates, and the motives which govern it. In the present case, we may be assured that all its duties, on both sides, were faithfully discharged. Young Brown was a conscientious and intelligent lad, whose spirit was docile and whose temper was without a flaw. It need hardly be said to those who knew the late Dr. Hedge at all, that he was a just, a good, and a benevolent man; and those who knew him well were aware that under a plain exterior he concealed much tenderness and delicacy of feeling. Every member of his household felt the influence and encouragement of his gentle and benignant nature; and the friendless youth from the country began at once to breathe the genial atmosphere of home. By the surviving members of Dr. Hedge's family he is well remembered as a well-grown stripling, but of a slender frame and pallid complexion, bearing the aspect of delicate health, and holding out no promise of that vigorous tread, erect bearing, and ample presence which he afterward attained. He was perfectly amiable in temper, irreproachable in moral conduct, of an obliging disposition and cheerful spirit, and especially remarkable for his insatiable love of knowledge—reading every thing in the shape of a book he could lay his hands upon, and by the energies of a healthy mind drawing nutriment from all.

Dr. Hedge himself, seeing his taste and aptitude for knowledge, gave him private instruction in mathematics and the Latin language; and the plan of his entering college was entertained and discussed, and might have been carried into effect but for a subsequent change in his position and prospects.

The whole period of Mr. Brown's residence with Dr. Hedge, extending through three or four years, was highly favorable to the growth of his mind and character. The light services required in a simple household left him both time and energy to gratify his love of knowledge; and in this praiseworthy pursuit he had not merely the sympathy, but the aid of his employer. Living, too, under the roof of a scholar, he was never without the means of obtaining books, the first want of an expanding mind. But in a gentle and sensitive nature like his these intellectual advantages would have borne but little fruit, had they not been attended, as they were, with a spirit of kindness, with a readiness to acknowledge cheerful and faithful service, and with a considerate thoughtfulness which laid no needless burdens upon him. In Dr. Hedge's family he was never tried with unreasonable requisitions, or capricious exactions, or harsh language; and always had the assurance that so long as he did his duty he might rely upon their friendly regard and substantial good-will.

Mr. Brown's feeling and judgment upon this part of his life were characteristic of the simple dignity of his nature. He never wished to conceal it, or keep it out of sight, or remove it from the contemplation of his own thoughts, as if there was any thing humiliating or mortifying in it. Nor, on the other hand, had he, in regard to it, that subtle vanity which Dickens so well delineates in the character of Mr. Bounderby, which delights to make a coarse and noisy proclamation of early disadvantages, and to find food for self-esteem in the contrast between present glories and past shadows. It was with Mr. Brown an episode in his life—no more and no less—not to be put out of sight and out of mind as something to be ashamed of, and not to be flauntingly displayed in order to challenge admiration and applause.

Some time during the year 1818, as Mr. Brown was walking through the streets of Cambridge, on a Sunday, he was met by the late Mr. William Hilliard, and asked by him if he would like to enter his service as a salesman and general assistant. Such a proposal was a piece of good fortune, as unexpected as it was gratifying, and it was very gladly accepted. For this offer on the part of Mr. Hilliard,

Mr. Brown was indebted to the thoughtful and considerate kindness of Dr. Hedge, who, seeing the moral worth and intellectual tastes of his young *protégé*, had warmly recommended him to Mr. Hilliard as an assistant, whenever any vacancy should occur in his business. Mr. Hilliard was at that time largely and actively engaged as a publisher and bookseller. He was an intelligent and estimable man; and had his love of money and care of small things been equal to his general capacity and enterprise, he could hardly have failed to accumulate an ample property.

Mr. Brown at once went into Mr. Hilliard's service, and entered upon an untried occupation. His position was at first rather difficult and perplexing. Besides opening and shutting the store, going on errands, attending to the wants of customers, he was employed during a portion of every day in pressing the sheets that came from the printing-office,—a labor that tasked severely his physical powers. Mr. Hilliard spent a portion of every day in Boston; and his former assistant, who had been expected to initiate Mr. Brown into his new duties, immediately left his post, without warning, as soon as the new-comer arrived; and he was thus left to grope his way, with very imperfect guidance, over an unknown path. But his natural quickness, aided by resolute industry, qualified him to meet the claims made upon him; and his duties were soon fulfilled with ease to himself and satisfaction to his employer.

Mr. Brown's engaging in the service of Mr. Hilliard was the decisive fact of his life, and from that moment his progress, though slow at first, was sure and uninterrupted.

But there were no unexpected incidents, no sudden turns, no lucky windfalls in his career. It was all substantially moulded of the same elements; each portion bound by natural relation to what had gone before. His subsequent prosperity was as much the inevitable result of the qualities which he showed in the very first week of his engagement with Mr. Hilliard, as the oak is of the acorn. He had found an occupation which suited his tastes, and for which his faculties and capacities were singularly well fitted. He was fond of books; he liked not merely to read them, but to see them, to handle them, and to have them about him. He was orderly and methodical in his habits; never idle, and never in a hurry; never permitting his business to get ahead of him; possessed of a most retentive memory, always knowing whether he had a book or not, and if he had it, able to put his hand upon it in the dark.

For some years his principal occupation was that of selling books at retail. The success of a salesman, as is well known among men of business, depends mainly upon certain natural endowments, which may be improved by culture, but can neither be taught nor learned; they are innate, and dependent upon organization and temperament. But in a person who sells books, and thus deals with scholars and men of letters, these qualities must be more nicely tempered and harmonized, than in one who sells shoes or domestic goods to country customers. In Mr. Brown the elements were happily mingled for this object. He was born with the feelings and instincts of a gentleman. He had an unerring power of observation, and a delicate tact that never failed him. His manners were winning, because they were the natural language of a good heart and a sweet temper; and their effect was increased by the open and ingenuous expression of his countenance. But his success in this department came mainly from those sources from which the whole success of his life was derived—from his entire truthfulness and perfect honesty. Nothing is more difficult to assume than the simplicity of truth. An artful man may make his manners fine, but hardly natural. But every one who dealt with Mr. Brown, felt that he was dealing with a thoroughly honest man, and that every word that fell from him could be taken at its full value, with no qualifications and reservations. In his intercourse with those who came to buy of him, there was no alloy of coaxing, or wheedling, or fawning; no subtle flattery; no politic use of weaknesses; no disingenuous concealments; and no loud vaunting of the merits of his merchandise.

During the period of his residence in Cambridge, Mr. Brown, though zealous in business, was by no means ascetic in his habits; but he gladly sought the society of congenial friends, and did not deny himself such amusements as did not interfere with the main objects on which his thoughts were fixed. He founded a sort of social meeting, which, in imitation of a well-known society in college, was called the Hasty-pudding Club, at the meetings of which a subject was discussed, and afterward the members partook of a simple repast. On one occasion the subject of discussion was, "How may eminence in life be attained;" and after the other members had given their views, Mr. Brown took a piece of chalk from the table, and made a mark on the wall so high that no others could reach it, saying at the same time, "Make your chalk high enough."

At one time he was in the habit of meeting with some of his friends to make a thorough study of the principles of grammar. He also read much, and his favorite reading lay among the English poets.

'He occasionally indulged himself in shooting and fishing, but never allowing his amusements to encroach upon the hours of business. He thus acquired some practical knowledge of ornithology, and was able to assist his friend, Mr. Nuttall, in the preparation of his work on the birds of America. On one of these sporting occasions, an incident occurred which showed his self-possession and presence of mind. He was with his friend, Mr. N. J. Wyeth, his usual companion on these expeditions. They were obliged to cross a decayed dam. Mr. Wyeth got safely over, but Mr. Brown slipped and fell into the water, where it was of considerable depth. He disappeared for a moment, but soon emerged dripping like a water-god; and as he scrambled up the bank, his friend noticing that he had his boots in one hand and his gun in the other, asked him why he did not let them go; to which Mr. Brown, with the utmost composure replied, "Because I thought I should want to use them again."

At this period of his life, as soon as the burden of business was removed, he was overflowing with animal spirits, and as full of frolic as a schoolboy on a holiday. His joyous temperament sometimes broke out in practical jokes; but they were of a kind that never wounded the feelings, nor left a sting in the memory.

Mr. Brown continued in the service of Mr. Hilliard till 1826, constantly growing in the confidence of his employer, and gradually assuming a larger share of the management of the business. In that year the relations between them were substantially, though not apparently, changed by the formation of a copartnership. The articles were dated September 4th; and the copartnership was to continue for five years.

In May, 1832, soon after the copartnership with Mr. Hilliard had expired by limitation, Mr. Brown formed a new connection with the late Mr. Harrison Gray and Mr. John H. Wilkins, under the style of Hilliard, Gray & Company. In June, 1832, a copartnership was formed between Mr. Lemuel Shattuck, on the one part, and the firm of Hilliard, Gray & Company, on the other, under the style of Brown, Shattuck & Company, which had its place of business in Cambridge; and its management was under the personal superintendence of Mr. Brown. In August, 1832, Mr. Wilkins withdrew from the firm of Hilliard, Gray & Company, and Mr. Gray and Mr. Brown continued to carry on the business under the same name, until March, 1833, when Mr. Charles Browne was admitted a member of the firm, no change taking place in its designation. The firm of Brown, Shattuck & Company continued till some time in the year 1834.

In August, 1837, Mr. James Brown withdrew from the firm of Hilliard, Gray & Company, and entered into copartnership with Mr. Charles C. Little, under the style of Charles C. Little & Company,* the new firm taking the law-books and foreign books of Hilliard, Gray & Company. In this business connection Mr. Brown continued till his death; Mr. Augustus Flagg, and his son, Mr. James Perry Brown, subsequently becoming members of the firm. These dates and facts complete the record of Mr. Brown's business life. We turn back to resume his personal biography, and to set down those events by which his character was ripened, his mind expanded, and his affections quickened and deepened.

In May, 1825, he married Miss Mary Anne Perry, daughter of Mr. James Perry, of West Cambridge, a lady to whom he had been for some time attached, and with whom he united his fortunes as soon as he felt that his position and prospects justified his assuming the care of a family. A nature and a heart like his would be sure to form an early, but not a rash marriage. His affectionate temper, and his need of quick and constant sympathy, drew him strongly toward domestic life; and for domestic life he was well fitted by his loving and gentle spirit, his refinement of feeling, his taste for quiet pleasures, and his perfect good temper. In this last quality—so large an element in the happiness of a happy home—Mr. Brown could hardly be surpassed. There are men who, by vigorous exercise of the habit of self-command, can repress the sallies of an impatient spirit; but the effort can not be

* The name of the firm always appeared in the imprint of books as Charles C. Little and James Brown; and it was also popularly known as Little & Brown. The present style is Little, Brown & Company.

concealed from an observant eye, and the enforced virtue has not the grace and sweetness of the natural growth. Mr. Brown had no rebellious impulses to subdue, for the pure gold of his temper never contracted the slightest stain of irritability, and his gentle and gracious bearing had all the charm of spontaneous movement.

Mr. Brown resided in Cambridge from the time of his marriage till 1829, when he removed to West Cambridge, and took a house upon Wellington Hill, now occupied by his second son, Mr. Edward Wyeth Brown. In 1835, he came into Boston, and lived for a year or two in a house upon Washington Place, Fort Hill; but his love of rural pleasures and rural occupations was too strong to make him contented in a city, and he returned to his former residence upon Wellington Hill, where he remained till 1840, when he moved into the house in Watertown, which he built, and in which he continued to reside till his death.

The children of his marriage were five in number, three sons and two daughters; and they formed an affectionate and a happy household. Mr. Brown was a kind and indulgent father; winning from the first the confidence of his children; never repelling their young hearts by coldness or sternness, nor darkening them by the shadow of fear. Nor did he live—as is often the case with men absorbed by the cares of a prosperous and increasing business—in practical ignorance of the minds and characters of his children. He was a conscientious as well as a loving father, and faithfully discharged the trusts of a parent by his care as well as his tenderness.

When he first set up housekeeping he had very little property and but a moderate income, and was obliged to live frugally and in a plain way. But love makes all sacrifices light; and looking at life from the beginning to the end, it is beyond question a gain, in happiness even, to start under the rule of strict economy and self-sacrifice.

Hope is the sunshine of the heart; and those young people who begin life with a free gratification of wants, and a full sense of prosperity, lose the fine relish that comes with each new and hard-earned indulgence, and the delight of adding to another's pleasure by self-sacrifice and renunciation. They may well be pitied for not knowing the enjoyment of gradual progress through their own power and perseverance.

Mr. Brown's business career was uniformly prosperous. For some years after his marriage his progress was not very rapid, nor were his gains large. He was not of a scheming and speculating turn: the foundations of his success were laid slowly and deeply in industry, economy, sagacity, and a rigid adherence to plain and safe rules in the conduct of business. He was thus spared the corroding anxieties and the wasting cares that haunt the path, and murder the sleep, of reckless and daring spirits. In common with the whole business community, he passed through more than one of those periods of pecuniary pressure which recur from time to time in our country; and there were doubtless moments of grave examination into his affairs, not unmingled with uneasiness; but he never suffered serious embarrassment or long-continued perplexity. The clouds never darkened round him so as to shut out the light. And from the time of his entering into partnership with Mr. Little, success flowed in upon him in a deeper and broader stream. In the management of the business of this new firm, each partner found the distinct sphere which was in unison with his tastes and his capacities; neither interfering with the other, and both working harmoniously together.

In seeking the causes which led to Mr. Brown's success in business—and which contributed to the success of the copartnerships of which he was a member—we find them in a combination of qualities not so rare in themselves as in their harmonious union. They may be briefly summed up by saying that he had the tastes of a scholar, the manners of a gentleman, and the habits of a man of business. He was born with the instincts and perceptions of good-breeding; and he had nothing to learn or to forget in order to qualify him to stand in the highest social place. He was born, too, with a strong love of knowledge, and consequently a strong love of books; and having had more than common opportunities in his youth for indulging this taste, he began active life with an amount of literary and miscellaneous acquisition not common among men who have not had what is usually termed a liberal education. These acquirements were of daily use to him as a publisher and a seller of books. He understood books as a scholar, as a bibliographer, and as a tradesman; he knew their substantial worth, their factitious or artificial value in the eyes of collectors, and their popular estimation. But these scholarly accomplishments would have been of doubtful value had they not been tempered and controlled by a sound practical understanding. Booksellers and book publishers sometimes fail of success because they love books not wisely but too well; because they push the scholar's tastes and habits into the region of pure business, and regard the contents of their shelves more as a library than as a stock in trade. Mr. Brown was a man of accurate and careful habits of business as well as a lover of books. These habits did not, perhaps, so much belong to his original constitution as did his literary tastes, but a strong sense of duty and a resolute will gave them all the energy of natural impulse.

The principal part of the business of the firm of Little & Brown consisted in the publication and sale of law-books, and in the importation and sale of foreign books. Their publications in general literature have been, for the most part, of a grave, solid, and substantial character, such as works in theology, history, politics, political economy, and biography—rarely meddling with those lighter and more ephemeral publications that come with the leaves of spring and go with the leaves of autumn. In their sales of law-books they were, it is believed, the first to apply that well-known rule in political economy, that in articles of permanent demand the increase of purchasers is greater, in proportion, than the decrease of price. It was formerly the usage to print a small edition of a law-book, and to sell the copies at a high price—a custom transmitted from England, and there founded on the limited demand presented by a bar neither numerous nor rapidly increasing. But Messrs. Little & Brown had the sagacity to perceive that the lawyers in our country were a numerous body, that their increase would keep pace with the progress of the country; and they drew the ready inference that if they could offer them at three dollars such books as had formerly cost five, the difference in price would be more than made up in the difference in sales. The result justified their enterprise; and thus they and the members of the legal profession were alike benefited. For obvious reasons, the price of law-books must always be more than that of works in general literature; but in the legal publications of Messrs. Little and Brown the difference is less than that which the profession were previously accustomed to.

The importation and sale of foreign books was the department of their business which came under Mr. Brown's especial control. For this he was particularly well fitted by his tastes and accomplishments. He knew the worth and the value of books; and he had an intuitive sagacity in discerning what the public wanted. This branch of their business was much increased during the latter years of his life, and after his successive visits to Europe. His temperament was hopeful and sanguine; and he bought very largely both of old works and new editions. The result did credit to his judgment and discernment; but his latest purchases were on a scale beyond which he could hardly have gone with safety.

During the last fourteen years of his life, Mr. Brown made five voyages to Europe. With the exception of his second visit, in 1845, he had always the companionship of one or more members of his family. The formation or extension of his business connections was the main inducement to these excursions, and London and Paris were his chief points of interest; but he allowed himself time to visit many places interesting from associations or attractive from natural beauty. He saw England and Scotland more thoroughly and deliberately than most American tourists; and he visited Ireland, Holland, Belgium, North Germany, the Rhine country, Switzerland, and parts of France. These brief trips to Europe were sources of high enjoyment to him. His good health and his stock of animal spirits made him sensitive to the pleasures of traveling and indifferent to its discomforts. He took great delight in examining places and objects familiar to him in books. His simple, cordial manners, and the unaffected worth and intelligence which they expressed, made him everywhere welcome; and many of his transatlantic acquaintances ripened into enduring and valuable friends. The London publishers and booksellers with whom he was brought in contact—a shrewd and observant body of men—at once recognized his claims as a man and as a man of business; and the favorable relations he established with them were due not merely to the ample pecuniary credit he commanded, but also to the confidence inspired by his presence.

His first visit to Europe was in 1841. He was absent about four months; leaving Boston in June and returning in October. He was accompanied by Mrs. Brown; and on this account, and from the fact that his children were too young for any thing more than brief communications, there are no memorials of this tour to be found among his papers. Much of his time and thoughts were given to business, and to the establishment of his relations with European publishers. During this visit he made the acquaintance of that eminent publisher, the late Mr. John Murray. By this gentleman—a sagacious observer of men and manners—Mr. Brown was treated with a cordial and hospitable kindness which was in itself a compliment, and which was always warmly and gratefully remembered. His youngest son—born after his return—received the name of John Murray, in honor of his transatlantic friend.

Upon his return home, Mr. Brown wrote a brief account of his tour to a friend in the western country. His letter appeared, but without the writer's name, in the Cincinnati Daily Republican of October 27, 1841, and is here reprinted.

"BOSTON, October 17, 1841.

"We left Boston in the Caledonia, on the first of June, and reached Halifax in forty hours. Halifax harbor looks pretty as you approach it, but is as dull a city within, as was ever built of shingles or inhabited by Blue Noses. We remained only a few hours, and set sail with a fine wind and smooth sea for Liverpool. Excepting some trifling sea-sickness we were well, and enjoyed the remainder of the voyage as well as any one can on shipboard; for after all it is a most uncomfortable life at sea, and it was well said that 'it is a poor home that is not better than a ship.' On the eleventh morning we saw Mizen Head, in Ireland, and the next the shores and mountains of Wales, and on the thirteenth were safely landed in Liverpool. This is a fine city, full of activity, and about the size of New York. On the morning of the fourteenth, we took our seats in the cars, and, passing through a most delightful country, arrived at London, a distance of two hundred and twenty miles, in the evening. In the course of the day, we went through Birmingham and several other large manufacturing towns; but the charm of the ride was the rich agricultural country, and especially the Vale of Aylesbury, a spot unequaled for rural beauty perhaps in the world.

"I made direct for the London Coffee-House, Ludgate Hill, of course. Besides being one of the best houses in London, it is the place where Franklin lived, and I sat in the very stall where he and Strahan used to dine and hold their political discussions. This house, too, is within a stone's throw of St. Paul's, Paternoster Row, Fleet-street, and in fact is in the very heart of Old London. I called several times at Dr. Johnson's old home in Bolt-court, and drank a glass of ale to his memory. In the same dingy, dirty lane, is the Printing-office where Franklin worked journeywork, if you know what that means. The building is occupied for the same purpose now. I looked into Wills and Button's also, and did not forget the Boar's Head, nor the Saracen's, made classic by Dickens, as the haunt of the hero of Dotheboy's Hall. Paternoster Row I was greatly disappointed in. Instead of a fine street, full of splendid bookseller's shops, it is a narrow lane (not even a thoroughfare) barely admitting a carriage, dirty, dark, full of foul odors, gloomy, and disgusting. It is for the most part filled with booksellers; but what gives a character to the whole lane is a large tallow-chandler's establishment, and the beef-market. It resembles in size Bromfield-street, in Boston, but is perhaps twenty rods longer, and narrower than any of your streets in Cincinnati, that I saw last winter. In this mean street, however, as you know, are sold more fine books than in any other in the world. Here, too, booksellers with their families live; and here, as elsewhere in London, you meet the bookseller's wife assisting in the labors of the shop,—busy with the pen, or assorting parcels for distant customers, and in the retail shops, discussing the comparative value of the different editions of Bayle and

Domat; and if you call to dine with her, you will find her at home also in all matters which with us are thought to be a woman's exclusive province—the management of household affairs.

"The bookselling business is much more subdivided than with us. Law booksellers sell only law-books. Medical booksellers only medical books, &c. None of them keep what with us is called 'an assortment.' If you want several books, you call on your bookseller and give him a list, and he procures them. No single bookseller, as with us, pretends to keep every book, new and old.

"At a dinner given by one of the trade, I became acquainted with Mr. Murray, the justly celebrated publisher. He is now about seventy, but still in good health and the full enjoyment of a green old age. I afterward dined with him and his family at Albemarle-street, and spent a Sunday with them at Twickenham, at a delightful country residence on the Thames, within a few rods of Pope's house, and ten minutes' walk from Strawberry Hill, where Horace Walpole wrote his charming letters. In the afternoon we rode down the Thames to Richmond, walked over the celebrated park, and enjoyed the richest view in the world—the valley of the Thames, Windsor Castle, a glimpse of the gothic towers of Eton College, and the thousand delightful palaces and country-seats which are imbedded in the deep green fields and woods of Old England.

"Mr. Murray has published for most of the celebrated authors of England, from the time of Sheridan to the present, and he has a rich fund of anecdote which he might, and I hope will, embody in a book, that would be as interesting a one as has been given to the world in that eventful period in literary history. He told me many which I have not time or room to give you. He doubtless knows as much of Byron's private life as any other person alive, and his publications are among the best, and their style infinitely superior to that of any of his contemporaries. His splendid editions of Lockhart's Ballads and of Childe Harold, now just before the public, bear full testimony to this fact. He has a delightful family, and lives in the exercise of that hospitality peculiar, I believe, to Old England—the perfect personification of the 'Old English gentleman,'—the finest character on earth.

"Bound on business, I had not time to go into the details of England. I went to Eton College, and Windsor, and Virginia Water; to Oxford, Hampton Court, and Bushy Park and Palace; Chelsea, Greenwich, &c.; to Edmonton, and in the city spent a day or two visiting Westminster Abbey, the Tower, the Houses of Parliament, Westminster Hall, the courts, the tunnel under the Thames, the galleries, &c., &c. After passing five weeks in London, we went by Southampton to Havre, and thence up the Seine, by Rouen, to Paris; remained ten days; thence by diligence through Coutraî, Cambrai, &c., to Liege; thence to Brussels, Antwerp, Waterloo, &c.; thence to Aix-la-Chapelle, Cologne, and then up the Rhine to Ehrenbreitstein, Coblentz, and Mayence; thence to Frankfort-on-the-Maine, which was the end of our journey. From that place we retraced our steps to the Rhine, and down through Holland to Rotterdam; remained there a day, and took steamer to London; thence to York, Newcastle, Alnwick Castle, &c., to Edinburgh and Glasgow. From Glasgow I went to Ayrshire, and saw the birthplace of Burns, followed Tam O'Shanter from Ayr to the Bridge of Doon, by old Kirk Alloway; saw the grand monument to Burns on the banks of Doon, &c.; returned by Androssan to Fleetwood in England; thence to Liverpool, and here I am.

"Though driven by business, I saw much, and enjoyed myself to the full extent of my capacity. Within the last eight months, and since I saw you in Cincinnati, I have traveled at least fifteen thousand miles, and seen all sorts of 'life and manners,' from the interior of Arkansas to Paris; from the swamps of Georgia to the gardens of England and Belgium. I can hardly realize that I have gathered cotton and moss from the fields and woods of the Mississippi, wheat from Waterloo, and roses and relics from 'the banks and braes of bonny Doon,' in so short a time. But so it is; they are all before me, and here I am without accident—not even the loss of a farthing."

In October, 1844, a severe affliction fell upon him in the death of his wife, who had been for some time in declining health. Mrs. Brown was an amiable and affectionate woman, of retiring manners, and rather delicate health, who found her happiness in the faithful discharge of her duties as a wife and mother. Her husband was tenderly attached to her, and she deserved all the love and confidence she enjoyed.

Here it may not be inappropriate to introduce a portion of a letter written to his three youngest children, during a brief absence from home, which shows his kindly and playful temper, as well as the warm and expressive affection which marked his domestic relations.

"Washington, January 28, 1843.

"My dear Children:—I wrote a letter from this place last summer to your brothers, and now I shall try to write something to you. Last Tuesday I wrote to your mother, and gave her some account of my journey up to that time. On Thursday I left Philadelphia on the railroad for Baltimore and Washington. The weather was fine, and has been during all my journey. The ride through Pennsylvania and Delaware was very pleasant, though not new to me, as I have been over the ground many times before. * * *

"Here I have been about selling books and looking at the curiosities, &c. From the western part of the Capitol you can see the Potomac River far down—almost to Mount Vernon, where Washington lived, and where his tomb is. You also have a fine view of Alexandria and Georgetown as well as Washington City. The weather is very warm here, and the negroes are plowing in the fields. Sometimes I have counted ten or twelve all driving their horses and plows round a great field. They are very merry, and sing and laugh as loud as a fish-horn.

"In the market are plenty of deer, duck, and fish; also spinach, sweet potatoes, &c., and the little negroes bring mocking-birds in abundance. They bring their chickens alive. One negro woman had half a dozen cackling hens in one hand, and a baby almost as big as John Murray, and as black as the shiniest blacking, in the other, and cried, 'Who'll buy?' I don't know which she meant to sell, but I thought I would not buy the baby, because your mother said, some time ago, she had enough of them.

"This afternoon I had to go from the Treasury Office to the Capitol; so, as I was tired, I asked a negro coachman what he would carry me for. 'Oh, massa,' he said, 'for two levies' (twenty-five cents). 'That's too much,' I said; 'it is hard times.' 'Oh, massa,' he said, 'hard times for poor nigger, but, massa, he no hard times for you. You neber see hard times, nor you neber will; you don't look like him.' So I had to give him his two levies.

"There are rows of carriages all down the great street, and as a great many of them have little to do, the drivers, all negroes, have a plenty of fun. They sing queer negro songs, and I suppose, by their laughing, tell very funny stories. They are very polite to the ladies. Several of them met this morning in front of our hotel, and made more bows and courtesies than your dancing parties make in a whole evening, though all of them had either baskets of marketing or something else in their hands.

"To-morrow morning, if it does not storm badly, I shall

go back to Philadelphia, and on Monday hope to be in New York, where I shall have to stay a day or two, and then I shall come home, where I hope to be on Thursday or Friday. * * * *

"Your affectionate father,
"JAMES BROWN."

In 1845, Mr. Brown made a second visit to Europe, leaving home in the steamer of April 1st, and returning in that of July 19th. This was the only occasion on which he was entirely alone during these foreign excursions. To relieve the irksomeness of the solitude which was always distasteful to his genial and social nature, he kept an ample journal of his movements and observations, some extracts from which are here appended. It is an unstudied record of his daily life, hastily jotted down in such brief intervals as he could snatch from his many engagements and occupations; but it will interest his friends alike from the ease and animation of the style, and from the unconscious revelations which it makes of his own amiable and kindly nature.

"*April* 14*th*, 1845.—Took cars for London. The day was stormy and cold, and the country showed few marks of spring. Even the Vale of Aylesbury looked gloomy and cheerless. Arrived at Old London Coffee-House at six o'clock, P. M., being nine hours from Liverpool, a distance of two hundred and ten miles. The road is much of the distance uneven, and on the whole appears not so good as our best roads.

"15*th*.—Breakfasted in the stall where, seventy-five years ago, Franklin usually took his meals, and discussed with Strahan the then growing troubles with the mother country. There is a permanency about things here that does not exist with us. What stall in America will be found 'unimproved' seventy-five years hence, or has remained so that length of time?

"21*st.*—Took tea and supped with Pickering, the celebrated publisher, in Piccadilly. Saw a large collection of Burns's manuscript poems; among others, the original of 'Mary in Heaven,' 'Auld Lang Syne,' and 'Bruce's Address;' also a copy of the first edition (1785) of his poems. Mr. Pickering is an enthusiast in his profession, to which he is most devoted. He has done more for the advancement of the printing art, and the dissemination of the best class of English literature, than any other man alive. He lives over his shop, as is the habit of some of the wealthiest tradesmen here. We sat at the table, and drank Old Port, and talked of old books, till nearly two o'clock. Mr. Pickering understands the value of both. This was a 'red-letter day.'

"25*th.*—Called on several of the trade, and also on Mr. Rogers, the poet, at the request of Mr. Moxon. He received me very cordially, and opened his most curious collection of paintings and curiosities to my inspection. He has, among other rare things, the original contract of Milton with Simmons, for the sale of Paradise Lost, for £5, and the first edition of that work. Spent two hours in the library, then returned to the drawing-room, and was introduced to Mr. Wordsworth the poet, who is on a visit to Mr. Rogers. He had a long conversation with us; asked after Pennsylvania, in which he is interested, as his relatives hold a large amount of her bonds. Invited us to visit him at Rydal Mount. Told us not to follow the example of many of our countrymen, and pass our time in the frivolities of Paris, and the ruins of Italy, to the neglect of our fatherland. I told him that we did not intend to do so, that I preferred to know the people of England to any other object. He then said that he was glad his advice was not needed by us; that he thought it a poor way to go abroad to learn German metaphysics, which could be as well learned at home; but the study of man must be made on the spot. I told him also that I first published his poems in America. He remembered the edition, and said he had the copy I sent to him. Mr. Rogers made us promise to breakfast with him on Monday, and we then took our leave.

"28*th*.—Breakfasted at nine o'clock, with Mr. Rogers, according to appointment. Mr. R. delighted us with his literary anecdotes of the last sixty years. Showed us numerous autographs of Dryden, Pope, Goldsmith, Sheridan, &c. He takes a warm interest in America,—remembers his father's decided friendship for the colonies when the war of the Revolution broke out. The Recorder, his father's friend, when he heard of the battle of Lexington, went into mourning, and the Master of Ordnance at the Tower gave up his place, worth £1,000 a year, rather than ship guns to America, to be used against us. Mr. Rogers directed our attention to Dryden's house, and Milton's garden. He is now eighty-one years old—hale and cheerful.

"*May 5th*.—Went to the Tower—once a prison of State, now a museum of curiosities and arms. There is a complete series of arms, from about 900, down to the present time, arranged by Sir Samuel Meyrick, in a most beautiful manner. Horses and horsemen, knights, esquires, yeomanry,—all dressed and armed according to the times in which they lived. Many of the kings so mounted, are likenesses as well in person as armor. In another apartment we were shown the various instruments of torture, those venerable arguments for the spread of faith and the advancement of truth. The axe used in the execution of Lady Jane Grey, Anne Boleyn, and the Countess of Salisbury, is here. No Englishman could be found who would act as executioner to Lady Jane Grey, and a Frenchman was sent for, for the purpose. He was left-handed, and the axe was made expressly for his use. The block is here, too, on which the Scottish lords were beheaded in the time of the Pretender (1745). The seams on it, which the axe-man made, when he struck through the neck, are deep, and show with what zeal he did his work. Here is the little prison-room, with walls eighteen feet thick, where Sir Walter Raleigh was confined for twelve years.

"11*th.*—Breakfasted with Mr. Vertue, and then took railroad and steamboat to Gravesend, twenty miles, to visit Colonel William and Major James Burns, sons of the poet. After an agreeable ride down the river, the shores of which are highly cultivated, and often ornamented with fine country-seats, we arrived at Gravesend at one o'clock. Called on Mrs. Burns, whom we found at home, and pleased with our visit. The daughter of James (the one pictured with a daisy in her hand, standing by the side of her grandmother), is a very intelligent and pretty Scotch lassie, and strongly resembles her grandfather. She talked with much interest of the poet. Her father (James), the youngest son of Burns, has no resemblance in person or mind to the poet: William, on the contrary, resembles him strongly in person and expression. His face is what would be called a perfect likeness. He appeared under some disadvantage, being ill, but his conversation was animated, and his eye showed the original fire. He manifested a lively interest in his father's fame in America, which country he intimated he might visit. Both these gentlemen are retired officers from the East India Company's service, and have both passed thirty-two years at or near Madras. I left them with a melancholy feeling that it was the last time I should ever see a living representative of the greatest poet since Shakspeare.

"13*th.*—Went with Mr. Pickering to Hampstead, to hear the nightingales in 'Caen Wood,' and was gratified with a full concert. The note is very much like that of the ferruginous thrush, but less varied, and not so loud. It is very quick and lively, and not, as I expected, slow and pensive. So much for impressions from poets. We had a fine moon, and remained in the wood listening to the warblers till after nine o'clock. Then walked through such lanes as are to be found only in England, to Highstead. Passed the cottage where Steele wrote his Essays, and which is pictured in Drake's Essays at Hampstead,—and Coleridge's residence (Mr. Gillman's) at Highstead. On the whole, had a delightful ramble, with a most intelligent and kind-hearted man, and returned to his house in Piccadilly, at ten. Supped with him, talking over literary anecdotes.

* * * * * * *

"*June 4th.*—Went to St. Denis to hear the organ. I am no musician, but I am sure it was played with surpassing skill. The imitation of a tremendous storm was perfect. The first grumbling of the thunder in the distance, its nearer approach, and finally the awful bursting of the whole storm, thunder, rain, and hail, was as frightful as any reality could be. A gentleman sitting near me, unconsciously grasped his umbrella, and was in the act of handing it to a lady when he woke from his dream, and was sensible of the deception. I am glad that I have witnessed so impressive a scene. On my way back to town, bought some sabots, or wooden shoes. The woman who sold them expressed her surprise that sabots were not worn in so cold a country as America,—said that she had no idea that we were so much behind in the arts of life, and expressed her belief that those bought by me would be greedily copied.

"*7th.*—The Belgian country over which I passed, is highly cultivated—to a remarkable extent by the spade, and the seed sown in drills, instead of broadcast. Neither of these methods can be practiced except when labor is very low. Much of the heaviest labor is done here by women, who seem to be treated more like beasts of burden than the men of the same rank. I saw this morning two women just beginning to spade a lot of, I should think, four acres, and I could hardly conceive a more discouraging prospect, the progress of the labor is so slow. Three or four of the lords of creation sat near, with their long, dirty beards, smoking, and observing the work go on. Yesterday, I passed a man and woman returning from the day's labor in the field, with the tools, and the man sat in the hand-cart, which the woman dragged, or rather shoved!

"12*th.*—Leipsic is a nice city, but remarkable for little except its University. The principal building is very plain, without any pretensions to the picturesque. In the evening, went with Mr. B. Tauchnitz, and Dr. Fluegel, to Mr. T.'s country-house, or castle (as it is in magnitude), about four miles out of town. Mr. Tauchnitz lives in a very expensive way, and is decidedly wealthy. He has a very interesting family. His house is surrounded by water (a branch of the Elbe), and single forest-trees, with gardens, and every thing belonging to a large landed estate in this country. Passed a pleasant evening. Both Mr. and Mrs. Tauchnitz speak English. Our supper would have surprised a New England teetotaller. In the first place, the servant presented me with what I supposed was a plate of soup, but which I found to my surprise was quite another thing. It was a plate of Hock wine, sweetened and spiced, and with bits of toast floating on it, resembling, in all but the taste, a soup-maigre. It was delicious. Then followed pigeons, fowls, &c., &c., with a constant flow of delicious wines, sweetmeats, and a long list of delicacies, which I did not venture upon. * * * * *

"20*th.*—Rejoiced to be once more in Old England, among a people that can *talk*, and that have always received me as an old friend. Looked about for lodgings, but could find none that I would occupy. The London Coffee-House, so long the resort of Americans, is dark, dirty, and ill-attended. Inquired of my friend William Smith, bookseller, 113 Fleet-street, who told me there were fine rooms at Stoke Newington that I could obtain, belonging to a 'very decent person.' As it was only four miles out of town, and the communication constant by omnibus, I decided to go and look at them. Accordingly at evening he accompanied me, and I was agreeably surprised to find myself (willy-nilly) his guest. He said he was alone, having no children, and having lately lost his wife, and should feel obliged if I would remain with him as long as I stayed in London. Of course, I could not resist such an invitation.

"*22d.*—Walked with Mr. Smith over the village of Stoke Newington. It is an extremely pleasant village, having Highbury, Hampstead, Tottenham, Clapton, and Islington, as boundaries. It is quite in the country, and the gardens and villas of the Londoners are scattered in the rich farms and orchards of the cultivators. The new river, which supplies a portion of London with water, runs through the village, and the River Lea, which was one of Walton's haunts, runs for some distance parallel with it, in the neighboring town of Clapton. This village seems to have been the favorite resort of authors. Goldsmith lived near it, and wrote his Vicar in a house near the one I occupy. Dr. Watts lived and died here, and his chapel is now used as a lecture-room. Priestley, too, preached here. De Foe's house is still in fine repair, and indicates a thrifty and opulent proprietor, as De Foe is said to have been when he resided here.

"*July 6th, Sunday.*—Went by railroad to Slough, and then walked through the largest and finest wheat-fields to Stoke Pogis Church, the burial-place of the poet Gray. It was here that he took his hints chiefly for his Elegy. It is a spot of unequaled beauty,—approached only by footpaths,—stands in a crescent of groves in the grounds of Mr. Penn, a descendant of William Penn, who has erected a statue to Gray, in another part of his grounds. The yew-trees still shade the graves, 'in many a mouldering heap,' and the ivy still literally covers the little, but singularly beautiful, church. I heard service in the church; the music was fine, and the sermon dull and sensible. The congregation was almost entirely of rustics, and it required a poet indeed to imagine that any 'inglorious Milton,' or 'village Hampden,' were among them. They were the most wooden-headed looking persons I have ever seen. A rural tablet, outside the church, tells that Gray is buried in the tomb hard by, with his mother. I looked in vain for any other distinguished name both in the church and churchyard. Every image, except the 'elms,' recorded or alluded to in the Elegy, may be traced to this stop. A bell surmounts the tower. The church and grounds are included in the farm of Mr. Penn, and the lowing herds feed on the very borders of the 'yard.' The 'plowman,' and the 'owl,' are at home in the fields,—dark woods are to be seen on all sides, and the 'rude forefathers of the hamlet sleep' beneath many a heaving turf, in this little home of the dead, covered with deep-green moss. If I had seen nothing more, this day's pilgrimage is worth a journey to England. After lingering around this lovely spot until the shades of evening began to close in, I took a private way through long fields of beans in blossom, and wheat, oats, and barley, back to the station, and returned to the house of my hospitable friend at Stoke Newington.

"17*th*.—Went to Prescott, to see Mr. Nuttall at Nutgrove. Found him beautifully situated on his estates, and pleased to see me. Went over his grounds, and saw his tenantry, who are mostly old men who have occupied under his uncle for many years. They are small farmers, occupying from thirty to sixty acres; and the rents seemed to me low, but they pay all taxes, and those are monstrous.

For sixty acres of good grass and grain land, the net rent to Mr. Nuttall was only £70. In the morning went to Knowesly Park, the seat of Earl Derby, with Mr. Nuttall, —a delightful walk through wheat and bean fields—beans in full bloom. Innumerable private ways are kept open in England, through fields, parks, &c. One might almost travel over the whole country, without setting his foot on a carriage-way. Earl Derby's seat is surrounded by an immense grove of fine oaks, the whole ranged by deer, and covered with hares and other game. His fruits are of the finest varieties, and the gardens of great extent. I tasted the grapes, peaches, and nectarines, all of course protected by glass, but all of fine flavor. His gardener estimated that there were two thousand pineapples in various stages of growth in the hot-houses. He has also a fine and very extensive aviary, and many rare quadrupeds. Returned to Mr. Nuttall's, and after dinner visited his orchards and gooseberry plantations. One of the last covered six acres, and every bush seemed crowded with fruit to its greatest capacity. We supposed there were two hundred barrels of fruit nearly fit to be gathered.

"*July* 19*th.*—At twelve o'clock was under way for Boston, in the Cambria steamer. I am so fortunate as to have for a room-mate Dr. Sharp, who accompanied me over.

"The passage home was as agreeable as a pleasant companion and fine weather could make it. It was monotonous, but the quickest passage ever made from Europe to America—being only eleven days and four hours, including twenty hours' delay by visiting Halifax. Arrived at my house at nine, after an absence of four months, lacking two days. In all this time, and having traveled at least ten thousand miles, I have not met with the slightest accident, or unpleasant circumstance. I have been everywhere received with the kindest attention, and most liberal hospitality, and not in a single instance have I met with a rude action or an unkind word."

In April, 1846, Mr. Brown was married to Miss Mary Derby Hobbs, daughter of Dr. Ebenezer Hobbs, of Waltham—a connection in every way fortunate; securing to himself the society and conversation of an intelligent and sympathizing companion, and to his younger children that affectionate maternal care of which they stood in need; and increasing his social resources by his adoption into a most amiable and cultivated family circle.

In 1847, Mr. Brown, accompanied by his wife, visited Europe; leaving home on the first day of April, and returning on the first day of September. They remained in London till the early part of June, and then went to Paris, to which a fortnight was given. Another fortnight was spent in an excursion through Belgium and the Rhine country. They then returned to London, where Mr. Brown completed his business engagements; after which a tour was made through Scotland and the north of England, before embarking for home.

In 1849, Mr. and Mrs. Brown again visited Europe, accompanied by Dr. and Mrs. Hobbs; leaving home on the 21st day of March, and returning at the close of August. Their tour comprised London and Paris, the English lake country, parts of Scotland, Germany, and Switzerland. They had proposed to visit Italy also, but this was prevented by an illness of Mr. Brown, which detained them three weeks in London.

While in Switzerland, a brief separation of the traveling party took place at Lucerne, Mr. Brown and Dr. Hobbs going over the Brunig Pass, and rejoining their friends at Interlaken—it being deemed unadvisable for the ladies, one of whom was ill, to tempt the fatigue of a mountain excursion. While at Grindelwald, Mr. Brown wrote an account of their journey, to his wife, the greater part of which is here copied.

"GRINDELWALD, June 26, Tuesday.

"MY DEAR WIFE:—To compensate you as far as I can for the loss of *seeing* with me, the last two days, I will attempt some description of our little journey from Lucerne. We left, as you know, in a row-boat, with our guide Francis, a most intelligent and obliging Swiss, for Alpnach, about nine miles up the lake. Our guide amused us with his shrewd remarks, queer stories, and broken English. He was particularly severe on the priest at Lucerne, who blessed the boat that went out on Sunday with music—you recollect it—that is, blessed it for that trip, for which Francis says he had money. Well, the boat had just left the wharf when one of the men went into the engine-room for something, when the engineer let go the engine and killed him! Now, Francis says the priest has to say a long list of prayers gratis for the poor boatman whom his blessing did not save.

"The shores of the lake are pretty on this side, but without the grandeur of the Altorf trip which we made on Saturday. We called at the inn at Alpnach, and took some bread, honey, and wine, whilst Francis hired a carriage to take us to Lungern, fifteen miles, where we dined pretty well. We then took horses for the Brunig Pass, the Bernese Oberland, and Meyringen. In passing from Alpnach to Lungern we saw the opening made into the lake by which a large portion of its waters were drawn off, and its beauty spoiled. The road was so precipitous we were obliged to walk several miles, and through quite a smart shower. The passage from Lungern to Meyringen was very grand and varied, giving us at different times views of the valley of the Aar, Lake Lucerne, and the Brunig mountains. On the whole, we thought it inferior to the ride up the Righi, but it was at times frightfully grand. Parts of it were hard and difficult for the traveler, and we were obliged to walk a good deal. In looking over the books at the stopping-places, we saw but few ladies' names; our guide says the journey should only be made by ladies in chairs. We had a nice supper of tea, strawberries, and cream! and went early to bed, intending to be off at six in the morning. I took a bath, as the guide said it would take the tired out of us. Slept well, and in the morning went down to the dining-room, where the usual stores of carved wooden-ware were offered. I bought none, but I found a very nice herbarium at ten francs, and another at three francs, both of which I secured for you. Agreeably to our orders, every thing was ready at six to start—we had before taken some coffee, eggs, and strawberries,—and we took to our horses, and after passing a mile or more out of the straggling village, began to rise on the great Scheideck, by the side of the Wetterhorn, Wellhorn, the Black Forest, and the upper and lower Grindelwald glacier. We had not rode above a mile, when our attention was fixed by the grandeur of the scene around us. The valley of the Aar, the village of Meyringen, and the thousand little waterfalls that come down like silver threads, give to the scene a surpassing beauty. We now left our horses, and took a road for a mile or so impracticable for them, and went to the fall of the Reichenbach, one of rare beauty. We saw it from a small house built to protect observers from the spray. The sun shone its brightest, and I think I never witnessed a more truly beautiful spectacle, a complete rainbow formed in the spray, and really within our reach. This fall is about one hundred feet high, but the river falls in its course two thousand, and we followed it to its source in the Black Forest glacier, and the neighboring Alpine snows. After leaving the fall, the way became very steep, and on the edge of the mountain, the shelf which served for a road, being for a great distance hardly more than three feet in width. We now passed on through scenes of majestic grandeur, which I can not attempt to describe. Waterfalls on all sides, rushing streams and deafening rapids, mountains far above the clouds, capped with snow, and distant glaciers, all presenting new views at every angle of the path. The chalets of the shepherds were scattered through the valleys, and numerous flocks of goats and cattle, tinkling their bells, served to beautify a scene oppressive by its solemn majesty. At first we would call each other's attention to the more striking scenes, but we soon neglected this, each being absorbed in his own reflections. I felt something of the confused feeling that I do when visiting a gallery of fine paintings without time to examine. The scene shifted so fast, that an object that I could have stood before and wondered at for days, had no time to make a distinct impression. As we began to descend, we passed the little hamlet of Rosenlaui, where there is a fine waterfall and sulphur bath. We now came in full view of the upper Grindelwald glacier, stretched out into the valley before us. The bad state of the road compelled us to leave our horses for nearly two hours, and walk over morasses and steep banks. At about ten we reached the borders of the glacier, and, in company with a peasant who cut steps for us in the ice, went on to it. It is truly an astonishing spectacle. Full of frightful crevices, some of them of great depth, of the most solid and transparent ice, that bids defiance to sun and rain, rising to an unknown height, and spreading to an almost unknown extent, the glacier is still surrounded, to within a few feet of its margin, with delicate flowers and fruit-trees,—the apple, pear, cherry, &c., in full fruit, within five minutes' walk of the lower Grindelwald. We reached our inn tired and hungry, feelings that we had forgotten until then in the excitement of the scenes we were passing through. We enjoyed our dinner with the nice

Alpine strawberries, and after a short siesta, I am writing these recollections. Before finishing, I must tell you that our window, literally *au premier*, looks out on the immense Wetterhorn, rising like a great gothic ruin some eight thousand feet on my left,—the lower Grindelwald with its silver peak, the Schreckhorn covered with snow of dazzling whiteness, sometimes enveloped in clouds, and then as they melt away seeming to rest on the cerulean blue behind, far up in the heavens, more than thirteen thousand feet from me, but as distinct as the glaciers at my feet; this makes the center and the background. On the right the Eigher, or Giant, a rude mass of brown stone, naked, except where a few lines of snow relieve his savage grandeur, rises to an immense height, and seems to support his fair and brilliant neighbor, the Jungfrau. Imagine all this within twenty minutes' walk (I mean, of course, their bases), and I think you will agree with me that such a scene is not witnessed more than once in any life."

Some further account of this tour is contained in a letter from Paris, addressed to his eldest daughter, a portion of which is here given.

"PARIS, May 28, 1849.

"MY DEAR MARY,—Your mother has given such full accounts of our travels in her letters, that I can not add much that will interest you. I must expect that almost all the value my letter can have to you, will be in the fact that it is mine. Since I saw you, as you know, I have been sick for a long time, and when I have been well my business has been so pressing that I have had but little time to write letters. I hope now to be a better correspondent. We have been in Paris now a week, and have seen many of its curiosities. Few of them, of course, were new to your mother or me, but they are so beautiful that they very well bear seeing twice. Mr. and Mrs. Bossange, and other of our friends, have been very polite to us, and contributed very much to make our journey pleasant. We live in the fine rooms overlooking the beautiful gardens of the Tuileries and the palace of the king (when there is a king). This garden, or rather park—for it is as thickly covered, for the most part, with trees, as our grounds around the pond—is filled every fine day with thousands of people who sit there and read and smoke or sew, according to their various tastes. Children of all ages, from a month old to eighty years, come there for fine air and various games. In the street, between our rooms and this garden, a thousand interesting scenes are constantly passing. Now a troop of horse, with flourish of trumpets, go clattering over the pavements, while near them, busy chiffoniers are collecting from the refuse of the streets, their foul and scanty fare. Then a regiment of infantry, with fine music, pass before us on their way to the *Place du Carrousel*, or to the *Champ de Mars*. Omnibuses, carriages, crowds of gentlemen and ladies, beggars, grisettes, vagabond-looking soldiers in undress, market-women with their whole wealth on their head, or *en crochet*, on their backs, vary and fill up the always-shifting and never-tiresome scene.

"Every thing here is scenic—picturesque. The old houses, five or six stories high, with their Norman capped windows and turreted chimneys, and standing so near each other that in many streets you can not drive a chaise between them. The lamp-posts are covered with allegorical emblems, and surmounted in many instances with elaborately carved statues. At every turn, you meet with palaces or churches or monuments, some of them dating before the Christian era, and others the work of the Emperor Napoleon, on which the labors of the most celebrated men have been bestowed, and the wealth of nations compelled by conquests to contribute to these works as well as to the resources of the kingdom of France. Even the trees are trimmed to represent Gothic arches and other architectural forms. You may walk for miles under the shade of elms and beeches shaped in this manner, and so perfectly done, that you doubt whether you are not in the solemn aisle of some great cathedral. In Père-le-Chaise, with the nightingales for choristers, and the service for the dead going on in the midst, the deception is complete.

"We visited this celebrated cemetery last Sunday, after hearing high mass at the cathedral church of Notre Dame. It is filled, even crowded, with monuments; some of them in fine taste and of exquisite workmanship. But it wants the natural beauties which will always give Mount Auburn a beautiful pre-eminence over all other burial-places. It is not well kept either, and has many monuments that give evidence of a perverted taste, which should never have been admitted.

"Near the gate where you enter, is the monument of the celebrated lovers and more celebrated scholars, Abelard and Heloise; the term scholar only applies to the first, except what his fame has reflected on his pupil. The monument, removed from a church, destroyed, I believe, in some of the commotions of the first French Revolution, is the most interesting one in the grounds, both for its architectural ornament and historical associations. But as a whole the cemetery is full of interest, for it contains a large portion of the great men of the nation—scholars, civilians, marshals, &c., &c.; and it commands from its high grounds the finest view of Paris and the surrounding country that can be had anywhere. You will see that I have referred to several things in this letter, that you will wish to consult books in order to understand. The great Cyclopædia in the library will help you in any difficulty. You are now enjoying your (too?) long vacation. You must not neglect to read regularly from some good book, which

Mr. Emerson will recommend, nor let the thimble I gave you rust for want of use.

"Your affectionate father,

"James Brown.

"Miss M. A. E. Brown."

In the summer of 1852, Mr. Brown again visited Europe, accompanied by his second son, Mr. Edward Wyeth Brown. They sailed from Boston in the packet-ship Daniel Webster, on the seventh day of July, and were absent exactly twelve weeks. A large portion of this time was spent in London and Paris, and devoted to business engagements; but a rapid glance was given to some of the most interesting points in England and Scotland.

The next summer, Mr. Brown made his fifth and last voyage to Europe. He was accompanied by his wife, his eldest daughter, and Miss Eliza Hobbs, a sister of Mrs. Brown. They left home on the 13th of April, and returned early in September. They saw Paris, Switzerland, the Rhine country, and the English and Scotch lakes; for the sake of the young ladies, who had never been in Europe before, going over ground already somewhat familiar to Mr. and Mrs. Brown. Mr. Brown's business arrangements kept him in London a considerable time; during which period the ladies of the party lived in the immediate neighborhood, at such distance as to permit Mr. Brown to join them after his daily work was over. During the hours that he was busy in London, they made short excursions to the interesting spots in the vicinity of the great metropolis, such as Hampton Court, Kew, Finchley, Hammersmith, and Norwood. One pleasant week was passed at Richmond; and the long, silvery twilights of the early English summer were spent in rowing up and down the Thames—a river so rich in natural beauty, and so crowded with historical associations.

Having thus presented a continuous narrative of Mr. Brown's successive visits to Europe, as a sort of distinct chapter in his experience, we now go back a few years, and resume our sketch of his domestic and business life at home.

As Mr. Brown's partnership with Mr. Little was the crown and consummation of his business career, so the building of his house, and the establishment of his family, at Watertown, in 1840, was an event of similar moment in his domestic and private life. The feeling of attachment which gathers round the spot in which we dwell, depends much upon the fact whether we look upon it as a permanent, or only a temporary, home. A man will often live long in a house, his children will grow up around him in it, and yet his affections will never take deep root there, because he is looking forward to something better. His imagination, his hopes, his thoughts, are dwelling upon some point not yet reached. He says to himself that at some future period, when his means are greater or his occupations less, he will rear a house which shall be and have all that he desires—which shall realize his visions of a home, where he shall be content to rest. It often happens that the dream never comes to pass—that year after year slips by, and the final summons reaches him in the midst of fruitless wishes and hopes postponed. But it is not always so. The airy mansion is sometimes fixed upon the firm earth, and the husband and the father gathers his household round him in a home from which his feet shall wander no more on earth, and where he may permit his affections to strike into the soil, because he means that no hand but that of death shall uproot them.

And this assuredly was Mr. Brown's sentiment in regard to the spot in which he lived during the last fourteen years of his life. He had previously resided, as the head of a family, in four different houses; two in Cambridge, one in

West Cambridge, and one in Boston; but when he had settled himself in this home, he felt that he had made the last of his earthly removals; that here he had found his haven of rest, in which his anchor was dropped and his sail furled. The house itself is a wooden structure, of moderate size, in its exterior making no great architectural pretensions, and in its situation happily blending with the objects and scenery in its immediate vicinity. It stands in Watertown, near the line which divides it from West Cambridge, to the south of Wellington Hill, just where the lower spurs of this beautiful elevation subside, by gentle gradations, into the broad plain which clasps the waters of Fresh Pond with its belt of verdure. It faces nearly east. A lawn, of about an acre in extent, lies between it and the road. To the north—between Wellington Hill and the house, but only a few feet distant from the latter—is a thick grove of trees, mostly elms and maples—the natural growth of the soil. They overshadow, and with their thick-woven canopy of leaves, keep dark, amid the blaze of noon, a steep gorge, or chasm, at the bottom of which runs a clear stream, mingling its liquid voice with the whisper of the overhanging trees. The rocky bed, along which the waters trip and sing, has been artificially enlarged, and exotic trees have been planted among those of native growth; but the essential character of the spot has not been changed by the hand of improvement. The brook is near enough to the house to be heard in the pauses of speech during the stillness of a summer's day, but not near enough to be obtrusive in its claims. In the dust and drought of August, it mocks the ear with a delusive sound of rain; and at all times it falls upon the sense like an audible pulse of nature, ever in movement and yet ever the same.

This stream passes under the road which runs in front of the house, and reappears in a broader and gentler form upon the other side. Here it flows, in shape like a bended bow, through an ample meadow of the richest verdure, which, in its soft slopes and in the marks of finished cultivation which it presents, recalls some of the characteristic features of English scenery. To the left, the view is closed in by the hills of Medford; and directly in front, at the distance of about three miles, rises the rounded elevation upon which the flaring red brick of Tufts' College certainly sheds no grace. The white houses and spires of Medford, West Cambridge, and Somerville stand clearly shown in the bright and smokeless air; but Boston is hidden by the rising ground on the right. Directly in front, a broad, green plain is unrolled to the eye—a waveless sea of verdure—richly cultivated, and thickly sprinkled with fruit-bearing and ornamental trees.

The environs of Boston, beautiful as they are, can show few scenes more beautiful than the site of Mr. Brown's house. It stands in what may be called the border land between the region of agriculture and the region of horticulture, strictly speaking. On the one side, we see trim gardens, ornamented pleasure-grounds, smooth-shaven lawns, fair houses, and all the indications of that wealth which is drawn from the city and expended in the gratification of rural tastes; and on the other are plain farm-houses and farms, which have come down from father to son, orchards, pastures, and grain-fields—a district not yet whirled into the vortex of the metropolis, where land is still sold by the acre and not by the foot, and where old manners and primitive habits are yet found. Thus, the grace of nature and the grace of art are shed over the landscape. And it has the further advantage of being thickly wooded with trees, some of native growth and some planted by the hand of man. In early summer, when the grass is bright and fresh, and the foliage wears its hue of "glad, light-green,"—when the vault of heaven rings and overflows with the joyous notes of the bobolink and the liquid warble of the wood-thrush—when the breeze seems to caress the trees that bend to its touch, and the flying clouds dapple the broad plain with their shadows—the whole scene is stamped with rich and glowing beauty; not grand, not strictly picturesque, but made up of those soft and gentle elements that are equally fitted to refresh a wearied spirit and soothe a saddened heart.

When fairly settled in his new home, Mr. Brown began to indulge himself in the gratification of two tastes, which had previously been kept somewhat restrained by the circumstances of his life; and these were his love of land and his love of books. Born with a love of nature, and having a strong relish for agricultural pursuits, his purchases of land kept steady pace with the increase of his substance. One small farm after another was gradually added to his estate; until at his death he was the owner of about one hundred and forty acres* in the vicinity of his residence. This homestead farm, if it may be so called, stretched along the slopes and over the upland of Wellington Hill—so well known for the superb view which it commands. It comprised wood-land, arable land, and pasture-land. Some of it was what farmers call rough, and presented rather a discouraging aspect to an unprofessional eye; but much of it was fertile, and some of it was well situated for building-lots. Even the most unfavorable portions were of a kind to invite and reward the application of skill and capital.

In the cultivation of his land, Mr. Brown found a constant occupation and interest during the latter years of his life. If as a mere pecuniary investment, he might have employed his capital better, he could not have disposed of it in a way to yield larger returns of happiness and health. His agricultural occupations supplied him with regular and attractive employment during the hours he rescued from

* Besides these, he owned a parcel of land, of about eleven acres, on the banks of Fresh Pond, and several lots and houses in Cambridge.

business, so that no moment ever hung heavy upon his hands. He had gained some practical knowledge of farming in his boyhood, which he now revived; and he also made himself acquainted with the best methods which experience and observation had recorded in print. His farm was not one of those showy, model establishments, which require a fortune to carry it on; nor was it conducted exactly as it would have been done by a sharp New England farmer, who looked at nothing but the main chance. It was managed in a liberal spirit; more with reference to prospective benefit than present gain; but there was no extravagant expenditure, no whimsical outlay, no fantastic indulgence of unprofitable tastes.

Among other things, he took pains to provide himself with specimens of the best cattle that could be procured, both of foreign and domestic breed; and in these he took great delight. His kindly nature led him to become attached to every living thing that was put under his charge, and his four-footed dependents shared in this feeling. His Alderneys and Durhams were objects of constant and growing interest to him. Their arrival was impatiently waited and eagerly welcomed; he made them almost daily visits, to examine their condition and watch their progress; he took pleasure in showing them to his friends, and in helping ignorant eyes to discern their peculiar points of excellence. The expression of his countenance, as he looked upon them, seemed to be asking them if they were contented in their new home, and if he could do any more than he had already done to make them comfortable.

The last few years of Mr. Brown's life do not present much for his biographer to record. His visits to Europe, and occasional journeys to other parts of our own country, were the only interruptions to the uniform channel in which his days glided by. Happy, it has been said, is the nation whose history is dull; happy, it may be added, is the man whose life is uneventful. Certainly the lot of humanity can hardly permit one to be more happy than was Mr. Brown during the last ten years of his sojourn upon earth. His business was, of course, his primal and paramount interest; it was the mainspring of his mind, calling forth all its energies, and allowing no faculty to gather rust by inaction. But while his business occupied, it never absorbed or exhausted him; it never left him in such a state of prostration as to require the sting of some sharp excitement to rouse his languid spirit. He did not bring back to his home a brain so worn out by long-continued toil as to be incapable of any thing but absolute repose. His days were wisely divided and happily ordered. He paid to duty its just tribute, but from the hours of every day something was reserved for the domestic affections, something for the claims of health, something for the cultivation of the mind, something for the gratification of pure and elevating tastes. His life turned upon two poles; one was his place of business, and the other was his home, his library, and his farm —and it turned harmoniously, because it was proportionably distributed between the two. And this double interest contributed to the health of both body and mind. The management of his farm, the overseeing of his laborers, the interest he took in his cattle and the growth of his crops, gave him an object for long walks and drives, and prevented his falling into those habits of bodily inaction which are so apt to creep over men in our country after middle life. And the hours not devoted to out-of-door employments were happily filled up by his books and the society of his family and friends. Thus, without hurry, without feverish excitement—and equally without apathy and inaction—his life glided by, passing from resort to retirement, as the stream steals from sunshine to shade. His business was securely prosperous, an affectionate family was growing up around him, he was rich in friends, his influence in the community was increasing, his past was without reproach, and no cloud seemed to rest upon his future.

Mr. Brown was—as the apostle would have a bishop to be—"a lover of hospitality and a lover of good men." His sympathies were generous and comprehensive, but by no means without discrimination and preference. He valued men for their personal qualities, and not for their accidental advantages; and his simple self-respect inspired a natural independence of spirit, which had nothing to assume and nothing to suppress. He had many friends among the favored classes—among those who had drawn prizes in the lottery of life—who were in the enjoyment of wealth, intellectual superiority, social distinction, widespread influence—but these friendships did not in the least cool his heart toward those who had none of these things to commend them, but who had earned his confidence and won his affection by their personal worth, their substantial services, or their attachment to him. He was of a truly catholic spirit; and though holding decided opinions upon the controverted points of the day, he did not limit his regards to those who thought as he did, or insist that his friends should be also his partisans. Under his benignant and reconciling influence, men of discordant views met together and learned from his example lessons of charity and tolerance. His guests will ever recall with melancholy pleasure the hours they spent under his roof. His smile of welcome, his outstretched hand of greeting, will live forever in their memories. Had an artist sought an embodied type of the spirit of hospitality, he might have found it in him, as he stood at his door to receive a friend that he loved. When presiding over his generous but never ostentatious board, his cordial manner and beaming countenance diffused around him an atmosphere of happiness which "outdid the meats, outdid the frolic wine." The sunshine of his spirit thawed all the icy chains of coldness and reserve; and nowhere did men appear to better advantage—nowhere did they bring forth more of their intellectual resources—than at the table of a man who used no other art of drawing out than the magic of a warm heart and a genial nature.

Mr. Brown's love of books was a native taste, like his love of nature and of rural pursuits; and as soon as his means permitted, he began to indulge himself in the purchase of them. This was especially the case after he had removed to Watertown, and felt himself settled for life. So long as a man is a wanderer upon the earth, he will hardly buy books on a large scale; for a lover of books does not like to have them exposed to the mischances of conveyance from one place to another. Scholars are often discontented with the smallness of their libraries; but they will find much comfort therein when they wish to move them. Mr. Brown's business relations gave him peculiar facilities in the selection of his library; and from his large purchases for the public he generally reserved some choice specimens for his own collection. Year by year, this collection increased, and at his death it numbered about twenty-five hundred volumes. This statement of its amount, however, gives a very imperfect notion of its value; for it had been slowly gathered together with great judgment and taste, and it comprised many costly and many rare works. It was confined, with few exceptions, to the English language; and it may be described, in one word, by saying that it contained the best editions of the best books. All the great lights of English literature were here, as well as the best products of our own; and in a form and garb worthy of their claims. Mr. Brown was a little touched with that disease of bibliomania of which Dr. Dibdin writes in a vein of such pleasant exaggeration. He liked tall copies, fine impressions, ample margins; and was nice and fastidious in binding. Mingled with those works, the value of which is as universally recognized as that of gold and silver, were many chosen for their rarity; which the common reader would pass by without heeding, but which would make the eyes of a bibliomaniac to sparkle with joy, and his hands to tremble with eager longing.

The library contained some very valuable works in Natural History, especially Ornithology, always a favorite pursuit with Mr. Brown. Among these were Cuvier's Histoire Naturelle, Hardwicke's Indian Zoology, Lambert's "Genus Pinus," Poitéau's Pomologie Française, Gray's Genera of Birds, and the magnificent publications of Gould on Ornithology, in sixteen folio volumes. These were all devised by him to the Boston Society of Natural History. There were also fine copies of Wilson, and of the quarto Audubon; a complete set of Dr. Dibdin's works, and of the bibliographical productions of Sir Egerton Brydges; a copy of Neale's Views of English Seats; a fine set of the Publications of the Percy Society; Scott's editions of Dryden and Swift; the works of Ritson; Watt's Bibliotheca Britannica; Lodge's Portraits; and Renouard's Works on the early printers, Aldus and Stephanus.

Mr. Brown was a warm admirer of the genius of Burns, and read with the liveliest interest every thing connected with his life and fortunes. He made it a point to visit every spot that was in any way associated with his name, and we have seen with what animated pleasure he records his meeting with the poet's sons. His collection of the editions of Burns's poems, and of works illustrating his life and genius, could not, to say the least, be paralleled by any other single library in this country. He had every edition, of any note and value, which had appeared in England or Scotland; including that of Kilmarnock, in 1786, in which this splendid luminary of song first broke upon the admiring gaze of his countrymen, and that of Edinburgh, in 1787.

He had the copy of Currie's first edition, which had belonged to Clarinda (Mrs. McLehose), with whom the poet, under the name of Sylvander, carried on a correspondence, in a style of extravagant, falsetto sentiment, hardly worthy of the honors of publication, which it has recently attained. Another copy of Currie in his possession is profusely illustrated with autographs, views of places, and portraits of persons mentioned in Burns's letters and poems—making a work of great interest to every admirer of the poet's genius, the materials of which must have been collected with a patient assiduity, which nothing but hearty admiration could have inspired.

Mr. Brown's library was not an assemblage of books ranged in handsome cases to please the eye,—to be looked at merely and not handled,—but it was for daily use. To his singularly truthful nature it would have seemed a little disingenuous to buy books which he never meant to read; and it is not too much to say, that there was not a volume in his library with the contents of which he was not more or less acquainted. His day was not so wholly given to his business, his farm, his family, and his friends, as not to leave some time for reading; and his residence in the country, while it cut him off from some social privileges and from some attractive forms of amusement, left him long, unbroken hours, especially in the winter season, for this occupation, such as the hurry of a city life rarely affords.

Such was Mr. Brown's life at the age of fifty-four; such were his sources of usefulness and of happiness. The bounty of Providence had been showered upon him with a most liberal hand; and it was acknowledged with a proportionably grateful spirit. Possessed of an ample fortune, rich in friends, happy in his domestic relations, occupied but not absorbed by his business, enjoying a daily increasing confidence and respect—he had won, with no exhausting struggle, all the best prizes of life. And he had known enough of privation and sacrifice to enjoy with keen yet temperate relish the blessings of his lot. The flavor of prosperity was heightened by the remembrance of difficulties subdued and obstacles overcome. The delight he took in aiding others was enhanced by his recollection of a period when he was in a condition to receive but not to bestow favors. He had the happiness, in the closing years of his life, to see his two eldest sons established in business, and settled in homes of their own; and the birth of a grandchild, while it served to remind him of the lapse of time, by the beginning of a new generation, touched his heart with the sense of that new relation, which seems to have the sweetness and tenderness of the parental tie, without its anxiety and responsibility.

And to his friends—even those who knew him most intimately and saw him most frequently—there seemed to be no reason why this happy, useful, and generous life should not be prolonged to a good old age. No preparatory stroke of warning was sounded, to give them note of the coming separation. His frame and face betokened more than ordinary constitutional vigor, and were those of a man in whom the tide of life had not begun to turn. The casual stranger would have seen in him the promise of that full measure of threescore and ten years which is allotted to man. But it was not so ordained; and he was called from an earthly to a heavenly home, in the prime of life, and in the fullness of his powers—taken away from plans unripened, and unblown hopes.

Some three or four years before his death, he had suffered from an attack of diabetes; a disease which so affects the constitution, that the subject of it is constantly exposed to fatal effects from causes which but slightly disturb the system when in health. This illness was not known to his most intimate friends, or even to all the members of his family; but he took medical advice upon his case, both here and in Europe, and the remedies prescribed for him gave him material relief, but, as it appeared, did not effect an entire cure.

About a year before his death, on a slippery day, he fell at the railroad station, and slid down several steps, sustaining some heavy bruises. This accident brought on a recurrence of his former illness, and he was detained at home a few days; but he did not think it of sufficient importance to take medical advice.

In January, 1855, a large carbuncle broke out upon him, just below the shoulder-blade, which much reduced his strength, and was very slow in healing; and the physician* who attended him found his former disease unabated. He was kept at home several weeks by this illness, and compelled to postpone the journey to Washington which he was accustomed to take in the winter season. But in time he recovered; his strength and flesh returned; he seemed to have gained his usual health; and he felt himself well enough to go to Washington, where he was called by a matter of business.

Upon his return home, he was attacked by a sharp recurrence of his old disease. Dr. Hodgdon was called to him on Saturday, March 3, and found him in much suffering. The fatigue of his journey had probably irritated those parts of the system which had been injured by the fall of the previous year, and much inflammation was the result.

Leeches were applied, and other means tried, but they gave only temporary relief. Tuesday night and Wednesday were periods of great suffering. On Thursday, he was not in great pain, but his strength was fast declining. On Friday, his brain began to be affected by his disease; and during that night he was in a state of high fever, and slightly delirious. On Saturday, he became insensible,

* Dr. Hodgdon, of West Cambridge.

sank rapidly through the day, and breathed his last at about five in the evening.

His illness had been so short, that the news of his death fell with startling surprise upon the community; and the expressions which it called forth were marked with the sense of an unexpected, as well as a great loss. His funeral took place on Tuesday, March 13, and the number and character of those who were present bore touching testimony to the wide circle of affection, esteem, and confidence which had gathered round his life.

The foregoing brief sketch comprises a delineation of Mr. Brown's leading traits of character, and of those mental and moral qualities to which his success in life was due, and by which he laid up such treasures in the hearts of his friends. An obituary notice, written by the author of this biography, appeared in the Boston Daily Advertiser of March 20, 1855. It was prepared under the fresh sense of a great personal loss, and bears obvious marks of the feeling from which it flowed; but the author, looking at it after an interval of more than a year, sees in it no extravagance or overstatement, but only a just tribute to a strong, pure, noble, and affectionate nature. It is here reproduced in its original form. The writer's eyes grow dim at the pictures and memories which it recalls; but mingled with the sense of an ever-present loss is a feeling of gratitude that he has been permitted to lay an offering upon the grave of his friend which may help to keep his memory green in the hearts of those who knew him, and justify their love to those who knew him not.

When a man like the late Mr. James Brown dies, it is due to the esteem and affection with which he was regarded by his friends, that his eminent worth should be set forth with somewhat more of fullness and distinctness than belongs to most men whose lives were so private as his. Few men not clothed with official trusts—not set in conspicuous stations—whose way of life was so far removed from the glare of public applause—could have left, by their death, a wider chasm in our community, or will be more lovingly remembered or more tenderly mourned. And the love and honor which he enjoyed while living, and which have followed him to his grave and beyond his grave, were fairly earned by a rare combination of fine and high qualities.

At the close of a man's life, we naturally and instinctively first consider the place which he held in the profession, or employment, to which the strength of his days was given. He who fails in the calling of his choice must needs decline in our regards, unless such failure be made up by the display of uncommon virtues or capacities outside of it. Mr. Brown was a publisher and bookseller, and, as such, eminently successful. The position which he held in his profession at the time of his death, and the wide influence he exerted, would alone have made him a marked man. His whole career was honorable to him, and encouraging to those who start as he did. He was born in Acton, about the beginning of the present century, of a virtuous but poor household; and his childhood was passed under influences favorable to the growth of the character, but not to the cultivation of the mind. His book education was not beyond that which is the common heritage of every New England boy, but he was well trained in the school of circumstances. He began life with a vigorous constitution, a resolute will, a cheerful spirit, and an affectionate heart. His time, up to the dawn of manhood, was passed in modest toils, which earned for him no more than a decent subsistence. And here it may be remarked, that, to his intimate friends, the feeling with which Mr. Brown looked back upon these days of struggle and privation, formed an interesting trait in his character. He recalled them with a modest pride, mixed with a certain grateful tenderness. He never attempted to conceal any event in his life, and yet he was free from the subtle vanity which delights to make proclamation of difficulties subdued and disadvantages overcome. His boyhood was a happy period, after all; especially, linked as it was by ties of such "natural piety" to the prosperity of his maturer years.

While yet quite young, and residing in Cambridge, he was invited by the late Mr. William Hilliard to enter his service, as salesman and assistant generally. He once expressed to the writer of this notice his surprise and pleasure at this proposition, made to him at an accidental meeting in the street, and remarked upon his utter ignorance of the duties he was called upon to discharge. But he bent his powers to the task committed to him, and soon learned his work; and from this point his progress in business was rapid and uniform. He soon began to be known as a man diligent in his calling, and sagacious and successful in his enterprises; and a continually widening sphere of action was opened to him. He early took his place as a man of influence and consideration in the trade, so called, inviting and rewarding the largest confidence. For many years past, he has been a member of the widely-known bookselling and publishing firm of Little, Brown & Company; and it is doing no injustice to any living man to say, that much of the position held and power wielded by this eminent house was due to his personal qualities. And as a man of business merely, his endowments and accomplishments were of a high order. He was sagacious, liberal, penetrating, and wise; he saw far, and he saw truly; he was always prompt, and never in a hurry; his speculations and enterprises were always well-timed and resolutely pursued. His knowledge of men was instinctive, and he rarely or never made a mistake in his estimate of them. He perfectly understood his own interests, and stoutly maintained them, and no man could either overreach or overbear him. And then he was probity itself. He abhorred any thing mean, or shuffling, or equivocating. What he said, he stood by; and everybody who knew any thing about him knew this, so that no word of his ever fell to the ground. The foundations of his nature were laid in frankness and simplicity, and these flowed out into his business. The stranger, who saw his open, cordial countenance for the first time, felt that he was in the presence of an honest man, and that the air of truth breathed from him. An Arab in the desert would have trusted such a face with uncounted diamonds.

His great success in business was mainly owing to his instinctive and unerring judgment. Few men who have published so many books have made so few mistakes. He understood the literary wants of the country, and was ready with the right work at the right time. And it was the same in the choice of the extensive stock which he kept on hand for sale. He had a considerable amount of bibliographical knowledge, which was turned to good practical account in this way. He has more than once returned from Europe with a very large collection, over which a desponding man might well shake his head; but the books never cumbered his shelves long. He would walk through the salesrooms of London or Paris, and tell at a glance what would suit the literary meridian of home. All book-buyers and book-collectors in this neighborhood—and to our honor be it said they are numerous—will find his loss irreparable. He never forgot or neglected a commission, however trifling; and if a rare or curious work were wanted, he would be sure to find it if it were anywhere to be found.

His taste was as good as his judgment was sound. He was just enough touched with the bibliomania of which Dr. Dibdin so pleasantly writes, to make book-buying and book-collecting a labor of love. He had a quick eye for tall copies, fine bindings, wide margins, and fair type; and this good taste stamped itself upon his business. He had a just pride in the external aspect of the books which he published; and the great improvement which has taken place within the last twenty years in New England, in the style and appearance of books, is due to him more than to any other man.

The house to which he belonged, as is well known, has been for many years largely engaged in the publication and sale of law-books; a branch of their business to the success of which Mr. Brown essentially contributed. He had the same sagacious comprehension of what was wanted in this department as in that of miscellaneous literature. He saw that in this class of books, as in others, the true rule of success was moderate profits upon large sales; and thus, while his law-books were gotten up in better style than the profession had been accustomed to, while his scale of remuneration to authors and editors was more liberal than had been before known, his prices were lower, a far wider range of sale was secured, and the highest anticipations of success were met.

The whole community was a gainer, directly and indirectly, by the enterprising and liberal spirit in which Mr. Brown conducted his business, by the energies which he wielded, and the direction in which they were moved. He made good books more abundant and more accessible, and thus created and diffused a taste for them, which is in itself a substantial service to the public. He also helped to elevate the growing profession of authorship; not only by his generous way of dealing with writers, but by his courteous and considerate bearing toward them personally. He was not only just and prompt, but liberal and friendly. He never wounded the feelings of the most sensitive among them by even a thoughtless word.

He made more than one visit to Europe in the way of

his business; and there left the most favorable impression upon all who met him. His credit there, in the technical sense of the term, was unlimited; and he secured the confidence and esteem of many persons, whose regard is not lightly won. He was an honorable representative of the country, and any American abroad might have pointed to him with pride as a specimen of what might be done and gained among us by a man's unaided energies. Into whatever society he was thrown, he maintained the same simple self-respect, and the same modest manliness of manner which marked him at home. His bearing was ever that of a true man and a well-bred gentleman; never claiming more than was due to him, never yielding any thing of what was due to him.

All that has thus far been said of Mr. Brown might be true, without his having been so loved, and without his being so mourned. It is no very rare thing for a poor boy in our country to become a prosperous man, to accumulate a large property, and to have a commanding influence in the business world. He might have been a sagacious, a respectable, an estimable man, even a just and a true man, and yet not a lovable man. The liberal scale on which he did business might have been the result of a far-seeing thrift. Even his courteous manner might have been the easy growth of a smooth temperament, the cold and politic varnish of an essentially selfish nature. Men who have fought their way from poverty to wealth, from obscurity to distinction, are apt to retain some marks and scars of the conflict. They are apt to be hard, narrow, restless, and grasping, even if not sordid and unscrupulous. But Mr. Brown's title to the hearts of his friends was founded upon those qualities which lay outside of his calling, and had no other relation to his prosperity than that this enabled him to display them on a larger scale and in a more conspicuous sphere. He was a remarkable instance of a man who had achieved great success without paying the price at which it is usually bought. It seemed hardly possible that one so energetic and strong-minded should have so much sweetness, gentleness, and affectionateness; but it was so. They were as salient and conspicuous traits as were his sagacity, his judgment, his enterprise, and his perseverance. Their charm was the greater, from their contrast with his resolute will and vigorous understanding. Few men had more feminine tenderness and softness than he. These qualities could be heard in the quick changes of his voice, and seen in the ready suffusion of his eye, and in the lights of expression which passed over his countenance, and gave to his features all the beauty of a beautiful soul. His warm affections and cordial sympathies were not clouded by reserve or chilled by self-distrust, but they were ever prompt to reveal themselves. They were deep, and at the same time easily moved. He greeted his familiar friends as if, since their last meeting, he had found some new cause to love them. It is hardly necessary to say that the life of such a man, blessed as he was with ample means, was marked by a constant succession of kind acts. His bounty flowed out in all directions, upon every form of desert that came under his observation. He delighted to give, and his benefactions had all the charm and grace of spontaneous impulse. His charities were as natural to him as blossoms to the tree in spring, or fruits in autumn. And his kindness was as thoughtful and considerate as it was hearty.

There was nothing neutral or indifferent in Mr. Brown's feelings or affections. As he had warm sympathies, so he had strong dislikes and antipathies. But these were founded on solid and substantial grounds, and were not the growth of fastidious caprice. And as they were justified to his conscience and his reason, they were always as frankly expressed as were his preferences and his affinities. He had a vehement and intolerant scorn of insincerity, meanness, and treachery; and the strongest expressions that his gentle nature ever indulged in were called forth by manifestations of these qualities. But even here the kindness of his heart interposed; for he contented himself with an energetic word or two, and passed on to more genial subjects. He never dwelt long in the region of dislike and distaste; and when he could not speak well of a man, he ceased to speak of him at all.

A mind, a character, a heart like Mr. Brown's were surely formed to win large measures of respect, esteem, and love. But there was yet another charm in his nature, flowing from the purity and refinement of his tastes. He was a living refutation of the notion, that there is any thing necessarily coarsening or narrowing in a life devoted to trade. Here was a man born in poverty, reared in privation, the architect of his own fortunes, cut off from opportunities of intellectual cultivation in the forming period of life, displaying, the moment he had the means of indulging them, such tastes as would seem to be the fine growth of the choicest elements and the happiest influences. Pope said of Wycherly that he had the nobleman look; it might have been said of Mr. Brown, that he had the nobleman spirit. No man had a better sense of the true value of wealth, or ever contrived to extract from it a greater amount of happiness. He fixed his home in a region of varied and picturesque beauty; he gradually acquired a large and valuable farm, which he stocked with the choicest cattle, and cultivated after the most approved methods of husbandry; he adorned and improved his grounds, and called forth all their capacities of embellishment; and here, in the society of his family, his friends, his books, and in rural employments, he found the purest and most elevating pleasures. And the time which he spent here was no meager fragment, grudgingly torn from the desk and the counter, but a liberal measure—enough for refreshment, enough for repose, enough to permit the peace and loveliness of nature to fall upon his spirit with soothing and elevating power. He knew his fields, his cattle, his trees; he watched the growth of every growing thing upon his farm; he was the friend and companion, as well as the father, of his children.

His modest nature would have disclaimed the praise of scholarship, and yet he had the tastes and the spirit of a scholar. He was fond of books, and had collected a library very valuable for its extent, containing many rare and curious books, chosen with judgment and discrimination. These were not kept merely to look at, or to show to his educated friends, but they were read, comprehended, and enjoyed. He took especial pleasure in the poetry of Burns, and had gathered a large amount of materials illustrative of the life and genius of that splendid meteor of song. He had a considerable knowledge of natural history, especially ornithology; and his library contained a complete collection of books on this subject.

He had also a poet's love and a poet's comprehension of nature. Every "dingle and dell and bosky bourne" of the wooded and hilly region in which he lived, was familiar to him, under all the aspects of the changing year; in the light, glad green of early spring, in the rich ripeness of summer, in the gold and purple of autumn, and in the winding-sheet of wintry snow. His powers of observation were acute and practiced. He knew the names and properties of every tree and shrub and flower that grew in his fields. He had no trained ear for music, but he would stand and listen in rapt attention, and with suffused eyes, to the full-throated and deep-hearted song of the brown thrush, in the early summer. A fine maple, in its autumn red—an apple-tree, with its shower of vernal blossoms—would arrest his steps and call forth expressions of admiration. There was not a latent charm in the broad landscape that spread around his house—there was not a fleeting grace thrown over it by the sunshine, the cloud-shadows, the rippling breezes, the showers of summer—which he had not noted and enjoyed.

No one could be said to know Mr. Brown who had not seen him in his own house. No spot on earth deserved the sacred name of home more than this. Here the sun of hospitality never set. He received his friends as if he were an idler in the land, grateful to any one who would help him to speed the sluggish hours. No shadow of business ever sat upon his brow; but his face glowed with the light of welcome. His greeting—the clasp of his hand—were as cordial as the breezes that blew over his hills. To see him presiding over his hospitable but never ostentatious board, was warming and refreshing to the heart. Under the genial influence of his affectionate and sympathetic presence, the most various natures were brought into unison, and yielded their best tones to swell the general harmony of feeling. Nor had he one set of company manners, and another set for home consumption. Toward the members of his own household, his bearing was indulgent, affectionate, and tender. It may be doubted whether his children ever saw a frown upon his brow. No heavier yoke was ever laid upon them than the silken cord of love. To all who stood to him in the relation of service or dependence, he was kindly, considerate, and abounding in good offices. His bounty to the poor was constant, ample, but always secretly bestowed.

It is not to be wondered at that a man such as has been described, should have been very rich in friends. He had a right to be proud of his friendships; and his children have a right to be proud of them, now that he is gone, for they start in life with a large inheritance of transmitted interest. Few men not liberally educated, in the technical sense of the word—not belonging to either of the learned professions — not engaged in intellectual pursuits — have ever had so many friends among the cultivated and educated classes. His list of friends embraced statesmen, scholars, men of science, men of letters—names widely and favorably known—who yielded to him an unconstrained and unbought tribute of regard and affection. They valued him for what he was, not for what he had. They would have been as much repelled by any thing like obsequiousness as by ignorance or coarseness. His relations to them were founded upon a fair interchange of equivalents. No man ever patronized him; no man ever put on an attitude of condescension toward him; his dignity of character and the manly self-respect of his bearing forbade this.

And there was another and an unconscious tribute to Mr. Brown's worth, which should not be forgotten in summing up his merits. His life had been eminently successful; he had acquired a large measure of those things for which most men struggle, and many unavailingly; he had accumulated an ample fortune; he held a commanding influence in the world of business, and enjoyed a high social position—and yet no man grudged him all this. Everybody contemplated his prosperity with satisfaction; and the reason was, that his increase of substance not only did not remove him further from his fellow-men, but brought him into nearer and more intimate relations with them. The more means he had, the more happiness he diffused. His grateful heart repaid the sunshine and the dew of prosperity with a softer green of sympathy and a quicker growth of affection. Before good fortune so gently worn, envy dropt its envenomed arrows, and forgot to feed upon its own heart.

And now this rich, vigorous, and happy life has been brought to a close. In the midst of unripened schemes and unfinished plans—of enterprises that ran far ahead, and projects of wider sweep and broader range, when, in the course of nature, many active years seemed yet in store for him—he has been called away from earth. But the spirit which animated his whole life forbids his friends to mingle any bitterness in the grief which his death has called forth. He was a man of deep and sincere religious feeling, and his heart was penetrated with gratitude to God that he had been permitted to accomplish and enjoy so much. He was well aware of the insidious nature of the disease to which his frame finally yielded, and had long contemplated with a steady gaze the prospect of his departure. He was as resigned to the future as he was grateful for the past. His cup had been early made to run over with blessings, and he felt that he had no right to murmur if it were taken from his lips before the full measure of days had been allotted to him. With gentle submission, he obeyed the summons that called him from an earthly to a heavenly home; and we, on whom the shadow of his departure rests, should mourn him tenderly and serenely, mingling with our grief a sense of gratitude for a life so rounded and finished, so rich in action, so crowned with happiness.

PROCEEDINGS AT THE TRADE SALE IN NEW YORK.

At the Trade Sale Rooms of Messrs. Bangs, Brothers & Co., of New York, which were filled with booksellers from all parts of the country, the death of Mr. James Brown, their late colaborer, was announced this (Thursday) afternoon, the fifteenth day of March, 1855, whereupon the sale was adjourned, and a meeting organized for the expression of sympathy with the family of the deceased, and with his late partners in business, the following gentlemen being appointed officers:

Mr. James Harper, of New York, President; Messrs. W. A. Blanchard, H. Cowperthwait, of Philadelphia, C. S.

Francis, of New York, Vice-presidents; J. S. Redfield, of New York, Secretary.

The Chairman, on taking his seat, announced the object of the meeting in a few appropriate remarks, after which Mr. George P. Putnam offered the following resolutions:

"*Whereas*, It has pleased the Almighty Disposer of events to remove from among us, by death, our highly esteemed friend and fellow-laborer, Mr. James Brown, publisher and bookseller of Boston, and

"*Whereas*, In the distinguished position so long and so honorably filled by our departed friend, he has won for himself our hearty admiration and respect as the worthy leader of the trade, pre-eminent alike for intelligent enterprise and judgment, extensive knowledge of books, uncompromising integrity, and uniform courtesy and kindness of heart; therefore,

"*Resolved*, That the booksellers and publishers from various parts of the United States, here assembled, have heard, with deep and sincere regret, the intelligence of the death of Mr. Brown.

"*Resolved*, That we respectfully tender to the family of our late respected associate our earnest sympathy in their affliction.

"*Resolved*, That we also sympathize sincerely with the surviving partners of the deceased in the great loss they have sustained—a loss which will be felt by our whole fraternity."

Mr. James T. Fields, of Boston, moved the adoption of the resolutions with the following remarks:

"It is difficult, Mr. Chairman, to speak of our buried friend during the first sharp agony of grief, and while his loss is so recent and startling. His cheerful smile, his cordial greeting, his ever ready sympathy—those 'small, sweet courtesies in which there is no parade'—were so lately present to us, that our lips almost refuse to utter how much we feel in this sad bereavement. Our deceased brother was a genuine, hearty friend. We all rejoiced in his prosperity, for it seemed natural and right that he should be happy and successful. His excellent qualities we all recognized. He was a man of large culture, modest in his pretensions, but always competent in whatever affairs engaged his attention and his energy. He was a merchant in the fullest and best sense of that term; his sterling sense and wide comprehension of business matters claiming for him something more than the qualities of a mere buyer and seller. Abroad, as well as at home, he was extensively known and respected; nay, more, he was always, wherever he was known, beloved. His charity was liberal, never ostentatious. Doing good by stealth seemed his vocation. While the sun of prosperity warmed his own mansion, he never forgot those humble dwellings where poverty and want and hunger are constant visitors. His tastes were remarkably simple; and he delighted to walk under the open sky, abroad in the summer fields and woods, gathering health and instruction in the free air. No one came beneath his hospitable roof, as many here can testify, without a sensation of unalloyed pleasure in his hearty welcome.

"In that quiet home, at the close of the last week, at the ending of the day, he died. Tranquil, and without conscious suffering, he gently yielded up his spirit to the God who gave it. Those who loved him best were about his bedside,—his wife, his children, a few intimate friends.

'They watch'd his breathing through the day,
His breathing soft and low,
As in his breast the wave of life
Kept heaving to and fro.
Their very hopes belied their fears,
Their fears their hopes belied;
They thought him dying while he slept,
And sleeping when he died.'

"So calmly passed our brother to his rest. We shall never see his form again on earth; but we shall not cease to cherish his memory with an affectionate and endearing interest. He has gone to his reward. Let us think of him with a cheerful reliance on the goodness of God, and let us be ready to meet that messenger which sooner or later comes not unbidden to every human being."

On motion of Mr. Lemuel Bangs, it was resolved that copies of the proceedings of this meeting be sent to the family and partners of the deceased, and that they be published.

PROCEEDINGS OF THE BOOKSELLERS OF BOSTON.

A MEETING of the Book Trade of Boston was called on Monday afternoon, March 12, at four o'clock, in the room over Messrs. Ticknor & Fields's store, to consider what action should be had in relation to the death of the late James Brown, Esq., of the firm of Little, Brown & Company. The meeting was largely attended, nearly every firm in the city being represented.

William D. Ticknor, Esq., was called to the chair, and Charles Sampson, Esq., was appointed Secretary.

It was voted, that a committee of five be appointed to retire and draw up resolutions expressive of the sense of the meeting.

The following gentlemen were appointed:

Messrs. Osmyn Brewster, Charles J. Hendee, E. P. Tileston, William D. Swan, and William J. Reynolds.

The Committee reported the following:

"*Whereas*, we have learned, with deep and sincere regret, of the sudden death of our friend and colaborer, Mr. James Brown, therefore

"*Resolved*, That we cherish in our memories his noble qualities as a man; his reliable and steadfast integrity; his firm and conscientious purpose; his devoted and affectionate friendship; and his unbounded liberality of heart and hand; and that in his death we have sustained the loss of one of the brightest ornaments of our profession.

"*Resolved*, That we sympathize with the afflicted family of our departed friend, and earnestly commend them to the care and blessing of Him who is the Father of the fatherless and the widow's God.

"*Resolved*, That in token of our respect for the deceased we will attend his funeral, and that we will close our places of business dnring the services, and the remainder of the day."

The resolutions were unanimously adopted.

Appropriate remarks were made by Messrs. Ticknor, Marvin, Jenks, Dennett, Crocker, and others, and the meeting dissolved.

JOHN HANCOCK.

If there is a name upon the page of American history, which should be cherished by our merchants with a warmer love and a deeper veneration than any other, it is that of John Hancock. His memory should be their pride, for he was one of them; and among the many distinguished men of his time, the annals of our country boast of none more noble or patriotic. It will be our aim in this notice to give, in a condensed form, a few of the most striking periods of his life, that his disinterested character may serve as a model for imitation.

John Hancock was born in 1737, at Quincy, near Boston, in the then province of Massachusetts Bay. His father was a clergyman—learned, eloquent, and influential—beloved by all who knew him, and admired and reverenced for his noble liberality in patronizing and sustaining the literary institutions of his native land. He died during the infancy of his son, who was then placed under the care and protection of his paternal uncle; an individual who, from an humble condition of fortune, became the most eminent merchant in New England, and was for many years a member of the provincial council. He bestowed the utmost attention upon the education of his nephew, who was graduated at Harvard College, in 1754, and immediately entered the counting-house of his uncle. There he remained until 1760, when he visited England; and soon after his return his kinsman and patron died, leaving him, at the age of twenty-seven, with a larger fortune than was possessed by any other individual in the province. The appearance of Mr. Hancock was extremely prepossessing. His person was handsome, his countenance expressive and highly intellectual, and his manners were naturally graceful. His mind had been richly cultivated, and was endowed with sentiments of a lofty and refined character. He was passionately fond of society, and intimately versed in the elegant accomplishments of his time. Possessed of so many natural advantages, combined with superior acquirements, and a generous liberality where pecuniary interests were concerned, he soon became exceedingly popular; and when to all his other qualities we add that of eloquence, which he possessed to an unusual degree, it is not surprising that in a community where the elements of society were still unsettled, and where popular talent was ever rewarded by popular favor, he should be early called upon to encounter the turbulent storms and tread the thorny path of a public life. Associating with men of education, station, and wealth, and removed by his large fortune far above the common wants of life, courted by the rich and powerful, and taught by the prevailing spirit of the age to regard the king as the great source of power and legitimate fountain of the people's rights, we should be led to expect from him more of loyalty to the former, than of patriotism to the latter. But his character and feelings were not of the ordinary mould. His was a noble nature, which amalgamated with and poured forth its sympathies with every grade of men. His love of liberty was enthusiastic and ardent, and he expressed it in language bold, convincing, and eloquent. That he soon became a favorite with the people, it is hardly necessary to state, and as a distinguished mark of their esteem and confidence, after having for some time occupied the municipal office of selectman of Boston, he was elected in 1766, with James Otis, Samuel Adams, and Thomas Cushing, a representative to the general assembly of the province. Here, side by side with Adams, he stood up the unwavering friend and champion of the people, battling monarchical power when its exercise clashed with popular rights, and fearlessly opposing official tyranny and executive usurpations. His readiness and power in debate, and the captivating influence of his manners, combined with an independence of action which even his enemies admired, soon placed him at the head of a most powerful and influential party.

The first act of importance which served to arouse the revolutionary spirit among the people, was the imposition of heavy duties upon the importation of foreign goods, and this tyrannical and oppressive measure was resisted by Hancock from its inception, and, aided by his influence and address, associations were formed for prohibiting the importation of British goods into the colony. The boldness and energy with which he opposed the will of the governor and his royal master, marked him for proscription; and when, a short time after his election, he was chosen speaker of the assembly, the governor's sanction was refused, and his seat bestowed upon another. In 1767 he was chosen to the executive council, where the same opposition and official rejection awaited him. In proportion as he became an object of royal hatred, the affection evinced toward him by the people continued to increase. By many he was almost idolized, and all reposed in him the most unlimited confidence. His weight and influence with the popular party soon rendered him formidable to the British crown, and his corruption to its interests was resolved upon by Lord North, then prime minister of England. This wily noble saw the powerful elements that were forming in the colonies against the usurpations of their mother-land, and resolved to hush them into silence by conciliating their most prominent author, and thus binding him to royalty.

The ambition of Hancock, his fondness of elegant society, his polished manners, and his luxurious style of living, all combined to render him, in the opinion of the minister, peculiarly susceptible to the influence of a bribe, when proffered in the seductive form of station and power; and as one golden link in the chain which was to bind him to the pillars of the throne, by the orders of Lord North his nomination to the executive council was approved by the royal governor. The marked disapprobation which had been so long evinced toward Hancock by the minions of royalty, being thus suddenly withdrawn, and replaced by smiles of patronage and proffered honor, fears were excited on the part of his friends that his patriotism would swerve from its purity, and the envious and base-hearted assailed his noble name by poisonous insinuations that his devotion to the interests of the colonists had been sacrificed to the acquirement of kingly favor. But speedily and triumphantly did he vindicate his reputation from the dark suspicion which these assassin-like aspersions had cast upon its brightness. He indignantly refused to take his seat in the council-chamber, and became still bolder in his denunciations against the measures of the British ministry. But that which forever placed him beyond the pale of royal pardon, was his connection with the popular demonstrations of indignation which immediately succeeded the "massacre of Boston," as it is called. The particulars of this massacre it is unnecessary to describe. They dwell in the memory of every American, who sees in them the germs of the Revolution, and the first of a series of blood-stained acts which at length drove our forefathers to arms. The next day after the enactment of this fearful drama, a large meeting of the citizens was held, and Hancock was appointed, with some others, to wait upon the governor and request him to withdraw the British troops from Boston. Although the latter dared not openly refuse to order their removal, yet he endeavored to shield himself under the plea that his authority was not sufficient. But this did not avail him. A second committee was immediately appointed, with Hancock as chairman, who again waited upon him, and fearlessly and peremptorily urged their immediate withdrawal from the town; and the governor, fearing some terrible outbreak of popular indignation if they remained, was compelled to order their departure. Hancock had still another duty to perform in connection with the mournful event we have mentioned. It was to deliver an oration in commemoration of the massacre. His style and manner upon this occasion were bold, dignified, and impressive. The murder of the unoffending citizens by the soldiery was pathetically described, and its barbarity severely execrated. The injudicious policy of the government of Great Britain toward her colonies was fearlessly exposed, and condemned in terms of the severest reprobation; and the character of the mercenary troops which had been so recently quartered in Boston was examined, and their cruelty and infamy commented upon in a manner that gave deep offense to the British officers, civil as well as military.

Denunciations against the colonial government so open and daring, as were expressed in this oration, were sure to bring down upon the head of their author the swift vengeance of the British authorities, but he feared it not. To him personal interests were slight, when compared with the good of a suffering people; and although well aware that his commercial affairs, then in the most flourishing condition, must suffer irreparable injury in the event of a collision between the haughty mother-land and her infant colonies, he preferred freedom and a ruined fortune to luxury and political slavery. The path he pursued was plain, open, and independent, unawed by the frowns of a British king, or the threats of his minions in power. The executive of the royal will found in Hancock a candid, yet powerful enemy; and the people saw in him a firm, unflinching, and patriotic friend. His large fortune was ever open to their necessities and wants, and his readiness to expend it in improving the civil, political, and moral condition of those around him, and in protecting them from the tyranny of their rulers, soon rendered him formidable as an opposer of the crown.

We need not relate the noble career of "Hancock and Adams," which continued unsullied until the battle of Lexington. The history of those times is well known throughout the country. When the British troops marched into the village of Lexington, Hancock and Adams were there secreted; and as the house which formed their asylum was entered in front by the soldiers, the hunted patriots escaped by the rear, and thus eluded the vigilance of their pursuers. From this time forth, we find them proscribed, tracked, outlawed, and rewards offered for their apprehension, until Hancock, the arch and dangerous rebel, as he was called, was at length appointed a delegate to the "Continental Congress;" and in 1776, that body conferred upon him its highest honor. He was unanimously chosen their president. Being younger than most of his associates when the appointment was announced, he experienced that diffidence and embarrassment which are ever the accompaniments of genius; and it was not until Benjamin Harrison, a strong-nerved, noble-hearted member from Virginia, had borne him in his stout arms to the chair, that his wonted self-possession returned; and the rare and almost unequaled dignity with which he had adorned other stations, became apparent.

When the Declaration of Independence first appeared, it was for some time circulated over the name of Hancock alone, as president of the Congress; and the bold and striking characters which form his signature, were the first to proclaim the fact. The station which he occupied, surrounded as it was by innumerable difficulties, and responsibilities of the most arduous character, could not have been more honorably filled by any among the noble band over whom he presided. Even the few who were opposed to him, bore the highest testimony to the courteous and dignified manner which marked his official career; and when, in October, 1777, having for two years and a half of the darkest period of our revolutionary struggle sustained himself in his high seat, he was compelled, from severe bodily infirmities, brought on by great mental exertions, to resign, he carried with him the esteem and respect of his colleagues, and was received by the citizens of his native colony with the warmest demonstrations of veneration and attachment, at times amounting almost to adoration.

The repose which he so much needed, appeared now within his reach; the enjoyment of the calm and quiet retirement, to secure which he had left the council-chamber of his country, seemed about to be realized; but in this he was disappointed. Soon after his arrival in Massachusetts, he was chosen a member of a convention appointed to frame a constitution for that State; and feeling a deep interest and earnest solicitude respecting the provisions of so important an instrument, he accepted the trust, and by his experience, love of liberty, and profound knowledge of the principles upon which a republic should be based, assisted greatly in the deliberations and labors of the convention.

In 1780, he was elected governor of Massachusetts, being the first appointed under the new constitution, which he had assisted to frame, and was annually re-elected to that office until 1785, when he resigned. In 1787, he was re-elected at a period when the spirit of fierce rebellion raged throughout New England, and when the safety of Massachusetts was threatened by a powerful faction composed of men dissatisfied with the government, many of whom demanded that all debts and taxes should be swept away, and that an equal distribution of property should be made, as a just and merited reward for the dangers and toils they had undergone during the war, and who were led on by dangerous and designing demagogues of broken fortunes and reputations. The measures which were adopted by him for the suppression of these riotous and dangerous proceedings were prompt, energetic, and efficacious. They were soon dispersed, and the ringleaders, fourteen in number, having surrendered, were tried for treason, and condemned to suffer death, but were pardoned by the merciful interposition of the governor.

When the creation of the federal constitution was agitated throughout the States, Hancock was appointed president of the convention which met in Massachusetts to deliberate upon its adoption. A majority of the members were believed to be opposed to it, and it was owing to his efforts in its favor, which sickness prevented him from making until the last week of the session, that his native State was led to adopt an instrument which his statesmanlike sagacity enabled him to perceive would bind together the States in the closest alliance, while it would increase, to a vast extent, their power and prosperity.

On the 8th of October, 1793, Hancock, still governor of Massachusetts, died, in the fifty-fifth year of his age. His death was felt and mourned as a great national loss, and his enemies forgot the faults they had once condemned, and united in praising the noble, virtuous, and disinterested merchant—the statesman and patriot—who had periled his fortune in defending his country against British tyranny.

To him, among others, we owe our independence, our liberty, our prosperity, and our national greatness, and the high rank we hold among the nations of the earth. We are indebted to him for the aid which, in our revolutionary struggle, was derived from the arms and influence of France; for it was his generosity that furnished the means, when our country was utterly destitute of money or credit, to fit out the Alliance frigate, to carry Colonel Laurens, our first accredited diplomatic agent to the court of the French king; through whose influence and exertions during the darkest period of our revolutionary history, the co-operation of France was secured and her assistance extended, to help us break the chains of that political slavery with which we were bound.

As the first signer of the Declaration of American Independence, his name will not be forgotten while the history of mankind preserves among its records one of the noblest deeds ever performed in the cause of liberty; but while this act alone will perpetuate his fame, his services in behalf of his oppressed country demand from us—to whom he has been so instrumental in transmitting a greater degree of religious, civil, and political liberty, than was ever enjoyed by any other nation on the globe—some rich and lasting monument to his memory.

We do not think it necessary to imitate the love of the ancients for their heroes, by building a temple and consecrating it to his memory; but we do believe that it is our duty to raise at least one stone in commemoration of him, who, in the name of freedom, was the first to protest against British aggression; who sacrificed his property, and risked his liberty and life, in defense of our infant rights; affixed his name to an instrument which was once the wonder, and has ever since been the admiration of the whole civilized world; and who, as president of the Continental Congress, signed the commission constituting the immortal Washington commander of the armies of the United States.

We have long been ungrateful to his memory, for though we may have cherished it fervently and reverently in our hearts, yet no public monument or statue has been carved to the honor of his name in our whole country. To the memory of many others we have erected monuments and sculptured statues, and their deeds are imperishably recorded upon the undying marble. At Savannah, a monument has been erected to the memory of the brave Pulaski;

and one to Montgomery, another to Hamilton, and another to Lawrence, in the city of New York. We find one to the memory of Spurzheim, a foreigner, at Mount Auburn, in Cambridge; and another at Charlestown, to Harvard, the founder of the university at Cambridge which bears his name; and another at Groton, near New London; and upon the consecrated battle-ground of Lexington. While a column rears its giant proportions and lofty height to the memory of Washington at Baltimore, a monument has also been erected at Boston, in the same burying-place where repose "unknowing and unknown" the remains of Hancock, to the PARENTS of Franklin.

It is strange that among all these, and many more that we could mention, not one exists to the memory of "John Hancock." His remains sleep unnoticed beneath the soil which he, with others, freed from a tyrant's grasp, and the land which now echoes with the glad shouts of millions of freemen, contains no offering to the departed spirit of him to whom it is indebted for a large portion of its unrivaled blessings. This neglect to his memory can not be palliated, far less justified. It can not be said we are too poor to do him reverence; for to perpetuate the memory of others, we have seen our country pour out its treasure with a lavish hand; and to say that his deeds and actions alone are sufficient to immortalize his name, and that no monument need tower above his tomb, would be but the excuse for meanness and national ingratitude. From the earliest period of demi-civilization, nations and communities have ever testified their approbation of the services of great men, by engraving the history of their noblest acts upon columns of brass or marble; and let not our republic be the first to disregard a custom not more honorable in the observance than beneficial to succeeding generations.

Statues of brass were erected in the name of the people to Æschylus, Sophocles, and Euripides, the three great tragic poets of ancient Greece, to whom their country owed infinitely less than we owe to the memory of John Hancock. The Carthaginians erected altars and paid divine honors to the memories of two brothers, who, at the time of a dispute between the city of Carthage and the powerful city of Cyrene, in respect to the extent of territory which each possessed, had determined the controversy by running to meet two persons from the latter city, whom they beat in the race, and upon being accused of starting before the appointed moment, consented to be, and were actually buried alive, as an evidence of their honorable conduct. A splendid monument was erected by the Magnesians to Themistocles, the celebrated Grecian general; and a magnificent mausoleum, surrounded by nine vast towers, was reared by the Syracusans to the memory of Gelon, their sovereign, who was distinguished as a statesman and a warrior; and the Athenians, after murdering Socrates, caused a statue of brass to be erected to his memory, of the workmanship of the celebrated Lysippus, and even dedicated a chapel to him, as a hero and demigod, which they called the "Chapel of Socrates." Statues of brass were erected to Harmonius and Aristogiton, the deliverers of Athens; and also to Phocion, whose just and noble qualities and love of his country had obtained for him the appellation of the "Good."

The idea of all nations, in thus immortalizing their heroes and statesmen, was pure and exalted. The object was to express, by these honorable distinctions, their high sense of gratitude, and at the same time to inspire in the hearts of their citizens a noble thirst for glory, and a burning love and devotion for their country.

The same rewards for distinguished services have, among all modern nations, been heaped upon the tombs of their great men; and let it not be inscribed upon the annals of our republic, to its disgrace, that we alone have proved ungrateful to the first, the greatest, and the noblest of our patriots.

In the city of New York, the merchants of that great emporium of the western world are erecting* an Exchange which, when completed, will rank with the noblest and most splendid edifices upon the earth. In the interior of this stately pile, let one simple niche be reserved for the statue of John Hancock, the American merchant, whose wealth was freely given, and whose life was nobly periled, in the cause of human liberty. Let an American sculptor breathe into chiseled marble the soul, and invest it with the form, of him who should be the merchant's pride and boast; and let it stand the presiding genius of a temple reared and consecrated to the commercial interests of our great city.

---

* This biography is printed in this volume as originally published in *Hunt's Merchants' Magazine* of December, 1840.

ROBERT MORRIS.

The paths to renown are as numerous and diversified as the shades of human character and the ramifications of human genius. Over mountains crimsoned with slaughter, and through valleys seared with desolation, is marked the warrior's course: the poet's way winds amid groves of changeless verdure and inspiring shade, along dells carpeted with spontaneous flowers, and among all the gorgeous but unsubstantial architecture of imagination: deeper, thornier, and more dark is the historian's crooked road, through labyrinths of mouldering lore, which the glance of truth can scarcely penetrate, surrounded with the shadows and clouds of obscuring traditions, which impede his progress, and render its termination unsure: in the very bosom of nature the philosopher's orbit appears, insinuating itself into the mysterious coil of creation: the path of the orator skims the graceful sphere of science, explores all the rich empire of the arts, wanders amid the enchanted dominion of fancy, and unreservedly plucks the fruits and the blossoms which invite him to plunder at every step: while the statesman's more elevated and dangerous causeway, bounded by temptations alluring to destroy, lifts its traveler into the native region of wealth and influence, where the enmity of vicious nature and the hostility of party rancor are watchful to detect his errors, and to hurl him, should he swerve from rectitude, into the dark gulf of ignominy which opens at his feet.

Each of these roads, however, has its subordinate branches, the description of which, in this place, is neither necessary nor desirable. To connect this exordium with the character we now present, it is merely requisite to notice that division of political fame which runs into the intricacies of national finance. If this be a department which demands no dazzling superiority of natural ability, which calls for no extraordinary extensiveness of artificial knowledge, it brings into action the nobler acquisitions of a wakeful prudence and an inflexible integrity; and by their united operation, gives solidity and duration to the credit and prosperity of a people. Here the civic wreath decreed for useful services, and the edifice of public wealth and reputation they have contributed to erect, may be allowed to stand in honorable competition with the more gaudy laurels of genius, and the frailer homage of a fastidious and inconstant taste.

Such is the chaplet with which impartial history will invest the brow of Robert Morris. This eminent financier was born at Liverpool, on the 20th day of January (O. S.), 1733–4. Of his family very little is known, except that his father was a respectable English merchant; and, for a long time, held the agency of a very considerable tobacco-house in that wealthy and enterprising town. The nature and extent of his concerns required his frequent visits to this country, and it was in one of these trips that his son Robert, at the age of thirteen, became the companion of his voyage, and received an introduction to the scene of his future greatness. The rudiments of his education he had previously obtained in England; but, with a view to render it complete, his father, immediately on his arrival, placed him under the tuition of the Rev. Mr. Gordon, of Maryland, who was well qualified to finish the mould of the youthful mind.

That nature had bestowed on Robert a liberal capacity of mind, the circumstances of his maturer life sufficiently prove: to give effect to her bounty, education went no further than his endowment with the materials which might enable him to fill the character of a merchant. Had a more considerable allotment of his early years been devoted to the cultivation of polite literature and the sciences, he would, most undoubtedly, have become a very distinguished scholar; yet, as was well remarked by one of his bosom friends, "it is doubtful whether he would have become a better or a greater man:—he *might* have been more useful, but it is probable that this rare intellect would have been expended on the mere frivolities of learning, which was afterward destined to rear the moral edifice of a nation." And it is reasonable to conclude, that his acquaintance with the various branches of learning would have been more extensive, but for the melancholy catastrophe which, by rendering him an orphan, effectually interrupted the course of his studies, and cast him upon a sphere, where his unripened energies were to be called into premature employment. The circumstances of this fatal event are too interesting, as well as too nearly connected with this history, to be omitted.

About two years had elapsed since his father's establishment in this country as a merchant, during which period he had gained greatly on the love and respect of those who knew him. On the fatal morning he had received information of the arrival in the Delaware, of a ship from Liverpool, consigned to himself: he immediately went on board, and having made the necessary inquiries and arrangements, left the vessel to return to the shore. At this moment, just as he had reached the boat, the captain, as a tribute of particular respect to his visitor, ordered a gun to be fired—it was the flattery of death;—the wadding of the gun lodged in his shoulder; and, notwithstanding the promptest and most able exertions of medical skill, a mortification took place, which, in a few days, terminated his existence, leaving Robert, in his fifteenth year, fatherless.

This lamentable event, in a subsequent part of his son's life, was forcibly recalled to his memory, during a season of festive enjoyment; and, although the introduction of the anecdote in this place is chronologically incorrect, it might be difficult to find a more apt opportunity. In the zenith of his mercantile fame, a friend had presented him with a fine turtle. Unwilling to incur the trouble of dressing it at home, Mr. Morris sent it to a celebrated refectory a few miles from the city, on the banks of the Schuylkill, and invited thither a large party of ladies and gentlemen to partake of his hospitality. Festivity was at its height; every countenance was clothed in smiles; when suddenly the cheeks of the lively host grew pale; his gayety forsook him, and every attempt to rally his paralyzed spirits was ineffectual. A general anxiety to discover the cause of this change was evident through the whole circle; yet a restraining delicacy prevented a too minute inquiry: until, at length, Mr. Morris himself, taking one of the company aside, addressed him thus:—"A circumstance has occurred which has greatly affected me. I am at this moment informed that the man who killed my father is in this house." The association of ideas produced by this accident was too powerful to be subdued: adding, to the information of the cause of his distress, a request that his friend would apologize for his weakness, he retired from a scene, the cheerfulness of which was now become irksome, and its mirth a scene of intolerable anguish.

Remote from his native land, and deprived of his natural protector, whatever was the strength and elasticity of Robert's mind, misfortune seemed to have received a charter to break its energies, and destroy its anticipations. The dark uncertainty which hung over his path, the consequence of past, and the probable prelude to future adversities, would have cramped, if not wholly destroyed, an ordinary ambition; but his was not the ardor of chance, nor the aspiration of circumstances: he felt his own vigorousness of spirit, and relied upon it for ultimate success.

Soon after the death of his father, Robert was received into the counting-house of Charles Willing, Esq., at that time the most distinguished merchant in Philadelphia, to whom he appears to have been indentured, and, after remaining in this subordinate station the usual term of years, he was established in business by his patron, in conjunction with his son, Thomas Willing, Esq. Embarked in an extensive and profitable West India trade, he made several voyages, as supercargo, in the ships belonging to the company, in one of which he was unfortunately captured by the French, and, during a close imprisonment for some time, suffered cruelty of treatment, not to be justified by the laws of war, nor the usages of civilized nations. In this state of distress, without a shilling, by exercising his ingenuity, and repairing the watch of a Frenchman, he raised the means of his own liberation, and enabled himself to return to Philadelphia, to resume the mercantile station from which he had been torn.

Under his active superintendence, the house of Willing and Morris rapidly rose to the summit of commercial reputation. Their foreign freightage employed an incredible number of ships; while the management of their finances at home, marked with a regularity and an integrity which could not be surpassed, procured them the confidence and credit of the world. Business was pleasure to Mr. Morris, yet it encroached not upon the sphere of social cheerfulness; the simple and admirable arrangements of his counting-house leaving him sufficient time to indulge his inclination for the enjoyment of his friends, to whom he attached himself with all the ardor and sincerity of a generous and ingenuous mind.

Did the limits of this biographical sketch allow of such amplification, it would be easy to detail instances in proof of the solidity of his friendships; but, as the proper end of this brief portraiture will be best obtained by a summary of his political life, a single reference to such facts must suffice. A gentleman of the Jewish persuasion, who had lived on terms of intimacy with him, fell into sudden embarrassments, and became greatly distressed. As soon as Mr. Morris was acquainted with the matter, he advised an immediate removal to Baltimore, for the purpose of attempting to retrieve his broken fortunes; at the same time placing in his hands five hundred pounds, with a written agreement never to demand its repayment, and taking, as a nominal security, the personal bond of the party obliged: to this sum he subsequently added another £500, neither of which loans was ever repaid him.

About the year 1769, he renounced the unnatural solitude of bachelorship, and intermarried with Mary, the daughter of Colonel White, and sister of the late learned bishop of that name. She was elegant, accomplished, and rich, and, in every respect, qualified to carry the felicity of connubial life to its highest perfection.

The objects and employments of Mr. Morris's life, for some years after this change in his domestic character, were entirely of a commercial nature. On the appearance of a rupture with the British government, however, he was sent to Congress, as member for Pennsylvania, at the close of the year 1775; and, during that session, was employed in some financial arrangements of the greatest importance to the operations of the army and navy.

During the march of the British troops through the Jerseys, in 1776, the removal of Congress to Baltimore is well known. For reasons of a commercial nature, Mr. Morris was left at Philadelphia, to remain as long as circumstances would permit. At this crisis, a letter from the commander-in-chief was received by the government, announcing, that while the enemy were accurately informed of all his movements, he was compelled, from the want of hard money, to remain in complete ignorance of their arrangements, and requiring a certain sum as absolutely necessary to the safety of the army. Information of this demand was sent to Mr. Morris, in the hope that, through his credit, the money might be obtained; the communication reached him at his office, in his way from which to his dwelling-house, immediately afterward, he was met by a gentleman of the Society of Friends, with whom he was in habits of business and acquaintance, and who accosted him with his customary phrase—"Well, Robert, what news?" "The news is," said Mr. Morris, "that I am in immediate want of a sum of hard money," mentioning the amount, "and that you are the man who must procure it for me. Your security is to be my note of hand and my honor." After a short hesitation the gentleman replied—"Robert, thou shalt have it;" and, by the punctual performance of his promise, enabled Congress to comply with the requisition of the general.

The situation of General Greene, in South Carolina, was equally critical, his distresses rendering it scarcely practicable to keep his troops together, when a gentleman, Mr. Hall of that State, by stepping forward and advancing the necessary sums, enabled him to stem the danger. On the return of General Greene to Philadelphia, after the war had terminated, he repaired to the office of finance to settle his accounts, when the secret was divulged, that Mr. Hall had acted under the direction of Mr. Morris. The general was hurt at such an apparent want of confidence in him; but, on reconsidering the subject, at the request of the financier, he admitted the wisdom of the caution which had been used. "I give you my opinion," said he, "that you never did a wiser thing: for, on other occasions, I was sufficiently distressed to have warranted my drawing on you, had I known that I might have done so, and I should have availed myself of the privilege." Mr. Morris rejoined, that, even as matters had been conducted, the southern expedition had gone nearer than the operations in any other quarter to the causing an arrest of his commercial business.

By a resolution of Congress, the office of financier was established in 1781, and Mr. Morris was unanimously elected as the superintendent. Previous to this election he had formed a mercantile connection with I. & R. Hazlehurst, and his fear lest the duties of an official situation of such importance should interfere with his engagements in business, prevented his acceptance of office, until Congress had specifically resolved, that his fulfillment of his commercial obligations was not incompatible with the performance of the public services required of him.

To trace him through all the acts of his financial administration, would be to make this biography a history of the last two years of the Revolutionary war. When the exhausted credit of the government threatened the most alarming consequences; when the soldiers were utterly destitute of the necessary supplies of food and clothing; when the military chest had been drained of its last dollar; and even the intrepid confidence of Washington was shaken; upon his own credit, and from his own private resources, did Mr. Morris furnish those pecuniary means, but for which the physical energies of the country, exerted to their utmost, would have been scarcely competent to secure that prompt and glorious issue which ensued.

One of the first acts of his financial government was the proposition to Congress of his plan for the establishment of the Bank of North America, which was chartered forthwith, and opened on the 7th of January, 1782. At this time "the States were half a million dollars in debt on that year's taxes, which had been raised by anticipation, on that system of credit which Mr. Morris had created:" and, but for this establishment, his plans of finance must have been entirely frustrated. On his retirement from office, it was affirmed, by two of the Massachusetts delegates, that "it cost Congress at the rate of eighteen millions per annum, hard dollars, to carry on the war, till he was chosen financier, and then it cost them but about five millions."

By the representations of a committee of Congress, Mr. Morris was induced to abandon his intention of quitting office in 1783, and he accordingly continued to superintend the department of finance to the 30th September, 1784, when, in a letter to the commissioners of the treasury board, he resigned his office, and immediately issued an advertisement, pledging himself to the payment of all his outstanding notes, as they should arrive at maturity.

In 1786, he was elected a member of the convention which framed the federal constitution. No man had more often and severely felt the want of an efficient government. He had incessantly asked for a stronger bond, or instrument, than the old confederation, for "a firm, wise, manly system of federal government;" and he strenuously co-operated in devising and recommending the present. In 1788, the general assembly of Pennsylvania appointed him to represent the State in the first senate of the United States, which assembled at New York. As a member of that body he distinguished himself by wise counsels, and particularly by an irresistible speech for the repeal of the tender laws.

Fatigued with political cares, which, from the time of his election to a seat in the senate of the first Congress, under the federal constitution, had so completely engrossed his mind, he was now anxious to retire to the relaxation of private life. That he was not avaricious after influence, may be sufficiently established from the fact of his refusal to accept the situation of secretary of the treasury, which General Washington wished him to fill. On his being requested to name a gentleman for that office, he nominated Colonel

Hamilton; and, on the expression of some surprise by the general, who was not acquainted with the colonel's qualifications in that department, Mr. Morris decidedly declared his own knowledge of his entire competency, and he was accordingly elected to that important post.

That his long continuance in the public service, and his unremitted attention to the business of his country, had caused some confusion in his private affairs, he assigned as a reason for declining to comply with the solicitations of the city of Philadelphia, which had sent a delegation to request he would become its representative in Congress. It is true, indeed, that he was subsequently induced to resume his situation as a delegate from Pennsylvania, and that he continued to fill this distinguished character for several years after his retirement from the financial department; but it is equally true, that this compliance with the public wish was rather the effect of a powerful sense of political duty than of inclination. His long inattention to his private affairs was productive of great embarrassments of mind and circumstances, the results of which cast a shade over those declining years which unembarrassed repose and honorable affluence ought to have soothed and cherished.

In his old age Mr. Morris embarked in vast land speculations, which proved fatal to his fortune. The man to whose financial operations the Americans were said to owe as much as to the negotiations of Franklin, or even the arms of Washington, passed the latter years of his life in prison, confined for debt.

After a life of inestimable utility, Mr. Morris died in Philadelphia, on the 8th of May, 1806, in the seventy-third year of his age. That his arrangements for the raising of pecuniary supplies, and the support of the credit of his country, in her greatest need, essentially conduced to the glorious termination of the contest for liberty, is established by the evidence of the illustrious Washington himself; and it may be as truly said of him, as it was of the Roman Curtius, that he sacrificed himself for the safety of the commonwealth.

Mr. Morris was of large frame, with a fine, open, bland countenance, and simple manners. Until the period of his impoverishment, his house was a scene of the most liberal hospitality. It was open, for nearly half a century, to all the strangers of good society who visited Philadelphia. He was temperate in food, but fond of social meetings. No one parted with his money more freely for public or private purposes of a meritorious nature.

His expansive faculties, his habits of order, his energy and rigid justice in the transaction of business, enabled him to acquit himself creditably in his financial sphere. His extensive commercial and private correspondence with Great Britain and the continent, furnished him with early and important political information. His constant manifestations of confidence in the issue of the revolutionary struggle inspired many others with the same sentiment. His whole example did incalculable service.

His general situation, and the impossibility of relieving all the wants which were referred to his department, exposed him to slanderous charges and harsh suspicions, which have in no instance withstood a fair inquiry.

Mr. Morris was a fluent, correct, and impressive orator; he wrote with ease and tenderness; his fund of political knowledge could not but be ample; his acquaintance with the affairs of the world exceeded, in extent and diversity, that of any of his fellow-patriots, Franklin excepted; and his conversation was therefore replete with interest and instruction.

END OF VOL. II.

www.ingramcontent.com/pod-product-compliance
Lightning Source LLC
LaVergne TN
LVHW021105110826
845150LV00001B/180

* 9 7 8 1 4 2 5 5 6 5 2 0 6 *